Exoskeletons

…rostheses

AI for Robotic Exoskeletons and Prostheses

Guest Editor

Claudio Loconsole

MDPI

Basel • Beijing • Wuhan • Barcelona • Belgrade • Novi Sad • Cluj • Manchester

Guest Editor
Claudio Loconsole
Department of Engineering
and Sciences
Universitas Mercatorum
Rome
Italy

Editorial Office
MDPI AG
Grosspeteranlage 5
4052 Basel, Switzerland

This is a reprint of the Special Issue, published open access by the journal *Robotics* (ISSN 2218-6581), freely accessible at: www.mdpi.com/journal/robotics/special_issues/AI_robotics_exoskeletons_prostheses.

For citation purposes, cite each article independently as indicated on the article page online and as indicated below:

Lastname, A.A.; Lastname, B.B. Article Title. *Journal Name* **Year**, *Volume Number*, Page Range.

ISBN 978-3-7258-8227-4 (Hbk)
ISBN 978-3-7258-8228-1 (PDF)
https://doi.org/10.3390/books978-3-7258-8228-1

Contents

About the Editor . . . . **vii**

Claudio Loconsole
Special Issue "AI for Robotic Exoskeletons and Prostheses"
Reprinted from: *Robotics* **2026**, *15*, 77, https://doi.org/10.3390/robotics15040077 . . . . **1**

Gianmarco Cirelli, Christian Tamantini, Luigi Pietro Cordella and Francesca Cordella
A Semiautonomous Control Strategy Based on Computer Vision for a Hand–Wrist Prosthesis
Reprinted from: *Robotics* **2023**, *12*, 152, https://doi.org/10.3390/robotics12060152 . . . . **3**

Ebenezer Raj Selvaraj Mercyshalinie, Akash Ghadge, Nneka Ifejika and Yonas Tadesse
NOHAS: A Novel Orthotic Hand Actuated by Servo Motors and Mobile App for Stroke Rehabilitation
Reprinted from: *Robotics* **2023**, *12*, 169, https://doi.org/10.3390/robotics12060169 . . . . **20**

Domenico Chiaradia, Gianluca Rinaldi, Massimiliano Solazzi, Rocco Vertechy and Antonio Frisoli
Design and Control of the Rehab-Exos, a Joint Torque-Controlled Upper Limb Exoskeleton
Reprinted from: *Robotics* **2024**, *13*, 32, https://doi.org/10.3390/robotics13020032 . . . . **46**

Szilvia Kóra, Adrienn Bíró, Nándor Prontvai, Mónika Androsics, István Drotár, Péter Prukner, et al.
Investigation of the Effectiveness of the Robotic ReStore Soft Exoskeleton in the Development of Early Mobilization, Walking, and Coordination of Stroke Patients: A Randomized Clinical Trial
Reprinted from: *Robotics* **2024**, *13*, 44, https://doi.org/10.3390/robotics13030044 . . . . **75**

Ali KhalilianMotamed Bonab, Domenico Chiaradia, Antonio Frisoli and Daniele Leonardis
A Framework for Modeling, Optimization, and Musculoskeletal Simulation of an Elbow–Wrist Exosuit
Reprinted from: *Robotics* **2024**, *13*, 60, https://doi.org/10.3390/robotics13040060 . . . . **88**

Tomislav Bazina, Goran Mauša, Saša Zelenika and Ervin Kamenar
Reducing Hand Kinematics by Introducing Grasp-Oriented Intra-Finger Dependencies
Reprinted from: *Robotics* **2024**, *13*, 82, https://doi.org/10.3390/robotics13060082 . . . . **110**

Saqib Zafar, Hafiz Farhan Maqbool, Muhammad Imran Ashraf, Danial Javaid Malik, Zain ul Abdeen, Wahab Ali, et al.
Towards Prosthesis Control: Identification of Locomotion Activities through EEG-Based Measurements
Reprinted from: *Robotics* **2024**, *13*, 133, https://doi.org/10.3390/robotics13090133 . . . . **135**

Riccardo Bezzini, Giulia Bassani, Carlo Alberto Avizzano and Alessandro Filippeschi
Design and Experimental Evaluation of Multiple 3D-Printed Reduction Gearboxes for Wearable Exoskeletons
Reprinted from: *Robotics* **2024**, *13*, 168, https://doi.org/10.3390/robotics13110168 . . . . **150**

Hongquan Le, Marc in het Panhuis, Geoffrey M. Spinks and Gursel Alici
Hybrid LDA-CNN Framework for Robust End-to-End Myoelectric Hand Gesture Recognition Under Dynamic Conditions
Reprinted from: *Robotics* **2025**, *14*, 83, https://doi.org/10.3390/robotics14060083 . . . . **180**

Abhaya Pal Singh and Antonio Candea Leite
Neuromorphic Control of Robotic Systems with Numerical Simulations
Reprinted from: *Robotics* **2025**, *14*, 166, https://doi.org/10.3390/robotics14110166 . . . . **203**

Cristian Camardella, Tommaso Bagneschi, Federica Serra, Claudio Loconsole and Antonio Frisoli
A Synergistic Rehabilitation Approach for Post-Stroke Patients with a Hand Exoskeleton: A Feasibility Study with Healthy Subjects
Reprinted from: *Robotics* **2026**, *15*, 21, https://doi.org/10.3390/robotics15010021 . . . . **224**

About the Editor

Claudio Loconsole

Claudio Loconsole (Eng., Ph.D.) received his B.S. and M.S. degrees, both with honors (cum laude), in Computer Engineering from Politecnico di Bari, Italy, in 2007 and from Politecnico di Torino, Italy, in 2009, respectively. In 2012, he earned a Ph.D. in Innovative Technologies from Scuola Superiore Sant'Anna, Pisa, Italy. He was a postdoctoral research fellow at the PERCeptual RObotics (PERCRO) Laboratory, Scuola Superiore Sant'Anna, Pisa, Italy, and an assistant professor at Politecnico di Bari. Since 2021, he has been an Associate Professor of Information Processing Systems at Universitas Mercatorum, Rome, Italy, and an affiliate professor at the Institute of Mechanical Intelligence, Scuola Superiore Sant'Anna, Pisa, Italy. He has served as principal investigator for three research projects and has received several international awards and recognitions. He has authored or co-authored more than 70 papers published in international journals and conference proceedings, and he is the co-inventor of four national and international patents. He serves as an Associate Editor for two international scientific journals. His research interests include human–machine interaction, human–robot interaction, data analysis, assistive technologies, computer vision, and artificial intelligence.

robotics

MDPI

Editorial

Special Issue "AI for Robotic Exoskeletons and Prostheses"

Claudio Loconsole

Department of Engineering and Sciences, Universitas Mercatorum, 00182 Rome, Italy;
claudio.loconsole@unimercatorum.it

This Special Issue was conceived to explore how Artificial Intelligence can meaningfully empower robotic exoskeletons and prosthetic systems, enhancing modeling, control, perception, and real-world applicability to ultimately improve the quality of life of individuals that rely on these technologies.

The published works clearly demonstrate that reliable intention detection remains one of the central challenges in wearable robotics. EEG-based locomotion classification has been investigated to advance brain-controlled prostheses, showing robust activity recognition across varied walking conditions [1]. In parallel, a hybrid Linear Discriminant Analysis–CNN framework has been proposed to improve myoelectric hand gesture recognition under dynamic and non-stationary conditions, effectively combining classical robustness with deep learning adaptability [2]. The importance of exploiting physiological synergies has also been highlighted through synergistic rehabilitation strategies that promote coordinated activation patterns and functional recovery, enabling more natural and effective interaction with hand exoskeletons [3]. Complementing neural and muscular decoding, semiautonomous vision-based strategies have been introduced to integrate object recognition, grasp selection, and wrist orientation estimation with EMG-based control, reducing cognitive burden while preserving user embodiment [4].

Beyond perception and intention recognition, several contributions advance intelligent control architectures and system design. Neuromorphic control strategies based on spiking neural networks have been explored and supported by formal stability analyses, opening new perspectives for biologically inspired robotic control [5]. At the level of physical human–robot interaction, a joint torque-controlled upper limb exoskeleton has demonstrated how full-state feedback and nonlinear compensation can significantly enhance transparency and haptic rendering performance [6]. Mechanical innovation remains equally crucial: a systematic evaluation of 3D-printed reduction gearboxes provides valuable insights into lightweight and cost-effective actuation solutions for wearable devices [7], while the development of a servo motor–actuated orthotic hand controlled via a mobile application emphasizes usability, accessibility, and functional characterization in stroke rehabilitation contexts [8].

This Special Issue further includes substantial advances in modeling and biomechanical optimization. A comprehensive framework is presented for modeling, optimizing, and simulating an elbow–wrist exosuit, integrating dynamic modeling with musculoskeletal simulation to optimize anchor point placement and analyze muscular loading and offering a quantitative foundation for ergonomic and biomechanically sound design [9]. In parallel, large-scale statistical analyses of hand kinematics have demonstrated how intra-finger dependencies can significantly reduce the degrees of freedom required to represent grasping tasks, with important implications for prosthetic and rehabilitation device design and control [10]. Finally, clinical validation remains fundamental to demonstrating real-world impact: a randomized clinical trial evaluating a soft robotic exoskeleton for post-stroke rehabilitation has shown significant improvements in walking performance, balance, and functional independence, confirming the translational potential of intelligent wearable robotics [11].

Taken together, the contributions of this Special Issue confirm that AI is not merely an auxiliary component, but a foundational enabler of next-generation exoskeletons and prostheses. The integration of multimodal sensing, adaptive control, biomechanical modeling, and user-centered design is progressively transforming wearable robots into intelligent, responsive, and clinically meaningful systems. At the same time, challenges remain in ensuring long-term robustness, personalization, safety certification, and seamless integration into daily life.

Acknowledgments: Thanks are given to all the authors and peer reviewers for their valuable contributions to the first edition of this Special Issue "AI for Robotic Exoskeletons and Prostheses".

Conflicts of Interest: The authors declare no conflict of interest.

References

1. Zafar, S.; Maqbool, H.F.; Ashraf, M.I.; Malik, D.J.; Abdeen, Z.U.; Ali, W.; Taborri, J.; Rossi, S. Towards Prosthesis Control: Identification of Locomotion Activities through EEG-Based Measurements. *Robotics* **2024**, *13*, 133. [CrossRef]
2. Le, H.; Panhuis, M.; Spinks, G.M.; Alici, G. Hybrid LDA-CNN Framework for Robust End-to-End Myoelectric Hand Gesture Recognition Under Dynamic Conditions. *Robotics* **2025**, *14*, 83. [CrossRef]
3. Camardella, C.; Bagneschi, T.; Serra, F.; Loconsole, C.; Frisoli, A. A Synergistic Rehabilitation Approach for Post-Stroke Patients with a Hand Exoskeleton: A Feasibility Study with Healthy Subjects. *Robotics* **2026**, *15*, 21. [CrossRef]
4. Cirelli, G.; Tamantini, C.; Cordella, L.P.; Cordella, F. A Semiautonomous Control Strategy Based on Computer Vision for a Hand–Wrist Prosthesis. *Robotics* **2023**, *12*, 152. [CrossRef]
5. Singh, A.P.; Candea Leite, A. Neuromorphic Control of Robotic Systems with Numerical Simulations. *Robotics* **2025**, *14*, 166. [CrossRef]
6. Chiaradia, D.; Rinaldi, G.; Solazzi, M.; Vertechy, R.; Frisoli, A. Design and Control of the Rehab-Exos, a Joint Torque-Controlled Upper Limb Exoskeleton. *Robotics* **2024**, *13*, 32. [CrossRef]
7. Bezzini, R.; Bassani, G.; Avizzano, C.A.; Filippeschi, A. Design and Experimental Evaluation of Multiple 3D-Printed Reduction Gearboxes for Wearable Exoskeletons. *Robotics* **2024**, *13*, 168. [CrossRef]
8. Selvaraj Mercyshalinie, E.R.; Ghadge, A.; Ifejika, N.; Tadesse, Y. NOHAS: A Novel Orthotic Hand Actuated by Servo Motors and Mobile App for Stroke Rehabilitation. *Robotics* **2023**, *12*, 169. [CrossRef]
9. Khalilian Motamed Bonab, A.; Chiaradia, D.; Frisoli, A.; Leonardis, D. A Framework for Modeling, Optimization, and Musculoskeletal Simulation of an Elbow–Wrist Exosuit. *Robotics* **2024**, *13*, 60. [CrossRef]
10. Bazina, T.; Mauša, G.; Zelenika, S.; Kamenar, E. Reducing Hand Kinematics by Introducing Grasp-Oriented Intra-Finger Dependencies. *Robotics* **2024**, *13*, 82. [CrossRef]
11. Kóra, S.; Bíró, A.; Prontvai, N.; Androsics, M.; Drotár, I.; Prukner, P.; Haidegger, T.; Széphelyi, K.; Tollár, J. Investigation of the Effectiveness of the Robotic ReStore Soft Exoskeleton in the Development of Early Mobilization, Walking, and Coordination of Stroke Patients: A Randomized Clinical Trial. *Robotics* **2024**, *13*, 44. [CrossRef]

https://doi.org/10.3390/robotics15040077

robotics

MDPI

Article

A Semiautonomous Control Strategy Based on Computer Vision for a Hand–Wrist Prosthesis

Gianmarco Cirelli [1], Christian Tamantini [1], Luigi Pietro Cordella [2] and Francesca Cordella [1,*]

1 Research Unit of Advanced Robotics and Human-Centred Technologies, Universitá Campus Bio-Medico di Roma, 00128 Rome, Italy; gianmarco.cirelli@alcampus.it (G.C.); c.tamantini@unicampus.it (C.T.)
2 Universitá di Napoli Federico II, 80125 Naples, Italy; cordel@unina.it
* Correspondence: f.cordella@unicampus.it

Abstract: Alleviating the burden on amputees in terms of high-level control of their prosthetic devices is an open research challenge. EMG-based intention detection presents some limitations due to movement artifacts, fatigue, and stability. The integration of exteroceptive sensing can provide a valuable solution to overcome such limitations. In this paper, a novel semiautonomous control system (SCS) for wrist–hand prostheses using a computer vision system (CVS) is proposed and validated. The SCS integrates object detection, grasp selection, and wrist orientation estimation algorithms. By combining CVS with a simulated EMG-based intention detection module, the SCS guarantees reliable prosthesis control. Results show high accuracy in grasping and object classification ($\geq$97%) at a fast frame analysis frequency (2.07 FPS). The SCS achieves an average angular estimation error $\leq$18° and stability $\leq$0.8° for the proposed application. Operative tests demonstrate the capabilities of the proposed approach to handle complex real-world scenarios and pave the way for future implementation on a real prosthetic device.

Keywords: hand–wrist prosthesis; artificial vision; semiautonomous control

1. Introduction

The loss of an upper limb has profound physical, psychological, and social consequences [1]. It significantly impacts an individual's ability to perform activities of daily living and work-related tasks [2], limiting their independence and overall quality of life. Despite advancements in prosthetic technology, statistics show that less than half of amputees (44.7%) use their prosthetic device for more than eight hours per day. Additionally, the majority of amputees (76.9%) use their prostheses for cosmetic purposes rather than for functional ones. This highlights the challenges faced by amputees, where functional limitations and discomfort still influence their decision to utilize the prosthesis [3,4].

To address these issues, alleviating the burden on amputees regarding the control of prostheses is crucial. Hence, researchers are actively developing new strategies to intuitively control multiple degrees of freedom (DoFs) [5].

Traditionally, myoelectric prostheses rely on recognizing user motion intention through electromyographic (EMG) signals [6]. Various strategies based on pattern recognition [7] have been proposed to classify different muscle activation patterns, improving prosthesis control performance with respect to simple threshold-based methods. However, sequential control of different DoFs is still mainly adopted, limiting the naturalness, intuitiveness, reliability, and performance of the prosthesis control [8]. More recent and sophisticated approaches enable parallel control of multiple DoFs to naturally control prosthetic devices [9]. Nevertheless, their performance, as that of all the EMG-based systems, is heavily dependent on a trade-off between the number of possible outputs, i.e., the number of possible classes, and the system robustness: the higher the number of classes, the lower the performance and robustness of the system. Specifically, the classification accuracy drops to 90–95% when the number of motion classes is increased by more than 10, compared to the initial accuracy of 99% achieved when only four classes are considered [10]. This effect can be observed as a limitation arising from both the utilized algorithms, as well as from the inherent difficulty faced by upper-limb amputees in generating precise and consistent contractions. They also exhibit noticeable performance degradation over time, which can be attributed to various factors such as repositioning of the prosthetic socket, sweating, and muscle fatigue resulting from prolonged use or physical exertion [11]. These inaccuracies in detecting user intentions may significantly affect the performance and reliability of the prosthesis control.

To ensure significant improvements in the accuracy, naturalness, and intuitiveness of prosthesis control, and therefore to reduce users' cognitive burden, Semiautonomous Control Strategies (SCS) [12] were introduced to combine user inputs with automated or intelligent systems to control the prosthetic device [13]. Specifically, Computer Vision systems (CVS) can be exploited to predict the grasping configuration from the geometric properties of the framed object, allowing the accomplishment of the task.

The first CVS-based SCS did not consider any user input but only relied on the information retrieved from exteroceptive sensors. For instance, in [14], an RGB camera with an ultrasonic sensor was mounted on the back of a prosthetic hand to control its motion. Geometrical features of the object were extracted from the gray-scale image (320×240 pixels) acquired by the camera, using a threshold segmentation method. Wrist rotation, grasp type, and hand opening were determined based on visual and distance information [15]. More specifically, four types of grasp were considered, while the size of the aperture was determined based on the estimated size of the object. The control was run on a standard personal computer, using a DAQ board for communication with sensors. Another approach relies on an RGB-D camera for preshaping the robotic hand and estimating grasp type, size, and wrist orientation [16]. However, in both approaches, the cameras were not integrated into the hand–wrist prosthesis due to their weight and size. Moreover, this approach is based on the estimation of the desired prosthesis configuration by considering the properties of the segmented object, retrieved from the fitting model which well-approximates its shape. Specifically, only three geometrical models were taken into account, i.e., three different grasp types: sphere, cylinder, and cuboid.

Further approaches introduced EMG signals to activate the movement of the prosthesis, and left the identification of the gestures to be performed to the exteroceptive sensors.

In [17], EMG signals were used only to trigger the grasp phase, while Convolutional Neural Networks (CNNs) [18] were trained to categorize the objects framed by an RGB camera into four different hand gestures. All offline and real-time tests were implemented on a personal computer, leaving the integration of the system onto prostheses among future developments. In [19], a similar approach was proposed, where EMG signals recorded from two electrodes were used only to initialize the control strategy and to confirm hand gestures identified by the CNN-based control. Furthermore, the prosthesis user can receive feedback and decide whether to reset, adjust, or continue the movement.

The CNN-based approaches proposed in the literature present an important limitation: a shift towards object detection strategies results in relinquishing the autonomous and fine control of prosthetic hand orientation, i.e., pronation/supination (P/S) rotation, resorting to coarse control solutions or leaving the manual management of the prosthetic hand orientation to the user, significantly impacting user-side control.

Recent studies explored the use of a multimodal system with EMG and CVS in prosthetic control [20,21], proposing a strategy for combining these two types of information to improve the accuracy with respect to an EMG classifier. The hand gesture determined based on information gathered from an environmental CVS was used as an additional feature alongside those extracted from EMG signals to infer the final grasp to be executed [22], neglecting wrist orientation. From the state-of-the-art analysis, the need for a novel SCS that manages both hand and wrist configuration by simultaneously taking into account the user's motion intention is therefore evident. It will foster the inclusion of the user in the prosthesis control loop enhancing the prosthesis embodiment and the naturalness of the control. The objective of this paper is to fill this gap by proposing a novel SCS based on a CVS embedded in a wrist–hand prosthesis and integrating user motion intention, derived from a simulated EMG classifier, and exteroceptive information about the type and orientation of the object to grasp.

The proposed approach compares the output of the EMG classifier with that of the vision system to obtain the optimal grasp to be executed and the corresponding wrist orientation. More specifically, it starts with a limited set of grasp classes, identified by the EMG classifier, to determine object-specific sub-classes, ensuring the appropriate grasp execution. In the vision-based control strategies currently proposed in the literature, the user may feel estranged from controlling the prosthesis, because he/she only triggers the control via EMG sensors, while the grasp to be performed is autonomously determined by the control strategy. The proposed approach addresses this limitation, since the user can decide the grasp to be performed through EMG signals, and the SCS is responsible for determining the most appropriate wrist orientation and for confirming the recognized motion intention or suggesting corrections. More specifically, the EMG classifier is responsible for determining four grasp macro-categories, and the vision-based control strategy enables the assignment of grasp configurations belonging to that macro-category, but object-specific, considering object geometrical characteristics [23]. Furthermore, the implemented control strategy has the capability to handle real-life scenarios, enhancing the overall usability of the system in practical situations.

The proposed approach was validated in two different experimental settings. The first one is a structured environment to quantify the computational burden of the algorithm and its performance in accurately detecting the framed objects and their orientation. The outcome of this phase also guided the choice of the vision system's characteristics, i.e., the camera model to be used and the image resolution. The second experimental setting reproduces a realistic operative scenario. Once the optimal CVS positioning on the hand–wrist prosthesis was determined, the camera was mounted on the corresponding location of a human subject hand to assess the algorithm's capability for handling coherence between the user intention and the vision system, and for properly identifying approaching conditions with the object to be grasped.

The paper is structured as follows: Section 2 details the proposed approach and describes the methodological steps used for validation. Section 3 presents and discusses the results obtained in the different experiments. Lastly, Section 4 draws the conclusion of this work and provides possible future works.

2. Materials and Methods

An overview of the proposed approach is shown in Figure 1. The vision-based hand–wrist control strategy (blue box in Figure 1) takes as input an RGB image of the environment the hand has to interact with, captured from the CVS integrated into the prosthesis, and the user's intention, obtained from an EMG classifier, in terms of desired hand gesture. The combination of these two pieces of information makes it possible to simultaneously cope with coherent and non-coherent situations and accurately estimate wrist orientation to optimize hand preshaping, i.e., to output the hand gesture to be performed by the prosthesis and the wrist orientation (in terms of P/S angles) most appropriate to the object's geometric properties. Specifically, the proposed SCS is composed of 3 sequential processing steps: Object Detection, Grasp Selection, and Orientation Estimation. Visual feedback, based on the output of the control algorithm, is provided to the prosthesis user through two colored LEDs to report whether an object has been detected in the scene and any non-coherence with the output from the EMG classifier. Each block shown in Figure 1 is detailed in the following.

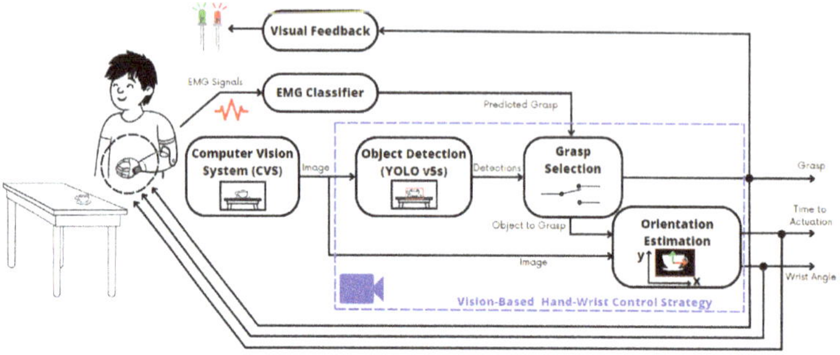

Figure 1. Block scheme of the proposed approach: the control strategy is outlined by the blue box.

2.1. Proposed Approach

2.1.1. EMG Signal Classifier

User motion intention about the grasp to be performed is retrieved by the EMG signal classifier. It is a simulated classifier that, considering the hand gestures commonly performed by commercial prostheses, is able to classify 4 grasp macro-categories in addition to the *Rest*, i.e., *Power*, *Lateral*, *Precision*, and *Pointing*.

2.1.2. Computer Vision System (CVS)

A CVS was introduced to recognize the objects to be grasped and their properties, as explained in Section 2.1.3, with the aim of estimating the most appropriate hand and wrist configuration. The system must be such that it can be integrated into one prosthetic hand. Therefore, the camera sensor and the electronic components should be miniaturized in order not to add weight and bulk to the prosthetic hand. To achieve this goal, a single-board computer (SBC) has been exploited to host the proposed algorithm and perform preliminary tests.

2.1.3. Vision-Based Hand–Wrist Control Strategy

The image of the scene retrieved by the CVS is the input for the Object Detection module. It is responsible for detecting any objects in the scene and associating them with a bounding box (x-coordinate and y-coordinate, width and height of the bounding box), a class label, and a classification confidence level, i.e., the probability the object was correctly classified, organized into an $(N, 6)$ tensor, where N is the number of objects detected and 6 is the computed information. The objects are sorted with descending confidence levels.

To detect the object in the scene, among the several CNN models in the literature, such as VGG16, ResNet50, YOLO, and MobileNet [24], YOLOv5 (You Only Look Once) [25,26] in its small version was chosen. Compared to other models, YOLOv5 provides a favorable trade-off between classification accuracy and processing speed, making it highly suitable for real-time object detection applications. The model was trained on the Microsoft COCO (Common Objects in Context, [27]) dataset, a large-scale image recognition dataset for object detection and segmentation.

Starting from the macro-categories of grasp that can be obtained from the EMG classifier, the vision-based control strategy enables the assignment of grasp configurations belonging to that macro-class, but object-specific, identified on the basis of the Feix taxonomy [28]. Thus, the EMG classifier maintains a high classification performance, as the number of considered classes is limited, while, at the same time, the grasping capabilities of the prosthesis are enhanced, as the implemented control strategy takes into account object-specific grasping sub-classes. Figure 2 shows the list of gesture sub-categories considered in the proposed control strategy and the objects associated with them.

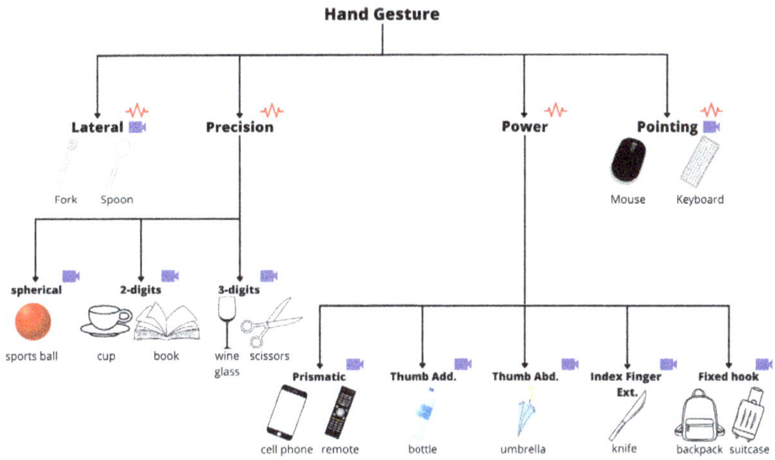

Figure 2. Diagram of all the hand gestures considered and objects associated with them: the symbols indicate the grasps the EMG classifier (red) and the developed SCS (blue) are able to recognize, respectively.

This information is then provided as input to the Grasp Selection module, which compares the hand gesture, obtained from the EMG classifier, with the one estimated by the vision system. The module identifies coherence or non-coherence between the two proposed grasps and the object that the user is most likely intending to grasp. Specifically, a decisional tree is proposed to autonomously respond to all cases that may occur in the scene:

- *If* there are no objects detected in the scene, *then* the control algorithm returns the *Rest* gesture. This information is given back to the user via visual feedback, as explained in Section 2.1.4.
- *If* there is non-coherence between the output from the EMG classifier and the hand gestures associated with the detected objects, *then* priority is given to the visual information. It means that the output of the Grasp Selection module is the hand gesture corresponding to the object with the highest confidence level. The correspondence between the object and the grasp is shown in Figure 2.
- *If* there is coherence between the output of the EMG classifier and the grasp associated with an object in the scene, *then* the object is taken into account, and the other objects not belonging to the class recognized by the EMG classifier are removed from the list of detections. In this case, the number of objects is variable and depends on how many of them can be grasped with the hand gesture obtained from the EMG classifier. In particular, *If* there are multiple objects that can be grasped with the class obtained from the user EMG classifier, *then* only objects framed in the central portion of the scene are considered. It is assumed that the object the user wants to grab is framed in the central region of the image [29], thus the one towards which the prosthetic hand will move. Even in this case, the number of objects is variable and depends on how many of them are in the central portion of the acquired image. *If* there are multiple objects in the central portion of the image, *then* the one that was recognized with a higher confidence level is selected.

The Orientation Estimation module is responsible for continuously estimating the wrist P/S angle by segmenting the Region of Interest (ROI) of the selected object and by applying Principal Component Analysis (PCA).

Selecting only the ROI is crucial, since it improves segmentation accuracy by focusing solely on the target object, eliminating noise areas in the image, and it reduces computational burden by analyzing only the bounding box, thereby increasing analysis speed.

The ROI is transformed from RGB to gray-scale and subjected to threshold segmentation using Otzu's method [30]. It allows for determining the optimal threshold by analyzing the intensity histogram to separate the foreground, i.e., the selected object, from the background. The resulting binary image undergoes the closure morphological operation involving dilation and erosion procedures to remove residual noise in the binary mask.

Contours are detected after segmenting the image, and only contours within the 5–95% area range of the ROI are considered to ensure a single region for the PCA. A method based on PCA has been chosen to retrieve the optimal wrist P/S angle, since PCA reduces the dataset's dimensionality while preserving maximum information and variance. PCA is specifically designed to capture the directions along which the data exhibit the highest variance, making it a valuable method for identifying the principal direction of variability within a segmented region, i.e., the detected object. The proposed method relies on some constraints the camera placement should satisfy: the image plane must be perpendicular to the wrist P/S rotation axis and the y-axis of the image reference system must be aligned with the longitudinal axis of the long fingers, while the x-axis must be perpendicular to it. If the aforementioned constraints are met, the P/S angle α the hand–wrist prosthesis has to reach is determined as the angle between the first Principal Component (PC) of the segmented region in the ROI and the x-axis of the image plane [31]. In this configuration, the first PC is perpendicular to the long finger's longitudinal axis, enabling grasping along the object's smallest dimension. However, some objects require a different procedure. For example, the ones without a principal axis, like spheres, cannot have their wrist orientation estimated. In this case, the optimal P/S angle is the one that allows the palm of the prosthetic hand to be parallel to the plane on which the object is located, which is an angle of 90°. For objects like the mouse, where the pointing hand configuration is required, the first PC should be parallel to the long finger's longitudinal axis, resulting in a rotation angle that complements α.

The approach works continuously and is capable of recognizing the reaching phase. Once the reaching occurs, the hand–wrist prosthesis shapes itself in the configuration estimated by the proposed approach. Specifically, the ROI area is tracked among subsequent frames and, if a 50% area increase is computed with respect to the initial value, the hand gesture obtained with the proposed strategy is actuated.

2.1.4. Visual Feedback

The developed system includes a feedback module that provides visual feedback to the prosthetic user about the detection of an object in the scene. Specifically, it consists of a pair of LEDs, one green and one red, connected to the SBC. The green one indicates the successful detection of an object in the scene. The red one is turned on for a fixed time whenever a mismatch between the user motion intention, obtained by the EMG classifier, and the gesture class, computed by the vision-based hand–wrist control strategy, occurs. This real-time visual feedback aims at improving user confidence, facilitating error detection and enabling effective control of the prosthetic device. More specifically, with the green LED, the user is informed that at least one object in the scene has been recognized by the control algorithm, whereas the red LED indicates a non-coherent condition that might lead to issues in the interaction with the object. This approach allows the user to opt for repeating the muscle contraction to correct the output from the EMG classifier, rather than proceeding with the grasping task solely relying on the information from the CVS.

2.2. Experimental Validation

Extensive tests of the proposed approach performance have been carried out. The experimental setup and protocol, and the key performance indicators used for the system validation are detailed in the following.

2.2.1. Experimental Setup

The vision-based control algorithm was executed on the Raspberry Pi 4 Model B, which was chosen as a single-board computer (SBC) due to its compact size (88 × 58 × 19.5 mm) and computing power, making it an ideal choice for small-scale system development. Moreover, the 64-bit OS Raspbian provides support for Python, the high-level programming language selected for writing the control algorithm. The SBC desktop was remotely controlled via virtual network computing (VNC) and a power bank was used as an energy supply (5V DC and 3A via a USB-C port) to make the system portable.

To develop the CVS, the following requirements were considered for the camera selection: *(i)* integration capability into a hand–wrist prosthesis, which imposes the use of a miniaturized RGB camera; *(ii)* high native resolution to ensure optimal algorithm performance; *(iii)* compatibility with the selected SBC for communication purposes; *(iv)* cost-effectiveness to not raise the prosthesis cost. After evaluating commercial options, two cameras were selected: the Arducam 16MP High-Resolution camera, with 16 MP resolution and autofocus capabilities, and the Joy-it Wide Angle camera, with 160° wide field of view. The technical specifications of the two cameras are reported in Table 1.

Table 1. Cameras technical specifications.

Camera Model	Arducam 16 MP	Joy-It Wide Angle
Sensor	Sony IMX519	OV5647
Resolution [pixels] (Static Images)	16 MP (4656 × 3496)	5 MP (2952 × 1944)
Resolution [pixels] (Video)	1080p30, 720p60, 640 × 480p90	1080p30, 960p 45, 720p60, 640 × 480p90
Field of View(FoV)	80°	160°
Autofocus	✓	N.A.
Dimension [mm]	25 × 23.86 × 9	25 × 24 × 18
Weights [g]	3	5
Cost	33.95 €	20.17 €

Figure 3 shows the scheme of the connections that characterize the CVS, with both the identified cameras.

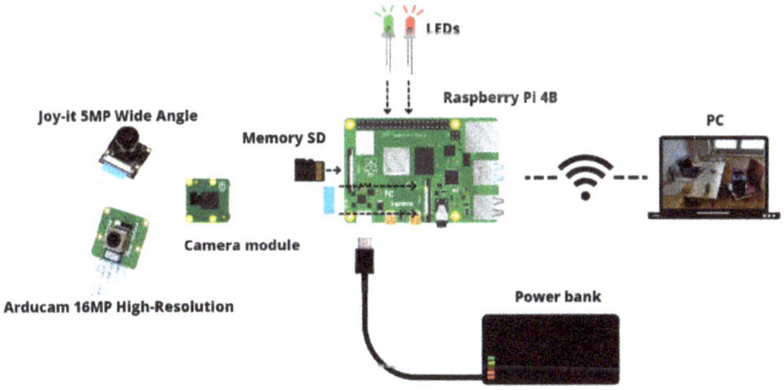

Figure 3. Connections scheme of the CVS.

The PiCamera2 and OpenCV libraries in Python were used to obtain images from the vision sensors. PiCamera2 facilitates communication with the camera and parameter configuration, while OpenCV is used to perform the image processing pipeline described in Section 2.1.3. Specifically, both cameras are configured at their best native resolution, which means an initial frequency of 10 FPS and 15.63 FPS, respectively.

In order to ensure a good compromise between speed and performance, the algorithm was tested by taking as input different image resolutions, i.e., 640 × 480 pixels [32,33], which are commonly used and the largest, and 320 × 240 pixels [14,15], which are widely employed and provide a 50% reduction in size compared to the former option. In this way, it was possible to quantify whether the input image size could affect computational burden and performance.

The Vicon VERO system was introduced for evaluating the orientation estimation of the proposed control strategy. It is an optoelectronic system gold standard in motion capture applications, capable of tracking the movement of objects and/or subjects in a 3D environment; specifically, Vicon is composed of 8 cameras called VERO; they are compact and super-wide infrared cameras with a resolution of 2.2 MP. The acquisition frequency was set to 100 Hz. Cameras are placed in the environment to optimally frame the scene and record the movement of reflective markers attached to the monitored objects. After the acquisition, raw data are used for kinematic reconstruction, giving back the 3D markers' position with respect to a reference frame defined at the beginning.

2.2.2. Experimental Protocol

To evaluate the performance of the proposed control strategy, the experimental protocol was divided into three sessions called Classification Performance, Orientation Estimation Validation, and Operative Tests.

The first session of the experimental protocol aimed at characterizing the performance of the proposed control algorithm, specifically of the Object Detection module, in correctly classifying the various objects shown individually, considering different setup configurations, i.e., various combinations of camera and input image resolution. The environment was structured with the camera framing the objects from above, not perfectly parallel to the image plane: in fact, the camera was held at a pre-defined angle to the plane on which the objects were standing, simulating a real context. In this part of the protocol, 16 objects were taken into account, divided among the 10 considered hand gestures: fork and spoon for Lateral; keyboard and mouse for Pointing; sports ball for Spherical (Precision); book and cup for 2-digits (Precision); scissors and wine glass for 3-digits (Precision); cell phone and remote for Prismatic (Power); bottle for Thumb Adducted (Power); umbrella for Thumb Abducted (Power); knife for Index Finger Extension (Power); backpack and suitcase for Fixed Hook (Power). Five trials were performed for each object per setup configuration, and in each of them, the object was framed for 25 frames for a total of 125 samples. To also verify if the position of the objects with respect to the camera influences the algorithm performance in associating the grasp class to the framed object, the objects were moved within the workspace to predefined positions.

The second session aimed at characterizing the performance of the algorithm in wrist orientation estimation and evaluating its computational burden, i.e., of the Orientation Estimation module, for each of the aforementioned setup configurations. Even in this case, the environment was structured as shown in Figure 4a and the camera was located in a fixed position and framed the scene in which the objects were placed one by one. Moreover, 2 markers were placed on each of the 8 considered objects, 2 per grasp macro-category (shown in Figure 4b) along their largest dimension, to have information on both object orientation, and 3 on the camera module to obtain the image plane.

For each object, 5 trials were performed for each configuration. In each test, the object was rotated by an angular displacement previously fixed to make the results comparable across different configurations. To evaluate the capability of the proposed control algorithm in estimating wrist orientation, the angular displacement obtained from the control algorithm was compared with the one calculated from the Vicon system's data processing. Markers' positions were elaborated on MATLAB and used to compute the camera plane and the Principal Component of the object.

The results obtained from the first two experimental sessions led us to identify the best setup (in terms of camera model and image resolution) among the four considered for obtaining the best algorithm performance. Once the best setup was found, the third part of the experimental protocol focused on finding the best position for the CVS in a hand–wrist prosthesis and evaluating the performance of the proposed control strategy, more specifically of the Grasp Selection module, in 3 more complex operative conditions (i.e., in a less structured environment) named Grasp selection test: Coherent Condition, Grasp selection test: Non-Coherent Condition, and Approaching Condition.

Figure 4. Experimental setup for Control Validation phase; VERO v2.2 cameras are shown in red circles (**a**). Objects used in the second session of the experimental protocol (**b**).

Firstly, the optimal camera placement was evaluated by positioning it in 4 different anatomical locations on the upper limb of 10 healthy subjects and assessing the different levels of hand occlusion. The test was conducted in an operational scenario with 5 men and 5 women (average age = 33.4 ± 13.6 years) of different anthropometric features, in order to characterize the level of occlusion with different wrist and hand sizes. The camera was placed at the wrist level, respecting all the positioning constraints defined in Section 2.1.3. Secondly, considering the so-obtained optimal camera placement, the CVS was placed on the upper limb of a healthy subject, as shown in Figure 5a, and the 3 operative tests were conducted considering the setup in Figure 5b.

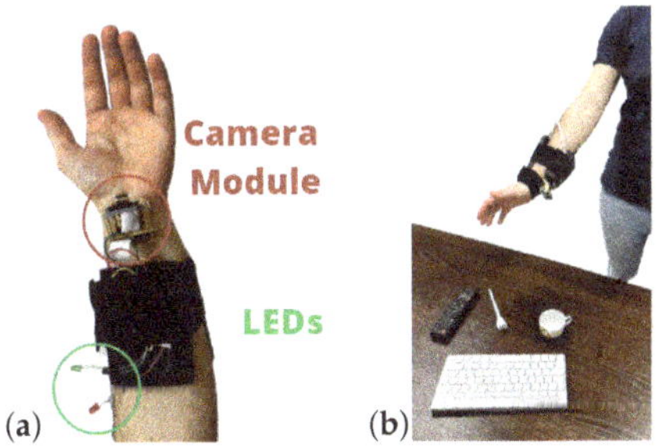

Figure 5. Positioning of CVS on the arm of the subject (**a**) and experimental setup for operative test (**b**).

In the first test, the performance of the control algorithm was analyzed whenever more than one object was detected and the user's intention changed. Four distinct items were displayed, each associated with a particular hand gesture, and the system was evaluated to see if it could select the proper object based on the EMG classifier input. This test aims at validating the capability of the proposed approach to identify the proper object according to the user's intention in a real-life scenario, where multiple tools/objects are often found close together.

The algorithm's ability to determine the proper hand gesture even when there was a discrepancy between the EMG-based user's intention and the hand gesture linked with the framed object was evaluated in the second test. Four items were provided, each representing a distinct grasp type, and the ability to accurately identify the hand gesture when the output from the EMG classifier was constant (Pointing) was tested.

The last test assessed the algorithm's capacity to detect when the prosthetic hand was approaching an object and required to shape the hand to grab it. The goal of this test was to use only information prior to the reaching phase for hand-shaping. Again, 4 objects were considered and the test was repeated twice for each.

In accordance with ethical guidelines and regulations governing research involving human subjects, this study has been determined to be exempt from obtaining approval from a relevant review board since the research poses minimal risk to the participants. The study primarily involves observations and does not involve any invasive or potentially harmful procedures. Participants have not been exposed to any physical, psychological, or social harm.

2.2.3. Key Performance Indicators (KPIs)

As explained in Section 2.2.2, each phase of the experimental protocol aims at assessing different aspects of the proposed control strategy. In order to assess the capability of the proposed pipeline to accurately detect the framed objects, the classification accuracies were quantified during the Classification Performance validation phase. In particular, the following accuracies were computed: *(i)* The Accuracy in Object Classification (AOC) assesses the correspondence between the real object and the predicted one, returned by the Object Detection module. *(ii)* The Accuracy in Grasp Classification (AGC) measures the correspondence between the true hand gesture and the predicted one.

During the Orientation Estimation Validation, the performance of the proposed control strategy in estimating object orientation and the computational burden of the implemented algorithm were characterized. The computed performance indicators were: *(i)* The Angular error (AE), which assesses the accuracy of the proposed system in estimating the object angular displacement and can be computed as

$$AE = |\Delta\theta_V - \Delta\theta_P|, \quad (1)$$

where $\Delta\theta_V$ and $\Delta\theta_P$ represent the angular displacement obtained from Vicon VERO and that computed by the proposed SCS, respectively. *(ii)* The Angular Estimation Stability (AES), which was analyzed considering the standard deviations of angles computed by the proposed algorithm and those obtained by the Vicon VERO data elaboration. The higher the value of the total standard deviations, computed per setup configuration, the lower the stability. These two KPIs were used in the first session of the protocol. *(iv)* The Analysis Frequency (AF), which quantifies, in frames per second (FPS), the approach to computational burden, i.e., the frequency at which the control algorithm analyzes the images.

Lastly, during the Operative Tests, the following performance indicators were computed: *(i)* The Occlusion Area (OA) , which is the area of the hand that occludes the scene and it is expressed as

$$OA = \frac{N_H}{N_{tot}} \cdot 100, \quad (2)$$

where N_H and N_{tot} are the number of pixels in which the hand is present and the total number of pixels, respectively. *(ii)* The Success Rate (SR), which is the success rate obtained in the Approaching Condition test, defined as the ratio between the number of trials in which the approaching phase (n) was recognized and the total trials N. It is expressed as

$$SR = \frac{n}{N} \cdot 100. \quad (3)$$

2.2.4. Statistical Analysis

The mean values and standard deviations of the above-mentioned KPIs were computed, specifically for AE and AF. Moreover, the Wilcoxon paired-sample test was performed for AE to analyze the differences between the two input sizes and the two camera sensors. In this way, identifying the best configuration among the four possible ones by comparing the angular errors for each object and each setup configuration was possible. Since all the performed tests are carried out on a couple of datasets, the significance level was set at p-value = 0.05.

3. Results and Discussions

Figure 6 shows the outputs of the proposed SCS for the same object, from Object Detection to Orientation Estimation, for both resolutions. As evident, the proposed approach was capable of *(i)* correctly detecting the framed spoon, *(ii)* segmenting it from the background, and *(iii)* estimating its orientation in the image plane.

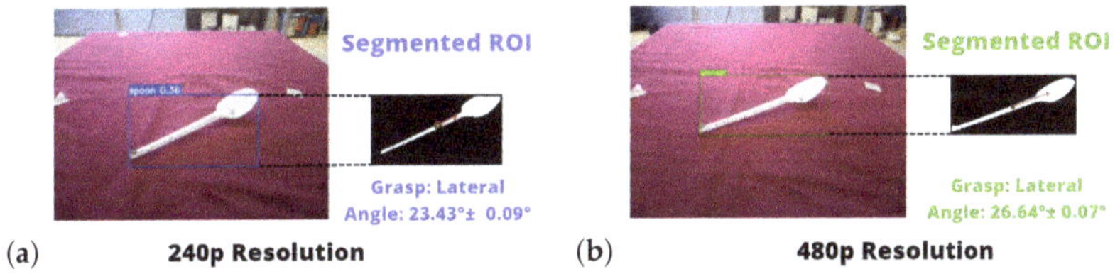

Figure 6. Example of Output in the first session of the experimental protocol for the 240p (**a**) and 480p (**b**) resolution and the same object.

Table 2 summarized the KPIs computed during the experimental validation of the proposed approach.

Table 2. Results obtained for each setup configuration in the first two sessions of experimental protocol.

	KPI 1		KPI 2	KPI 3	KPI 4
	AOC	*AGC*	*AE* [deg]	*AES* [deg]	*AF* [FPS]
5 MP 240p	97.80%	98.15%	14.17 ± 10.53	0.70	2.02 ± 0.13
5 MP 480p	97.35%	97.55%	11.40 ± 8.12	0.38	0.87 ± 0.13
16 MP 240p	97.85%	99.80%	16.26 ± 8.62	0.20	2.07 ± 0.15
16 MP 480p	99.35%	99.55%	17.35 ± 8.80	0.34	0.88 ± 0.17

As emerged from Table 2, each setup configuration obtained both AOC and $AGC > 97\%$. Misclassification errors for the 5 MP camera were due to fish-eye lens distortion and low confidence in detected objects. The majority of the errors were encountered for objects with spherical surfaces since fish-eye lens distortion modifies the shape of the objects and they were not detected with high confidence in many frames. On the contrary, the 16 MP camera sensor correctly classified spherical objects since the fish-eye lens distortion is absent. Since the autofocus of this camera requires 3 frames to properly focus the object, the algorithm was not capable of providing stable classification in the initial framing phase. Moreover, it emerged that $AGC \geq AOC$ objects associated with a certain hand gesture category are misclassified with another that can be manipulated with the same hand gesture. This highlights how the proposed approach is not significantly affected by object misclassification.

During the Orientation Estimation session, the average AE of the proposed system in estimating the object orientation did not exceed 18° and the AES was $\leq 0.8°$. The box plots of the AE for each object are divided with respect to the hand gestures and per setup configuration (Figure 7). It is worth observing that the median AE does not exceed 20°, except for the mouse and phone, considering the 16 MP camera with 480p resolution.

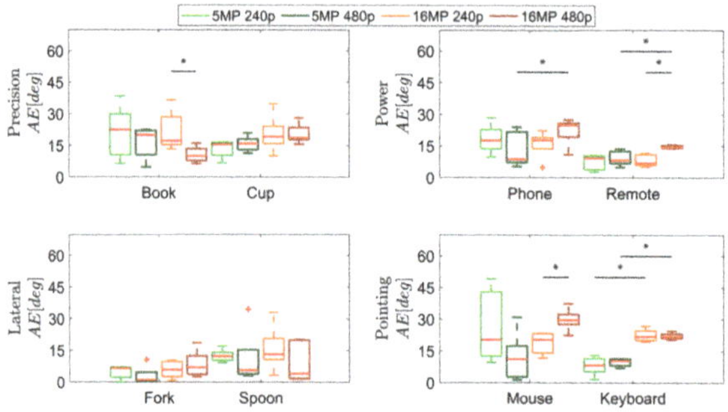

Figure 7. Box plot of angular errors for each object and setup configuration. The * denotes comparison in which p-value < 0.05.

Moreover, the statistical analysis highlights significant differences between the 16 MP camera module with two different resolutions only for the book (p-value = 0.032), remote (p-value = 0.008), and mouse (p-value = 0.032), with a higher AE for 240p resolution only in the first case. Considering 480p resolution for both cameras, the AE is lower for 5 MP one than the 16 MP in the case of the remote (p-value = 0.008), and keyboard (p-value = 0.008), whereas the phone is at the limit of statistical significance (p-value = 0.057). Furthermore, there is a statistical difference between the AE of the two different cameras at 240p resolution only for the keyboard.

Lastly, considering the computational burden of the proposed SCS, as expected, the execution time of the entire control cycle strongly depends on the chosen input image resolution rather than on the camera. AF is 2.02 ± 0.13 FPS and 0.87 ± 0.13 FPS for 240p and 480p resolutions, respectively, for the 5 MP camera sensor. Similarly, AF is 2.07 ± 0.15 FPS and 0.88 ± 0.17 FPS for 240p and 480p resolutions, respectively, for the 16 MP camera. The lower the resolution, the higher the AF of the proposed control algorithm. Regardless of the selected resolution, the Object Detection module takes three orders of magnitude longer than other parts, resulting in being the bottleneck of the control algorithm. In fact, the time required for Object Detection in the scene is >97% of the cycle time.

The comparative analysis highlighted that the 240p resolution outperformed the 480p one. It resulted in having a lower computational burden without affecting the AOC, AGC, AE, and AES. If the camera dimensions are taken into account, the 16 MP one can be considered the best choice since it can be more easily integrated into a prosthesis due to the absence of the fish-eye lens. Furthermore, the 16 MP camera module has the capability of automatically regulating focus: when integrating a camera into a prosthesis that is continuously in movement, automatic focus adjustment reduces the burden on the algorithm, which will always have to work under the condition where the objects of interest are in focus. Thus, the best configuration among the tested ones is the 16 MP Arducam High-Resolution Camera with a 320 × 240 pixels (240p) resolution. This configuration was employed for the last validation phase.

Moreover, the accuracy values in grasp classification are higher than or generally consistent with what has been observed in the literature [17,19], despite a substantial increase in the number of grasps [20,34] and the management of the prosthetic wrist orientation [21,22].

Figure 8a displays the average OA scores obtained for male and female subjects in all the four examined camera positions shown in Figure 8b. It emerged that the ventral position obtained the lowest OA (<15%). Furthermore, in this position, an object is framed until the moment it should be grasped, ensuring a more robust control of hand and wrist preshaping. The Operative tests were carried out by exploiting this camera positioning.

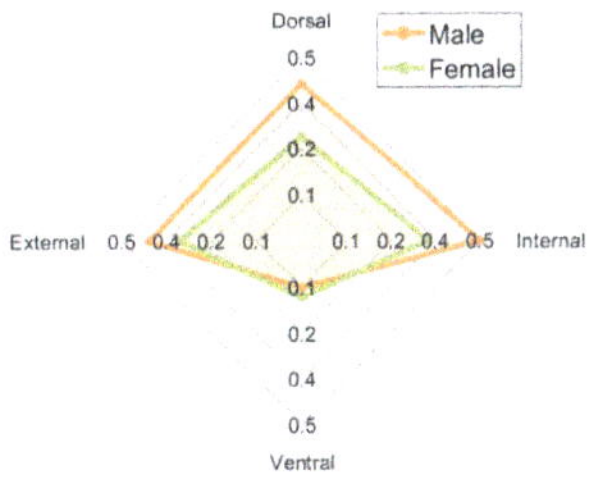

(**a**)

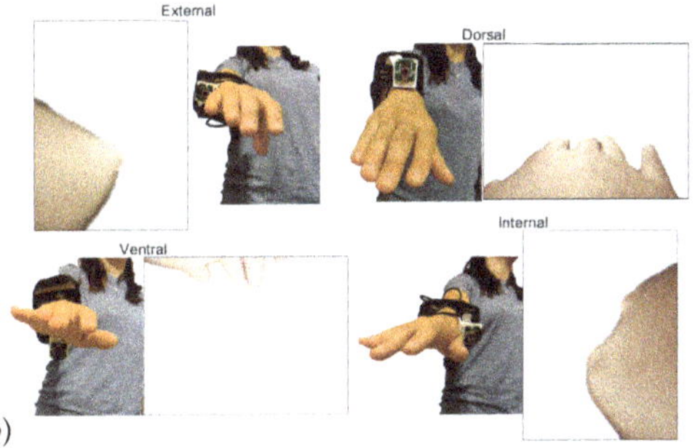

(**b**)

Figure 8. Spider plot of the average OA obtained (**a**). Positioning of the CVS on one subject for all the positions considered, with an example of a frame acquired at each of the four positions (**b**).

In the coherent condition, the proposed algorithm was able to select only the object whose hand gesture matches the EMG classifier output. Figure 9 shows the capability of the proposed SCS to change its output instantly. This occurs because the algorithm always identifies an object in the scene that is graspable with the gesture the user wants to perform. Furthermore, since an object of the user's motion intention class was always present, the red LED never turned on, i.e., the green LED never turned off. Consequently, the orientation estimation was smoothly aligned with the desired object.

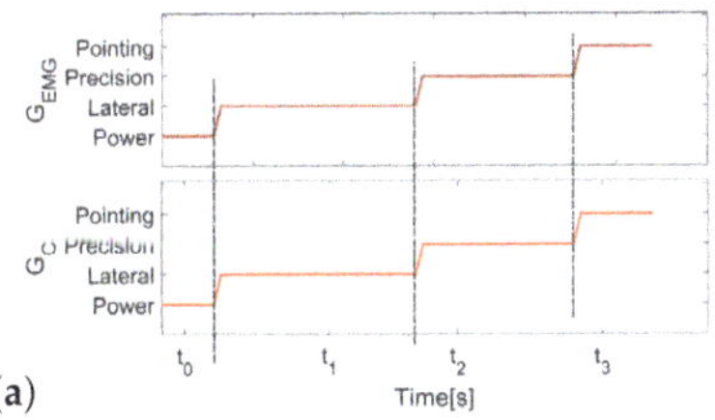

(**a**)

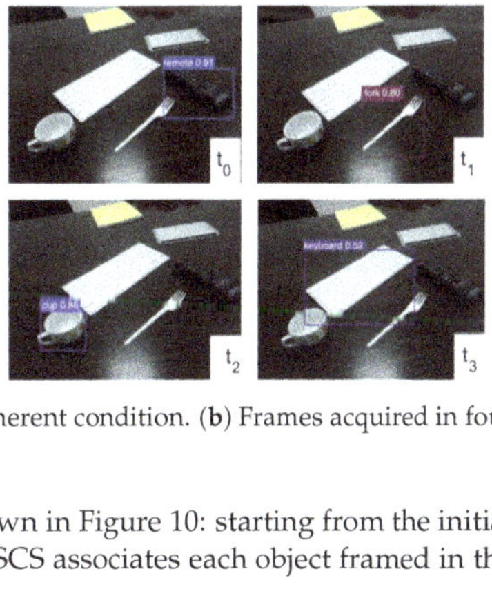

(**b**)

Figure 9. (**a**) Output from the Grasp selection test: coherent condition. (**b**) Frames acquired in four different time instants are reported on the right.

The non-coherent condition results are shown in Figure 10: starting from the initial output of the EMG classifier (dashed line), the SCS associates each object framed in the scene with the correct hand gesture (in orange) to return the correct selected grasp (in red). These discrepancies were fed back to the user by turning on the red LED.

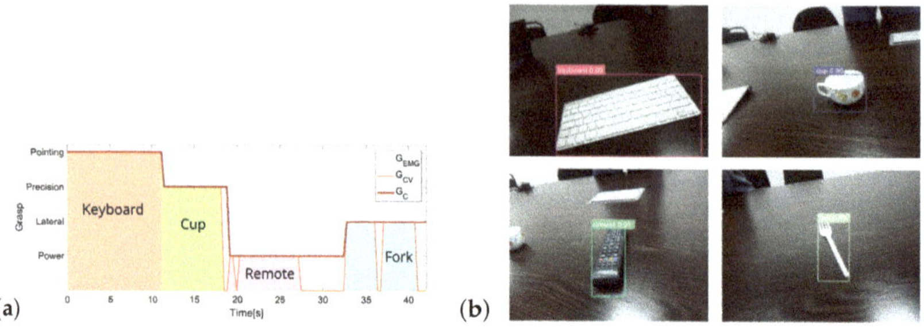

Figure 10. (**a**) Output from the Grasp selection test: non-coherent condition. (**b**) Four frames acquired by the camera are shown on the right.

The SR for the approaching condition test was 100%. The proposed algorithm was always capable of detecting the approach of the tested objects. Figure 11 shows a representative test conducted with the fork: the value of Area in pixels along with its variation at each frame is plotted.

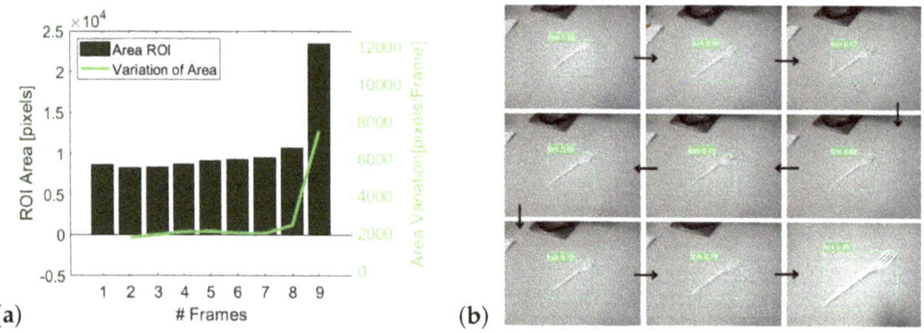

Figure 11. Output from Approaching condition test for the trial with a fork. (**a**) ROI area and its variation over time. (**b**) frames of the acquired video.

A preliminary analysis of the ease of use and the need to perform non-natural movements was carried out on one healthy subject wearing the system. As shown in Figure 5b, the user was asked to position himself in front of the objects in a natural way. In this configuration, the objects are recognized by the proposed algorithm without requiring the user to make non-natural or compensatory movements.

4. Conclusions

In this paper, a semiautonomous control system based on a computer vision system for wrist–hand prostheses was developed and tested. The SCS integrates a CNN-based object detection module, a grasp selection module, and an automatic thresholding algorithm for wrist orientation estimation. By combining exteroceptive information from the CVS with the user's intention via simulated EMG signals, the SCS aims at enhancing prosthesis control performance. The proposed SCS incorporates object detection, selective segmentation of the image, and dynamic thresholding. The results show promising outcomes, including high levels of accuracy in grasping and object classification (above 97%) and an average frame analysis frequency of 2.07 FPS. The developed SCS allows for the recognition of additional grasps beyond those detected by the EMG, ensuring the appropriate grasp for the specific object. The average angular error and angular estimation stability are below 18° and 0.8°, respectively, for all setup configurations. The proposed control strategy is capable of handling more complex situations as demonstrated by the conducted operative tests, reporting a success rate of 100% in recognizing the object approaching phase. Overall, the developed SCS grounded on CVS shows promising results in terms of accuracy, speed, angular estimation, and handling complex situations. Moreover, the proposed approach can be easily applied on different prosthetic hands [35] and robotic grippers [36], as long as they allow a range of hand gestures to be replicated. Indeed, in the design of the proposed solution, particular attention has been paid to build a CVS of reduced dimension to guarantee its portability and interoperability.

In the design of the proposed solution, particular attention has been paid to building a CVS of reduced dimension to guarantee its portability and interoperability.

Future efforts will be devoted to integrating the proposed CVS into a prosthetic hand and testing the developed SCS user-comfort, accuracy, and effectiveness in reducing the cognitive burden on a population of users. Moreover, the implemented SCS will be thoroughly characterized in the use case scenario, to quantify usability aspects in terms of acceptability, ease of use, and performance, i.e., grasp execution times, success rate, and compensatory movements.

Author Contributions: G.C. conceptualized the approach, performed the experiments, analyzed the data, and wrote the paper. C.T. performed the experiments, took care of the visualization of the results, and wrote the paper. L.P.C. conceptualized the approach, and reviewed the paper. F.C. conceptualized the approach, supervised the study, and wrote the paper. All authors have read and agreed to the published version of the manuscript.

Funding: This research received no external funding.

Informed Consent Statement: Informed consent was obtained from all subjects involved in the study.

Data Availability Statement: Data are contained within the article.

Conflicts of Interest: The authors declare no conflict of interest.

Abbreviations

The following abbreviations are used in this manuscript:

DoF	Degrees of Freedom
EMG	Electromyography
SCS	Semiautonomous Control Strategy
CVS	Computer Vision System
CNN	Convolutional Neural Network
P/S	Pronation/Supination
SBC	Single-Board Computer
COCO	Common Objects in Context
ROI	Region Of Interest
PCA	Principal Component Analysis
PC	Principal Component
VNC	Virtual Network Computing
KPI	Key Performance Indicator
AOC	Accuracy in Object Classification
AGC	Accuracy in Grasp Classification
AE	Angular Error
AES	Angular Estimation Stability
AF	Analysis Frequency
FPS	Frames Per Second
OA	Occlusion Area
SR	Success Rate

References

1. Yamamoto, M.; Chung, K.C.; Sterbenz, J.; Shauver, M.J.; Tanaka, H.; Nakamura, T.; Oba, J.; Chin, T.; Hirata, H. Cross-sectional international multicenter study on quality of life and reasons for abandonment of upper limb prostheses. *Plast. Reconstr. Surg. Glob. Open* **2019**, *7*, e2205. [CrossRef] [PubMed]
2. Tamantini, C.; Cordella, F.; Lauretti, C.; Zollo, L. The WGD—A dataset of assembly line working gestures for ergonomic analysis and work-related injuries prevention. *Sensors* **2021**, *21*, 7600. [CrossRef] [PubMed]
3. Jang, C.H.; Yang, H.S.; Yang, H.E.; Lee, S.Y.; Kwon, J.W.; Yun, B.D.; Choi, J.Y.; Kim, S.N.; Jeong, H.W. A survey on activities of daily living and occupations of upper extremity amputees. *Ann. Rehabilit. Med.* **2011**, *35*, 907–921. [CrossRef]
4. Smail, L.C.; Neal, C.; Wilkins, C.; Packham, T.L. Comfort and function remain key factors in upper limb prosthetic abandonment: Findings of a scoping review. *Disabil. Rehabilit. Assist. Technol.* **2021**, *16*, 821–830. [CrossRef] [PubMed]
5. Igual, C.; Pardo, L.A., Jr.; Hahne, J.M.; Igual, J. Myoelectric control for upper limb prostheses. *Electronics* **2019**, *8*, 1244. [CrossRef]
6. Roche, A.D.; Rehbaum, H.; Farina, D.; Aszmann, O.C. Prosthetic myoelectric control strategies: A clinical perspective. *Curr. Surg. Rep.* **2014**, *2*, 44. [CrossRef]
7. Atzori, M.; Cognolato, M.; Müller, H. Deep learning with convolutional neural networks applied to electromyography data: A resource for the classification of movements for prosthetic hands. *Front. Neurorobot.* **2016**, *10*, 9. [CrossRef]
8. Hahne, J.M.; Schweisfurth, M.A.; Koppe, M.; Farina, D. Simultaneous control of multiple functions of bionic hand prostheses: Performance and robustness in end users. *Sci. Robot.* **2018**, *3*, eaat3630. [CrossRef]
9. Leone, F.; Gentile, C.; Cordella, F.; Gruppioni, E.; Guglielmelli, E.; Zollo, L. A parallel classification strategy to simultaneous control elbow, wrist, and hand movements. *J. NeuroEng. Rehabilit.* **2022**, *19*, 10. [CrossRef]
10. Yadav, D.; Veer, K. Recent trends and challenges of surface electromyography in prosthetic applications. *Biomed. Eng. Lett.* **2023**, *13*, 353–373. [CrossRef]
11. Zhang, Q.; Zhu, J. The Application of EMG and Machine Learning in Human Machine Interface. In Proceedings of the 2nd International Conference on Bioinformatics and Intelligent Computing, Harbin, China, 21–23 January 2022; pp. 465–469.
12. Tomovic, R.; Boni, G. An adaptive artificial hand. *IRE Trans. Autom. Control* **1962**, *7*, 3–10. [CrossRef]
13. Stefanelli, E.; Cordella, F.; Gentile, C.; Zollo, L. Hand Prosthesis Sensorimotor Control Inspired by the Human Somatosensory System. *Robotics* **2023**, *12*, 136. [CrossRef]
14. Dosen, S.; Cipriani, C.; Kostić, M.; Controzzi, M.; Carrozza, M.C.; Popović, D. Cognitive vision system for control of dexterous prosthetic hands: Experimental evaluation. *J. Neuroeng. Rehabilit.* **2010**, *7*, 42. [CrossRef] [PubMed]
15. Došen, S.; Popović, D.B. Transradial prosthesis: Artificial vision for control of prehension. *Artif. Organs* **2011**, *35*, 37–48. [CrossRef] [PubMed]
16. Castro, M.N.; Dosen, S. Continuous Semi-autonomous Prosthesis Control Using a Depth Sensor on the Hand. *Front. Neurorobot.* **2022**, *16*, 814973. [CrossRef]
17. Ghazaei, G.; Alameer, A.; Degenaar, P.; Morgan, G.; Nazarpour, K. Deep learning-based artificial vision for grasp classification in myoelectric hands. *J. Neural Eng.* **2017**, *14*, 036025. [CrossRef]
18. Dhillon, A.; Verma, G.K. Convolutional neural network: A review of models, methodologies and applications to object detection. *Prog. Artif. Intell.* **2020**, *9*, 85–112. [CrossRef]
19. Weiner, P.; Starke, J.; Rader, S.; Hundhausen, F.; Asfour, T. Designing Prosthetic Hands With Embodied Intelligence: The KIT Prosthetic Hands. *Front. Neurorobot.* **2022**, *16*, 815716. [CrossRef]
20. Perera, D.M.; Madusanka, D. Vision-EMG Fusion Method for Real-time Grasping Pattern Classification System. In Proceedings of the 2021 Moratuwa Engineering Research Conference, Moratuwa, Sri Lanka, 27–29 July 2021; pp. 585–590.
21. Cognolato, M.; Atzori, M.; Gassert, R.; Müller, H. Improving robotic hand prosthesis control with eye tracking and computer vision: A multimodal approach based on the visuomotor behavior of grasping. *Front. Artif. Intell.* **2022**, *4*, 744476. [CrossRef]
22. Deshmukh, S.; Khatik, V.; Saxena, A. Robust Fusion Model for Handling EMG and Computer Vision Data in Prosthetic Hand Control. *IEEE Sens. Lett.* **2023**, *7*, 6004804. [CrossRef]
23. Cordella, F.; Di Corato, F.; Loianno, G.; Siciliano, B.; Zollo, L. Robust pose estimation algorithm for wrist motion tracking. In Proceedings of the 2013 IEEE/RSJ International Conference on Intelligent Robots and Systems, Tokyo, Japan, 3–7 November 2013; pp. 3746–3751.
24. Boshlyakov, A.A.; Ermakov, A.S. Development of a Vision System for an Intelligent Robotic Hand Prosthesis Using Neural Network Technology. In Proceedings of the ITM Web of Conference EDP Sciences, Moscow, Russia, 28–29 November 2020; Volume 35, p. 04006.
25. Redmon, J.; Divvala, S.; Girshick, R.; Farhadi, A. You Only Look Once: Unified, Real-Time Object Detection. In 2016 IEEE Conference on Computer Vision and Pattern Recognition (CVPR), Las Vegas, NV, USA, 27–30 June 2016.
26. Phadtare, M.; Choudhari, V.; Pedram, R.; Vartak, S. Comparison between YOLO and SSD mobile net for object detection in a surveillance drone. *Int. J. Sci. Res. Eng. Manag.* **2021**, *5*, b822–b827.
27. Lin, T.Y.; Maire, M.; Belongie, S.; Hays, J.; Perona, P.; Ramanan, D.; Dollár, P.; Zitnick, C.L. Microsoft COCO: Common Objects in Context. In Proceedings of the Computer Vision—ECCV 2014, Zurich, Switzerland, 6–12 September 2014; Fleet, D.; Pajdla, T., Schiele, B., Tuytelaars, T., Eds.; Springer International Publishing: Berlin/Heidelberg, Germany, 2014; pp. 740–755.
28. Feix, T.; Romero, J.; Schmiedmayer, H.B.; Dollar, A.M.; Kragic, D. The grasp taxonomy of human grasp types. *IEEE Trans. Hum.-Mach. Syst.* **2015**, *46*, 66–77. [CrossRef]

29. Flanagan, J.R.; Terao, Y.; Johansson, R.S. Gaze behavior when reaching to remembered targets. *J. Neurophysiol.* **2008**, *100*, 1533–1543. [CrossRef] [PubMed]
30. Otsu, N. A Threshold Selection Method from Gray-Level Histograms. *IEEE Trans. Syst. Man Cybern.* **1979**, *9*, 62–66. [CrossRef]
31. Tamantini, C.; Lapresa, M.; Cordella, F.; Scotto di Luzio, F.; Lauretti, C.; Zollo, L. A robot-aided rehabilitation platform for occupational therapy with real objects. In Proceedings of the Converging Clinical and Engineering Research on Neurorehabilitation IV: 5th ICNR2020, Vigo, Spain, 13–16 October 2022; pp. 851–855.
32. Gardner, M.; Woodward, R.; Vaidyanathan, R.; Bürdet, E.; Khoo, B.C. An unobtrusive vision system to reduce the cognitive burden of hand prosthesis control. In Proceedings of the 13th ICARCV, Kunming, China, 6–9 December 2004; pp. 1279–1284.
33. DeGol, J.; Akhtar, A.; Manja, B.; Bretl, T. Automatic grasp selection using a camera in a hand prosthesis. In Proceedings of the 38th Annual International Conference of the IEEE Engineering in Medicine and Biology Society (EMBC), Orlando, FL, USA, 16–20 August 2016; pp. 431–434.
34. Castro, M.C.F.; Pinheiro, W.C.; Rigolin, G. A Hybrid 3D Printed Hand Prosthesis Prototype Based on sEMG and a Fully Embedded Computer Vision System. *Front. Neurorobot.* **2022**, *15*, 751282. [CrossRef]
35. Devi, M.A.; Udupa, G.; Sreedharan, P. A novel underactuated multi-fingered soft robotic hand for prosthetic application. *Robot. Auton. Syst.* **2018**, *100*, 267–277.
36. Sun, Y.; Liu, Y.; Pancheri, F.; Lueth, T.C. Larg: A lightweight robotic gripper with 3-d topology optimized adaptive fingers. *IEEE/ASME Trans. Mechatronics* **2022**, *27*, 2026–2034. [CrossRef]

robotics

MDPI

Article

NOHAS: A Novel Orthotic Hand Actuated by Servo Motors and Mobile App for Stroke Rehabilitation

Ebenezer Raj Selvaraj Mercyshalinie [1,2], Akash Ghadge [1], Nneka Ifejika [3] and Yonas Tadesse [1,2,*]

1 The Humanoid Biorobotics and Smart Systems Lab (HBS Lab), Department of Mechanical Engineering, University of Texas at Dallas, 800 W Campbell Rd, Richardson, TX 75080, USA; ebbyandsam@gmail.com (E.R.S.M.); akashashok.ghadge@utdallas.edu (A.G.)

2 Bioengineering Department, University of Texas at Dallas, 800 W Campbell Rd, Richardson, TX 75080, USA

3 Department of Physical Medicine and Rehabilitation, Department of Neurology, UT Southwestern Medical Center, 5323 Harry Hines Blvd, Dallas, TX 75390, USA; nneka.ifejika@utsouthwestern.edu

* Correspondence: yonas.tadesse@utdallas.edu

Abstract: The rehabilitation process after the onset of a stroke primarily deals with assisting in regaining mobility, communication skills, swallowing function, and activities of daily living (ADLs). This entirely depends on the specific regions of the brain that have been affected by the stroke. Patients can learn how to utilize adaptive equipment, regain movement, and reduce muscle spasticity through certain repetitive exercises and therapeutic interventions. These exercises can be performed by wearing soft robotic gloves on the impaired extremity. For post-stroke rehabilitation, we have designed and characterized an interactive hand orthosis with tendon-driven finger actuation mechanisms actuated by servo motors, which consists of a fabric glove and force-sensitive resistors (FSRs) at the tip. The robotic device moves the user's hand when operated by mobile phone to replicate normal gripping behavior. In this paper, the characterization of finger movements in response to step input commands from a mobile app was carried out for each finger at the proximal interphalangeal (PIP), distal interphalangeal (DIP), and metacarpophalangeal (MCP) joints. In general, servo motor-based hand orthoses are energy-efficient; however, they generate noise during actuation. Here, we quantified the noise generated by servo motor actuation for each finger as well as when a group of fingers is simultaneously activated. To test ADL ability, we evaluated the device's effectiveness in holding different objects from the Action Research Arm Test (ARAT) kit. Our device, novel hand orthosis actuated by servo motors (NOHAS), was tested on ten healthy human subjects and showed an average of 90% success rate in grasping tasks. Our orthotic hand shows promise for aiding post-stroke subjects recover because of its simplicity of use, lightweight construction, and carefully designed components.

Keywords: powered hand orthosis; ADLs; grasping; stroke rehabilitation; characterization; design of hand orthosis

1. Introduction

Stroke ranks as the second leading cause of death globally, accounting for approximately 5.5 million deaths annually. The significant impact of stroke extends beyond its high mortality rate, as up to 50% of survivors face chronic disabilities. Consequently, stroke emerges as a disease of considerable public health significance, carrying substantial economic and social consequences. The public health burden associated with stroke is anticipated to escalate in the coming decades due to demographic shifts, especially in developing nations [1].

Activities of daily living (ADLs) are essential daily self-care tasks performed by individuals, including feeding, grooming, dressing, toileting, and mobility. Hand orthoses are assistive devices that aid in improving hand function, grasp strength, and dexterity, which allows individuals with hand impairments and spasticity to perform ADLs independently.

The development and testing of hand orthotic devices have been reported in many academic journals and conference proceedings, where innovative approaches have been explored, such as the use of shape memory alloys (SMAs), twisted and coiled polymer (TCP) actuators, and 3D printing technologies. The orthotic devices designed are personalized, portable, and aid in specific activities such as grasping and hand extension. The effects of hand therapy and rehabilitation involving orthoses on the independence of individuals in performing ADLs have been examined, underscoring the crucial role of hand function. They emphasize the importance of developing effective and personalized hand orthoses that aid in improving hand function and independence in performing ADLs for individuals with hand impairments [2–5].

Servo motors are used in hand orthoses for providing precise and smooth movements to the fingers and wrist. In an article by Dindorf and Wos in [6], an elbow orthosis with a bimuscular pneumatic servo drive which uses bioelectric signals for control is proposed. One key challenge in the integration of a bimuscular pneumatic servo drive using bioelectric signals within a virtual reality-based system lies in achieving seamless coordination and precision to ensure accurate and responsive control of the orthotic hand. Another issue of pneumatic systems for ADLs is portability. Cartagena et al. in [7] developed a multifunctional orthosis for hand rehabilitation based on virtual reality, which incorporates servo motors for finger flexion and extension. Megalingam et al. [8] designed a wearable hand orthotic device for rehabilitation with multimode control and real-time feedback which also uses servo motors to provide precise movements to the fingers. Veale and Xie in [9] reviewed current and emerging actuator technologies for developing compliant and wearable orthoses, including servo motors. Gretsch et al. in [10] developed a novel 3D-printed robotic prosthetic for amputees which incorporates servo motors to provide precise finger movements. The use of servo motors in hand orthoses ensures precise and smooth movements, which are crucial for effective rehabilitation and assistance to individuals with hand disabilities [11]. Hence, we focus on servo motors in this paper.

In terms of interfaces, the combination of a brain–computer interface (BCI) and a robotic hand orthosis has shown potential for improving motor function in stroke patients [12]. BCIs use electroencephalography (EEG) or near-infrared spectroscopy (NIRS) to detect motor intention signals from the user's brain and translate them into control signals for the servo motors that control hand orthoses. Studies evaluating the performance of BCI-driven hand orthoses showed promising results in stroke patients' neurorehabilitation. Therefore, BCIs coupled with servo motors in hand orthoses could be an effective rehabilitation tool for stroke patients [13–19]. Challenges may arise in the harmonious synchronization of bioelectric signals and the precise actions of servo motors, necessitating careful optimization to ensure seamless functionality and enhance the overall efficacy of the orthotic hand system. Advanced brain–computer interfaces (BCIs) are undoubtedly impressive. However, we believe that utilizing a mobile app controlled via Bluetooth to operate hand orthoses simplifies the actuation process, makes it more accessible, and transforms it into a versatile tool for both rehabilitation and as an assistive device.

The myoelectric concept is a technology used to control a prosthesis or orthosis using the electrical signals generated by muscles during contraction. Several studies have explored the use of myoelectric hand orthoses in different applications, including stroke rehabilitation, Duchenne muscular dystrophy, and spinal cord injury. A myoelectric orthosis typically consists of sensors that detect the electrical signals generated by the muscles, which are then translated into movement commands for the servo motor that actuates the orthosis. The servo motor, in turn, produces the desired movements of the orthosis, allowing the user to perform a range of functions with their affected limb. The studies reviewed here describe the design, development, and use of custom myoelectric elbow–wrist–hand orthoses for upper extremity paresis and loss of function in chronic stroke, as well as the use of electromyography to characterize muscle activation in Duchenne muscular dystrophy. The development of 3D-printed myoelectric hand orthoses for patients with spinal cord injury and the importance of user-centered design methodology are also discussed. Overall, the myoelectric concept has shown promise in improving upper limb function and quality of life for individuals with various neurological and muscular conditions [20–24].

The acoustic noise generated by servo motors can be a significant problem in various applications, such as cost-effective systems. We emphasized noise measurement because the major problem of servo motor-based actuation is their noise and size. We quantified the noise level in such designs to make sure this variable is quantified. To reduce the noise level, different techniques have been proposed in the literature. One approach is to use dual servo loops and digital filter implementation, which can provide ultraprecision positioning. Torsional oscillations can also contribute to the noise level, and the suppression of these oscillations is necessary in high-performance speed servo drives. In the case of controlling traveling-wave ultrasonic motors, pulse width modulation techniques can be used. Overall, reducing noise levels in servo motor systems can improve their performance and reliability in various applications. Velocity control of servo motor systems using an integral retarded algorithm can control the servo motor's velocity smoothly and accurately. In general, reducing noise in servo motor systems involves identifying and addressing the sources of vibration, optimizing control algorithms, and ensuring proper system design and maintenance. Techniques such as vibration analysis, frequency analysis, and signal processing can also be used to identify and quantify the sources of noise [25–31].

The use of soft robotics in rehabilitation for stroke and related disorders has been explored in recent studies [32,33]. Soft robotics allow for the development of lightweight and adaptable devices that can conform to the user's body, providing a more natural and comfortable fit. A challenge in implementing soft robotics in orthotic hands is achieving the necessary balance between flexibility and precision to effectively mimic natural human movements while providing adequate support and functionality. Using cotton gloves and evaluating users' preferences could be a much better option than using soft elastomeric materials. In a bioinspired soft robotics study, researchers discuss the selection of materials and actuation methods for creating soft robotic devices. In another study, "A helping hand", the integration of optical strain sensors and electromyography (EMG) control in a soft orthosis for hand rehabilitation is explored. These studies demonstrate the potential of soft robotics in developing effective rehabilitation devices for stroke and related disorders [34,35]. Our device, NOHAS, incorporates the soft robotic concept using fabric gloves.

Stroke rehabilitation can be conducted using various approaches such as virtual task-specific training guided by a wearable robotic orthosis (UL-EXO7), actual task-specific training guided by a physical therapist, and spring-assisted orthosis training. Home-based technologies have also been studied for stroke rehabilitation. In all these approaches, the aim is to improve the motor function of stroke patients through repetitive training and assistance provided by various technologies or therapists [36–38]. These technologies and approaches can help stroke patients to regain their strength, coordination, and mobility, and ultimately improve their quality of life. This is the goal of the design of NOHAS, but the construction of the devices mentioned above could be difficult and involve expensive components.

Spinal cord injuries, traumas, aging, and strokes are significant contributors to arm impairment and chronic disabilities, necessitating the development of robotic devices for rehabilitation and daily assistance. Surface electromyography (sEMG) control has gained prominence as an intention control method in these devices [39]. A review on control methods by Hameed et al. highlighted key sEMG control criteria such as muscle selection, channel count, and sensor types. Notably, sEMG-based control often faces challenges such as weak signals and abnormal muscle activation in stroke patients, necessitating supplementary control paradigms for effectiveness. In another prosthetic hand study [40], a hand known as FLUIDHAND III was shown to have enhanced functionality, cosmesis, and adaptive grasping, utilizing flexible fluidic actuators and myoelectrodes for pattern selection. A limitation in comparison to servo motor actuation is that the utilization of flexible fluidic actuators and myoelectrodes for pattern selection may pose challenges in achieving the same level of precision and force control needed for certain tasks. Additionally, 3D-printed transitional prosthetic hands offer cost-effective solutions to enhancing the range of motion, strength, and anthropometric variables for children with upper limb deficiencies [41]. Despite factors such as durability and environmental considerations, these prosthetic devices show potential for patients in developing countries who are looking for enhanced functionality and accommodative sizing for their forearm circumference [39–42].

Advancements in medical technology are addressing the challenging issue of hand mobility recovery in stroke therapy, as stroke severely affects hand and locomotor movement. Wearable devices, including EMG-controlled 3D-printed hand exoskeletons, are emerging as valuable tools. Hand exoskeletons help with gripping and can potentially aid in broader hand rehabilitation. Additionally, active hand exoskeleton technologies for rehabilitation, augmentation, and haptic applications are being reviewed, emphasizing specific requirements and challenges posed by the complex anatomy and biomechanics of the hand. The utilization of additive manufacturing, particularly in soft 3D-printed robotic hands, presents lightweight and cost-effective alternatives for robotics and prosthetics. These developments also extend to socially assistive robots (SARs), which can be used in public places. A systematic review of robot-aided upper extremity rehabilitation systems highlights the need for personalization, improved human–robot interaction, and lifelike environments to enhance the adoption of robot-based rehabilitation in clinical practice. EMG-controlled robots need to be used with a great amount of care. Also, EMG signals need significant signal processing and circuits for controlling hand orthoses. Raw EMG signals can be used but their accuracy is limited. An inherent challenge in EEG- and EMG-controlled orthotic hands, compared to mobile app-controlled servo motors, is fine tuning and precise controlling that impacts the intricacy of certain movements. Overall, these technological advancements hold promise for improving the quality of life and mobility of individuals with neurological and upper limb impairments [43–48].

In terms of software interfaces, in 2019, Lin et al. showed a rehabilitation device called *Quality of Movement Feedback-Oriented Measurement System (QM-fOrMS)*, which was designed for individuals with chronic upper limb motor deficits to monitor the motor functions of stroke patients during hospital rehabilitation sessions. QM-fOrMS, developed in Buffalo, NY, USA incorporated cost-effective portable sensors, including an eTextile pressure-sensitive Smart Mat and Smart Can, along with a mobile device. It offered a personalized and adaptive upper limb rehabilitation program that includes unilateral and bilateral functional activities [49]. Another study known as SpECTRUM, shown in [50], was based on a smart object ecosystem inspired by the Action Research Arm Test and consisted of objects like a hand grasping monitor and an arm dynamic monitor equipped with various sensors to monitor finger pressure, position, orientation, movements, and tremors during manipulation tasks. These objects connect to an Android mobile application for data transmission and performance assessment, allowing therapists to evaluate upper arm motor abilities and adapt rehabilitation programs. Health care professional evaluations indicate the utility of the objects and visualization interfaces, while a preliminary study of stroke patients confirms their willingness to use the ecosystem during rehabilitation sessions due to its user-friendliness [49,50]. These two devices are like the functioning of NOHAS but involve user interfaces for making the rehabilitation process easy. Hence, we considered the user interface of the device in our design of hand orthosis.

With regards to innovation, a range of innovative approaches and designs for hand exoskeleton systems tailored for applications in rehabilitation and virtual reality interfaces have been presented in [51–55]. A team of researchers in [51] introduces a dual-cable hand exoskeleton system optimized for virtual reality scenarios, focusing on the measurement of finger joint angles and the implementation of force feedback. Additionally, an index finger rehabilitation system known as HandeXos-Beta (HX-β) is presented, which offers a finger–thumb exoskeleton solution for hand rehabilitation, with independent actuation of thumb movements and the incorporation of series elastic actuators (SEA) to enable precise torque control [52]. The control of this orthotic device is seamless and accurate. The research contributions mentioned above collectively advance the field of hand exoskeleton technology, benefiting applications in rehabilitation and virtual reality interfaces. Our device's novelty is also in the unique features of NOHAS that will be discussed in this paper in detail in various sections.

This paper is organized as follows. As outlined, key advancements in hand orthosis and prosthetics have been explained in the introduction. The next section will introduce the design of a novel hand orthosis actuated by servo motors (NOHAS). Next, two studies on device characterization or testing are presented. The first one is non-human testing which involves evaluation of NOHAS as an effective orthotic device. Next comes human subject testing, which involved humans in experiments with approval from the Institutional Review Board (IRB). A conclusion and summary are provided at the end. An overview video of NOHAS is provided and can be found in the supplementary video (Supplementary Materials) at the following link: https://youtu.be/RtTiUP9PP94 (accessed on 6 December 2023).

The key limitations of the current solutions and technologies can be summarized with the following key points:

- **Limited precision and control**: One key challenge in the integration of hand orthoses based on pneumatic servo drives using bioelectric signals lies in achieving seamless coordination and precision to ensure accurate and responsive control of the orthotic hand. Bioelectric-based control like EEG- and EMG-based control often faces challenges, such as weak signals and abnormal muscle activation in stroke patients, necessitating supplementary control paradigms for effectiveness. An inherent challenge in EEG- and EMG-controlled orthotic hands, compared to mobile app-controlled servo motors, is fine tuning and precise control, which impact the intricacy of certain movements;
- **Acoustic noise, size, and cost**: Many hand orthosis systems utilizing servo motors generate significant acoustic noise, which is a drawback in various scenarios, especially those requiring cost-effective and quiet operations. The noise level should be determined as it may impact user comfort and acceptance. This necessitates studying and overcoming the challenges in undesired acoustic noise in medical devices. Some hand orthoses are very expensive and unaffordable;
- **Limited adaptivity and individual needs**: Some hand orthosis devices may lack adaptability to the specific needs and preference of individuals. The one-size-fits-all approach may not help to meet diverse requirements. Soft robotics can be a solution for fitting various groups. A challenge in implementing soft robotics in orthotic hands is achieving the necessary balance between flexibility, adaptability, and precision to effectively mimic natural human movements while providing adequate support and functionality.

2. Design and Components

The main requirements of the design of our hand orthosis are the following: (1) **lightweight**—less than 500 g including battery, (2) **low profile**—fits average adult hand size (breadth 190–200 mm) with adjustable features, (3) **inexpensive**—material cost USD ~400, (4) **actuated by simple wireless interface**—for in-house operation, (5) **untethered** connection—powered on board by a battery, and (6) **essential for ADLs** as well as rehabilitation. Recently, these design specifications and other aspects were discussed in a review article [56] and we suggest it to readers for more detail. In the design of this hand orthosis, we brainstormed different ideas, and a group of students from a senior design team and graduate students worked on this collaboratively, supervised by the principal investigator from the concept stage to final development. Our final model is shown in Figure 1, and we evaluated the functionality mainly using a standard ARAT kit. The design of the hand orthosis consists of a few components: casing, fabric glove, velcro straps, tendons, servo motors, rechargeable battery, microcontroller, and a cell phone driver app. Servo motors are commonly used as actuators due to their unparalleled precision and control. Their ability to provide accurate and repeatable movements makes them ideal for applications requiring fine-tuned motion, such as in robotics, automation, and orthotic devices. Servo motors offer precise angular positioning and speed control, ensuring a reliable and controlled execution of tasks. Their closed-loop feedback systems enable real-time adjustments, enhancing overall performance. Additionally, servo motors are versatile, capable of handling various loads and operating conditions, making them an excellent choice in applications where precision and reliability are paramount. They have higher energy efficiency than other smart materials and can be operated for longer periods using rechargeable batteries. The CAD model of NOHAS is shown in Figure 1a and the back is shown in Figure 1b. The model was developed using SolidWorks (2022) software while the rendering was created using Autodesk Fusion 360 (V.2.0.15995). Each finger is operated by a fishing line which is connected to the tip of the finger with the help of a distal interphalangeal (DIP) joint hook, while the other end is attached to a corresponding servo motor. The fishing lines are guided with the help of metacarpophalangeal (MCP) joint hooks; each finger has two such hooks.

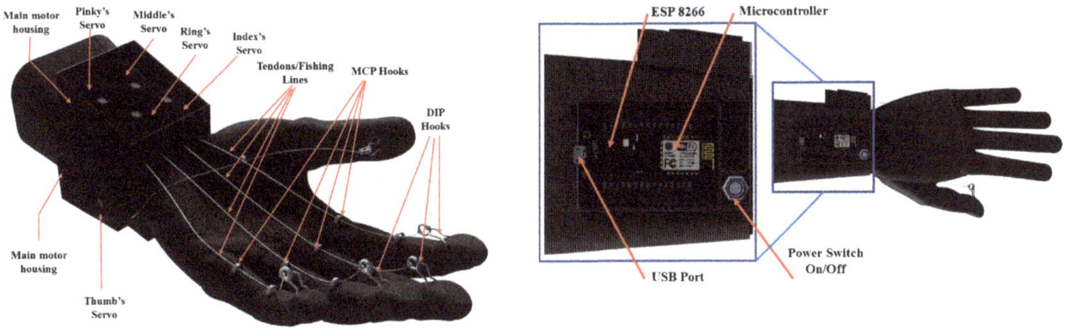

(**a**) (**b**)

Figure 1. CAD model of NOHAS. (**a**) Palm side without fabric—actuators and tendons. (**b**) Back side with electronics.

2.1. Materials Used in Construction

Casings: There are three major casings in our hand orthosis, namely (1) main motor housing, which has four servo motors that sit on the bottom of the user's wrist; (2) thumb motor housing, which has one motor frame on the right side of the user's wrist, and (3) final motor housing, which has one microcontroller and one battery power supply;

Microcontroller: An ESP8266 Wi-Fi microcontroller was selected based on its ability to transmit wireless communication, size, cost, and input/output capabilities. This model was obtained from Espressif Systems, Shanghai, China. The primary benefits of the ESP8266 are its web-friendly embedded technology and wireless capability. Other advantages include affordability, compact size, good speed, and processing power;

Rechargeable battery: A 3000 mAh lithium-ion rechargeable battery (Model Number 103665) is employed in the hand orthosis as a power supply. The battery is 10 × 36 × 66 mm in size and the weight is 47 g. It can actuate the servo motors for several hours (4 h of continuous use). We can also use an ESP8266 type B port by connecting it directly to a PC;

Servo motors: Servo motors (TowerPro SG92R and Sparkfun ROB-10189) with small 3D-printed PLA pulleys actuate the glove by pulling tendons that are connected to the fingertips and passing through guide wires. When the servo motors are actuated, they pull the tendons inside and cause the fingers to bend. The servo motors have position-sensing units that control the desired angles based on input. The ESP8266 Wi-Fi microcontroller is powered by a 9V battery, which also powers other components, including the servo motor;

Tendon: A 25 lb. monofilament fishing line that serves as the artificial tendon is connected to the glove and to the motor housing. The fishing line can spool around a pulley-style connection, which is attached to each motor. The fishing lines pass through holes in the housing along the palm area and are connected to the fingers at attachment points;

Velcro straps: For extra adjustability and customization to different users, the casings are joined by velcro straps; the wiring for the motors follows these straps. The region which is beneath the strap is rubberized to avoid the occurrence of slipping. This region also acts as a point of anchoring for the tendons and prevents the hyperextension of the DIP joint. These components can be securely attached to the fingers while reducing the amount of discomfort, hardness, and slipping due to foam padding and non-slip fabric straps. Mesh rings are used to maintain the finger's equilibrium (Figure 2b);

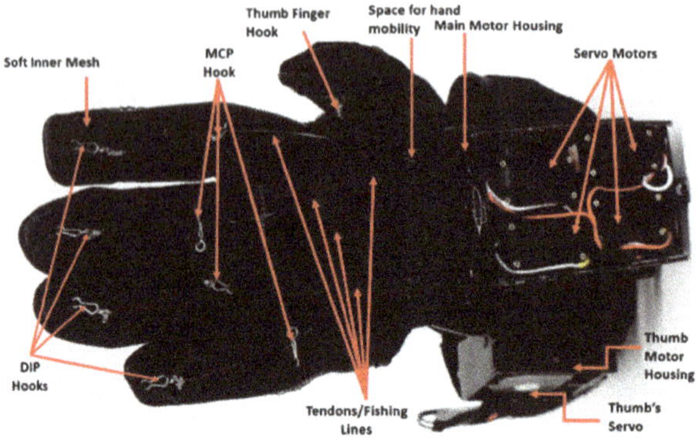

(**a**)

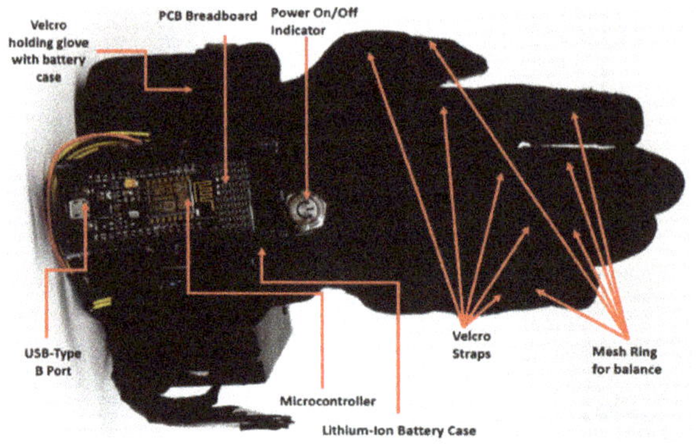

(**b**)

Figure 2. NOHAS, a powered hand orthosis actuated by servo motors. (**a**) Front side and (**b**) back side.

Blynk app: Blynk is a smartphone or tablet device application that is used to operate the servo motors. It is an Internet of Things (IoT) app that allows users to control the device over the cloud. Blynk is a user-friendly app which can be customized and modified any time according to the user's needs. The user will be able to set up specific control tasks or sequences to connect with the servo motors over the Wi-Fi chip using Blynk's user-friendly interface;

Return elastic rubber bands: Elastics bands at the back of the glove serve as spring-returning mechanisms that direct the fingers to their original positions after actuation;

Glove: The fabric glove is made of cotton and wool. The glove increases the stability of ligaments and tendons in the wrist, which substantially increases the overall stability of the hand. Generally, the material of the glove is safe and does not cause allergies for most people, but it can be replaced as needed as some individuals may be allergic to wool;

Safety aspect in our design: NOHAS is safe and comfortable. In the design phase, we added all the movable parts within a casing so that the user will only be wearing a fabric glove on their hand. Later, throughout our human subject testing, no issues or complaints were raised regarding the wearability of the glove. In our IRB, we provided a clear explanation of the glove's safety measures, highlighting that the use of compact and efficient servo motors ensures that there are no potential issues during finger flexion and extension. In the rare event that a user experiences even a minor discomfort, the device can be promptly deactivated, and the glove can be easily taken off the hand.

2.2. Prototype and Working Mechanism of the Hand Orthosis

The design comprises two independent parts in a right-handed configuration: the glove and electronics/motor housings. NOHAS is designed like other gloves used in hand rehabilitation. On the palmar side, active actuation occurs, and on the opposite side, a passive elastic band returns the finger back to its position. The thumb and each finger joint have two attachment points on the glove's fabric. The housings for the motors and controller consist of three distinct shells that are designed and 3D printed with PLA+ material to be worn on the wrist like a "watch". The primary motor housing, which contains four motors, is situated on the underside of the wrist. The thumb motor housing, which is on the right side of the wrist, contains just one motor. The prototype hand, when fully assembled, can be seen from the front and back sides as shown in Figure 2a,b, respectively.

The hypothesis of using servo motors for this application is that this technology provides a good combination of the desired attributes of a hand orthosis. Factors such as precise position, control, energy efficiency, compact size, and suitability for ADLs are among the key elements influencing our motor selection.

The working principle is shown in a schematic diagram in Figure 3a,b. When the servo motor is actuated to certain angles, the tendon connected to the guide structures will bend the fingers. The elastic band at the back of the glove returns the finger; at the same time, the servo motor should be actuated in the reverse direction to release the tendon.

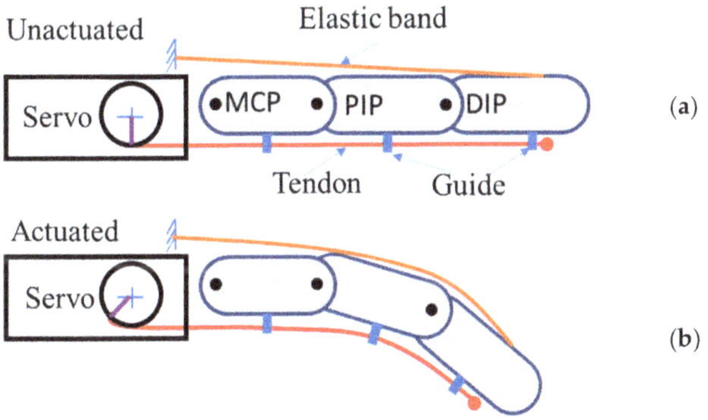

Figure 3. Working mechanism of NOHAS. (**a**) How the finger looks when unactuated and (**b**) when actuated.

2.3. Servo Motor Selection

Key properties were considered to select the proper servo motor for the design of the NOHAS hand orthosis. The servo motors must be able to rotate continuously at 360 degrees to be able to provide the necessary bending angle and torque to activate the fingers via the pulley system. An estimation based on data on men and women in their seventies says that their average gripping force is approximately 300 N [57]. If that is divided equally throughout all the fingers, then it will be 60 N per finger. NOHAS was designed using a TowerPro SG92R microservo and Sparkfun ROB-10189. SG92R has control arms and gears made of carbon fiber, which produces a torque of 2.5 kg-cm while weighing only 9 g. The SG92R can rotate about 180 degrees (90 degrees in each direction). Standard servo motors only operate inside a certain servo motor angle, typically 180 degrees. The ROB-10189 model has a stall torque of 2.2 kg-cm with 360-degree rotation. The servo motors are equipped with gears to reduce the motor speed and a potentiometer for position feedback. The motor may begin to vibrate and make noise if it is turned all the way to 0 or 180 because it is attempting to drive to an impassable position. It is preferable to either use it within the safety range or a usable range, such as 20–160 degrees. It is important to maximize the range because this results in a high stall current condition. This also has the potential to strip gears and it might lead to some unwanted damage to the motor. Because of the compact size, enhanced performance, and low-cost requirement of the glove, the RC servo motors discussed above were selected for the design. A dynamic equation using the Euler–Lagrange model for robotic or human fingers, including resistance and finger spasticity, can be expressed as [58]:

$$\tau = M(\theta)\ddot{\theta} + V\left(\theta,\ \dot{\theta}\right) + G(\theta) + J(\theta)^T F \tag{1}$$

where τ is the torque required to move the fingers, $M(\theta)$ is the mass and inertia matrix, which is an $n \times n$ matrix (n = 3 for the thumb and n = 4 for the other fingers), $V\left(\theta,\ \dot{\theta}\right)$ is the Coriolis and centrifugal terms, which is $n \times 1$ vector, $G(\theta)$ is the gravity term, which is $n \times 1$ vector. $J(\theta)$ is a Jacobian matrix that relates fingertip linear and angular displacement with joint velocity. F is applied force.

Equation (1) provides accurate modeling. However, it requires several variables and makes the selection of motors complicated. For simplicity, if we ignore gravity, Coriolis terms, and the resistance of fingers, the joint torque of the servo motors can be determined from a simple equation of force and offset distance from the following. A similar assumption was made in our previous analysis [59]:

$$\tau = F\ r\sin(\theta) \tag{2}$$

where τ is the torque required to move the fingers, F is the force needed to move the servo motor, r is the radius of the pulley/servo horn, θ is the bending angle of the finger/servo horn. Here, F = 60 N, r = 5 mm, and θ = 90, which yields τ = 2 kg-cm. Therefore, the minimum amount of torque required to actuate a finger with some safety factor will be approximately 2.6 kg-cm. Based on this calculation, all the servo motors for the hand orthosis are selected. Besides torque, size, weight, and cost are important properties of servo motors that determine the property of our orthotic hand.

3. Initial Characterization of NOHAS (Study 1)

In this section, we describe the methodology and experimental procedure for testing the orthotic hand by mounting it on a dummy hand. The experimental setup is shown in Figure 4a. The ESP 8266 chip's Wi-Fi mode is automatically turned on when the button is turned on in NOHAS, showing a blue light in the ESP casing. There are some cases when the blue light does not turn on which means that the battery needs to be replaced. The battery must be checked and fully operational before testing the device. In the case where the battery does not work, we need to manually plug in the port from the ESP chip to the laptop's port. Next, the mobile phone hotspot is turned on. In the list of available devices in our mobile phone, the ESP chip's name is displayed, and we connect to it. After this, Arduino IDE is opened on the laptop and is connected to NOHAS's ESP8266 chip port via a USB type-B cable. The next step is to verify the code in Arduino IDE. After the successful verification of the code in Arduino IDE, the code is uploaded to the ESP 8266 chip via the USB type-B cable. Generally, it takes less than a minute to successfully upload. The serial monitor displays that the connection is successfully established. The photograph of the real experimental setup is shown in Figure 4b, illustrating the device, laptop, cell phone, and a standard ARAT kit for grasping tasks [32]. The schematic diagram of the circuit was created using Cirkit Designer, and the codes were developed using integrated Arduino IDE. The circuit connections are shown in Figure 4c. Green wires represent positive connections, which are connected to the LED, resistor, all five servo motors, and ESP8266. Red wires establish a common ground for the circuit, ensuring proper voltage operation. Blue wires transmit the enable signal, allowing PWM signals to control the servo motors. LEDs indicate device status, and a resistor protects the LED. By actuating the servo motors according to a program in the mobile app, video recordings of the hand orthosis were taken and analyzed.

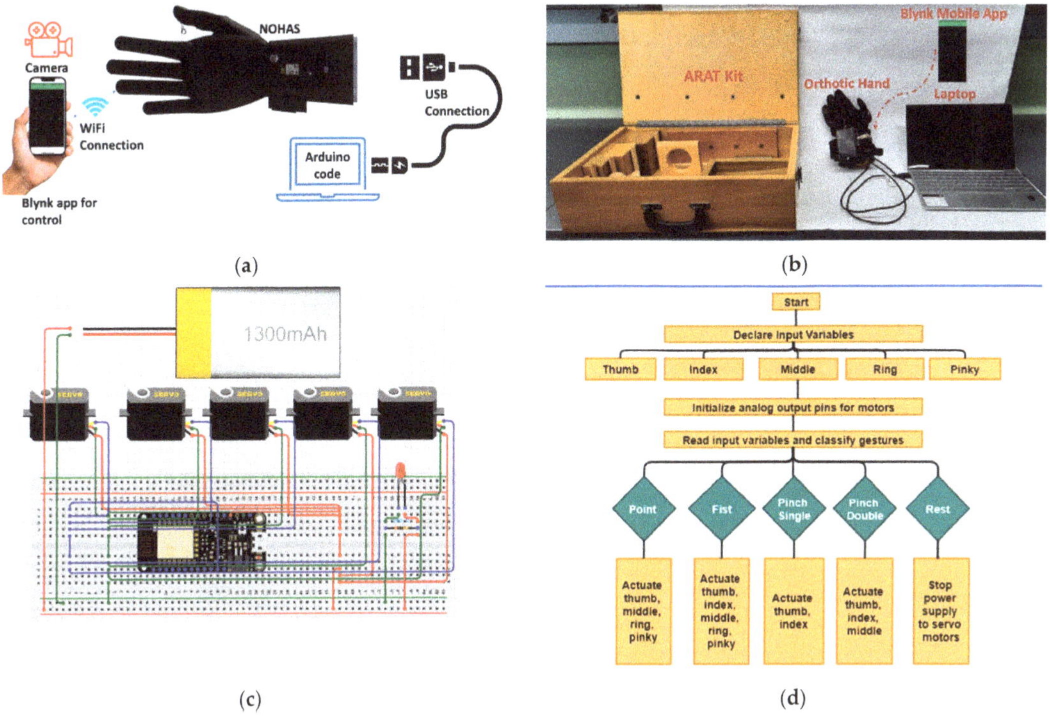

Figure 4. Actuation method. (**a**) Schematic diagram of the setup, (**b**) photograph, (**c**) circuit diagram, and (**d**) algorithm followed.

3.1. Basic Gesture Test

A basic gesture test was conducted using the Blynk mobile app by clicking the corresponding button in the program, as shown in Figure 5a. A dummy hand, which was made of silicone, was used to mimic a human hand and test the hand orthosis. For example, to actuate only the thumb, the button in the app is pressed once, then the servo motor will rotate approximately 30 degrees and move the finger. When the button is pressed again, it will move the thumb further by another 30 degrees. Typically, each finger is activated in three steps to complete full flexion. Finally, it will be set back to its position using the rest button. In ref. [60], researchers discussed two code states for a similar opening and closing orthotic hand. In our case, the code starts with declaring all the input variables. The input variables for the thumb, index, middle, ring, and pinky fingers are all presented separately, as shown in Figure 4d. Analog output pin initialization is carried out independently for each of the five servo motors. The next stage involves interpreting the input variables and categorizing the gestures.

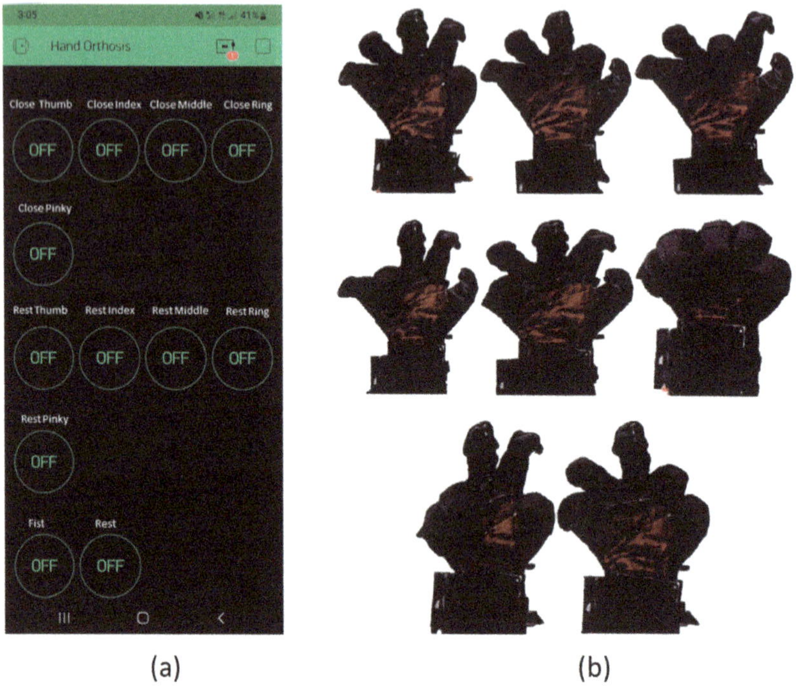

Figure 5. Testing NOHAS by mounting it on a dummy hand. (**a**) shows the layout of the Blynk mobile app. (**b**) shows some basic gestures performed by NOHAS. From top left: thumb close, index close, middle close, ring close, pinky close, fist close, peace gesture, and pinch gesture.

As seen in Figure 5b, NOHAS was designed to execute various ADLs. The main reason for conducting this test was the evaluation of how efficiently the servo motors and pulleys worked. The test was conducted by mounting the hand orthosis on the dummy hand for different gestures. This test also provided us with experience with dealing with tangling of the tendon or fishing line. Also, since we quickly trigger two or three fingers at once and relax them, this test was crucial in determining how well NOHAS handled multitasking. Similar to any other exoskeleton with stiff components across the hand, researchers in [61] created and tested a device that restricts the use of compensatory grasps that do not involve the thumb. Battery drain must be considered as a key factor in this stage as multitasking quickly depletes the battery. As a result, we had to recharge the battery often. To characterize the device, some simple hand gestures, including pointing, pinching, the peace sign, closing the fist, etc., were performed to validate NOHAS. But after performing each of these gestures, we had to bring NOHAS back to the initial rest position where no special gestures or actions are performed. This prevents the fishing lines from being tangled inside the servo motors. The tendons might get stuck and might damage the hook. This may damage the soft clothing on top of NOHAS. Thus, the relaxation step is essential.

3.2. *Agular Position Characterization and Maximum Angle Test*

Using video tracker software, the bending angles for each DIP, MCP, and PIP joint were estimated using the following approach. Several commonly used apparatuses which are generally used to investigate the angular locations of orthotic devices include anatomically accurate hands, a high-speed Phantom Miro camera, a computer which can collect theNI-cDAQ data, a power supply, and a K-type thermocouple. These were used in Saharan et al.'s work [62]. Other researchers used a similar approach on stroke patients who were affected with mild to moderate motor function impairment [63]. A high-speed camera was not needed to capture the actuation of NOHAS as a regular camera was sufficient. After this process, the data were retrieved and analyzed.

In this work, we characterized NOHAS by following a few processing steps. The index finger was initially chosen. Actuation in response to servo motor motion was recorded by a camera and then loaded into the tracker software. The video was then paused and cropped inside the tracker software in such a way that the tracking started as soon as we could see the finger actuation happening in the uploaded video. The result is shown in Figure 6. Coordinate axes were added to the video. This was used in the tracker software to accurately position the starting point and angle inside the video. A calibration stick was added to the video to inform the software about the finger's actual height. A point mass was positioned at the DIP joint, which is close to the tip of the index finger, to measure the DIP values. A similar process was conducted to automatically observe the other joints. The tracking was observed to be very smooth. Additionally, we can observe that the software appropriately plots the angle data vs. time.

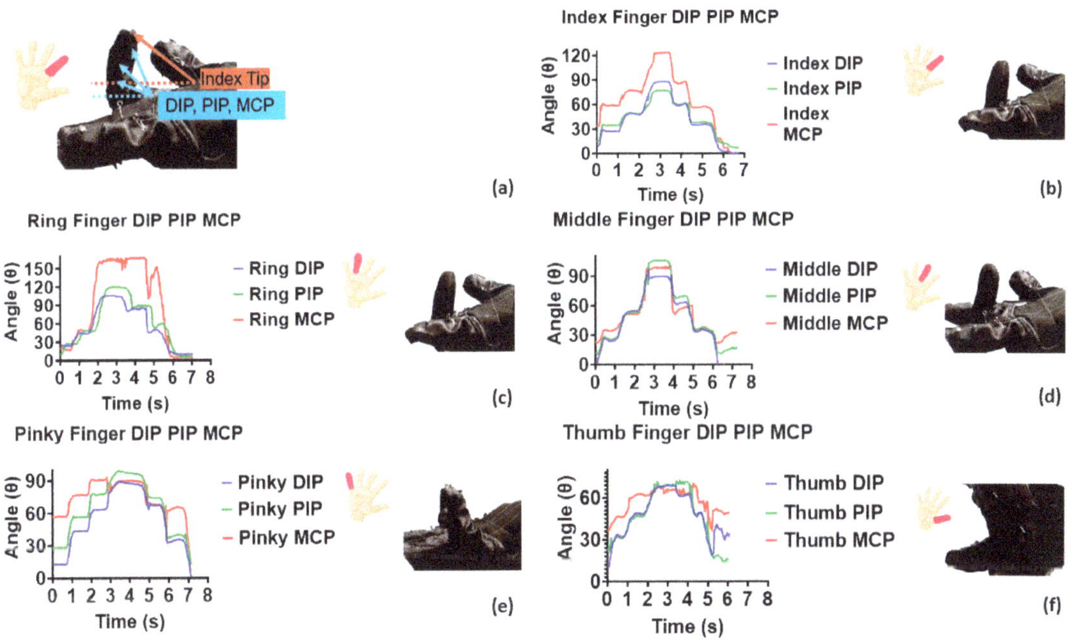

Figure 6. Characteristics of the DIP, PIP, and MCP angles obtained by the actuation of NOHAS's fingers. (**a**) represents the reference image. (**b**–**f**) represent the DIP, PIP, and MCP joint angles for the index, ring, middle, pinky, and thumb fingers, respectively. This was performed by mounting NOHAS on the right hand of a human subject.

The reference picture shown in Figure 6a explains the placement of the coordinate axes inside the tracker software. The procedure is the same for the index finger's PIP joint as shown in Figure 6b, showing all the three joints of a finger. The same steps are then carried out for the remaining four fingers, as shown in (c) to (f). So, we obtained five angle vs. time data in total. The maximum extension and flexion range of the fingers must be taken into consideration to prevent overstretching or overfolding, which causes discomfort to the fingers. DIP, PIP, and MCP plots are essential for monitoring the behavior of any orthotic hand. We can see that there are three steps in the DIP, PIP, and MCP lines for each graph. Considering the blue line in Figure 6b, when the "index close" icon in the mobile app is pressed, the index finger angle value increases from 40 to 60 degrees from 0 s to 0.2 s. There is no actuation from 0.2 s to 1 s. From 1 s to 1.2 s, we can see the next actuation. Then, from 1.2 s to 2 s, there is no actuation or change in angle. The same concept holds for the relaxation phase. The relaxation steps are performed until the device returns to 0. The same procedure was followed for all the other four fingers.

Regarding characterization using video tracking, studies [64–68] employed wearable devices and exoskeletons with sensors like potentiometers or encoders to measure angular movements of DIP, PIP, and MCP joints. In contrast, our approach utilized Tracker software, employing video recordings to measure bending and visually document hand movements. Tracker has been used in many studies [69–73], where it effectively captured angular deflections of analog instrument pointers. Their collective findings underscore Tracker's versatility, proving its value in cost-effective, straightforward experiments beyond mechanics, extending into various disciplines. The HBS lab group has successfully utilized Tracker software for characterizing dynamic motion, demonstrating its effectiveness in capturing angular motion [74–76].

3.3. Standard Object Grasping Test

The grasping test was primarily conducted to measure the time duration NOHAS can hold the objects with a firm grip. This was performed by mounting it on one subject and grasping objects from the ARAT kit. Healthy humans rely on pinch and power grasping techniques, which primarily depend on the utilization of the thumb. On the other hand, stroke survivors without proper thumb function generally make use of the other four fingers primarily. They also sometimes forcefully place the thumb away against the backs of the fingers. This action helps them to squeeze an object between the fingers and the palm. The texture and weight of the objects were taken into consideration during selection. Figure 7 illustrates how various grips were used to grasp various objects while actuating NOHAS. As indicated in Table 1, daily use objects of varying weights, sizes, and forms were assessed. Many gripping positions, namely tripod, extension, transverse volar, spherical volar, diagonal volar, lateral pinch, five finger pinch, and pulp squeeze [77] were tried and their outcomes are shown in Figure 7. The various objects used in Figure 7, the weights of individual objects, texture, size, and effective holding for NOHAS are provided in Table 1. These grasping techniques gave us a clear understanding of human muscles and their capacity to grasp various items.

Table 1. Different objects, their characteristics, and effective grasping time of NOHAS.

Object	Weight (grams)	Texture	Size	Dimensions (Length × Width × Height) mm	Weight: Type	Effective Time of Holding
Pen	15	Smooth	Small	140 × 10 × 10	Light	Until battery drains out
Box-Small	74	Smooth	Small	57 × 57 × 57	Light	Until battery drains out
PC Mouse	84	Rough	Medium	100 × 60 × 40	Light	Until battery drains out
Cardboard box	107	Rough	Big	300 × 200 × 100	Medium	5 min

Table 1. *Cont.*

Object	Weight (grams)	Texture	Size	Dimensions (Length × Width × Height) mm	Weight: Type	Effective Time of Holding
Ball-Stitched	154	Smooth	Medium	88.9 (diameter)	Medium	30 min
Box-Big	229	Smooth	Big	500 × 250 × 150	Medium	10 min
Water Bottle Empty	483	Smooth	Big	260 × 70	Heavy	1 min
Water Bottle Filled	1566	Smooth	Big	260 × 70	Heavy	25 s
Decoration stone	1862	Rough	Big	200 × 100 × 50	Heavy	15 s

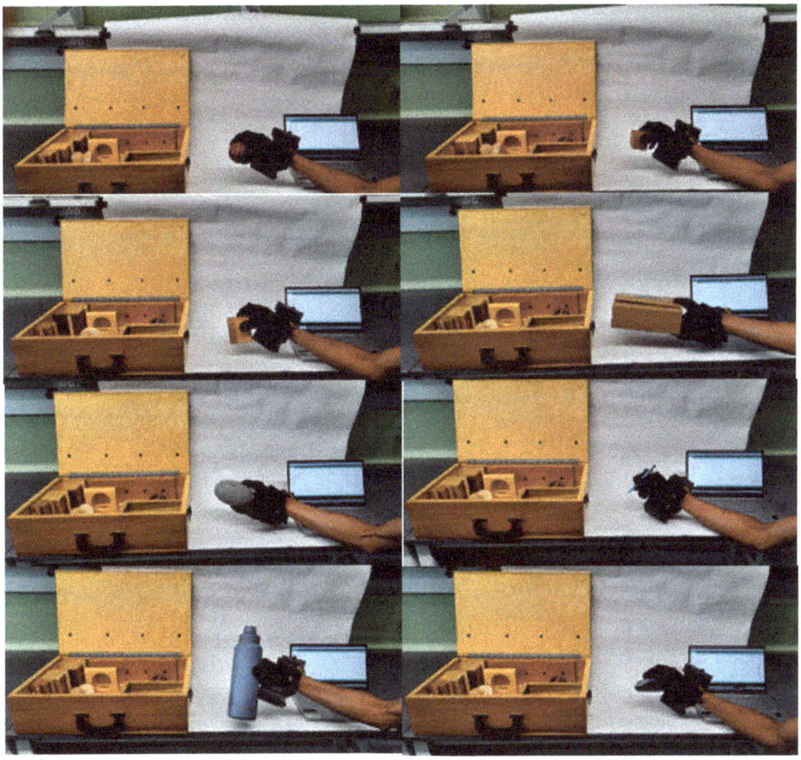

Figure 7. Standard object grasping test on a subject: horizontal and vertical grasping of objects from the ARAT kit with other commonly used items.

3.4. Variations in Finger Actuation Timing Test

The fingers of NOHAS were actuated and tested in a time interval of five, three, and one second, which are referred to as slow, medium, and fast, respectively. This test is like the test results shown in Figure 6, but here, the duration of actuation time is varied. First, the thumb was actuated and relaxed over a period of five seconds, resulting in slight movement from the initial position. After 5 s, the finger moved up a little bit more for the second actuation. In the third actuation, the finger was shown completely bent. This was a slow process. It was performed at the beginning to prevent the fishing lines from tangling and to watch if the device heats up. But, throughout the repeated actuation, there was no heating observed.

In a similar manner, all five fingers were gradually triggered over a period of five seconds. The thumb was triggered and actuated after three seconds in the next step. The second actuation happened a little bit quicker than the first. Like the prior phase, no obvious heating was noticed. The same procedure was followed for all the other four fingers. Finally, the thumb's actuation was completed after a 1 s delay. This actuation interval is the quickest since the delay is observed to be just 1 s. The primary motor housing clearly heated up because the actuation was nearly constant. Occasionally, the entanglement of tendons was also observed. In such cases, the "resting button" in the app should be pressed, and the orthosis should be rested to release the tangling. Due to high actuation frequency, the Bluetooth connection occasionally experienced some connectivity issues. However, these problems were resolved once the actuation was carried out once every second without any lag.

3.5. Force-Sensitive Resistors on NOHAS

Force-sensing resistors (FSRs) were used for testing the force output or, in other terms, the squeezing ability of NOHAS. In essence, FSRs change their resistance in response to external pressure, force, or stress placed on their surfaces. When we apply a notable amount of external force, the conductive film in an FSR is distorted against the substrate. FSRs generally have a vent or a space for forcing the air out. The resistance value was observed to decrease when the conductive ink region contacted the region of the conductive film. We tested different FSRs that could be used in our orthotic hand.

During our experiments, we tested FSRs and found that they have several advantages such as their small size, low cost, and high shock resistance. However, FSRs do have some limitations, such as low precision, and their sensitivity varies depending on the size. While force-sensing capacitors have better sensitivity and long-term stability, their driving circuits are bulky and more complex. We observed that a 1.5-inch FSR had very high sensitivity, with even a small amount of force causing a noticeable change in the FSR readings. On the other hand, A101 FSR and DF9–16 FSR had lower sensitivity, requiring more force to produce noticeable changes. However, for embedding the FSRs onto NOHAS, we determined that the A101 FSR was the best option due to its small size and ease of use. Figure 8a shows the experimental setup of NOHAS when analyzing the properties of the 1.5-inch FSR. The FSR reading corresponds to the voltage output and the mapping is as follows: 0 V corresponds to 0 FSR reading or 0 N force, and 5 V corresponds to 1024 FSR reading or 100 N force [78]. This relationship is dependent on the choice of pulldown resistor and supply voltage. The FSR reading is associated with 10-bit ADC used for reading.

Simulations were conducted to analyze the properties of the FSR, including its resistance and load bearing capacity. Figure 8d shows a simulation method which was carried out using a potentiometer for a three-terminal resistor with a sliding or revolving contact region to change the input force magnitude. We used potentiometers in our circuits to act as variable voltage dividers and to measure voltage accurately. In the simulation, changes in the signal level (FSR reading) were recorded from the LED display. During the simulation, a 10 kΩ resistor was connected to the FSR, which was then connected to the ground. The other end of the FSR was connected to the power supply. The simulation results showed changes in signal levels with variations in the applied force, which provided valuable insights into the properties and behavior of the FSR.

The result for the simulation is shown in Figure 8e. Initially, the FSR reading was 0. But when the force value was increased with an increment of 0.1 up to 1 N, we observed an increase in FSR value from 58 to 650, which is a rapid change in slope. After this, the values gradually increased to about 900 as the force magnitudes increased to 10 N with an increment of 1 N. We consider the two regions in Figure 8e for FSR reading to force in Newton conversion. The two regions are obtained by curve fitting using MATLAB as are shown in Figure 8b,c and the following relation provides the relationship between the FRS digital reading (x) and the Force output, $F(x)$ in Newton.

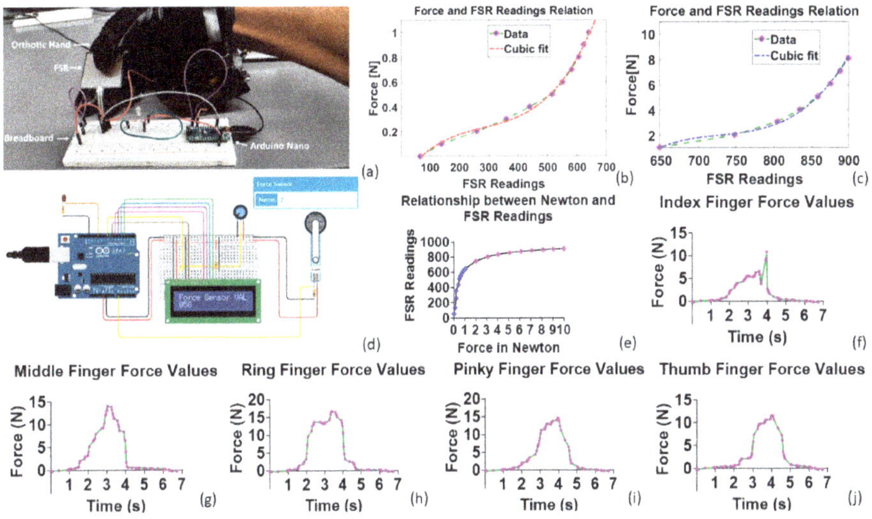

Figure 8. Experimental setup for obtaining FSR readings is shown in (**a**). Figures (**b**,**c**) show the curve fitting process for the relationship between FSR and force readings. The simulation of FSR with Arduino and other circuits to establish relationship between force input and FSR output is shown in (**d**). The relationship between force values in newton and FSR digital readings is shown in (**e**). Force characterization using FSR readings from index, middle, ring, pinky, and thumb fingers are shown in (**f**), (**g**), (**h**), (**i**) and (**j**) respectively.

$$F(x) = \begin{cases} f_1(x) = p_1x^3 + p_2x^2 + p_3x + p_4\,, & x \in [\,60 \;\; 650] \\ \\ f_2(x) = q_1x^3 + q_2x^2 + q_3x + q_4\,, & x \in [\,650 \;\; 900] \end{cases} \tag{3}$$

where the contestants are given by:

$$p_1 = 1.1578 \times 10^{-8} \quad p_2 = -9.7359 \times 10^{-6} \quad p_3 = 0.0033137 \quad p_4 = -0.18968$$
$$q_1 = 1.0343 \times 10^{-6} \quad q_2 = -0.0022575 \quad q_3 = 1.6483 \quad q_4 = -400.58$$

Figure 8f,j shows the force vs. time plots when all five servo motors (namely index, middle, ring, pinky, and thumb) are actuated individually. We can see a gradual increase in the force magnitude when NOHAS is actuated until 3.5 s. With a short gap after 3.5 s, we can see that NOHAS is in the relaxation phase, and we observe a steady decline in the force output. Notable changes in force happen only when an external force acts upon the FSR. The profiles are slightly different from each other, indicating variations in applying force while wearing the device and this is also dependent on the user.

The actuation of NOHAS was performed in a few steps. In the first step, the actuation was carried out by pressing the button in the app. During this time, the FSR values were about 200 (0.18 N force) in the display. In the next step of actuation, there was a higher amount of force acting and the values increased up to around 500 (0.48 N force) and in the next step, even more force was acted upon, and the readings went up to about 800 (2.82 N force). The maximum values in the output were observed at around 940 (13.16 N force). We did not want to actuate the servo motors even more because it may have led to the tangling of tendons on the servo motors and the device might have got damaged. Next, the relaxation phase was performed in steps and we can see that the FSR values displayed in Arduino decreased slowly until they dropped to 0. The same procedure was followed for all the five servo motors, and we found that in all cases, the FSR readings accurately reflected the squeezing ability of NOHAS. The FSR readings were converted to Force readings for easy understanding of squeezing ability. In Figure 8f,j, we may notice a few red connection lines with no green points. This is caused by the delay in the actuation of the servo motors. The main reason for this is the delay caused by ESP 8266 with respect to the hotspot and mobile phone.

3.6. Servo Noise Measurement Experiment

Servo motors are great for actuation due to their speed and energy efficiency [79–81]. However, their drawback is the audible noise that comes out of the motor during actuation. For noise measurement in our robotic hand, we followed a similar procedure to quantify actuator noise to the procedure published using the Qualtrics web platform by researchers in [82]. To record the noise, they connected each servo motor to a power supply. It was controlled using a 490 Hz pulse width modulation signal by Arduino IDE. To reduce resonance when recording, the equipment was turned on and the servo motors were kept on a tiny cloth. Each servo motor performed a 180-degree sweep when unloaded. It was coded in such a way that a similar back and forth movement of 2 s in each direction was made in continuous rotation. This made sure the sounds were comparable, even though the lengths of the clips varied from 0.5 s to 5 s due to speed differences. They used a Zoom H2N microphone for recording in a studio. After all noises were captured, each clip's volume was normalized, and it was cropped to distinguish the noise during the 0–180–0-degree change. In our case, we used a mobile phone to record servo motor noise.

Servo motors follow the same principles as standard AC and DC motors, except for the positioning device to which they are coupled. This makes closed-loop system control possible. Understanding and rectifying some of the most common problems that could occur is essential for successfully managing a servo motor system; in our case, where the servo motors are used for active finger actuation. Noise during actuation will heat up the servo motor. A motor that is heating up while running can cause problems that might eventually lead the motor or other machine parts to fail.

3.7. Understanding Servo Motor Audio Noise and Overheating

We suspected that the sharp noise could cause some level of discomfort to the people who are wearing it. If they wear this device for a long time and hear this noise continuously, they might feel they need to remove the glove. So, we want to quantify the level of noise. The audio noise of RC servo motors is caused by the vibration of components such as gears. This audio noise should be quantified as it may cause inconvenience to users. The magnitude of this noise could vary depending on other factors such as the surface quality of the gears. The servo motor noise problem could be either intermittent or constant, with the motor stopping and making a chattering noise. While the output shaft of the motor is stationary, it occasionally oscillates to some extent. The chattering noise observed is generally due to positioning blunders, with a drive module setup issue or loss of settings-related causes. Although servo motor bearings were usually sealed, moisture could still enter and cause the lubricant to dry out. The servo motor required a service that included a bearing swap when typical troubleshooting, such as checking settings and parameters. This issue needed to be resolved since it worsened over time and eventually led to the failing of the motors. For each of the five fingers individually, noise intensity was measured. The five servo motors' noise levels were tested using the free Sound Meter app from the Google Play store. The setup for this experiment comprised placing the microphone near the servo motors and actuating the fingers, as shown in Figure 9. The same experiment was conducted multiple times to verify the accuracy of the noise levels. But the noise levels of all the five servo motors are different from each other, which could be due to the loading conditions while pulling the tendons. Figure 9 shows the individual and combined noise levels for each servo motor.

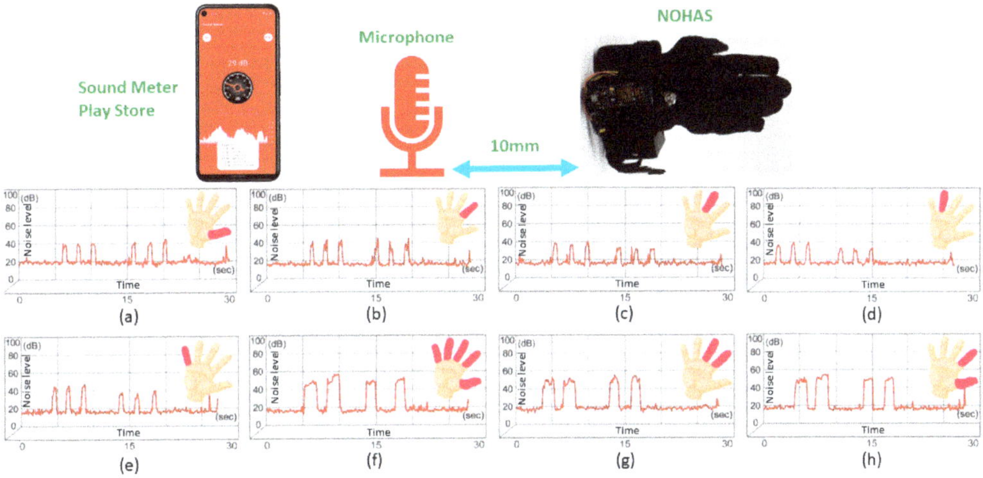

Figure 9. Experimental setup for measuring noise level. (**a**–**e**) represent the noise levels of the thumb, index, middle, ring, and pinky, respectively. Figures (**f**–**h**) represent the noise levels when the fist, peace, and pinch gestures are performed.

The noise level produced by the servo motors when they are operated fully, partly, or simultaneously was analyzed. The thumb finger servo motor's noise level is represented by Figure 9a. Here, the initial three peaks reflect the three successive steps of actuation, and the last three peaks represent the three successive steps of relaxation. The noise level of the servo motors of each finger is characterized one by one. The index finger, middle finger, ring finger, and pinky finger servos are designated as (a) to (e), respectively. (f) denotes the magnitude level and the width of the audio noise of all five servo motors operating simultaneously from all five fingers. This symbolizes the closing of the entire fist. The first two peaks denote the actuation phase. The relaxation phase from the fist close to its initial rest position is represented by the next two peaks of (f). (g) stands for the peace sign, in which the middle and index fingers are stretched, and the thumb is folded. This stage often involves the activation of two fingers. The pinch gesture is shown in Figure 9h, where just two fingers, namely the thumb and index finger, are actuated, leaving the other fingers in the resting position. The first two peaks show the actuation phase, while the last two peaks show NOHAS returning to the resting phase. The average noise level is around 40 dB. A noise level of up to 60 dB was observed when all the five servo motors were actuated at once in the first gesture. People might feel comfort or discomfort from the audible noise of NOHAS which cannot be solely determined based on peak noise levels alone. Factors such as frequency, duration, and temporal patterns of noise also significantly influence individuals' perception of the sound. Furthermore, even at low levels where direct damage to the hearing organ does not occur, noise can still induce stress to individuals.

According to the Centers for Disease Control and Prevention (CDC) [38], a soft whisper level of sound measures at approximately 30 dB. Normal conversation and air conditioner sounds measure at approximately 60 dB. These respective sounds were found safe and typically not causing any damage to the hearing organ. But the noise arising from a washing machine/dishwasher (70 dB) and city traffic (80–85 dB) were found to be annoying. Motorcycles (95 dB) and gas-powered machines (80–85 dB) were found to cause damage to hearing organs if there was continuous exposure to these environments. Therefore, we assessed the performance of the servo motors used in the hand orthosis from this standard and considered the comfort of the users [83,84].

Regarding the reliability of smartphone apps for noise measurement, some studies have been carried out. The findings in [85,86] indicate that the iOS platform's SLA Lite emerged as the best app, while the second-best app, namely Sound Meter, was associated with the Android platform, which we used to quantify the noise from NOHAS. On the Android platform, Sound Meter was identified as the most accurate app, exhibiting a slight undermeasurement of noise by 1.93 dB(A)—within the generally acceptable error threshold of ±2 dB(A). However, analysis across all reference levels revealed an average differential from the actual noise level ranging between 3 and 4 dB(A). It can be asserted that with a considerable number of sample measurements, Android apps like Sound Meter and Decibel Pro are likely to converge on a noise measurement level that is approximately within ±2 dB(A) of the true noise levels. The dB(A) measurements were compared to true noise levels obtained through a calibrated sound level meter. The investigation in [87] revealed that app-based measurements effectively captured average noise levels, exhibiting a variance of ±2 dB when compared to measurements obtained using the gold standard sound level meter. dB(A) represents the weighted average of the sound pressure in dB, which is tailored to match the human ear's frequency response.

4. Human Subject Testing (Study 2)

To enhance the gripping of objects and to prevent slipping while grasping fragile items, NOHAS's fingers were sealed with rubberized tips, as shown in Figure 10a,b. This enabled the human subjects to grasp items effectively.

4.1. Objective of Human Subject Testing

Human subject testing was conducted to collect feedback about the device's functionality and effectiveness in grasping objects because human subjects will not be able to voluntarily control their grasping. Hence, before wearing the glove, we instructed the human subjects not to control or move their wrist voluntarily. They can only control their wrist using the app in the mobile phone. The human subjects were allowed to use the mobile phone by themselves with their other hand.

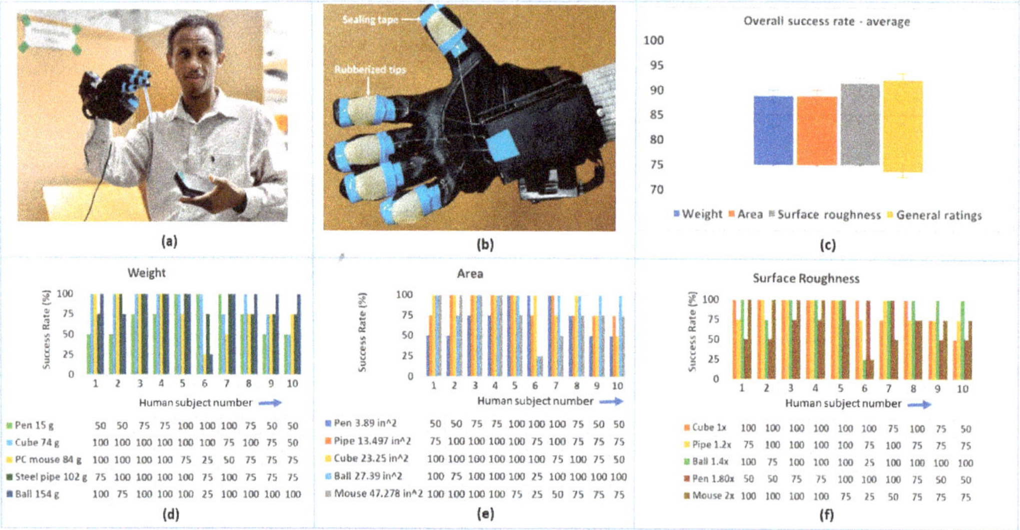

Figure 10. Human subject test results: (**a**) operation instruction, (**b**) grip enhancement in the glove, (**c**) box and whisker plot of test results based on categories of objects showing average overall success rates. (**d**) Success rate based on weight of objects, (**e**) success rate based on area of objects, and (**f**) based on relative surface roughness (1x is a smooth surface and 2x is relatively rougher). General feedback rating in (**c**) (yellow) does not consider any specific technical parameters but it includes overall feedback rating from our human subjects.

4.2. Eligibility

Healthy participants who did not have pre-existing health conditions, exhibit symptoms of fever or cold, have physical limitations, fractures, or allergies to wool or cotton were suitable for human subject testing. We set these as guidelines in our IRB application. Our study was approved by UT Dallas IRB.

4.3. Participant Inclusion and Exclusion Criteria

We selected participants from members of the HBS lab at UT Dallas. The HBS lab is dedicated to the study of fundamental and applied science of humanoid robots, biorobotics, smart materials, and structures. This group was well-suited for testing NOHAS as they can use their own research experiences to provide valuable insights into the design of the orthotic hand. We believed that testing the device with this group would yield accurate feedback. For instance, if the device is perceived as heavy or flexible, they can articulate these observations properly. A student researching soft robots might even propose innovative ideas, such as replacing noise-generating servos with other types of actuators. This was chosen to receive comprehensive and constructive comments from this group.

4.4. Recruitment Method

The principal investigator for this study sent out emails to the HBS lab mailing list after the approval of the director of HBS lab. Involvement was based on the response of the person to the mail request, after reviewing the consent form and the study plan. A written consent form signed by the participant was required before the start of the experiment. We did not record the age or name of the participants. The human subject test was conducted for a total of ten subjects aged between 20 and 45, consisting of eight males and two females following the approved IRB protocol (IRB-23-31).

4.5. Collection of Data

- Participants were asked to come to the HBS lab during their free time and the experimental procedure was explained to them during the first 10 min. The ARAT kit was opened, and the experimenter explained the mobile app layout to the participants. They were allowed to use the mobile app independently and operate the glove. We selected the ARAT kit as it is a frequently used tool in stroke rehabilitation and standard assessment for hand function;
- Next, participants were instructed to wear NOHAS and pick up standard objects from the ARAT kit, which included a ball, boxes of various sizes, plastic hard cups, metal tubes, etc. The entire activity was captured on video, focusing solely on the participants' hand movements and grasping actions, with their faces excluded from the recording. Throughout the process, participants used a mobile application to control the glove;
- Afterwards, participants were asked to remove the glove and safely place it in the provided location. Participants were not asked any demographic questions. Instead, they were requested to provide a rating as per the consent form, assessing the orthotic hand's performance on a scale of 4 to 1, where 4 denoted excellent, 3 very good, 2 good, and 1 poor. The entire process took around 15 min;
- Finally, participants were thanked for their time, and they left the lab. The video of this data collection is shown in the overview of NOHAS available on the HBS lab website at the following link: https://youtu.be/RtTiUP9PP94 (accessed on 6 December 2023).

The human subject test results and analyses were categorized based on three parameters, including object weight, area, and surface roughness, as shown in Figure 10c. We obtained feedback from the human subjects that these parameters directly affected the grasping task of different objects using NOHAS. People were able to give different ideas about NOHAS and its efficiency in grasping objects such as a pen, ball, box, PC mouse, and steel pipe. These objects were used in the test because they resembled most of the objects which we use in our day-to-day life. We were able to find out that the human subjects were able to grasp the ball very easily because when the glove closes, the ball was firmly placed next to the main servo motor housing case. Even though the ball had a smooth and shiny surface, the glove was able to provide an excellent grip. The motor case provided additional support for the ball. From this, we can understand that smooth objects can easily be grasped by NOHAS. While lifting boxes, the servo motor casing was able to provide excellent support because of the well-defined edges and smooth surface. For the pen, the rating was low because lifting it from the table in a flat position was difficult. This was because of the small diameter of the pen. If the pen was picked up from a pen stand in a vertical orientation, it would have been much easier to grasp, and the rating would have been much higher. We were also able to grasp the pen from a pen stand. Some subjects felt difficulty in lifting and moving the personal computer (PC) mouse because of its shape and slippery surface. The steel pipe received good ratings because of its perfect size, shiny surface, and easily graspable structure.

Figure 10d describes the grasping success rate for different objects when weight is considered. The objects are arranged in ascending order from lowest weight to heaviest. It was found that the average weight percentage ratings for the pen, cube, PC mouse, steel pipe, and ball were 72.5, 90, 77.5, 87.5, and 75, respectively, as per Figure 10d. From this, we can infer that considering the weight of objects, NOHAS was able to grasp the cube easier. The average area ratings for the pen, pipe, cube, ball, and mouse are 72.5, 87.5, 90, 90, and 77.5, respectively, as per Figure 10e. The human subjects felt it was easier to grasp the cube and ball. The average surface roughness ratings for the cube, pipe, ball, pen, and mouse are 90, 87.5, 90, 72.5, and 77.5, respectively, as per Figure 10f. Figure 10c shows a box and whisker plot for the human subject test. The yellow bar is the overall general feedback rating given by the human subjects. The median, lower quartile (Q1), upper quartile (Q3), lower extreme, and upper extreme values for the weight category are 75, 75, 87.5, 75, and 90 respectively. Similarly, for area category, these values are 75, 75, 87.5, 75, and 90. Regarding surface roughness, the values are 75, 75, 92.5, 75, and 92.5, respectively. Considering general feedback, the median, lower quartile (Q1), upper quartile (Q3), lower extreme, and upper extreme values are 80, 75, 90.5, 72.5, and 93.5 respectively. Our future work will focus on grasping tests with stroke subjects, considering patient outcomes and psychology.

Several recent studies [88–91] highlight the critical need to tailor rehabilitation treatments to patients' psychophysiological states, emphasizing personalized approaches in robotic-assisted therapies. The integration of advanced technologies, like hand exoskeletons and psychophysiological-aware control strategies, demonstrates a commitment to addressing the unique conditions of individual patients. These robotic systems aim to optimize therapy outcomes by sensing and adapting to psychophysiological states, ensuring accurate and efficient motor interventions while enhancing patient comfort and minimizing fatigue. The emphasis on active-assisted training, virtual reality games, and the integration of linguistic interaction further highlights a holistic approach to rehabilitation, acknowledging the multifaceted nature of patient well-being. These advancements collectively signify a paradigm shift towards tailoring the behavior of robotic systems to the individual complexities of patients, ultimately maximizing the effectiveness and impact of motor rehabilitation therapies. This personalized approach is particularly pertinent to devices like NOHAS, where understanding and adapting to the intricate conditions of everyone becomes paramount. NOHAS was developed using parametric CAD software, which can be easily modified to fit in varied sizes. There are some commercially available exoskeletons like Gloreha [58,92], which have good functionalities, especially for inpatient rehabilitation training. Despite its advantages, its bulkiness due to the accessories and noise from its pneumatic actuators may pose challenges in certain settings.

5. Conclusions

We have presented an app-controlled novel hand orthosis actuated by servo motors (NOHAS) which is cost effective, energy-efficient, easily worn, and has potential for use in activities of daily living and as an assistive device for persons with impaired hand function. Orthotic hands with servo motors play a pivotal role in stroke rehabilitation by facilitating motor recovery through a mechanism known as task-oriented repetitive training. These devices, often controlled by smartphone commands, enable post-stroke subjects to engage in purposeful and repetitive hand movements. The precision and adjustability of servo motor-driven orthotic hands allow for tailored rehabilitation exercises, targeting specific muscle groups and joint ranges affected by stroke-induced impairments. Repetitive movements aid in neuroplasticity, promoting the rewiring of neural pathways in the brain to enhance motor control and coordination. The smartphone-controlled interface provides a user-friendly and adaptable platform, allowing rehabilitation professionals to customize exercises based on individual patient needs and progress. This technology thus offers an innovative and effective means to augment traditional rehabilitation approaches, promoting functional recovery and enhancing the quality of life for post-stroke subjects, specifically for ischemic stroke. The characterization of the angle (i.e., the flexion of the PIP, DIP, and MCP joint with respect to time), cyclic actuation, and grasping capabilities were performed to quantify the properties of NOHAS. The amount of force NOHAS can apply or fasten is also a very important characteristic feature, which gives us a very good idea of NOHAS's ability to hold and carry heavy objects. The quantification of auditory noise indicated that the inexpensive servo motors do not generate audio noise significant enough to cause problems. This information provides us with a better understanding of noise levels while wearing NOHAS and helps assess the seamless functioning of the servo motors. We conducted a human subject test for NOHAS after IRB approval and it was found out that ten subjects successfully grasped few objects and were not able to do the same for other objects from a standard ARAT kit. The ideas we obtained after the human subject test will be used for the improvement of the device in terms of design and manufacturing. The device presented is a proof of concept and it needs further testing in practical scenarios in healthy subjects and post-stroke subjects. We will be able to improve the functioning of NOHAS by redesigning it further, considering design, manufacturing, and control aspects. One aspect is replacing our current servo motors with small and smoother ones which create less noise and are more efficient. This will be our future work. This may add cost, but optimization is needed to address all the issues.

Supplementary Materials: A video that shows the design, structure, properties, and function of our device is provided. It is also available on our YouTube Channel (HBS lab) https://youtu.be/RtTiUP9PP94 (accessed on 6 December 2023).

Author Contributions: Conceptualization, Y.T.; Methodology, E.R.S.M. and N.I.; Software, E.R.S.M. and A.G.; Formal analysis, E.R.S.M. and Y.T.; Investigation, E.R.S.M. and N.I.; Resources, Y.T.; Writing—original draft, E.R.S.M.; Writing—review & editing, A.G., N.I. and Y.T.; Project administration, Y.T.; Funding acquisition, Y.T. All authors have read and agreed to the published version of the manuscript.

Funding: The research was partially supported by Internal fund from Research Enhancement.

Data Availability Statement: Data are contained within the article.

Acknowledgments: We would like to thank our senior design team at UT Dallas for their initial contributions to this project. We would like to extend our special thanks to Taylor Hollers, Joe Torres, Roy Lara, Anothony Dyoub, Dominic Labarge, and Jin Sik Woo. Special thanks to Jin Sik Woo for the Blynk App. We also would like to thank Robert Hart and Todd Polk.

Conflicts of Interest: The authors declare no conflict of interest.

References

1. Donkor, E.S. Stroke in the century: A snapshot of the burden, epidemiology, and quality of life. *Stroke Res. Treat.* **2018**, *2018*, 3238165.
2. Toth, L.; Schiffer, A.; Nyitrai, M.; Pentek, A.; Told, R.; Maroti, P. Developing an anti-spastic orthosis for daily home-use of stroke patients using smart memory alloys and 3D printing technologies. *Mater. Des.* **2020**, *195*, 109029. [CrossRef]
3. Yurkewich, A.; Hebert, D.; Wang, R.H.; Mihailidis, A. Hand extension robot orthosis (HERO) glove: Development and testing with stroke survivors with severe hand impairment. *IEEE Trans. Neural Syst. Rehabil. Eng.* **2019**, *27*, 916–926. [CrossRef] [PubMed]

4. Park, C.B.; Park, H.-S. PorTable 3D-printed hand orthosis with spatial stiffness distribution personalized for assisting grasping in daily living. *Front. Bioeng. Biotechnol.* **2023**, *11*, 895745. [CrossRef] [PubMed]
5. Kaskutas, V.; Powell, R. The impact of flexor tendon rehabilitation restrictions on individuals' independence with daily activities: Implications for hand therapists. *J. Hand Ther.* **2013**, *26*, 22–29. [CrossRef] [PubMed]
6. Dindorf, R.; Wos, P. Using the bioelectric signals to control of wearable orthosis of the elbow joint with bi-muscular pneumatic servo-drive. *Robotica* **2020**, *38*, 804–818. [CrossRef]
7. Cartagena, P.D.; Naranjo, J.E.; Saltos, L.F.; Garcia, C.A.; Garcia, M.V. Multifunctional exoskeletal orthosis for hand rehabilitation based on virtual reality. In *Information and Communication Technologies of Ecuador (TIC. EC)*; Springer: Berlin/Heidelberg, Germany, 2018; pp. 209–221.
8. Megalingam, R.K.; Manoharan, S.K.; Mohandas, S.M.; Reddy, C.P.K.; Vijay, E.; Naveen, P.N.V.K.; Chandrika, D. Wearable Hand Orthotic Device for Rehabilitation: Hand Therapy with Multi-Mode Control and Real-Time Feedback. *Appl. Sci.* **2023**, *13*, 3976. [CrossRef]
9. Veale, A.J.; Xie, S.Q. Towards compliant and wearable robotic orthoses: A review of current and emerging actuator technologies. *Med. Eng. Phys.* **2016**, *38*, 317–325. [CrossRef]
10. Gretsch, K.F.; Lather, H.D.; Peddada, K.V.; Deeken, C.R.; Wall, L.B.; Goldfarb, C.A. Development of novel 3D-printed robotic prosthetic for transradial amputees. *Prosthet. Orthot. Int.* **2016**, *40*, 400–403. [CrossRef]
11. Dereshgi, H.A.; Hüseyin, D.; Demir, D.; Türe, N.F. Orthoses: A Systematic Review. *J. Smart Syst. Res.* **2021**, *2*, 135–149.
12. Cheng, N.; Phua, K.S.; Lai, H.S.; Tam, P.K.; Tang, K.Y.; Cheng, K.K.; Yeow, R.C.-H.; Ang, K.K.; Guan, C.; Lim, J.H. Brain-computer interface-based soft robotic glove rehabilitation for stroke. *IEEE Trans. Biomed. Eng.* **2020**, *67*, 3339–3351. [CrossRef]
13. Cantillo-Negrete, J.; Carino-Escobar, R.I.; Carrillo-Mora, P.; Rodriguez-Barragan, M.A.; Hernandez-Arenas, C.; Quinzaños-Fresnedo, J.; Hernandez-Sanchez, I.R.; Galicia-Alvarado, M.A.; Miguel-Puga, A.; Arias-Carrion, O. Brain-computer interface coupled to a robotic hand orthosis for stroke patients' neurorehabilitation: A crossover feasibility study. *Front. Hum. Neurosci.* **2021**, *15*, 656975. [CrossRef]
14. Chowdhury, A.; Raza, H.; Meena, Y.K.; Dutta, A.; Prasad, G. An EEG-EMG correlation-based brain-computer interface for hand orthosis supported neuro-rehabilitation. *J. Neurosci. Methods* **2019**, *312*, 1–11. [CrossRef]
15. Cantillo-Negrete, J.; Carino-Escobar, R.I.; Carrillo-Mora, P.; Elias-Vinas, D.; Gutierrez-Martinez, J. Motor imagery-based brain-computer interface coupled to a robotic hand orthosis aimed for neurorehabilitation of stroke patients. *J. Healthc. Eng.* **2018**, *2018*, 1624637. [CrossRef] [PubMed]
16. Pichiorri, F.; Morone, G.; Petti, M.; Toppi, J.; Pisotta, I.; Molinari, M.; Paolucci, S.; Inghilleri, M.; Astolfi, L.; Cincotti, F.; et al. Brain–computer interface boosts motor imagery practice during stroke recovery. *Ann. Neurol.* **2015**, *77*, 851–865. [CrossRef] [PubMed]
17. King, C.E.; Dave, K.R.; Wang, P.T.; Mizuta, M.; Reinkensmeyer, D.J.; Do, A.H.; Moromugi, S.; Nenadic, Z. Performance assessment of a brain–computer interface driven hand orthosis. *Ann. Biomed. Eng.* **2014**, *42*, 2095–2105. [CrossRef] [PubMed]
18. Delijorge, J.; Mendoza-Montoya, O.; Gordillo, J.L.; Caraza, R.; Martinez, H.R.; Antelis, J.M. Evaluation of a p300-based brain-machine interface for a robotic hand-orthosis control. *Front. Neurosci.* **2020**, *14*, 589659. [CrossRef] [PubMed]
19. Lee, J.; Mukae, N.; Arata, J.; Iihara, K.; Hashizume, M. Comparison of feature vector compositions to enhance the performance of NIRS-BCI-triggered robotic hand orthosis for post-stroke motor recovery. *Appl. Sci.* **2019**, *9*, 3845. [CrossRef]
20. Dunaway, S.; Dezsi, D.B.; Perkins, J.; Tran, D.; Naft, J. Case report on the use of a custom myoelectric elbow–wrist–hand orthosis for the remediation of upper extremity paresis and loss of function in chronic stroke. *Mil. Med.* **2017**, *182*, e1963–e1968. [CrossRef] [PubMed]
21. Nizamis, K.; Rijken, N.H.; Van Middelaar, R.; Neto, J.; Koopman, B.F.; Sartori, M. Characterization of forearm muscle activation in duchenne muscular dystrophy via high-density electromyography: A case study on the implications for myoelectric control. *Front. Neurol.* **2020**, *11*, 231. [CrossRef]
22. Yoo, H.-J.; Lee, S.; Kim, J.; Park, C.; Lee, B. Development of 3D-printed myoelectric hand orthosis for patients with spinal cord injury. *J. Neuroeng. Rehabil.* **2019**, *16*, 162. [CrossRef]
23. Peters, H.T.; Page, S.J.; Persch, A. Giving them a hand: Wearing a myoelectric elbow-wrist-hand orthosis reduces upper extremity impairment in chronic stroke. *Arch. Phys. Med. Rehabil.* **2017**, *98*, 1821–1827. [CrossRef] [PubMed]
24. Martins, H.V.; Setti, J.; Guimarães, C. Handy Orthotics: Considerations on User-Centered Methodology During Development Stages of Myoelectric Hand Orthosis for Daily Assistance. In *XXVII Brazilian Congress on Biomedical Engineering, Proceedings of CBEB 2020, Vitória, Brazil, 26–30 October 2020*; Springer: Berlin/Heidelberg, Germany, 2022; pp. 1277–1283.
25. Pahk, H.J.; Lee, D.S.; Park, J.H. Ultra precision positioning system for servo motor–piezo actuator using the dual servo loop and digital filter implementation. *Int. J. Mach. Tools Manuf.* **2001**, *41*, 51–63. [CrossRef]
26. Sevinc, A. A full adaptive observer for DC servo motors. *Turk. J. Electr. Eng. Comput. Sci.* **2003**, *11*, 117–130.
27. Vukosavic, S.N.; Stojic, M.R. Suppression of torsional oscillations in a high-performance speed servo drive. *IEEE Trans. Ind. Electron.* **1998**, *45*, 108–117. [CrossRef]
28. Chung, K.C.W. Servo speed control of traveling-wave ultrasonic motors using pulse width modulation. *Electr. Power Compon. Syst.* **2001**, *29*, 707–722.
29. Feng, G.-H.; Pan, Y.-L. Establishing a cost-effective sensing system and signal processing method to diagnose preload levels of ball screws. *Mech. Syst. Signal Process.* **2012**, *28*, 78–88. [CrossRef]

30. Ramírez, A.; Garrido, R.; Mondié, S. Velocity control of servo systems using an integral retarded algorithm. *ISA Trans.* **2015**, *58*, 357–366. [CrossRef] [PubMed]
31. Jung, D.; Levy, E.J.; Zhou, D.; Fink, R.; Moshe, J.; Earl, A.; Tsiotras, P. Design and development of a low-cost test-bed for undergraduate education in UAVs. In Proceedings of the 44th IEEE Conference on Decision and Control, Seville, Spain, 15 December 2005; IEEE: Piscataway, NJ, USA, 2005; pp. 2739–2744.
32. Dutta, D.; Aruchamy, S.; Mandal, S.; Sen, S. Poststroke grasp ability assessment using an intelligent data glove based on action research arm test: Development, algorithms, and experiments. *IEEE Trans. Biomed. Eng.* **2021**, *69*, 945–954. [CrossRef]
33. Kim, D.H.; Lee, Y.; Park, H.-S. Cooperative Hand Therapy via a Soft, Wearable, and Unilateral Telerobotic System. *IEEE Trans. Biomed. Eng.* **2022**, *70*, 366–377. [CrossRef]
34. Coyle, S.; Majidi, C.; LeDuc, P.; Hsia, K.J. Bio-inspired soft robotics: Material selection, actuation, and design. *Extrem. Mech. Lett.* **2018**, *22*, 51–59. [CrossRef]
35. Zhao, H.; Jalving, J.; Huang, R.; Knepper, R.; Ruina, A.; Shepherd, R. A helping hand: Soft orthosis with integrated optical strain sensors and EMG control. *IEEE Robot. Autom. Mag.* **2016**, *23*, 55–64. [CrossRef]
36. Byl, N.N.; Abrams, G.M.; Pitsch, E.; Fedulow, I.; Kim, H.; Simkins, M.; Nagarajan, S.; Rosen, J. Chronic stroke survivors achieve comparable outcomes following virtual task specific repetitive training guided by a wearable robotic orthosis (UL-EXO7) and actual task specific repetitive training guided by a physical therapist. *J. Hand Ther.* **2013**, *26*, 343–352. [CrossRef] [PubMed]
37. Woo, Y.; Jeon, H.; Hwang, S.; Choi, B.; Lee, J. Kinematics variations after spring-assisted orthosis training in persons with stroke. *Prosthet. Orthot. Int.* **2013**, *37*, 311–316. [CrossRef] [PubMed]
38. Chen, Y.; Abel, K.T.; Janecek, J.T.; Chen, Y.; Zheng, K.; Cramer, S.C. Home-based technologies for stroke rehabilitation: A systematic review. *Int. J. Med. Inform.* **2019**, *123*, 11–22. [CrossRef] [PubMed]
39. Hameed, H.K.; Hassan, W.Z.W.; Shafie, S.; Ahmad, S.A.; Jaafar, H. A review on surface electromyography-controlled hand robotic devices used for rehabilitation and assistance in activities of daily living. *JPO J. Prosthet. Orthot.* **2020**, *32*, 3–13. [CrossRef]
40. Gaiser, I.N.; Pylatiuk, C.; Schulz, S.; Kargov, A.; Oberle, R.; Werner, T. The FLUIDHAND III: A multifunctional prosthetic hand. *JPO J. Prosthet. Orthot.* **2009**, *21*, 91–96. [CrossRef]
41. Zuniga, J.M.; Peck, J.; Srivastava, R.; Katsavelis, D.; Carson, A. An open source 3D-printed transitional hand prosthesis for children. *JPO J. Prosthet. Orthot.* **2016**, *28*, 103–108. [CrossRef]
42. Ramaji, R.Y.; Daryabor, A.; Bani, M.A. The effect of ulnar deviation orthosis in patients with zigzag deformity due to rheumatoid hand. *JPO J. Prosthet. Orthot.* **2021**, *33*, 203–207. [CrossRef]
43. Plessis, T.D.; Djouani, K.; Oosthuizen, C. A review of active hand exoskeletons for rehabilitation and assistance. *Robotics* **2021**, *10*, 40. [CrossRef]
44. Qassim, H.M.; Hasan, W.W. A review on upper limb rehabilitation robots. *Appl. Sci.* **2020**, *10*, 6976. [CrossRef]
45. Deng, E.; Tadesse, Y. A soft 3D-printed robotic hand actuated by coiled SMA. *Actuators* **2020**, *10*, 6. [CrossRef]
46. Neto, A.R.; Fajardo, J.; da Silva, W.H.A.; Gomes, M.K.; de Castro, M.C.F.; Fujiwara, E.; Rohmer, E. Design of tendon-actuated robotic glove integrated with optical fiber force myography sensor. *Automation* **2021**, *2*, 187–201. [CrossRef]
47. Singh, A.P.; Palani, D.; Ahmed, O.; Matharu, P.S.; Linn, T.; Nguyen, T.; Tadesse, Y. HBS-1.2: Lightweight Socially Assistive Robot with 6-Ply Twisted Coiled Polymer Muscle-Actuated Hand. *Actuators* **2023**, *12*, 312. [CrossRef]
48. Oña, E.D.; Garcia-Haro, J.M.; Jardón, A.; Balaguer, C. Robotics in health care: Perspectives of robot-aided interventions in clinical practice for rehabilitation of upper limbs. *Appl. Sci.* **2019**, *9*, 2586. [CrossRef]
49. Lin, F.; Ajay, J.; Langan, J.; Cavuoto, L.; Nwogu, I.; Subryan, H.; Xu, W. QM-FOrMS: A portable and cost-effective upper extremity rehabilitation system. *Smart Health* **2019**, *14*, 100080. [CrossRef]
50. Bobin, M.; Bimbard, F.; Boukallel, M.; Anastassova, M.; Ammi, M. SpECTRUM: Smart ECosystem for sTRoke patient's Upper limbs Monitoring. *Smart Health* **2019**, *13*, 100066. [CrossRef]
51. Park, Y.; Jo, I.; Lee, J.; Bae, J. A dual-cable hand exoskeleton system for virtual reality. *Mechatronics* **2018**, *49*, 177–186. [CrossRef]
52. Marconi, D.; Baldoni, A.; McKinney, Z.; Cempini, M.; Crea, S.; Vitiello, N. A novel hand exoskeleton with series elastic actuation for modulated torque transfer. *Mechatronics* **2019**, *61*, 69–82. [CrossRef]
53. Conti, R.; Meli, E.; Ridolfi, A. A novel kinematic architecture for portable hand exoskeletons. *Mechatronics* **2016**, *35*, 192–207. [CrossRef]
54. Jo, I.; Bae, J. Design and control of a wearable and force-controllable hand exoskeleton system. *Mechatronics* **2017**, *41*, 90–101. [CrossRef]
55. Xiao, F.; Gu, L.; Ma, W.; Zhu, Y.; Zhang, Z.; Wang, Y. Real time motion intention recognition method with limited number of surface electromyography sensors for A 7-DOF hand/wrist rehabilitation exoskeleton. *Mechatronics* **2021**, *79*, 102642. [CrossRef]
56. Achilli, G.M.; Amici, C.; Dragusanu, M.; Gobbo, M.; Logozzo, S.; Malvezzi, M.; Tiboni, M.; Valigi, M.C. Soft, Rigid, and Hybrid Robotic Exoskeletons for Hand Rehabilitation: Roadmap with Impairment-Oriented Rationale for Devices Design and Selection. *Appl. Sci.* **2023**, *13*, 11287. [CrossRef]
57. Nilsen, T.; Hermann, M.; Eriksen, C.S.; Dagfinrud, H.; Mowinckel, P.; Kjeken, I. Grip force and pinch grip in an adult population: Reference values and factors associated with grip force. *Scand. J. Occup. Ther.* **2012**, *19*, 288–296. [CrossRef] [PubMed]
58. Kabir, R.; Sunny, M.S.H.; Ahmed, H.U.; Rahman, M.H. Hand rehabilitation devices: A comprehensive systematic review. *Micromachines* **2022**, *13*, 1033. [CrossRef] [PubMed]

59. Saharan, L.; Wu, L.; Tadesse, Y. Modeling and simulation of robotic finger powered by nylon artificial muscles. *J. Mech. Robot.* **2020**, *12*, 14501. [CrossRef]
60. Ochoa, J.M.; Kamper, D.G.; Listenberger, M.; Lee, S.W. Use of an electromyographically driven hand orthosis for training after stroke. In Proceedings of the 2011 IEEE International Conference on Rehabilitation Robotics, Zurich, Switzerland, 29 June–1 July 2011; IEEE: Piscataway, NJ, USA, 2011; pp. 1–5.
61. Chen, A.; Winterbottom, L.; Park, S.; Xu, J.; Nilsen, D.M.; Stein, J.; Ciocarlie, M. Thumb Stabilization and Assistance in a Robotic Hand Orthosis for Post-Stroke Hemiparesis. *IEEE Robot. Autom. Lett.* **2022**, *7*, 8276–8282. [CrossRef]
62. Saharan, L.; de Andrade, M.J.; Saleem, W.; Baughman, R.H.; Tadesse, Y. iGrab: Hand orthosis powered by twisted and coiled polymer muscles. *Smart Mater. Struct.* **2017**, *26*, 105048. [CrossRef]
63. Schabowsky, C.N.; Godfrey, S.B.; Holley, R.J.; Lum, P.S. Development and pilot testing of HEXORR: Hand EXOskeleton rehabilitation robot. *J. Neuroeng. Rehabil.* **2010**, *7*, 1–16. [CrossRef]
64. Wang, Y.; Zheng, S.; Pang, J.; Li, S.; Li, J. Design and experiment of a hand movement device driven by shape memory alloy wires. *J. Robot.* **2021**, *2021*, 6611581. [CrossRef]
65. Chen, Y.; Tan, X.; Yan, D.; Zhang, Z.; Gong, Y. A composite fabric-based soft rehabilitation glove with soft joint for dementia in Parkinson's disease. *IEEE J. Transl. Eng. Health Med.* **2020**, *8*, 1–10. [CrossRef] [PubMed]
66. Casas, R.; Sandison, M.; Chen, T.; Lum, P.S. Clinical test of a wearable, high DOF, spring powered hand exoskeleton (HandSOME II). *IEEE Trans. Neural Syst. Rehabil. Eng.* **2021**, *29*, 1877–1885. [CrossRef] [PubMed]
67. Peperoni, E.; Capitani, S.L.; Fiumalbi, T.; Capotorti, E.; Baldoni, A.; Dell'Agnello, F.; Creatini, I.; Taglione, E.; Vitiello, N.; Trigili, E.; et al. Self-Aligning Finger Exoskeleton for the Mobilization of the Metacarpophalangeal Joint. *IEEE Trans. Neural Syst. Rehabil. Eng.* **2023**, *31*, 884–894. [CrossRef] [PubMed]
68. Yang, J.; Xie, H.; Shi, J. A novel motion-coupling design for a jointless tendon-driven finger exoskeleton for rehabilitation. *Mech. Mach. Theory* **2016**, *99*, 83–102. [CrossRef]
69. Aguilar-Marín, P.; Chavez-Bacilio, M.; Jáuregui-Rosas, S. Using analog instruments in Tracker video-based experiments to understand the phenomena of electricity and magnetism in physics education. *Eur. J. Phys.* **2018**, *39*, 35204. [CrossRef]
70. Nurmayanti, D.; Jumadi, J.; Wilujeng, I.; Kuswanto, H. Developing of Learning Instruments based on Software Tracker in Measuring Cognitive Learning Outcomes. *J. Phys. Conf. Ser.* **2019**, *1233*, 12047. [CrossRef]
71. Bastos, R.O. Practical measurements in radioactivity with the electroscope and the Tracker software. *Phys. Educ.* **2020**, *55*, 55007. [CrossRef]
72. Wilujeng, I.; Kuswanto, H. Developing learning instruments using tracker in measuring students' science process skills. *J. Phys. Conf. Ser.* **2019**, *1233*, 12053.
73. Chiriacescu, B.; Chiriacescu, F.S.; Miron, C.; Berlic, C.; Barna, V. Arduino and tracker video–didactic tools for study of the kater pendulum physical experiment. *Rom. Rep. Phys.* **2020**, *72*, 1–14.
74. Matharu, P.S.; Wang, Z.; Costello, J.H.; Colin, S.P.; Baughman, R.H.; Tadesse, Y.T. SoJel–A 3D printed jellyfish-like robot using soft materials for underwater applications. *Ocean. Eng.* **2023**, *279*, 114427. [CrossRef]
75. Hamidi, A.; Almubarak, Y.; Rupawat, Y.M.; Warren, J.; Tadesse, Y. Poly-Saora robotic jellyfish: Swimming underwater by twisted and coiled polymer actuators. *Smart Mater. Struct.* **2020**, *29*, 45039. [CrossRef]
76. Joshi, A.; Kulkarni, A.; Tadesse, Y. FludoJelly: Experimental study on jellyfish-like soft robot enabled by soft pneumatic composite (SPC). *Robotics* **2019**, *8*, 56. [CrossRef]
77. Yun, Y.; Dancausse, S.; Esmatloo, P.; Serrato, A.; Merring, C.A.; Deshpande, A.D. An EMG-driven assistive hand exoskeleton for spinal cord injury patients: Maestro. In Proceedings of the IEEE International Conference on Robotics and Automation (ICRA), Singapore, 29 May–3 June 2017.
78. Using and FSR. Available online: https://learn.adafruit.com/force-sensitive-resistor-fsr/using-an-fsr (accessed on 29 July 2012).
79. Tadesse, Y. Actuation technologies suitable for humanoid robots. In Proceedings of the ASME 2012 International Mechanical Engineering Congress and Exposition, Houston, TX, USA, 9–15 November 2012; American Society of Mechanical Engineers: New York, NY, USA, 2012; pp. 1–10.
80. Tadesse, Y. Electroactive polymer and shape memory alloy actuators in biomimetics and humanoids. In Proceedings of the SPIE Smart Structures and Materials + Nondestructive Evaluation and Health Monitoring, San Diego, CA, USA, 10–14 March 2013; International Society for Optics and Photonics: Bellingham, WA, USA, 2013; p. 868709.
81. Wu, L.; Chauhan, I.; Tadesse, Y. A Novel Soft Actuator for the Musculoskeletal System. *Adv. Mater. Technol.* **2018**, *3*, 1700359. [CrossRef]
82. Moore, D.; Tennent, H.; Martelaro, N.; Ju, W. Making noise intentional: A study of servo sound perception. In Proceedings of the 2017 ACM/IEEE International Conference on Human-Robot Interaction, Vienna, Austria, 6–9 March 2017; pp. 12–21.
83. Heo, P.; Kim, J. Power-assistive finger exoskeleton with a palmar opening at the fingerpad. *IEEE Trans. Biomed. Eng.* **2014**, *61*, 2688–2697. [CrossRef] [PubMed]
84. Miller, L.C.; Ruiz-Torres, R.; Stienen, A.H.; Dewald, J.P. A wrist and finger force sensor module for use during movements of the upper limb in chronic hemiparetic stroke. *IEEE Trans. Biomed. Eng.* **2009**, *56*, 2312–2317. [CrossRef] [PubMed]
85. Murphy, E.; King, E.A. Testing the accuracy of smartphones and sound level meter applications for measuring environmental noise. *Appl. Acoust.* **2016**, *106*, 16–22. [CrossRef]

86. Murphy, E.; Eoin, K.; Rauhusen, S. Exploring the accuracy of smartphone applications for measuring environmental noise. In Proceedings of the 44th International Congress on Noise Control Engineering, San Francisco, CA, USA, 9–12 August 2015.
87. Lee, P.J.; Hampton, T. Smartphone applications for measuring noise in the intensive care unit: A feasibility study. *J. Crit. Care* **2024**, *79*, 154435. [CrossRef]
88. Lapresa, M.; Lauretti, C.; Scotto di Luzio, F.; Bressi, F.; Santacaterina, F.; Bravi, M.; Guglielmelli, E.; Zollo, L.; Cordella, F. Development and Validation of a System for the Assessment and Recovery of Grip Force Control. *Bioengineering* **2023**, *10*, 63. [CrossRef]
89. Lauretti, C.; Cordella, F.; Tamantini, C.; Gentile, C.; di Luzio, F.S.; Zollo, L. A surgeon-robot shared control for ergonomic pedicle screw fixation. *IEEE Robot. Autom. Lett.* **2020**, *5*, 2554–2561. [CrossRef]
90. Tamantini, C.; Cordella, F.; Lauretti, C.; di Luzio, F.S.; Campagnola, B.; Cricenti, L.; Bravi, M.; Bressi, F.; Draicchio, F.; Sterzi, S.; et al. Tailoring upper-limb robot-aided orthopedic rehabilitation on patients' psychophysiological state. *IEEE Trans. Neural Syst. Rehabil. Eng.* **2023**, *31*, 3297–3306. [CrossRef]
91. Tamantini, C.; di Luzio, F.S.; Hromei, C.D.; Cristofori, L.; Croce, D.; Cammisa, M.; Cristofaro, A.; Marabello, M.V.; Basili, R.; Zollo, L. Integrating Physical and Cognitive Interaction Capabilities in a Robot-Aided Rehabilitation Platform. *IEEE Syst. J.* **2023**. [CrossRef]
92. Gloreha Company, a Hand Rehabilitation Company Based in Italy. Available online: https://www.gloreha.us/ (accessed on 24 November 2023).

robotics

MDPI

Article

Design and Control of the Rehab-Exos, a Joint Torque-Controlled Upper Limb Exoskeleton †

Domenico Chiaradia [1,*], Gianluca Rinaldi [1], Massimiliano Solazzi [1], Rocco Vertechy [2] and Antonio Frisoli [1]

[1] Institute of Mechanical Intelligence and Department of Excellence in Robotics & AI, Scuola Superiore Sant'Anna, 56127 Pisa, Italy; gianluca.rinaldi@santannapisa.it (G.R.); massimiliano.solazzi@santannapisa.it (M.S.); antonio.frisoli@santannapisa.it (A.F.)

[2] DIN—Department of Industrial Engineering, University of Bologna, 40136 Bologna, Italy; rocco.vertechy@unibo.it

* Correspondence: domenico.chiaradia@santannapisa.it

† This paper is an extended version of our paper published in Solazzi, M.; Abbrescia, M.; Vertechy, R.; Loconsole, C.; Bevilacqua, V.; Frisoli, A. An interaction torque control improving human force estimation of the rehab-exos exoskeleton. In Proceedings of the 2014 IEEE Haptics Symposium (HAPTICS), Houston, TX, USA, 23–26 February 2014; pp. 187–193.

Abstract: This work presents the design of the Rehab-Exos, a novel upper limb exoskeleton designed for rehabilitation purposes. It is equipped with high-reduction-ratio actuators and compact elastic joints to obtain torque sensors based on strain gauges. In this study, we address the torque sensor performances and the design aspects that could cause unwanted non-axial moment load crosstalk. Moreover, a new full-state feedback torque controller is designed by modeling the multi-DOF, non-linear system dynamics and providing compensation for non-linear effects such as friction and gravity. To assess the proposed upper limb exoskeleton in terms of both control system performances and mechanical structure validation, the full-state feedback controller was compared with two other benchmark-state feedback controllers in both a transparency test—ten subjects, two reference speeds—and a haptic rendering evaluation. Both of the experiments were representative of the intended purpose of the device, i.e., physical interaction with patients affected by limited motion skills. In all experimental conditions, our proposed joint torque controller achieved higher performances, providing transparency to the joints and asserting the feasibility of the exoskeleton for assistive applications.

Keywords: physical human–robot interaction; joint torque sensor; elastic joint; upper limb exoskeleton; full-state feedback control; transparency; haptic rendering

1. Introduction

Exoskeletons are robotic interfaces for human–robot interaction where the highest physical symbiosis with the human operator is achieved. Unlike many industrial robots designed to exhibit a rigid structure and behavior, to be used with a stiff position control, exoskeletons are designed to satisfy compliance and safety requirements commonly employed by physical human–robot interaction (pHRI) devices [1]. Other performance metrics, inherently depending on actuation and control systems, need to be taken into account when designing an exoskeleton whose main purpose is to provide assistance to patients in need of rehabilitation treatments. An assistive device must be able to support the weight of any impaired limbs of the patient as well as provide sufficient forces to allow the correct completion of the task [2].

Therefore, two of the most relevant metrics for evaluating an assistive device are as follows:

Transparency: It relates to the ability of the robotic system to not apply any resistance to free motion when interacting with a human user who is moving voluntarily [3], or, equivalently, it means that the robot's reaction forces perceived by the user are minimal [4]. Although no standard procedures exist for measuring transparency in pHRI, there is a general consensus in the exoskeletons field to refer not only to end effector resistance forces but also to single-joint resistance torques or measurements coming from specific contact points [4];

Haptic rendering: It refers to the device's capability to render a desired dynamic behavior such as a virtual impedance or a virtual wall, i.e., a task featuring both very high impedance—when in contact with the wall—and very low impedance—when out of contact [5]. An efficient mechanical structure should be able to predict the maximum stiffness displayed by existing devices by including appropriate dimensioning of sensors and actuators combined with more effective control strategies [6].

In the last two decades, several exoskeleton prototypes have been proposed using different implementation principles depending on the field of application [2], such as neuro-rehabilitation and assistance [7–10], human power augmentation [11] and telepresence [12–14]. The majority of exoskeletons employed in the aforementioned fields—especially for rehabilitation purposes—are active, which means they employ an actuation system capable of actively providing and transmitting the required force to the human user. There are many types of actuator systems, each one employing different solutions for power transmission, such as geared actuators [15,16], tendon drives [17,18], hybrid solutions [19,20] and pneumatic or hydraulic systems [21–23]. According to how each actuation system adjusts the impedance displayed to the user, it is possible to classify the actuators employed in pHRI into two main categories, as shown in Figure 1a. There are actuation systems with *active impedance by control*— i.e., they render impedance by the means of a control system—which mainly rely on position and torque sensors, and others that present *inherent impedance*—i.e., the impedance is obtained by inherent mechanical properties of the actuator—such as compliance or damping [24].

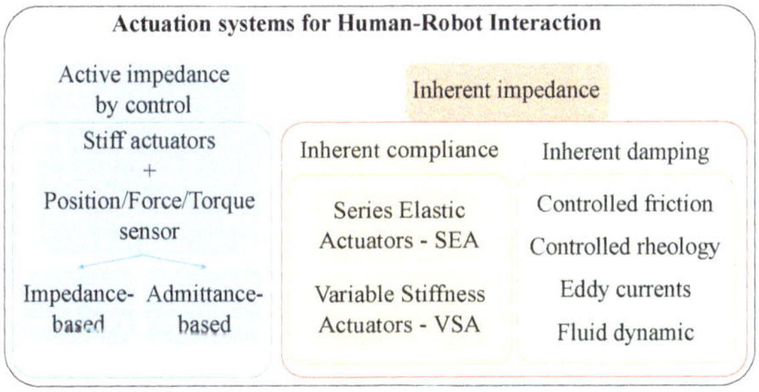

(a)

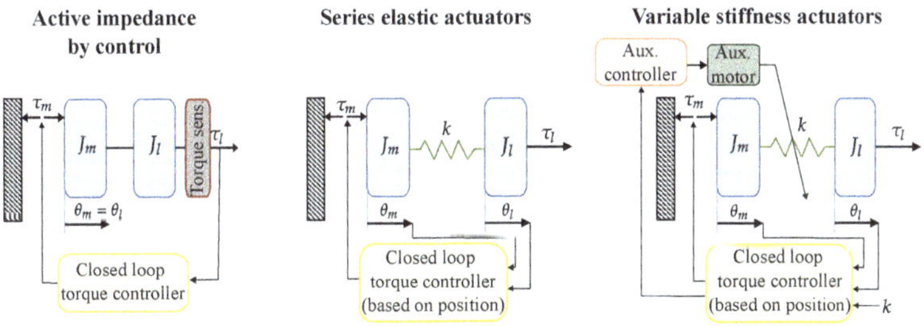

(b)

Figure 1. (**a**) Classification scheme for variable impedance actuation systems in pHRI. (**b**) Block diagrams of three different physical human–robot interaction solutions.

Actuators employing inherent compliance provide an electric motor coupled with a spring. Depending on whether the spring is fixed—i.e., its value does not change—like mechanical springs, or variable like silicone rubber springs, these actuators can be classified respectively into Series Elastic Actuators (SEAs) and Variable-Stiffness Actuators (VSAs). Both of the solutions are based on the principle that, by adding a series elastic element between load and actuator, it is possible to reduce the peak power requested from the motor. Inherent damping actuators are based on the control of friction by means of eddy currents, controlled rheology or fluid dynamics. Both SEAs and VSAs have been implemented in exoskeletons such as Lopes [25], the NEUROexos elbow exoskeleton [26], the ALTACRO locomotion exoskeleton [27] and the Harmony exoskeleton [28]. These actuators have the great advantage of impact absorption, thus enhancing the system safety. Moreover, SEAs and VSAs are eventually capable of mechanically storing energy during passive phases while releasing it in active phases of the motion cycle. VSAs generally employ two motors, which increase the size, weight and complexity of the whole actuator in comparison with an SEA [29].

On the other side, actuators employing active impedance by control are equipped with electric motors coupled with a transmission/reduction system; they can be classified according to the back-drivability and sensing system. Force-controlled actuators implement a force/torque sensor at the joint level, and they can achieve impedance behavior by closed-loop control. Generally, traditional actuators with no elastic or damping elements are lighter and more compact than passive variable impedance actuators, but their time response and dynamic bandwidth are limited by the control system as well as the electrical properties of actuators, such as motor maximum speed.

Simplified block diagrams of the solutions based on active impedance by control, an SEA and a VSA are reported in Figure 1b.

The majority of recent exoskeletons based on joint torque sensors have been mostly designed for lower limb solutions [30–32]. The main advantages of these systems are their compactness and robustness, though when the torque sensor is embedded in the joint, it becomes sensitive to the link inertia, thus affecting the system transparency. A mechanical solution is presented in Ref. [33], and the transparency of a lower limb exoskeleton is improved by positioning the force/torque sensor on the supporting cuffs, that is, at the interaction point between the human leg and the exoskeleton. Sensors generally employed to measure angular deflections are encoders [34] and potentiometers [35]—usually requiring custom mechanical supports to avoid errors related to sensitivity to misalignments. While deflection-based force estimation has become the most widely utilized method for SEAs and VSAs performing reliable force control in various robotic applications, there are still practical difficulties such as errors in spring deflection measurements or noise in the encoder signal [36]. These factors have a very negative impact on high-stiffness SEAs. In [37], a polymer optical fiber is mounted on the torsional spring of an SEA to read angles and torques in a more accurate way without considerably enlarging the actuator size at the cost of more specific (and complex) electronics.

Therefore, the adoption of inherent compliant actuation systems rather than achieving compliance by control is not a trivial choice; it mainly depends on the desired mechanical features, and it is the result of a trade-off among many factors such as compactness and weight, costs, safety and efficiency. The mentioned advantages and disadvantages of the SEA, VSA and active impedance by control solutions are summarized in Table 1.

In this paper, we propose a solution based on active impedance obtained by closed-loop control employing an elastic component to measure and transmit axial torques at the same time. This is a good trade-off favoring compactness and simplicity using just one motor. We implement a joint torque controller based on novel full-state feedback (JTFC1) to obtain a short time response and a high dynamic bandwidth by closed-loop control to achieve a desired impedance behavior.

Table 1. List of advantages and disadvantages of the SEA, VSA and active impedance by control solutions. This list is not exhaustive.

pHRI Actuator Solution	Advantages	Disadvantages
SEA	Smaller requested motor peak power; safety	Fixed stiffness; torque estimation relies on the encoder readings and sensor accuracy
VSA	Versatility; smaller requested motor peak power; safety	Increased complexity; need for auxiliary motor, mechanics and control; more weight
Active impedance by control	Lightness; compactness; robustness	Time response and dynamic bandwidth is limited by the control system and actuators' electrical properties

The design of a closed-loop feedback torque control is an essential aid for managing the identification of human intention in pHRI [2]. Among the broad variety of force/torque controllers available in the literature, and, particularly, among the ones based on direct joint torque sensor readings, Hashimoto et al. proposed a single-joint torque controller based on torque readings estimated from the harmonic drive elasticity [38]. The basic closed-loop controller was tested with different feedforward compensation terms in order to achieve high disturbance reduction and robustness to model error. Moreover, Kugi et al. proposed a passivity-based impedance controller configuration, providing an inner torque feedback loop based on joint torque readings in combination with an outer impedance control loop [39]. This controller configuration was tested with the DLR Light Weight Robot III (LWR III) in several experiments which verified the efficiency of this approach. Both of these aforementioned control approaches have the common goal of providing safe and efficient pHRI by designing a closed-loop controller able to compensate non-linear effects as well as offering accurate estimation of the interaction forces.

Moreover, in this paper, we introduce the design and the experimental characterization of the Rehab-Exos, an upper limb exoskeleton designed for rehabilitation purposes and equipped with actuators based on joint torque sensors and a high reduction ratio. We contribute by designing a joint torque controller based on novel full-state feedback (JTFC1) that takes into account the multi-DOF, non-linear system dynamics and provides compensation for other non-linear effects such as friction and gravity components. This is accomplished by employing a single-joint optimum observer that ensures joint torque tracking while a centralized controller estimates and compensates for the whole system's dynamics. To validate the proposed controller for the Rehab-Exos, in both transparency and haptic rendering experiments, the full-state feedback controller is compared with two alternative controllers: a feedback controller (JTFC2) inspired by Ref. [38] and a passivity-based feedback controller (JTFC3) inspired by Ref. [39]. The experiments performed with our proposed controller validate the Rehab-Exos as a device able to achieve satisfying pHRI performances, thus asserting the feasibility of the Rehab-Exos for human assistance and rehabilitation purposes.

This paper is structured as follows: Section 2 presents the design of the Rehab-Exos, with a particular focus on the design and issues related to its torque sensors based on strain gauges. Section 3.1 provides a mathematical model of the single joint, whereas, in Section 3.2, the full dynamics model of the Rehab-Exos is described. Section 4 explains the proposed full-state feedback controller and recalls two benchmark torque controllers already known from the literature. Section 5 presents the experiments and the obtained results. Finally, discussions and conclusions are respectively addressed in Sections 6 and 7.

2. System Design

The Rehab-Exos (Figure 2) is an active robotic exoskeleton designed to be modular and easily re-configurable. Since rehabilitation applications are its final purpose, it is designed to be capable of generating controlled contact forces/torques not only at its end effector handle but also at intermediate contact points with the human user's arm. By wearing the device, the patient is able to control the full force interaction with the exoskeleton as well as guide—or be guided by—shoulder and elbow articulations. The joint torque sensors monitor the physical interaction between the user and the exoskeleton.

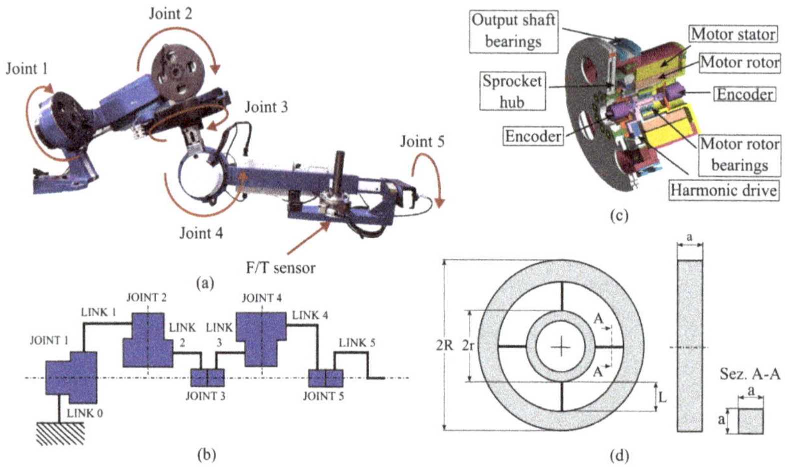

Figure 2. (**a**) The Rehab-Exos, a 5 DOF upper limb exoskeleton with four actuated joints. The joints J_1, J_2 and J_4 share the same characteristics: high reduction ratio (100:1) obtained by harmonic drive, an embedded torque sensor and maximum actuation torque of 150 Nm. The joint J_3 is composed of a semi-circular guide actuated by a DC motor through tendon transmission. Joint J_5 is passive. The exoskeleton is equipped with a force/torque sensor at the end effector that is used for evaluation purposes. (**b**) Joint and link schematic view of the Rehab-Exos exoskeleton. (**c**) The section view of the actuators of J_1, J_2 and J_4. (**d**) Two-dimensional dimensions of the torque sensor.

2.1. Mechanical Design of the Rehab-Exos

As depicted in Figure 2, the exoskeleton has a serial architecture which is isomorphic with human kinematics. It comprises a shoulder joint which is fixed in the space, and it is composed of three active joints, J_1, J_2 and J_3, an active elbow joint, J_4, and a passive revolute joint, J_5, allowing wrist prono/supination. For a more detailed description of both the Rehab-Exos and actuation groups, the reader can refer to Ref. [40]. The exoskeleton is grounded to a supporting structure that can be easily moved via passive wheels, and the height of the first link can be adjusted; thus, the position of the center of the shoulder of the exoskeleton can be set to fit the center of the shoulder of the user. The actuation stage of the joints J_1, J_2 and J_4 of the exoskeleton is identical. These joints integrate a compact harmonic drive (HD) component set—which implements a high reduction ratio of 100:1—and a custom-made frame-less, brushless torque motor. The maximum joint output torque of the actuator is equal to 150 Nm with an overall weight of 3.7 kg and a motor shaft inertia, reduced to the joint output shaft Jm, equal to 2.5 kgm^2. The adopted mechanical components limit both the back-drivability—when the motor is powered off—and the overall mechanical complexity. Nevertheless, the user never holds the weight of the joints because the gravitational and dynamic contributions are modeled and provided by the torque controller. Then, the reaction torques/forces to the first link are exerted by the supporting structure.

A CAD section of the J_1, J_2 and J_4 joints is depicted in Figure 2c. Joint J_3 is characterized by tendon transmission which is used to transmit the actuation torque through an open semi-circular guide. More detail on the J_3 joint can be found in Ref. [40].

2.2. Design Aspects of the Strain-Gauge-Based Torque Sensor

The three joints J_1, J_2 and J_4 have a torque sensor featuring a four-spoke shape geometry. Despite increasing the actuation group compliance, the embedded torque sensors enable multi-contact force control. Moreover, it allows the implementation of a stable, high-bandwidth torque closed loop around each joint that is weakly affected by the variable inertia of the robot links; suppresses robot vibrations produced by the inherent transmission compliance (harmonic drive); reduces internal disturbance torques caused by the actuator and reducer as, for example, friction losses, actuators torque ripples and gear-teeth-wedging actions; and measures externally applied forces/moments and complex non-linear dynamic interactions between joints and links.

Each sensor embeds two fully balanced strain gauge bridges, located on different beams of the spoke. The sensor is made of AISI 630 steel, a harmonic steel exhibiting a yield strength of 1950 MPa and a Young's modulus of 196 GPa, and it is designed to exhibit low weight and high sensitivity to axial moments. The axial torsional stiffness of the sensor k_s is equal to 30 KNm/rad, and it can be computed as in Equation (1).

$$k_s = \frac{\tau}{\theta} = \frac{Ea^4(r + L(1-Q))}{3L^2(1/2 - Q)}, \tag{1}$$

where the adimensional parameter Q is given by the following:

$$Q = \frac{3r + L}{6r + 3L}, \tag{2}$$

where, according to Figure 2d, r is the radius of the internal sensor ring, L is length of the beams and a is the side length of the beam section. The characteristic dimensions of the sensor are reported in Table 2. Moreover, the torsional stiffness of the joint reduced to its output shaft k is equal to 11.38 KNm/rad.

Table 2. Characteristic dimensions of the torque sensor.

Dimension	R	r	L	a
Value (mm)	78	38	24	4

The position of the strain gauges on the beam is selected according to a trade-off process. By locating them in the middle of the beam, the sensor sensitivity is low, while locating them near the extremities of the beam results in sensor readings being affected by the non-linearities coming from the beam fillets. Taking this into account, the selected distances from the extremities are selected as $p = 1/8$ and $L = 3$ mm. To estimate the strain of the beam at a given point with distance p from the inner ring under a certain axial torque τ, the normal tension σ_p that acts on that point p needs to be computed as follows:

$$\sigma_p = \frac{3\tau((1-Q)L - p)}{2a^3((1-Q)L + r)}, \tag{3}$$

and then the strain is computed as follows:

$$\epsilon_A = \frac{\sigma}{E}, \tag{4}$$

where E is the Young's modulus.

Theoretically, i.e., using (4), at 3 mm from the inner ring and under an axial torque of 120 Nm, a maximum strain of 2.7×10^{-3} is obtained. The same test is conducted using an FEM software tool (Ansys® v.2019 R3.0) because the surface of the strain gauge is not negligible compared to the beam one (see Figure 3). The FEM analysis results in a maximum strain of 1.98×10^{-3}. The strain of each strain gauge when a 1 Nm load is applied is shown in Table 3.

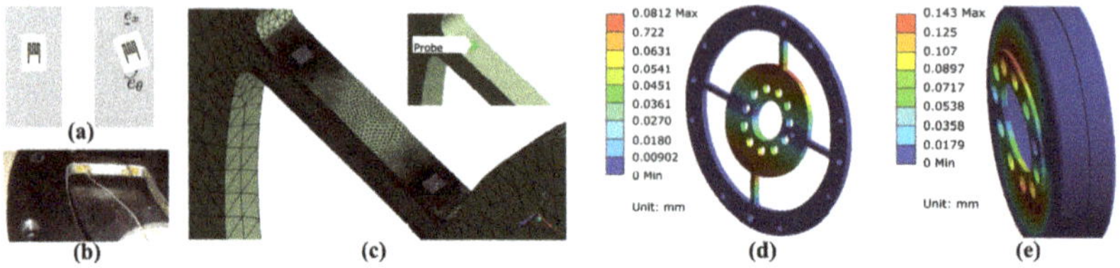

Figure 3. (**a**) A possible cause of the high sensitivity to non-axial load is the strain gauge mounting misalignment. The value e_x represents the linear displacement, while the angular one is represented by the value e_θ. (**b**) A detail of the mounted strain gauges on the torque sensor. (**c**) Regarding the FEM analysis, a more dense grid mesh for the zone of interest is used. For each area, the average strain along the radial direction is computed. (**d**) Results of the FEM analysis on the torque sensor and on the flexible spline deformation under non-axial load (**e**).

Table 3. Strain of the four strain gauges.

Probe 1	Probe 2	Probe 3	Probe 4
1.65×10^{-5}	-1.33×10^{-5}	-1.91×10^{-5}	2.2546×10^{-5}

An important feature of the torque sensor is represented by the sensitivity to non-axial moments. For this reason, an experimental test is conducted to compute the sensitivity, i.e., predetermined non-axial torque is exerted on the sensor in four configurations (angles) of the sensor. Experimental results are reported in Table 4, and the obtained sensitivity is equal to the following:

$$S_S = \frac{C_{mis}}{C_S} = 0.067, \tag{5}$$

Table 4. Sensor readings referring to non-axial moment sensitivity.

Applied Torque (Nm)	Sensor Readings Per Angle (Nm)			
	0°	45°	90°	180°
32	1.6	2.4	2.2	2.3
64	2.9	4.8	4.4	4.4
96	4.5	7.5	6.9	6.9

Observing the results in Table 4, it should be noted that the sensitivity to non-axial moments is relatively high if compared to the one mentioned in Ref. [41]. The issue is investigated according to the steps reported in the roadmap of Figure 4. Indeed, the correct estimation of the joint torque is crucial for obtaining a high level of transparency of the controlled exoskeleton in all the poses of the workspace. To explain the experimental evidence, two possible reasons (or a combination of them) are proposed: the first cause of error could be represented by a strain gauge mounting misalignment; the second one could be related to an excessive deformation of the sensor due to the non-axial moments. Considering the first hypothesis of error, the sensitivity of the strain gauges to non-axial load C_S due to strain gauge misalignment—when a flexible model of the HD is considered—can be modeled as follows:

$$S_{misal} = k_s \cdot (k_{ex} \cdot e_x + k_{e\theta} \cdot e_\theta), \tag{6}$$

where k_s is a scaling factor equal to $7.87e^{-3}$, k_{ex} is the sensitivity to linear mounting misalignment, which is equal to 3, and $k_{e\theta}$ is the sensitivity to angular mounting misalignment and is equal to 2.3, whereas e_x and e_θ are the positional and angular misalignment errors, respectively—see Figure 3a. Equation (6), together with the measured sensitivity of 0.067, leads to a misalignment error of millimeters and tens of degrees, but these values are higher than the actual misalignment the installation operator may have introduced, as can be seen in Figure 3b.

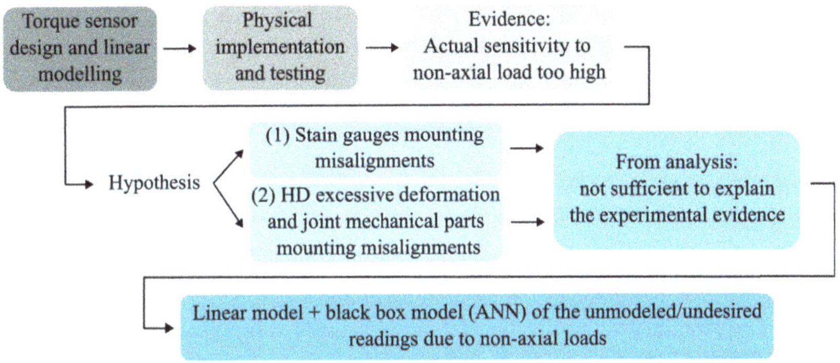

Figure 4. Roadmap of the analysis conducted on the sensitivity to non-axial load of the torque sensor.

Regarding the second hypothesis, it is worth noticing that the sensor from a structural point of view is in series with the HD, and both of them are in parallel with a couple of bearings. This parallel chain composes a hyper-static system (see Figure 5); therefore, the excessive sensitivity may be due to the mounting misalignment of the mechanical parts of the chain.

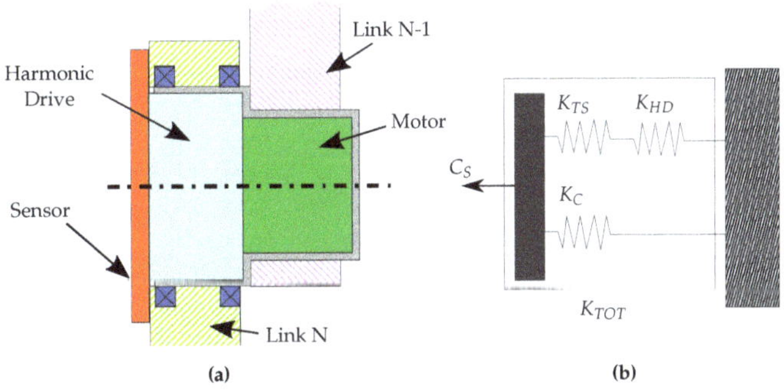

Figure 5. (**a**) Schematic view of the joint. The torque sensor connects in series the motor and the link n; nevertheless, it is not structural and is designed to transmit only axial torque. (**b**) The kinematic chain of the joint to non-axial loads. K_{TS} and K_{HD} represent the stiffness of the torque sensor and of the harmonic drive to non-axial load, respectively, whereas K_B is the bearing stiffness.

For the study of the hyper-static system, the system parts are supposed to behave in a linear, elastic way, while the system response at non-axial moments is modeled as mono-dimensional. The overall joint stiffness to non-axial moment K_{TOT} is experimentally evaluated, whereas the non-axial moment stiffness of the torque sensor K_{TS} and the HD K_{HD} are computed via FEM analysis. The FEM results are depicted in Figure 3, and the stiffness values are reported in Table 5.

Table 5. Stiffness of the components.

Component	Stiffness (kNm/rad)
K_{TS}	4.1
K_{HD}	0.4
K_B	23.6
K_{TOT}	24

A possible mounting misalignment of the hyper-static chain may consist of a collinear and/or concentric mounting misalignment between the sensor axis and the bearing axis. In this case, the HD works as a universal joint that connects the sensor—connected to the $n+1$ link—with the $n-th$ link. The sensitivity to non-axial moments defined in Equation (5) and the mechanical properties in Table 5 lead to a theoretical mounting misalignment of about 0.5 mm. However, this value does not agree with the design tolerances or the data-sheets of the components, from which a misalignment of about 0.05 mm is considered for the worst case.

To summarize, unwanted sensor readings related to non-axial load may be due to the combination of effects from sensor mounting misalignments and HD excessive deformation. In order to minimize this undesired effect, we adopt a model-free adaptive method based on Artificial Neural Networks (ANNs) to characterize and compensate this non-linear response of the sensors. This proposal represents an alternative method to modeling approaches, and the choice is justified by the complexity of the phenomenon.

Considering the ideal and linear response of the sensor, the torque readings can be expressed as follows:

$$\tau_s = k_v \cdot v, \tag{7}$$

where v is the measured voltage tension, and k_v represents the voltage constant of the torque sensor. In a real case, it is possible to write the following:

$$\hat{\tau}_s = k_v \cdot v + \delta\tau, \tag{8}$$

where $\delta\tau$ is the non-linear influence on the sensor readings due to the mounting and non-axial loads. By experimental evidence, it is possible to assert that the term $\delta\tau$ varies in a non-linear way with respect to the exoskeleton pose (joint angles) and load. The mounting errors influence the torque readings in a non-linear way with respect to the joint angle, whereas the non-axial torques depend partially on the interaction with the human user and partially on the dynamics and gravitational torques acting on the considered joint. For all three sensors, the k_v constants are experimentally evaluated. In order to minimize the effect of non-linear, undesired term $\delta\tau$, an ANN is involved in the process, with seven neurons in the hidden layer and sigmoid activation function. The goal is to estimate the error basing on the four angles and load on each axis. The angular information is useful for inferring the assembly error component, whereas, for the load influence, the gravitational torque is used. To train the neural network, the whole workspace is partitioned into 414 target points. The torque sensor readings are acquired while the exoskeleton is holding the target position. For each joint, the training is performed using the four angles and the gravity torque acting on the joint (and computed by the model) as input data, whereas the output is represented by the residual $\hat{\delta\tau}$ as follows:

$$\hat{\delta\tau} = G_i(\boldsymbol{\theta_m}) - k_v * v, \tag{9}$$

where G_i represents the gravity load on the i-th joint when the pose is given by the angle vector $\boldsymbol{\theta_m}$. The set of target points is divided into three parts: 70% for the training set, 20% for the validation set and 10% for the test set. The regression value between the ANN output and the target points is 0.99.

The actual sensor torque estimation $\bar{\tau}_s$ is computed as follows:

$$\bar{\tau}_s = k_v * v + \delta\tau(\boldsymbol{\theta_m}, G_i). \tag{10}$$

2.3. Control Hardware

The control architecture of the Rehab-Exos is decentralized and based on the EtherCAT communication bus in order to guarantee both an optimal signal-to-noise ratio in the acquisition of analogical signals—i.e., the force sensors—and higher safety standards. The EtherCAT communication network consists of one master controller and four EtherCAT Slave Controllers (ESCs), one for each actuation joint. The master controller is handled by the Simulink Real-Time™ Operating System, which executes the centralized control model at 2 KHz of frequency. The exoskeleton is equipped with three 170 VDC power-supplied brushless motors on the first, second and fourth joint, each one driven by programmable current drivers, and one 48 VDC power-supplied DC motor on the third joint. Each motor is provided with one incremental encoder and one torque sensor. Each ESC board is a custom control board featuring an ARM7 micro-controller of up to 72 Mhz; four 14-bit DAC output interfaces setting the reference of the current drives; ten 14-bit Analog-to-Digital Converter (ADC) channels acquiring the torque signals through two pre-amplified Wheatstone full-bridge channels; and an EtherCAT ET1100 controller connecting to the double-port Ethernet interface.

3. Dynamic Model

3.1. Single-Joint Model

Each joint is modeled with a two-mass system with a spring and damper (Figure 6) due to the elasticity of the harmonic drive speed reducer and torque sensor for joints J_1, J_2 and J_4 and due to the cable transmission for joint J_3. The selected single-joint model is as follows.

The single-joint dynamics are represented by the following system of equations:

$$I_{m,i}\ddot{\theta}_{m,i} + c_{m,i}\dot{\theta}_{m,i} + c_{t,i}(\dot{\theta}_{m,i} - \dot{\theta}_i) + k_{t,i}(\theta_{m,i} - \theta_i) = \tau_{m,i} + \tau_{d,i} \tag{11}$$

$$I_{l,i}\ddot{\theta}_i + c_{t,i}(\dot{\theta}_i - \dot{\theta}_{m,i}) + k_{t,i}(\theta_i - \theta_{m,i}) = \tau_{l,i} \tag{12}$$

where, referring to the i-th joint, $\theta_{m,i}$ and θ_i represent the motor and joint angles, respectively; $k_{t,i}$ and $c_{t,i}$ are the stiffness and viscous coefficient of the transmission identified from experimental characterization; the terms $I_{m,i}$ and $I_{l,i}$ represent the inertia of the motor and the average link inertia considered as constant, respectively; and $\tau_{m,i}$, $\tau_{d,i}$ and $\tau_{l,i}$ represent the torque of the motor, the disturbance torque acting on the motor rotor and the external torque acting directly on the output link, respectively. The term $\tau_{l,i}$ accounts for both the exogenous input due to the interaction with the human user and the endogenous input, which takes into account the unmodeled non-linear effects, such as dynamic or gravity forces.

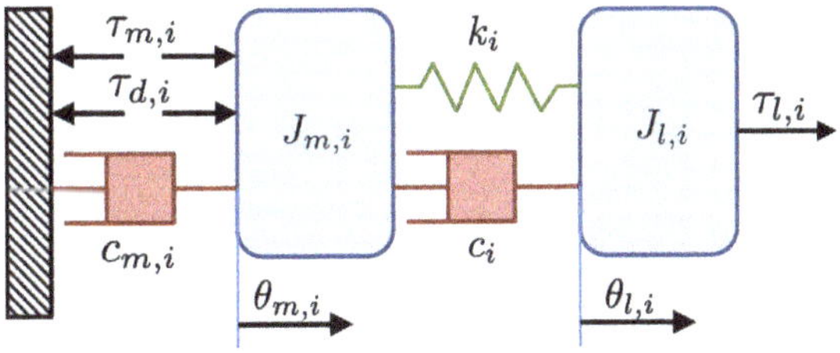

Figure 6. The two-mass model selected for each joint.

Experimental Characterization of the Single Joint's Performance

As described in Section 2.1, the joint is equipped with a torque sensor which is part of the transmission chain. It is also capable of measuring the elastic torque $\tau_{s,i}$, which acts between the motor's rotor and the joint output link. The elastic sensor torque can be expressed by the following:

$$\tau_{s,i} = k_{t,i}(\theta_i - \theta_{m,i}). \tag{13}$$

The joint dynamics can be rewritten by putting in evidence of the $\tau_{s,i}$ readings starting from the $\tau_{s,i}$ definition then taking into account its first and second derivatives, as well as using Equations (11) and (12). As a result, the following equation is obtained:

$$\ddot{\tau}_{s,i} + \frac{c_{t,i}}{I_i}\dot{\tau}_{s,i} + \frac{k_{t,i}}{I_i}\tau_{s,i} = \frac{k_{t,i}}{I_{l,i}}\tau_l + \frac{k_{t,i}}{I_{l,i}}\tau_g - \frac{k_{t,i}}{I_{m,i}}\tau_d - \frac{k_{t,i}}{I_{m,i}}\tau_m, \tag{14}$$

where $I_i = I_l I_m/(I_l + I_m)$. The natural frequency of this system is computed as follows:

$$\omega_n = \frac{\sqrt{\frac{k_{t,i}}{I_i}}}{2\pi}, \tag{15}$$

and it is experimentally evaluated for a single joint in a test rig by analyzing the response of the τ_s when a τ_m command torque signal of chirp type is fed to the motor.

From Figure 7, the use of the Half-Power Bandwidth method returns an overall damping coefficient c of the flexible joint equal to 11.8 Nms/rad. The obtained value is also validated via the Logarithmic Decrement method.

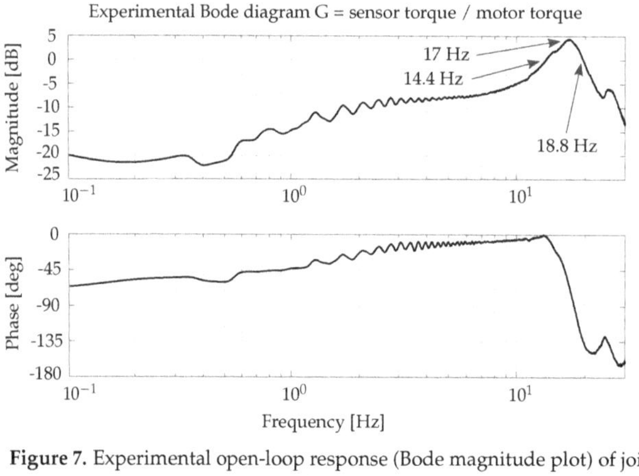

Figure 7. Experimental open-loop response (Bode magnitude plot) of joints J_1, J_2 and J_4: joint sensor torque vs. motor torque command in standardized testbed conditions.

Each exoskeleton joint perceives link inertia depending on the pose; thus, the natural frequency of each joint depends on the pose of the exoskeleton. Therefore, the natural frequency for each joint elastic transmission can be obtained by taking into account average link inertia. Results are shown in Table 6.

Table 6. The natural frequency of the joints.

Joint	Avg. Link Inertia (kg/m^2)	Natural Freq. (Hz)
1	0.9639	19.3930
2	1.11	18.3501
4	0.1925	39.6797

The three joints referenced in Table 6 share the motor inertia value, which is equal to 3.742 kg/m^2.

3.2. Multiple-Joints Model

Given the two-mass model employed for each single joint, the dynamic model of the whole exoskeleton can be formulated in matrix form as follows:

$$\begin{gathered}\overbrace{\mathbf{I_m D}\ddot{\theta}_m + \mathbf{B_m D}\dot{\theta}_m}^{\text{Motor Dynamics}} + \overbrace{\mathbf{C_t}(\mathbf{D}\dot{\theta}_m - \dot{\theta}) + \mathbf{K_t}(\mathbf{D}\theta_m - \theta)}^{\text{Elastic transmission torque}} = \tau_m + \tau_d \\ \underbrace{\mathbf{M}(\theta)\ddot{\theta} + \mathbf{C}(\dot{\theta},\theta)\dot{\theta}}_{\text{Joint dynamics}} + \underbrace{\mathbf{C_t}(\dot{\theta} - \mathbf{D}\dot{\theta}_m) + \mathbf{K_t}(\theta - \mathbf{D}\theta_m)}_{\text{Elastic transmission torque}} + G(\theta) = \mathbf{J^T} F_h,\end{gathered} \tag{16}$$

where $\mathbf{I_m}$, $\mathbf{B_m}$, $\mathbf{D}$, $\mathbf{K_t}$ and $\mathbf{C_t}$ are diagonal matrices; $\mathbf{I_m}$ and $\mathbf{B_m}$ represent, respectively, inertia and viscous friction at the motor; $\mathbf{K_t}$ and $\mathbf{C_t}$ represent stiffness and damping associated with the elastic transmission; $\mathbf{D}$ represents the transmission reduction factor introduced by joint gear-heads; G accounts for the gravity force effects on the links; and $\mathbf{J^T}F_h$ is the torques reflected on the joints due to the interaction forces exchanged between the human and the system where the transposed Jacobian matrix $\mathbf{J^T}$ is evaluated in the actual exoskeleton configuration. The multi-joint model introduces cross-coupling among joints and non-linearities by taking into account the term $\mathbf{C}(\dot{\theta},\theta)$, which is related to Coriolis effects, and the term $\mathbf{M}(\theta)$, representing the links' inertia. The latter term can be decomposed into a constant diagonal component and a variable one as follows:

$$\mathbf{M}\ddot{\theta} = \underbrace{\overline{\mathbf{M}}\ddot{\theta}}_{\text{constant}} + \underbrace{\Delta\mathbf{M}(\theta)\ddot{\theta}}_{\text{variable}} \tag{17}$$

By switching variables, this expression can also be introduced for the joint torque as follows:

$$\tau_s = -\mathbf{K_t}(\mathbf{D}\theta_m - \theta), \tag{18}$$

Then, the dynamics Equation (16) can be rearranged, highlighting the new variables τ_s and θ_m as follows:

$$\mathbf{I_m D}\ddot{\theta}_m + \mathbf{B_m D}\dot{\theta}_m = \mathbf{K_t}^{-1}\mathbf{C_t}\dot{\tau}_s + \tau_s + \tau_d + u \tag{19}$$

$$\ddot{\tau}_s + \mathbf{C_t I_i}^{-1}\dot{\tau}_s + \mathbf{K_t I_i}^{-1}\tau_s = \mathbf{K_t I_m}^{-1}(\mathbf{I_m}\overline{\mathbf{M}}^{-1}\mathbf{J}^T F_l + \mathbf{B_m D}\dot{\theta}_m - \tau_d - u), \tag{20}$$

where the term u represents the actual control command, while the external disturbance forces are collected within the external load force term F_l—see Appendix A for a detailed derivation of terms.

From the reshaped dynamics equation, we define the full-state feedback control law and the optimal observer to estimate the joint torque.

3.2.1. Joint Acceleration Estimation

The full dynamics model of the exoskeleton is dependent on the acceleration of each joint. In order to estimate and compensate for the dynamics of the device, an observer for the joint acceleration is designed. The observer estimates the acceleration, taking into account the motor encoder readings $\theta_{m,i}$, the joint torque $\tau_{s,i}$ and the commanded control torque $\tau_{m,i}$. The term $\tau_{s,i}$ represents the torque measured by the sensor at the joint and can be expressed as in Equation (18). The acceleration can be estimated starting from a model of the actuation group—motor plus gear-head—and, additionally, by modeling the torque acting on the actuation group as $\tau_{m,i} - \tau_{s,i}$ and by considering the losses as a static and velocity-dependent viscous friction. Thus, the acceleration can be estimated as follows:

$$\begin{cases} \ddot{\theta}_{m,i} = 0 & \text{for } -\tau_{A,i} < \tau_{m,i} - \tau_{s,i} < \tau_{A,i} \\ \ddot{\theta}_{m,i} = \dfrac{\tau_{m,i} - \tau_{s,i} - c_{m,i}\dot{\theta}_{m,i}}{J_{m,i}} & \text{otherwise} \end{cases} \tag{21}$$

where the terms $\tau_{A,i}$ and $c_{m,i}$ represent the static friction torque and the dynamic friction, respectively, both of them previously experimentally evaluated. The torque saturation effects due to power supply voltage limits are modeled as follows:

$$k_c \frac{-V_{max} - k_v \dot{\theta}_{m,i}}{R} < \tau_{m,i} < k_c \frac{V_{max} - k_v \dot{\theta}_{m,i}}{R}, \tag{22}$$

depending on the electric constants of each motor. Particularly, where k_c is the associated torque constant, the k_v is the velocity constant, R is the winding terminal resistance and V_{max} represents the maximum supply voltage to the motor.

An optimum observer is used to estimate the acceleration term $\ddot{\theta}_{m,i}$. Figure 8 shows a diagram scheme of the acceleration estimator, which uses both controller and measured torques.

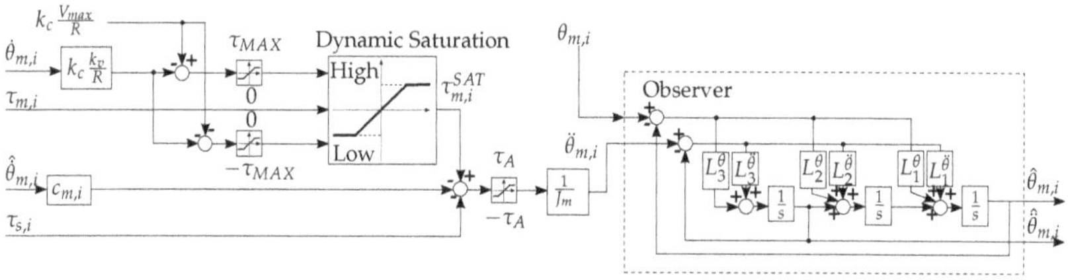

Figure 8. Block scheme of the acceleration estimator basing on torque measurements. The left side of the scheme models the motor dynamics, and it takes into account saturation effects. The right side of the scheme shows the implementation of the observer.

The model can be expressed in the state variable form as follows:

$$\begin{cases} \dot{x} = \mathbf{A}x + \Gamma d \\ y = \mathbf{C}x, \end{cases} \tag{23}$$

where

$$x = \begin{bmatrix} \theta_{m,i} \\ \dot{\theta}_{m,i} \\ \ddot{\theta}_{m,i} \end{bmatrix}, \mathbf{A} = \begin{pmatrix} 0 & 1 & 0 \\ 0 & 0 & 1 \\ 0 & 0 & 0 \end{pmatrix}, \Gamma = \begin{bmatrix} 0 \\ 0 \\ 1 \end{bmatrix}, \mathbf{C} = \begin{pmatrix} 1 & 0 & 0 \\ 0 & 0 & 1 \end{pmatrix}, \tag{24}$$

and $\boldsymbol{d}$ represents the process noise.

The observer can be formulated as follows:

$$\dot{\hat{x}} = \mathbf{A}\hat{x} + \mathbf{L}(y - \mathbf{C}\hat{x}), \tag{25}$$

where L represents the gain matrix of the observer. A scheme of the observer is depicted in Figure 8.

The gain L is found, resolving the problem of the Kalman optimum observer based on the experimental covariance data of measurement and process noise. Measurement noise is derived from motor encoder readings $\theta_{m,i}$, which mainly take into account the encoder quantization and motor acceleration estimate $\ddot{\theta}_{m,i}$ through (21) thanks to the available torque measurement.

As an example, the comparison between the real-time estimated acceleration—gray dotted line—and the off-line computed acceleration—black solid line—for the first two joints is shown in Figure 9.

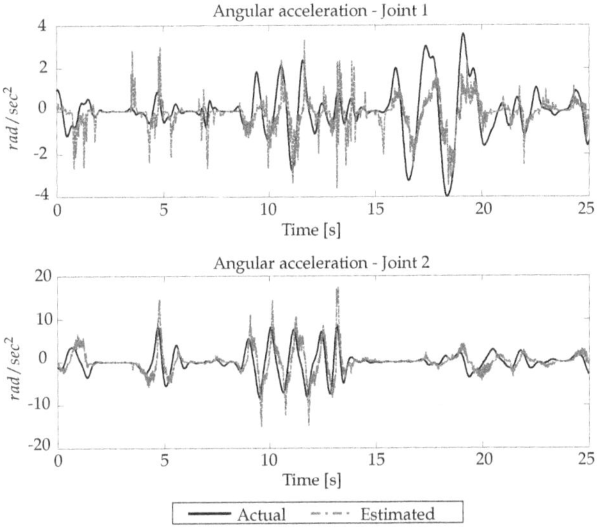

Figure 9. Comparison between estimated (gray dashed line) and actual (solid black line) joint acceleration. Joints J_1 and J_2 are chosen for reference only. Similar results are obtained for all the joints.

3.2.2. Dynamics Compensation

As reported by Equation (A4), the torques measured by joint sensors relate to the human force and to any load applied on the links (F_l). To obtain a good estimation of human forces by the torque sensors, it is necessary to remove the contributions of both gravity and dynamics loads applied to the links from torque measurements. The gravity contribution depends only on the pose of the exoskeleton, and it can be computed by the position signals acquired with the motor encoders. The gravitational term is already compensated in feedforward by the term $\hat{\mathbf{G}}(\mathbf{D}\hat{\theta}_m)$ in τ_m, except for the term δg. On the other side, the dynamics contribution depends on pose, velocity and acceleration of the links. These terms are not directly provided by any sensor, but they can be first approximated as $\mathbf{D}\hat{\ddot{\theta}}_m$ by the observer described in Section 3.2.1.

The dynamic torques—which are generated from the links' inertia and are measured by the joint torque sensors—can be estimated as the sum of the inertial contribution and the Coriolis effect as follows:

$$\hat{\tau}_{\mathrm{dyn}} \approx \hat{\mathbf{M}}(\mathbf{D}\theta_m)\mathbf{D}\ddot{\theta}_m + \hat{\mathbf{C}}(\mathbf{D}\theta_m, \mathbf{D}\dot{\theta}_m)\mathbf{D}\dot{\theta}_m, \tag{26}$$

where matrices $\hat{\mathbf{M}}$ and $\hat{\mathbf{C}}$ are computed by taking into account for each joint the inertia of each part supported by the torque sensor while discarding the inertia of joint actuator.

The estimated dynamic torques are then used to compensate the dynamic effects of the link. The compensation torques $\alpha\hat{\tau}_{\mathrm{dyn}}$, with $0 < \alpha < 1$, are a percentage of the estimated torques $\hat{\tau}_{\mathrm{dyn}}$. The compensation torques are added to the desired torques τ_s^D as input to the state feedback controller and then fed back with the estimated torque $\hat{\tau}_s$.

4. Full-State, Basic and Passivity-Based Feedback Controllers

From the full dynamic model of the exoskeleton, a novel full-state feedback control law is derived and implemented where the state of the system is estimated through a Kalman filter algorithm—see Section 4.1. This control law is identified in the following with the acronym JTFC1 and explained in Section 4.2. To evaluate the performance of the proposed full-state feedback control, two other torque control methods are implemented. These two control methods are inspired by the existing joint torque controls available in the literature, and, in this work, they are addressed with the acronyms JTFC2 and JTFC3.

The JTFC2 controller—presented in Section 4.3—was first introduced by Hashimoto [38], and it mainly consists of a torque control for a single joint based on torque sensor readings. In order to compare the basic torque control with our full-state feedback control, the Hashimoto formulation is extended and generalized to a multi-DOF case.

The JTFC3 controller—reported in Section 4.4—is inspired by the passivity-based control law designed in Ref. [39] and implemented for the DLR Light Weight Robot III (LWR III) in order to guarantee the passivity of the controlled system. The DLR LWR III is equipped with a joint configuration compatible with the Rehab-Exos one since both systems make use of the joint torque sensor to estimate the interaction of torques/forces with the environment/human.

4.1. An Optimal Observer for Joint Torque Estimation

Since the correct state estimation is essential for the design of a full-state feedback joint torque controller, knowledge of the interaction torques between the human arm and the exoskeleton is required for correct torque control implementation. The joint torque sensor provides a raw measurement $\tau_{s,i}$ that can be fused with the measured joint position $\theta_{m,i}$ to filter the sensed torque and to estimate the full system state, given by $[\tau_{s,i}, \dot{\tau}_{s,i}, \theta_{m,i}, \dot{\theta}_{m,i}, \tau_{d,i}, \tau_{l,i}]$, where $\tau_l = \mathbf{J}^T F_l$. Therefore, a full-state Kalman filter cleans out both $\theta_{m,i}$ from quantization noise $w_{\theta,i}$ and $\tau_{s,i}$ from measurement noise $w_{\tau,i}$, and it estimates the state variables.

Following Ref. [42], the dynamics of the two state components $\tau_{d,i}$ and $\tau_{l,i}$ can be modeled as two distinct Wiener processes—i.e., as two distinct, non-stationary random processes: $\dot{\tau}_{d,i} = v_{d,i}$ and $\dot{\tau}_{l,i} = v_{l,i}$. Starting from Equation (20), the following meta-system can be derived:

$$\begin{cases} \dot{\tau}_i = \mathbf{A_i}\tau_i + \mathbf{B_i}\tau_{m,i} + \Gamma v_i \\ y_i = \mathbf{C}\tau_i + w_i \end{cases} \tag{27}$$

where $\tau_i{}^T = [\dot{\tau}_{s,i}\ \tau_{s,i}\ \dot{\theta}_{m,i}\ \theta_{m,i}\ \tau_{l,i}\ \tau_{d,i}\ ]$ represents the meta-state vector, $v_i{}^T = [v_{l,i}\ v_{d,i}]$ represents the process noise vector with variances $V_{l,i}$ and $V_{d,i}$, $w_i{}^T = [w_{\tau,i}\ w_{\theta,i}]$ represents the measurement noise vector with variances $W_{l,i}$ and $W_{d,i}$. The matrices are built as follows:

$$\begin{gathered} \mathbf{A_i} = \begin{pmatrix} \frac{-c_{t,i}}{J_i} & \frac{-k_{t,i}}{J_i} & \frac{k_{t,i}b_{m,i}}{J_{m,i}} & 0 & \frac{k_{t,i}}{J_{l,i}} & \frac{-k_{t,i}}{J_{m,i}} \\ 1 & 0 & 0 & 0 & 0 & 0 \\ \frac{c_{t,i}}{k_{t,i}J_{m,i}} & \frac{1}{J_{m,i}} & \frac{-b_{m,i}}{J_{m,i}} & 0 & 0 & \frac{1}{J_{m,i}} \\ 0 & 0 & 1 & 0 & 0 & 0 \\ 0 & 0 & 0 & 0 & 0 & 0 \\ 0 & 0 & 0 & 0 & 0 & 0 \end{pmatrix} \\ \mathbf{B_i} = \begin{bmatrix} \frac{-k_{t,i}}{J_{m,i}} \\ 0 \\ \frac{1}{J_{m,i}} \\ 0 \\ 0 \\ 0 \end{bmatrix} \quad \Gamma = \begin{pmatrix} 0 & 0 \\ 0 & 0 \\ 0 & 0 \\ 0 & 0 \\ 1 & 0 \\ 0 & 1 \end{pmatrix} \quad \mathbf{C} = \begin{pmatrix} 0 & 0 \\ 1 & 0 \\ 0 & 0 \\ 0 & 1 \\ 0 & 0 \\ 0 & 0 \end{pmatrix} \end{gathered} \tag{28}$$

4.2. The Proposed Full-State Feedback Controller—JTFC1

The proposed control law is based on the full-state system obtained from the state observer described by Equations (27) and (28), where the input control u is split into one term u_f, implementing force control behavior, and another term u_g, providing gravity compensation, as shown in Equation (29).

$$u = u_f + u_g \tag{29}$$

The two above terms are expressed as follows:

$$u_g = G(\mathbf{D}\hat{\theta}_m) \tag{30}$$

$$u_f = -\underbrace{\boxed{\mathbf{I_i^{-1}}\mathbf{I_m}\tau_s^D}}_{\text{desired torque}} - \underbrace{\boxed{\mathbf{I_m}\mathbf{K_t^{-1}}(\ddot{\tau}_s^D - \mathbf{K_d}\dot{e} - \mathbf{K_p}e)}}_{\text{state feedback}} + \underbrace{\boxed{(\mathbf{I_m}\overline{\mathbf{M}^{-1}}\mathbf{J^T}\hat{F}_l + \mathbf{B_m}\mathbf{D}\dot{\theta}_m - \hat{\tau}_d)}}_{\text{unmodeled dynamics compensation}} \tag{31}$$

where $e = \tau_s - \tau_s^D$ is the error in sensor torque given its desired value τ_s^D. Moreover, let us assume the following:

$$\begin{cases} \dot{\tau}_s^D = 0 \quad thus \quad \dot{e} = \dot{\tau}_s, \\ \ddot{\tau}_s^D = 0 \quad thus \quad \ddot{e} = \ddot{\tau}_s. \end{cases} \tag{32}$$

The modified dynamics with the control laws (29)–(31) lead to the following stable error dynamics equation:

$$0 = \ddot{e} + (\mathbf{C_t}\mathbf{I_i^{-1}} + \mathbf{K_d})\dot{e} + (\mathbf{K_t}\mathbf{I_i^{-1}} + \mathbf{K_p})e \tag{33}$$

The convergence to zero of the error e can be adjusted to obtain the desired dynamic response by using $\mathbf{K_p}$ and $\mathbf{K_d}$ gains—proportional and derivative gain, respectively.

Based on the above, from the double derivation of Equation (18), we obtain the following dynamics:

$$\ddot{\theta}_m = \mathbf{D}^{-1}(\ddot{\theta} - \mathbf{K_t^{-1}}\ddot{e}) \tag{34}$$

Figure 10 reports the proposed full-state feedback control scheme. The selected control method takes into account the dynamic compensation contributions. It should be noted that the torque sensor readings $\tau_{s,i}$ and the commanded motor torques $\tau_{m,i}$ exclude the gravity compensation term u_g.

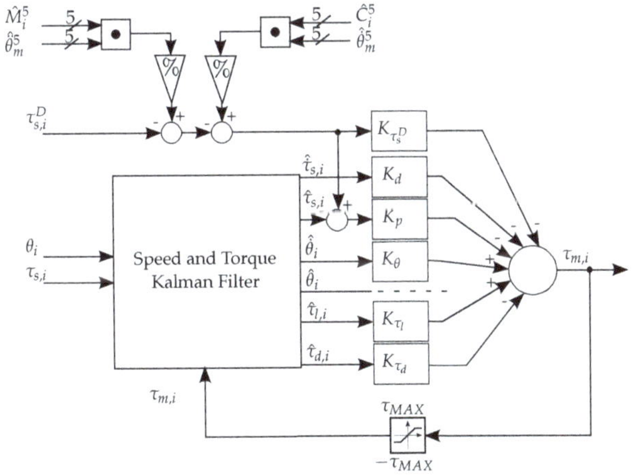

Figure 10. Schema of the full state feedback controller that implements the dynamic compensation. Inertial and Coriolis effects make use of the estimated joint accelerations and velocities (see scheme of Figure 8).

4.3. A Basic-State Feedback Controller—JTFC2

The basic-state feedback controller is derived assuming the following full model dynamics, extending the model already introduced for a single joint by Hashimoto [38], where feedforward compensation using desired torque values is presented for torque control by using torque sensors with a built-in harmonic drive. The JTFC2 model differs from Equation (16) since it has no damping contribution of the elastic transmission and external forces.

The basic control law used in Ref. [38] can be generalized in the case of a multi-joint robot. Therefore, using the same notation and conditions of Equation (32), the control law u_f can be written as a function of the desired torque value, where u_g refers to Equation (30).

$$u_f = -\underbrace{\boxed{\mathbf{I_i}^{-1}\mathbf{I_m}\tau_s^D}}_{\text{desired torque}} - \underbrace{\boxed{\mathbf{I_m}\mathbf{K_t}^{-1}(\dot{\tau}_s^D - \mathbf{K_d}\dot{e} - \mathbf{K_p}e)}}_{\text{state feedback}} \tag{35}$$

Considering the modified dynamics, and taking into account the control law shown in Equation (35), the following error dynamics equation is computed:

$$\mathbf{K_t}\overline{\mathbf{M}}^{-1}\mathbf{J}^{\mathbf{T}}F_l + \mathbf{B_m}\mathbf{D}\dot{\theta}_m - \mathbf{K_t}\mathbf{I_m}^{-1}\tau_d = \ddot{e} + (\mathbf{K_d} + \mathbf{I_i}^{-1}\mathbf{C_t})\dot{e} + (\mathbf{K_p} + \mathbf{I_i}^{-1}\mathbf{K_t})e \tag{36}$$

4.4. A Passivity-Based Feedback Controller—JTFC3

The passivity-based state feedback is derived assuming the following full model dynamics—introduced by Ott in Ref. [39]—which differ from the ones depicted in Equation (16) as there is an absence of the motor's viscous friction term $\mathbf{B_m}\mathbf{D}\dot{\theta}_m$.

In Ref. [39], the control law $\boldsymbol{u}$ is designed as in (29), where $\boldsymbol{u_g}$ is the torque due to the gravity, whereas the controller input $\boldsymbol{u_f}$ can optimize the matching with a desired impedance $\mathbf{I}_\theta$. Taking these computations into account, the term $\boldsymbol{u_f}$ can be written after some algebraic transformations as:

$$u_f = -\underbrace{\boxed{\mathbf{I_m}\mathbf{I}_\theta^{-1}\tau_s^D}}_{\text{desired torque}} - \underbrace{\boxed{(\mathbf{I} - \mathbf{I_m}\mathbf{I}_\theta^{-1})(\tau_s + \mathbf{C_t}\mathbf{K_t}^{-1}\dot{\tau}_s)}}_{\text{state feedback}} \tag{37}$$

Therefore, the modified dynamics adopting the control law described in Equation (37) lead to the following error dynamics equations, where the error convergence can be set according to the selected value for $\mathbf{I}_\theta$:

$$\mathbf{K_t}\overline{\mathbf{M}}^{-1}(-\tau_s^D + \mathbf{J}^{\mathbf{T}}F_l) + \mathbf{B_m}\mathbf{D}\dot{\theta}_m - \mathbf{K_t}\mathbf{I_m}^{-1}\tau_d = \ddot{e} + \mathbf{C_t}(\mathbf{I}_\theta^{-1} + \overline{\mathbf{M}}^{-1})\dot{e} + \mathbf{K_t}(\mathbf{I}_\theta^{-1} + \overline{\mathbf{M}}^{-1})e \tag{38}$$

4.5. Haptic Rendering

The three torque control laws are used as an inner feedback loop of the impedance controller used to test the exoskeleton in the haptic rendering task. The desired end effector force F_{ee}^D is due to the interaction with the virtual environment impedance. In more detail, the desired force is defined by the following:

$$\begin{cases} F_{ee}^D = 0, & x < x_d \\ F_{ee}^D = \mathbf{K_x}(x - x_d) - \mathbf{D_x}\dot{x}, & x \geq x_d \end{cases} \tag{39}$$

where $\boldsymbol{x}$ represents the coordinate along the axis which is perpendicular with respect to the surface, $\boldsymbol{x_d}$ represents the wall coordinate and $\mathbf{K_x}$ and $\mathbf{D_x}$ are, respectively, the desired stiffness and damping of the simulated virtual environment.

5. Experiments and Results

The controller performances are assessed in the transparency and haptic rendering task. In the first one, the user imposes a motion on the exoskeleton while the robot controller keeps the desired joint torque at 0 Nm. The second test is the haptic rendering task, consisting of a slanted flat surface with different simulated stiffness.

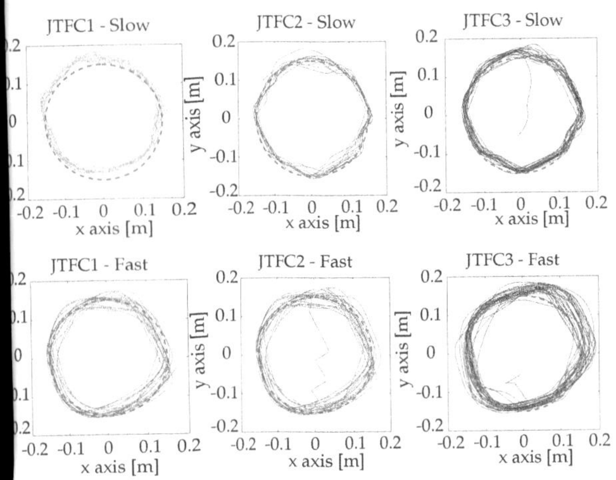

ure 14. The trajectories performed during the transparency test using the three control laws in the w-speed (first row) and fast-speed (second row) conditions. The red dashed lines are the circular erence trajectories.

Figure 13 shows that the full-state feedback controller (JTFC1) has the lowest mean que and mean peak torque values in the slow-speed scenario. Moreover, JTFC1 is re transparent with respect to JTFC2 and JTFC3 in terms of interaction torques. Data statistically compared with a paired t-test ($\alpha = 0.05$), first between JTFC1 and JTFC2, n between JTFC1 and JTFC3. Outliers are removed before any further analysis using a mpson Tau test. The obtained mean torque results are statistically significant ($p < 0.01$) joints J1, J2 and J4 in both slow-speed and fast-speed conditions. The joint J3 implements same PD feedback control in all the experiments, and it performs equally in all speeds l controller conditions. The obtained results for JTFC1 are comparable with the ones sented in Ref. [4] and are reported in detail in Table 8.

ble 8. Mean torque and mean peak torque for JTFC1.

	Speed	J1	J2	J3	J4
Mean rque (Nm)	Slow	0.54	0.77	0.57	0.39
	Fast	0.58	0.88	0.63	0.44
Mean peak rque (Nm)	Slow	1.35	2.05	1.07	0.93
	Fast	1.36	2.36	1.24	1.06

The control JTFC1 performs better because it manages to model the joint dynamics a more accurate and general way. Moreover, JTFC1 compensates for the modeled cts. Taking the joint behavior into account, the control JTFC3 behaves more similarly to C1 than JTFC2; indeed, the torque errors of the controls JTFC1 and JTFC3 seem to be related to the link inertia. Moreover, from the analysis of the control torque errors at joints (Figure 13), it can be seen that the control JTFC2 exhibits an average error that is ependent from the link inertia. The torque-error-to-link-inertia ratio for the elbow joint e highest.

For the sake of completeness, we report the measured end effector position, joint ues and end effector forces coming from a part of the transparency test in Figure 15 for litative analysis purposes.

The implemented control laws (30), (35) and (37) are set using the model parameters. For the proportional and derivative PD gains (K_p and K_d), we start from the analytical resolution of the free response of Equation (33) for JTFC1—and the same is performed for JTFC2 and JTFC3— where we impose as desired error dynamics in the form that guarantees the minimum ITAE index for a second-order system, as reported in Equation (40).

$$s^2 + 3.2\,\omega_0\, s + \omega_0^2 = 0 \qquad (40)$$

where ω_0 is the natural frequency of the error dynamics. Starting from the theoretical values, we manually fine-tune the control gains to prevent the occurrence of joint oscillations. The actual values of the PD gains are reported in Table 7 for the sake of completeness.

Notice that the control laws (30) and (35) have two degrees of freedom, i.e., K_p and K_d can be independently chosen, whereas the control law (37) exhibits only one degree of freedom; thus, the two control gains are linked, and they are computed as a function of the desired inertia I_θ.

Table 7. Values of the parameters of each joint for the JTFC1, JTFC2 and JTFC3 controllers.

	JTFC1			JTFC2		
	J1	J2	J4	J1	J2	J4
d	3.2	6	2	4	7	2
ω_0	$40 \cdot 2\pi$	$20 \cdot 2\pi$	$40 \cdot 2\pi$	$55 \cdot 2\pi$	$37.5 \cdot 2\pi$	$50 \cdot 2\pi$
K_p	15.89	0.82	0.33	34.39	13.89	12.01
K_d	0.26	0.25	0.16	0.45	0.54	0.21
	JTFC3					
	J1	J2	J4			
d	0.11	0.09	0.16			
ω_0	$33.21 \cdot 2\pi$	$27.17 \cdot 2\pi$	$48.3 \cdot 2\pi$			
K_p	9.43	5.21	9.84			
K_d	0.005	0.0027	0.005			

5.1. Transparency

For the transparency test, a performance measurement is adopted based on multi-joint transparency as in Ref. [4], where the pHRI torque on each joint was analyzed. In more detail, two kinds of trials are performed: the first type of trial uses the JTFC1 control law described in Section 4.2 in order to verify the amount of improvement the dynamics compensations provide to the desired torque tracking; the second type of trials aims to compare the three control laws in order to understand how the parameters of each controller are related to the desired torque tracking.

The transparency tests are performed by recruiting 10 healthy subjects—all males, eight right-handed—with an average age of 30.9 ± 5.2 years. All subjects are asked to sign a written informed consent form for participating in the study. The two transparency tests have a slight difference: in the first trials, the user moves the exoskeleton, grabbing the end effector handle with no constraints (interaction forces are exerted only at the end effector), whereas, during the second transparency test, the user is anchored at the exoskeleton at two points—arm and forearm—by grasping the end effector handle. An additional force sensor is mounted on the end effector of the exoskeleton to measure the actual forces F_h^* applied by the user at the handle interface.

For evaluating the transparency index, the mean absolute pHRI torque and the mean peak absolute pHRI torque are computed as in Ref. [4]. The measured end effector forces provide only a qualitative index in the transparency test when a multi-contact interaction with the exoskeleton occurs. On the contrary, the norm of the measured end effector force is used to quantitatively evaluate the controller performances during single-contact interactions.

5.1.1. How Dynamic Compensation Affects the Transparency

In order to understand how the dynamic compensation affects the transparency, the scheme depicted in Figure 10 is implemented using the JTFC1 control law plus the dynamics terms multiplied by the parameter α with $0 \leq \alpha \leq 1$. In this test, the subject is asked to perform sinusoidal movements at each joint with a range of 10° ($\simeq 0.2$ rad) with a frequency of 0.5 Hz; thus, similar acceleration is imprinted to the exoskeleton joint both with (w.) dynamic compensation and without (w.o.) compensation conditions. The experimental results for torque tracking, with a desired torque $\tau_s^D = 0$, are shown for J_2 in Figure 11, with J_2 being the joint with the highest link inertia. The controller is set to follow the motion at zero torque w. (Figure 11, left) and w.o. (Figure 11, right) dynamic compensation. The upper plots show the joint position (black solid line), and the central plots display the estimated acceleration (gray dashed line) to demonstrate how the movements are similar in both cases. The lower plots represent the interaction torques estimated by the observer (gray dashed line) and measured by the force sensor (black solid line). Even if the estimated torques are similar in both cases, with dynamic compensation, the actual interaction forces are lower, demonstrating that torque tracking is more precise, and the user has to compensate less for the link dynamics.

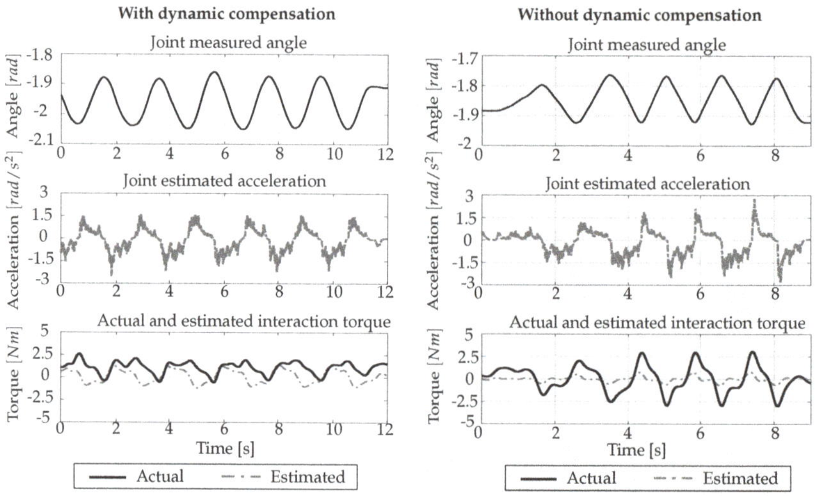

Figure 11. Comparison between the two experiment conditions: w. (**left**) and w.o. dynamic compensation (**right**, in gray). The three sets of rows show, respectively, the measured angular position of the joint, its estimated acceleration and a comparison between actual and estimated joint torque. The latter is computed by the force sensor for the joint J_2. Without dynamics compensations, the actual torques differ from the estimated ones, resulting in a loss of transparency.

5.1.2. Comparison between JTFC1, JTFC2 and JTFC3 Torque Controllers

For this kind of trial, the three joint torque controls presented in Section 4 are tested with the desired torque set to zero ($\tau_s^D = 0$). The tests are performed as in Ref. [4]; the participants are asked to track a reference point on a circular path displayed on a screen with the end effector parallel to the coronal plane in front of them. Figure 12 shows a subject while performing the transparency task. The diameter of the circle is equal to 0.3 m, and the center position is set taking the subject's chest height—as in a hypothetical daily task inside the workplace—as reference. Each circle is performed at two speed levels, a slow one of 45 deg/s and a faster one of 90 deg/s, in accordance with Ref. [4]. A total of 10 repetitions are performed for each speed level. Moreover, the sequence of the controllers is randomly assigned to each participant to mitigate potential order effects.

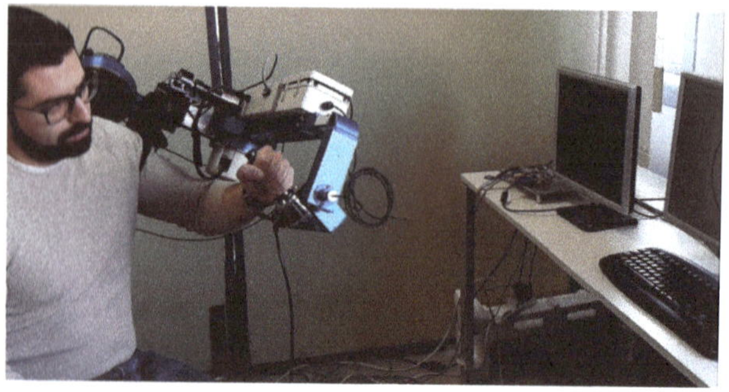

Figure 12. Experimental setup for the transparency test. The user is c
shoulder level and at the end effector, grabbing the handle. The user'
one are in contact during the trial execution. The subject moves the exo
trajectory at a constant angular speed, whose reference is displayed o

The comparative multi-joint transparency study is depicte
real trajectories performed by a representative subject are show

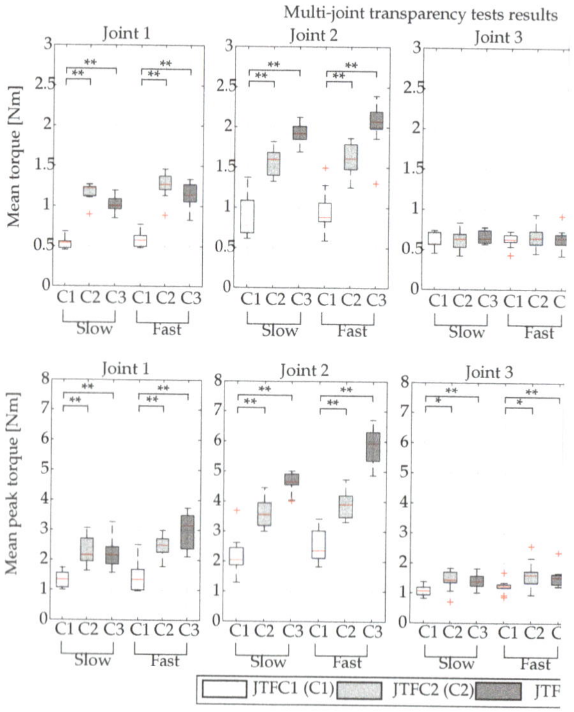

Figure 13. Multi-joint transparency study. Mean absolute torque and
the four Rehab-Exos actuated joints for the 10 subjects are visualiz
outlier samples). The interaction torques are evaluated for the three
and fast (90 deg/s) speed conditions, as proposed in Ref. [4]. JTFC1 o
in both conditions for all the joints with high statistical significance (

Robotics 2024, 13, 32

The implemented control laws (30), (35) and (37) are set using the model parameters. For the proportional and derivative PD gains (K_p and K_d), we start from the analytical resolution of the free response of Equation (33) for JTFC1—and the same is performed for JTFC2 and JTFC3— where we impose as desired error dynamics in the form that guarantees the minimum ITAE index for a second-order system, as reported in Equation (40).

$$s^2 + 3.2\,\omega_0\,s + \omega_0^2 = 0 \tag{40}$$

where ω_0 is the natural frequency of the error dynamics. Starting from the theoretical values, we manually fine-tune the control gains to prevent the occurrence of joint oscillations. The actual values of the PD gains are reported in Table 7 for the sake of completeness.

Notice that the control laws (30) and (35) have two degrees of freedom, i.e., K_p and K_d can be independently chosen, whereas the control law (37) exhibits only one degree of freedom; thus, the two control gains are linked, and they are computed as a function of the desired inertia I_θ.

Table 7. Values of the parameters of each joint for the JTFC1, JTFC2 and JTFC3 controllers.

		JTFC1			JTFC2	
	J1	J2	J4	J1	J2	J4
d	3.2	6	2	4	7	2
ω_0	$40 \cdot 2\pi$	$20 \cdot 2\pi$	$40 \cdot 2\pi$	$55 \cdot 2\pi$	$37.5 \cdot 2\pi$	$50 \cdot 2\pi$
K_p	15.89	0.82	0.33	34.39	13.89	12.01
K_d	0.26	0.25	0.16	0.45	0.54	0.21
		JTFC3				
	J1	J2	J4			
d	0.11	0.09	0.16			
ω_0	$33.21 \cdot 2\pi$	$27.17 \cdot 2\pi$	$48.3 \cdot 2\pi$			
K_p	9.43	5.21	9.84			
K_d	0.005	0.0027	0.005			

5.1. Transparency

For the transparency test, a performance measurement is adopted based on multi-joint transparency as in Ref. [4], where the pHRI torque on each joint was analyzed. In more detail, two kinds of trials are performed: the first type of trial uses the JTFC1 control law described in Section 4.2 in order to verify the amount of improvement the dynamics compensations provide to the desired torque tracking; the second type of trials aims to compare the three control laws in order to understand how the parameters of each controller are related to the desired torque tracking.

The transparency tests are performed by recruiting 10 healthy subjects—all males, eight right-handed—with an average age of 30.9 ± 5.2 years. All subjects are asked to sign a written informed consent form for participating in the study. The two transparency tests have a slight difference: in the first trials, the user moves the exoskeleton, grabbing the end effector handle with no constraints (interaction forces are exerted only at the end effector), whereas, during the second transparency test, the user is anchored at the exoskeleton at two points—arm and forearm—by grasping the end effector handle. An additional force sensor is mounted on the end effector of the exoskeleton to measure the actual forces F_h^* applied by the user at the handle interface.

For evaluating the transparency index, the mean absolute pHRI torque and the mean peak absolute pHRI torque are computed as in Ref. [4]. The measured end effector forces provide only a qualitative index in the transparency test when a multi-contact interaction with the exoskeleton occurs. On the contrary, the norm of the measured end effector force is used to quantitatively evaluate the controller performances during single-contact interactions.

5.1.1. How Dynamic Compensation Affects the Transparency

In order to understand how the dynamic compensation affects the transparency, the scheme depicted in Figure 10 is implemented using the JTFC1 control law plus the dynamics terms multiplied by the parameter α with $0 \leq \alpha \leq 1$. In this test, the subject is asked to perform sinusoidal movements at each joint with a range of $10°$ ($\simeq 0.2$ rad) with a frequency of 0.5 Hz; thus, similar acceleration is imprinted to the exoskeleton joint both with (w.) dynamic compensation and without (w.o.) compensation conditions. The experimental results for torque tracking, with a desired torque $\tau_s^D = 0$, are shown for J_2 in Figure 11, with J_2 being the joint with the highest link inertia. The controller is set to follow the motion at zero torque w. (Figure 11, left) and w.o. (Figure 11, right) dynamic compensation. The upper plots show the joint position (black solid line), and the central plots display the estimated acceleration (gray dashed line) to demonstrate how the movements are similar in both cases. The lower plots represent the interaction torques estimated by the observer (gray dashed line) and measured by the force sensor (black solid line). Even if the estimated torques are similar in both cases, with dynamic compensation, the actual interaction forces are lower, demonstrating that torque tracking is more precise, and the user has to compensate less for the link dynamics.

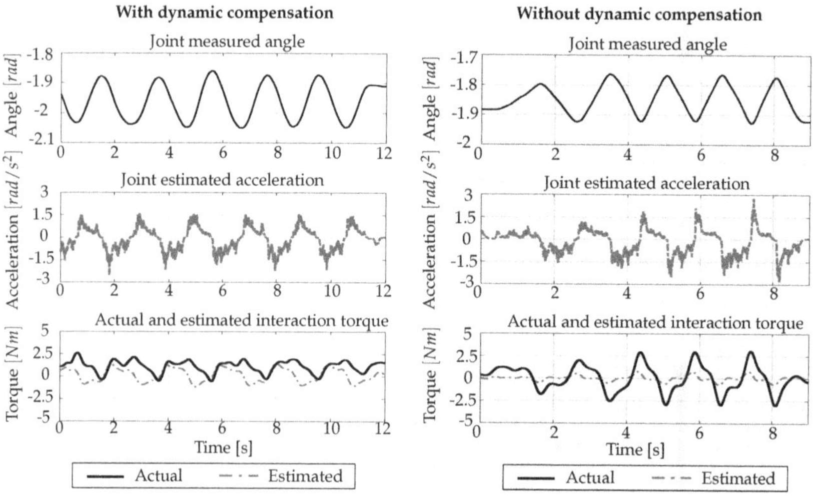

Figure 11. Comparison between the two experiment conditions: w. (**left**) and w.o. dynamic compensation (**right**, in gray). The three sets of rows show, respectively, the measured angular position of the joint, its estimated acceleration and a comparison between actual and estimated joint torque. The latter is computed by the force sensor for the joint J_2. Without dynamics compensations, the actual torques differ from the estimated ones, resulting in a loss of transparency.

5.1.2. Comparison between JTFC1, JTFC2 and JTFC3 Torque Controllers

For this kind of trial, the three joint torque controls presented in Section 4 are tested with the desired torque set to zero ($\tau_s^D = 0$). The tests are performed as in Ref. [4]; the participants are asked to track a reference point on a circular path displayed on a screen with the end effector parallel to the coronal plane in front of them. Figure 12 shows a subject while performing the transparency task. The diameter of the circle is equal to 0.3 m, and the center position is set taking the subject's chest height—as in a hypothetical daily task inside the workplace—as reference. Each circle is performed at two speed levels, a slow one of 45 deg/s and a faster one of 90 deg/s, in accordance with Ref. [4]. A total of 10 repetitions are performed for each speed level. Moreover, the sequence of the controllers is randomly assigned to each participant to mitigate potential order effects.

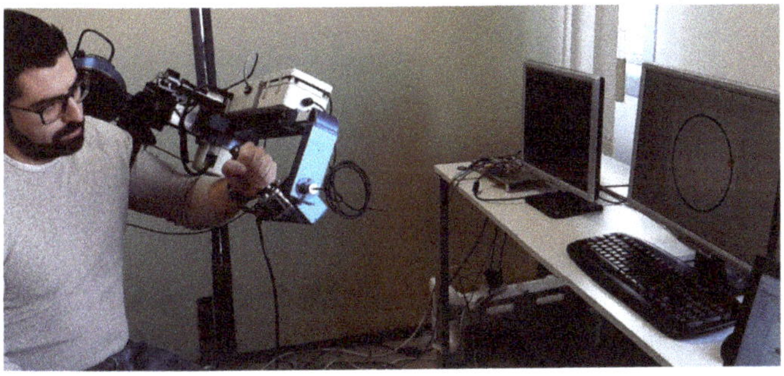

Figure 12. Experimental setup for the transparency test. The user is connected to the exoskeleton at shoulder level and at the end effector, grabbing the handle. The user's elbow and the exoskeleton's one are in contact during the trial execution. The subject moves the exoskeleton, performing a circular trajectory at a constant angular speed, whose reference is displayed on a screen.

The comparative multi-joint transparency study is depicted in Figure 13, whereas the real trajectories performed by a representative subject are shown in Figure 14.

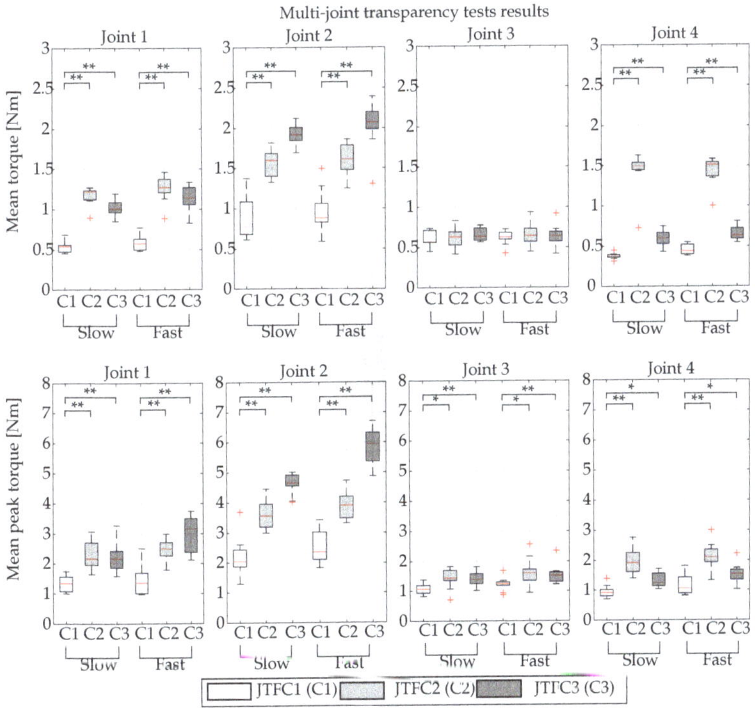

Figure 13. Multi-joint transparency study. Mean absolute torque and mean absolute peak torque for the four Rehab-Exos actuated joints for the 10 subjects are visualized as boxplots (+ indicates the outlier samples). The interaction torques are evaluated for the three controllers in slow (45 deg/s) and fast (90 deg/s) speed conditions, as proposed in Ref. [4]. JTFC1 offers the lowest resistive torque in both conditions for all the joints with high statistical significance (*, $p < 0.05$; **, $p < 0.01$).

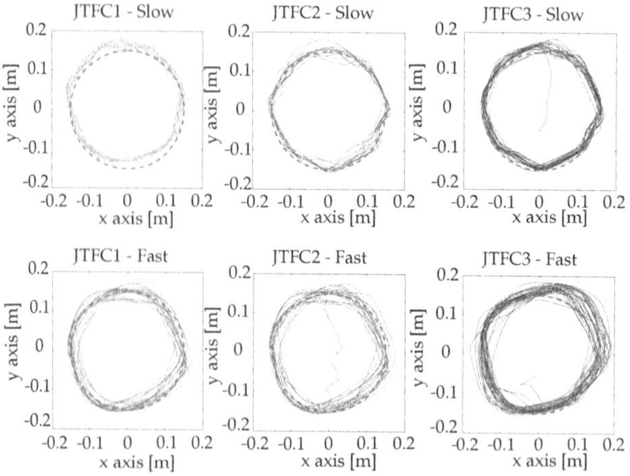

Figure 14. The trajectories performed during the transparency test using the three control laws in the slow-speed (first row) and fast-speed (second row) conditions. The red dashed lines are the circular reference trajectories.

Figure 13 shows that the full-state feedback controller (JTFC1) has the lowest mean torque and mean peak torque values in the slow-speed scenario. Moreover, JTFC1 is more transparent with respect to JTFC2 and JTFC3 in terms of interaction torques. Data are statistically compared with a paired t-test ($\alpha = 0.05$), first between JTFC1 and JTFC2, then between JTFC1 and JTFC3. Outliers are removed before any further analysis using a Thompson Tau test. The obtained mean torque results are statistically significant ($p < 0.01$) for joints J1, J2 and J4 in both slow-speed and fast-speed conditions. The joint J3 implements the same PD feedback control in all the experiments, and it performs equally in all speeds and controller conditions. The obtained results for JTFC1 are comparable with the ones presented in Ref. [4] and are reported in detail in Table 8.

Table 8. Mean torque and mean peak torque for JTFC1.

	Speed	J1	J2	J3	J4
Mean torque (Nm)	Slow	0.54	0.77	0.57	0.39
	Fast	0.58	0.88	0.63	0.44
Mean peak torque (Nm)	Slow	1.35	2.05	1.07	0.93
	Fast	1.36	2.36	1.24	1.06

The control JTFC1 performs better because it manages to model the joint dynamics in a more accurate and general way. Moreover, JTFC1 compensates for the modeled effects. Taking the joint behavior into account, the control JTFC3 behaves more similarly to JTFC1 than JTFC2; indeed, the torque errors of the controls JTFC1 and JTFC3 seem to be correlated to the link inertia. Moreover, from the analysis of the control torque errors at the joints (Figure 13), it can be seen that the control JTFC2 exhibits an average error that is independent from the link inertia. The torque-error-to-link-inertia ratio for the elbow joint is the highest.

For the sake of completeness, we report the measured end effector position, joint torques and end effector forces coming from a part of the transparency test in Figure 15 for qualitative analysis purposes.

Table 10. The average forces involved in the T1 and T2 trials, the average force peaks and the average slope of the T3 and T4 trials.

K_x D_x	**5 kN/m** **2 Ns/m**	**20 kN/m** **7 Ns/m**	**40 kN/m** **10 Ns/m**
Avg. force T1 (N)	22.22	22.81	24.98
Avg. force T2 (N)	50.79	66.14	59.37
Avg. peaks T3 (N)	83.33	103.97	88.32
Avg. slope T3 (N/s)	127.28	159.25	120.39
Avg. peaks T4 (N)	112.33	136.97	126.20
Avg. slope T4 (N/s)	518.49	550.99	616.03

To evaluate the performances of the three different torque controllers, the following three indexes are proposed:

- The mean of the norm of the error force vectors;
- The mean of the absolute value of the error of the orthogonal component;
- The mean of the angle between the desired forces and the measured ones.

The results are shown in Figure 17. The first graph shows the average difference between the forces rendered by the controllers and the desired forces with an aggregate index, i.e., the norm of the error vector. From this graph, the reader can see that, in all the conditions, the JTFC1 control performs better then the others; in fact, the mean of the error is around 10 N in all three cases.

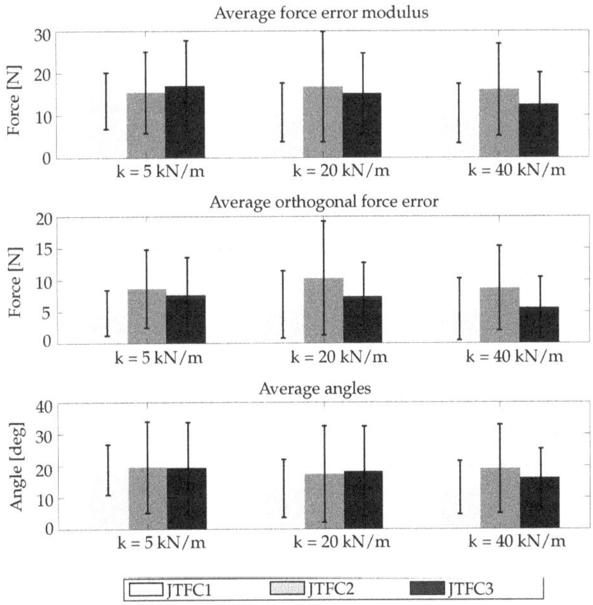

Figure 17. The first row shows the average of the modulus of the error force vectors at the end effector of the three controllers in the rendering task. For this test, three stiffnesses are evaluated: 5 KN/m (small), 20 KN/m (medium) and 40 KN/m (high). The second row shows the average error forces of the orthogonal component. The third row shows the average angle between the desired force vectors and the measured ones.

To decompose the information given in the first graph, another two indexes are considered: the average error of the orthogonal component of the force and the angle between the desired and the rendered forces. Unlike the norm of the error vector, these two indexes give information on the amplitude and the direction of the undesired force components. The second graph highlights that the JTFC1 control leads to an average error of 5 N along the task direction, independently from the environment parameters, which is a good result, coupled with the exhibited stable contact with the surface in every condition. The third graph is substantially in agreement with the previous ones.

6. Discussion

The results exposed in the previous sections highlight the advantages of using a full-state feedback controller that compensates for both estimated disturbance torques and for viscous torque losses of the motor. The major benefit coming from usage of the full-state feedback control is the high transparency exhibited during free motion tasks. This means that the exoskeleton is able to not affect the user's desired motion and, at the same time, more accurately identify the user's intention, i.e., the human forces/torques.

Although the basic-state feedback control (JTFC2) presents an average force modulus at the end effector which is similar to that of the passivity-based feedback control (JTFC3), it hinders the user's voluntary motion with a major impact with respect to the other controllers. Indeed, the end effector trajectory due to the controller JTFC2 is the farthest from the desired one. This is because JTFC1 and JTFC3 take into account (although in different ways) both the link and motor inertia, whereas the JTFC2 control considers only the motor inertia.

The high transparency—the average force modulus at the end effector is less than 6 N for JTFC1—is also due to the effect of the dynamic compensations. A correct estimation of the joint acceleration is crucial for obtaining a transparency enhancement. This is the reason why the dynamic contributions are weighted by a constant < 1. Indeed, a high transparency exhibiting a stable behavior can only be obtained with a very accurate acceleration estimation. The proposed estimation methodology using the torque sensor and motor data can help to further improve the estimation process.

Another important result is the wide range of stable impedance that the system is capable of rendering. The Rehab-Exos is able to render a flat surface with a stiffness equal to 40 kN/m with all the three compared control laws with different performances while still preserving stability. This is certainly due to inherent mechanical damping of the system.

The mechanical design of the Rehab-Exos influences its performances. The residual torques at the joint are basically the effects of unmodeled link inertia and joint friction. A lighter design consisting of smaller motors and a lower transmission ratio could lead to a more back-drivable solution, though at the cost of less torque being available at the joint. This could be a trade-off solution aimed at achieving a more transparent device. Lastly, the torque sensor requires a more robust design. In more detail, in order to obtain a smaller sensitivity to non-axial loads, a spoke with wider beams could be implemented for future developments.

The choice of a joint with active impedance by control based on a torque sensor presents a valid alternative to the passive inherent compliant actuators with the main purpose of achieving more compact and simpler mechanics and electronics. The proposed torque controller, combined with the joint mechanics, allows the building of safe and responsive control strategies suitable for rehabilitation and assistance purposes.

7. Conclusions

This paper presented the Rehab-Exos exoskeleton design and, particularly, the design of the joint torque sensors based on strain gauges. Some sensor issues were highlighted and explained, while two possible hypotheses were proposed related to these issues. In order to validate the design of the Rehab-Exos and its effectiveness towards rehabilitation applications, an interaction torque controller was developed and validated by experimental tests based on common pHRI metrics—transparency and haptic rendering. The kinematics and dynamics of the device were represented by a full dynamics model implemented in centralized torque control. The torque tracking for each joint was performed by a single-joint full-state Kalman filter plus a torque feedback controller. The centralized control provided each single-joint observer with both the desired torque for force feedback and an estimation of the joint torques due to the links' dynamic loads to be compensated as feedforward contributions. The developed full-state feedback controller was then compared with a basic feedback controller and a passivity-based feedback controller for benchmarking purposes. Results showed how the full-state approach we proposed is effective for estimating the human interaction force in a clean way, i.e., it is not affected by the inertial and gravity contributions due to the non-negligible mechanical properties of the exoskeleton structure. The full-state feedback control was more accurate and transparent with respect to the other two controllers. Our proposed control strategy, combined with the presence of a joint torque sensor, represents a valuable asset in enhancing the performances of exoskeletons in human–robot interaction, even in the presence of non-back-drivability.

We believe these results are promising and that our Rehab-Exos could pave the way towards an enhancement of safety, sustainability and effectiveness in rehabilitation therapies. Indeed, as a first future step, we plan to validate the device with more extensive and focused tests to evaluate the impact on the kinematics and physiology of the users, as well as the perceived ergonomics in prolonged use. Finally, a future direction for this work is the design of a more compact, portable and simple device with all the advantages of the Rehab-Exos but with a smaller level of assistance to be used in the final stage of the rehabilitation process.

Author Contributions: Conceptualization, D.C., G.R., M.S., R.V. and A.F.; methodology, D.C., M.S., R.V. and A.F.; software, D.C. and G.R.; validation, D.C., G.R., M.S., R.V. and A.F.; formal analysis, D.C., G.R, M.S., R.V. and A.F.; investigation, D.C. and M.S.; resources, D.C., G.R., M.S., R.V. and A.F.; data curation, D.C., G.R. and M.S.; writing—original draft preparation, D.C., G.R., M.S., R.V. and A.F.; writing—review and editing, D.C., G.R., M.S., R.V. and A.F.; visualization, D.C., G.R., M.S., R.V. and A.F.; supervision, M.S. and A.F.; project administration, D.C. and A.F.; funding acquisition, M.S., R.V. and A.F. All authors have read and agreed to the published version of the manuscript.

Funding: This research was funded in part by the European Union FSE-REACT-EU, PON Research and Innovation 2014–2020 DM1062/2021, and in part by the NEXTGENERATIONEU (NGEU) and the Ministry of University and Research (MUR), National Recovery and Resilience Plan (NRRP) through project BRIEF under grant IR0000036—Biorobotics Research and Innovation Engineering Facilities (DN. 103, 17 June 2022).

Informed Consent Statement: Informed consent was obtained from all subjects involved in the study.

Data Availability Statement: The raw data supporting the conclusions of this article will be made available by the authors on request.

Conflicts of Interest: The authors declare no conflicts of interest.

Appendix A

Let us study the effect under static condition when applying motor torque compensating for the non-linearity due to gravity, estimated as $\hat{G}(\mathbf{D}\hat{\theta}_m)$ with the following:

$$\tau_m = \hat{G}(\mathbf{D}\hat{\theta}_m) + u, \tag{A1}$$

where u represents the actual control command. Under static conditions, the following can be found:

$$u = -\mathbf{J}^T F_h + G(\theta) - \hat{G}(\mathbf{D}\hat{\theta}_m) \simeq -\mathbf{J}^T F_h \tag{A2}$$

since $\hat{G}(\mathbf{D}\hat{\theta}_m) \simeq G(\theta)$.

Under dynamic conditions, we can introduce a disturbance term $\delta g = G(\theta) - \hat{G}(\mathbf{D}\hat{\theta}_m)$ because of a not-perfect cancellation of the gravity component due to the elasticity of the joint transmission which can be summed up as F_h as a disturbance noise supported by the operator.

Therefore, a variable and apparent dynamic contribution of the force $\boldsymbol{F}_{dyn}$ can be modeled such that the following applies:

$$\mathbf{J}^T \Delta \boldsymbol{F}_{dyn}(\dot{\theta}, \theta) = -\Delta \mathbf{M}(\theta)\ddot{\theta} - \mathbf{C}(\dot{\theta}, \theta)\dot{\theta} \tag{A3}$$

The new variable $\Delta \boldsymbol{F}_{dyn}$, representing uncompensated and/or unmodeled dynamics, can be considered as a disturbance force and also as a term contributing to the overall external load force $\boldsymbol{F}_l$, as expressed by the following:

$$\boldsymbol{F}_l = \underbrace{F_h}_{\text{exogenous}} + \underbrace{\delta g + \Delta \boldsymbol{F}_{dyn}}_{\text{endogenous}} \tag{A4}$$

This generally states that the external forces are the sum of exogenous—F_h—and endogenous—$\delta g + \Delta F_{dyn}$—inputs. While exogenous inputs are unknown a priori and depend largely on the human subject's behavior, endogenous inputs can be estimated and compensated to some extent.

Therefore, by introducing the variable substitution expressed in (18), the dynamic equations can be reformulated as follows:

$$\mathbf{I_m}\mathbf{D}\ddot{\theta}_m + \mathbf{B_m}\mathbf{D}\dot{\theta}_m + = \mathbf{C_t}\mathbf{K_t}^{-1}\dot{\tau}_s + \tau_s + \boldsymbol{u} + \tau_d \tag{A5}$$

$$\overline{\mathbf{M}}\ddot{\theta} + \mathbf{C_t}\mathbf{K_t}^{-1}\dot{\tau}_s + \tau_s = \mathbf{J}^T \boldsymbol{F}_l \tag{A6}$$

Since we know that

$$\mathbf{K_t}^{-1}\ddot{\tau}_s + \mathbf{D}\ddot{\theta}_m = \ddot{\theta}, \tag{A7}$$

then substituting (A7) into (A6) to eliminate $\ddot{\theta}$ leads us to obtain the following:

$$\overline{\mathbf{M}}\mathbf{D}\ddot{\theta}_m + \overline{\mathbf{M}}\mathbf{K_t}^{-1}\ddot{\tau}_s + \mathbf{C_t}\mathbf{K_t}^{-1}\dot{\tau}_s + \tau_s = \mathbf{J}^T F_l \tag{A8}$$

Then, taking from (A5) the term $\mathbf{D}\ddot{\theta}_m = \mathbf{I_m}^{-1}\{-\mathbf{B_m}\mathbf{D}\dot{\theta}_m + \mathbf{C_t}\mathbf{K_t}^{-1}\dot{\tau}_s + \tau_s + u + \tau_d\}$ and defining $\mathbf{I_i}^{-1} = \overline{\mathbf{M}}^{-1} + \mathbf{I_m}^{-1}$, it is possible to replace these terms and rewrite the dynamics equations in the form (A9), which can help the definition of a full-state feedback controller and an optimal observer for joint torque estimation.

$$\ddot{\tau}_s + \mathbf{C_t}\mathbf{I_i}^{-1}\dot{\tau}_s + \mathbf{K_t}\mathbf{I_i}^{-1}\tau_s = \mathbf{K_t}\overline{\mathbf{M}}^{-1}\mathbf{J}^T F_l + \mathbf{K_t}\mathbf{I_m}^{-1}(\mathbf{B_m}\mathbf{D}\dot{\theta}_m - \tau_d - \boldsymbol{u}) \tag{A9}$$

References

1. Bajcsy, A.; Losey, D.P.; O'malley, M.K.; Dragan, A.D. Learning robot objectives from physical human interaction. In Proceedings of the 1st Annual Conference on Robot Learning 2017, Mountain View, CA, USA, 13–15 November 2017; Volume 78, pp. 217–226.
2. Gull, M.A.; Bai, S.; Bak, T. A Review on Design of Upper Limb Exoskeletons. *Robotics* **2020**, *9*, 16. [CrossRef]
3. Jarrasse, N.; Tagliabue, M.; Robertson, J.V.; Maiza, A.; Crocher, V.; Roby-Brami, A.; Morel, G. A methodology to quantify alterations in human upper limb movement during co-manipulation with an exoskeleton. *IEEE Trans. Neural Syst. Rehabil.* **2010**, *18*, 389–397. [CrossRef]
4. Just, F.; Özen, Ö.; Bösch, P.; Bobrovsky, H.; Klamroth-Marganska, V.; Riener, R.; Rauter, G. Exoskeleton transparency: Feed-forward compensation vs. disturbance observer. *At-Automatisierungstechnik* **2018**, *6*, 1014–1026. [CrossRef]
5. Colgate, J.E.; Brown, J.M. Factors affecting the z-width of a haptic display. In Proceedings of the 1994 IEEE International Conference on Robotics and Automation, San Diego, CA, USA , 8–13 May 1994; IEEE: New York, NY, USA, 1994; pp. 3205–3210.
6. Diolaiti, N.; Niemeyer, G.; Barbagli, F.; Salisbury, J.K. A criterion for the passivity of haptic devices. In Proceedings of the 2005 IEEE International Conference on Robotics and Automation, Barcelona, Spain, 18–22 April 2005 ; IEEE: New York, NY, USA, 2005; pp. 2452–2457.
7. Lo, H.S.; Xie, S.Q. Exoskeleton robots for upper-limb rehabilitation: State of the art and future prospects. *Med Eng. Phys.* **2012**, *34*, 261–268. [CrossRef]
8. Pirondini, E.; Coscia, M.; Marcheschi, S.; Roas, G.; Salsedo, F.; Frisoli, A.; Bergamasco, M.; Micera, S. Evaluation of the effects of the arm light exoskeleton on movement execution and muscle activities: A pilot study on healthy subjects. *J. Neuroeng. Rehabil.* **2016**, *13*, 1. [CrossRef]
9. Crea, S.; Cempini, M.; Moisè, M.; Baldoni, A.; Trigili, E.; Marconi, D.; Cortese, M.; Giovacchini, F.; Posteraro, F.; Vitiello, N. A novel shoulder-elbow exoskeleton with series elastic actuators. In Proceedings of the 6th IEEE International Conference on Biomedical Robotics and Biomechatronics (BioRob), Singapore, 26–29 June 2016; pp. 1248–1253. [CrossRef]

10. ALEx Arm. Available online: http://www.wearable-robotics.com/kinetek/ (accessed on 3 January 2024).
11. Kim, M.J.; Lee, W.; Choi, J.Y.; Park, Y.S.; Park, S.H.; Chung, G.; Han, K.L.; Choi, I.S.; Suh, I.H.; Choi, Y.; et al. Powered upper-limb control using passivity-based nonlinear disturbance observer for unknown payload carrying applications. In Proceedings of the 2016 IEEE International Conference on Robotics and Automation (ICRA), Stockholm, Sweden, 16–21 May 2016; IEEE: New York, NY, USA, 2016; pp. 2340–2346.
12. Buongiorno, D.; Sotgiu, E.; Leonardis, D.; Marcheschi, S.; Solazzi, M.; Frisoli, A. Wres: A novel 3dof wrist exoskeleton with tendon-driven differential transmission for neuro-rehabilitation and teleoperation. *IEEE Robot. Autom. Lett.* **2018**, *3*, 2152–2159. [CrossRef]
13. Rebelo, J.; Sednaoui, T.; Den Exter, E.B.; Krueger, T.; Schiele, A. Bilateral robot teleoperation: A wearable arm exoskeleton featuring an intuitive user interface. *IEEE Robot. Autom. Mag.* **2014**, *21*, 62–69. [CrossRef]
14. Porcini, F.; Chiaradia, D.; Marcheschi, S.; Solazzi, M.; Frisoli, A. Evaluation of an Exoskeleton-based Bimanual Teleoperation Architecture with Independently Passivated Slave Devices. In Proceedings of the 2020 IEEE International Conference on Robotics and Automation (ICRA), Paris, France, 31 May–31 August 2020; IEEE: New York, NY, USA, 2020; pp. 10205–10211. [CrossRef]
15. Mihelj, M.; Nef, T.; Riener, R. Armin ii-7 dof rehabilitation robot: Mechanics and kinematics. In Proceedings of the 2007 IEEE International Conference on Robotics and Automation (ICRA), Rome, Italy, 10–14 April 2007; IEEE: New York, NY, USA, 2007; pp. 4120–4125.
16. Carignan, C.; Liszka, M.; Roderick, S. Design of an arm exoskeleton with scapula motion for shoulder rehabilitation. In Proceedings of the 12th International Conference on Advanced Robotics 2005, Seattle, WA, USA, 18–20 July 2005; IEEE: New York, NY, USA, 2005; pp. 524–531.
17. Frisoli, A.; Salsedo, F.; Bergamasco, M.; Rossi, B.; Carboncini, M.C. A force-feedback exoskeleton for upper-limb rehabilitation in virtual reality. *Appl. Bionics Biomech.* **2009**, *6*, 115–126. [CrossRef]
18. Perry, J.C.; Rosen, J.; Burns, S. Upper-limb powered exoskeleton design. *IEEE/ASME Trans. Mechatron.* **2007**, *12*, 408–417. [CrossRef]
19. Garrec, P.; Friconneau, J.; Measson, Y.; Perrot, Y. Able, an innovative transparent exoskeleton for the upper-limb. In Proceedings of the 2008 IEEE/RSJ International Conference on Intelligent Robots and Systems, Nice, France, 22–26 September 2008; IEEE: New York, NY, USA, 2008; pp. 1483–1488.
20. Rinaldi, G.; Tiseni, L.; Xiloyannis, M.; Masia, L.; Frisoli, A.; Chiaradia, D. Flexos: A Portable, SEA-Based Shoulder Exoskeleton with Hyper-redundant Kinematics for Weight Lifting Assistance. In Proceedings of the 2023 IEEE World Haptics Conference (WHC), Delft, Netherlands, 10–13 July 2023; pp. 252–258. [CrossRef]
21. Tsagarakis, N.G.; Caldwell, D.G. Development and control of a soft-actuated exoskeleton for use in physiotherapy and training. *Auton. Robot.* **2003**, *15*, 21–33. [CrossRef]
22. Klein, J.; Spencer, S.; Allington, J.; Bobrow, J.E.; Reinkensmeyer, D.J. Optimization of a parallel shoulder mechanism to achieve a high-force, low-mass, robotic-arm exoskeleton. *IEEE Trans. Robot.* **2010**, *26*, 710–715. [CrossRef]
23. O'Neill, C.T.; Phipps, N.S.; Cappello, L.; Paganoni, S.; Walsh, C.J. A soft wearable robot for the shoulder: Design, characterization, and preliminary testing. In Proceedings of the International Conference on Rehabilitation Robotics (ICORR) 2017, London, UK, 17–20 July 2017; pp. 1672–1678. [CrossRef]
24. Vanderborght, B.; Albu-Schäffer, A.; Bicchi, A.; Burdet, E.; Caldwell, D.G.; Carloni, R.; Catalano, M.; Eiberger, O.; Friedl, W.; Ganesh, G.; et al. Variable impedance actuators: A review. *Robot. Auton. Syst.* **2013**, *61*, 1601–1614. [CrossRef]
25. Veneman, J.F.; Kruidhof, R.; Hekman, E.E.; Ekkelenkamp, R.; Van Asseldonk, E.H.; Van Der Kooij, H. Design and evaluation of the lopes exoskeleton robot for interactive gait rehabilitation. *IEEE Trans. Neural Syst. Rehabil.* **2007**, *15*, 379–386. [CrossRef]
26. Vitiello, N.; Lenzi, T.; Roccella, S.; De Rossi, S.M.M.; Cattin, E.; Giovacchini, F.; Vecchi, F.; Carrozza, M.C. Neuroexos: A powered elbow exoskeleton for physical rehabilitation. *IEEE Trans. Robot.* **2013**, *29*, 220–235. [CrossRef]
27. Cherelle, P.; Grosu, V.; Beyl, P.; Mathys, A.; Van Ham, R.; Van Damme, M.; Vanderborght, B.; Lefeber, D. The maccepa actuation system as torque actuator in the gait rehabilitation robot altacro. In Proceedings of the 2010 3rd IEEE RAS & EMBS International Conference on Biomedical Robotics and Biomechatronics, Tokyo, Japan, 26–29 September 2010; IEEE: New York, NY, USA, 2010; pp. 27–32.
28. Kim, B.; Deshpande, A.D. An upper-body rehabilitation exoskeleton Harmony with an anatomical shoulder mechanism: Design, modeling, control, and performance evaluation. *Int. J. Robot. Res.* **2017**, *36*, 414–435. [CrossRef]
29. Wolf, S.; Eiberger, O.; Hirzinger, G. The dlr fsj: Energy based design of a variable stiffness joint. In Proceedings of the IEEE International Conference on Robotics and Automation (ICRA) 2011, Shanghai, China, 9–13 May 2011; IEEE: New York, NY, USA, 2011; pp. 5082–5089.
30. Kim, J.-H.; Shim, M.; Ahn, D.H.; Son, B.J.; Kim, S.-Y.; Kim, D.Y.; Baek, Y.S.; Cho, B.-K. Design of a knee exoskeleton using foot pressure and knee torque sensors. *Int. J. Adv. Robot. Syst.* **2015**, *12*, 112. [CrossRef]
31. Aguirre-Ollinger, G.; Colgate, J.E.; Peshkin, M.A.; Goswami, A. Design of an active one-degree-of-freedom lower-limb exoskeleton with inertia compensation. *Int. J. Robot. Res.* **2011**, *30*, 486–499. [CrossRef]
32. Hwang, B.; Jeon, D. A method to accurately estimate the muscular torques of human wearing exoskeletons by torque sensors. *Sensors* **2015**, *15*, 8337–8357. [CrossRef]

33. Zanotto, D.; Lenzi, T.; Stegall, P.; Agrawal, S.K. Improving transparency of powered exoskeletons using force/torque sensors on the supporting cuffs. In Proceedings of the IEEE 13th International Conference on Rehabilitation Robotics (ICORR) 2013, Seattle, WA, USA, 24–26 June 2013; IEEE: New York, NY, USA, 2013; pp. 1–6.
34. dos Santos, W.M.; Caurin, G.A.; Siqueira, A.A. Design and control of an active knee orthosis driven by a rotary series elastic actuator. *Control. Eng. Pract.* **2017**, *58*, 307–318. [CrossRef]
35. Junior, A.G.L.; de Andrade, R.M.; Bento Filho, A. Series elastic actuator: Design, analysis and comparison. *Recent Adv. Robot. Syst.* **2016**, *36*, 1698–1705.
36. Lee, C.; Oh, S. Integrated transmission force estimation method for series elastic actuators. In Proceedings of the 2018 IEEE 15th International Workshop on Advanced Motion Control (AMC), Tokyo, Japan, 9–1 March 2018; IEEE: New York, NY, USA, 2018; pp. 681–686.
37. Leal-Junior, A.G.; Frizera, A.; Marques, C.; Sánchez, M.R.; dos Santos, W.M.; Siqueira, A.A.; Segatto, M.V.; Pontes, M.J. Polymer optical fiber for angle and torque measurements of a series elastic actuator's spring. *J. Light. Technol.* **2018**, *36*, 1698–1705. [CrossRef]
38. Hashimoto, M.; Kiyosawa, Y. Experimental study on torque control using harmonic drive built-in torque sensors. *J. Robot. Syst.* **1998**, *15*, 435–445. [CrossRef]
39. Ott, C.; Albu-Schaffer, A.; Kugi, A.; Hirzinger, G. On the passivity-based impedance control of flexible joint robots. *IEEE Trans. Robot.* **2008**, *24*, 416–429. [CrossRef]
40. Vertechy, R.; Frisoli, A.; Dettori, A.; Solazzi, M.; Bergamasco, M. Development of a new exoskeleton for upper limb rehabilitation. In Proceedings of the 2009 IEEE International Conference on Rehabilitation Robotics, Kyoto, Japan, 23–26 June 2009; IEEE: New York, NY, USA, 2009; pp. 188–193.
41. Kashiri, N.; Malzahn, J.; Tsagarakis, N.G. On the sensor design of torque controlled actuators: A comparison study of strain gauge and encoder-based principles. *IEEE Robot. Autom. Lett.* **2017**, *2*, 1186–1194. [CrossRef]
42. Solazzi, M.; Abbrescia, M.; Vertechy, R.; Loconsole, C.; Bevilacqua, V.; Frisoli, A. An interaction torque control improving human force estimation of the rehab-exos exoskeleton. In Proceedings of the IEEE Haptics Symposium (HAPTICS), Houston, TX, USA, 23–26 February 2014; pp. 187–193. [CrossRef]

robotics

MDPI

Article

Investigation of the Effectiveness of the Robotic ReStore Soft Exoskeleton in the Development of Early Mobilization, Walking, and Coordination of Stroke Patients: A Randomized Clinical Trial

Szilvia Kóra [1,2], Adrienn Bíró [1,3], Nándor Prontvai [3], Mónika Androsics [3], István Drotár [2], Péter Prukner [2], Tamás Haidegger [4,5,*], Klaudia Széphelyi [1] and József Tollár [1,2,3,6,*]

1 Doctoral School of Health Sciences, Faculty of Health Sciences, University of Pécs, 7600 Pécs, Hungary; kovacs.adrienn@pte.hu (A.B.); kai.szephelyi@gmail.com (K.S.)
2 Digital Development Center, Széchenyi István University, 9000 Győr, Hungary; prukpe@sze.hu (P.P.)
3 Somogy County Móricz Kaposi Teaching Hospital, 7400 Kaposvár, Hungary
4 Austrian Center for Medical Innovation and Technology, Viktor-Kalpan-str. 2, 2700 Wiener Neustadt, Austria
5 University Research and Innovation Center (EKIK), Óbuda University, Bécsi út 96/B, 1034 Budapest, Hungary
6 Department of Otorhinolaryngology-Head and Neck Surgery, University of Pécs Medical School, 7600 Pécs, Hungary
* Correspondence: haidegger@irob.uni-obuda.hu (T.H.); tollarjozsef86@gmail.com (J.T.); Tel.: +36-306994497 (J.T.)

Abstract: Medical robotics nowadays can prevent, treat, or alleviate numerous severe conditions, including the dire consequences of stroke. Our objective was to determine the effect of employing a robotic soft exoskeleton in therapy on the development of the early mobilization, gait, and coordination in stroke patients. The ReStore™ Soft Exo-Suit, a wearable exosuit developed by a leading company with exoskeleton technology, was utilized. It is a powered, lightweight device intended for use in stroke rehabilitation for people with lower limb disability. We performed a randomized clinical intervention, using a before–after trial design in a university hospital setting. A total of 48 patients with a history of stroke were included, of whom 39 were randomized and 30 completed the study. Interventions: Barthel Index and modified Rankin scale (mRS) patients were randomly assigned to a non-physical intervention control (n = 9 of 39 completed, 30 withdrew before baseline testing), or to a high-intensity agility program (15 sessions, 5 weeks, n = 30 completed). The main focus of assessment was on the Modified Rankin Scale. Additionally, we evaluated secondary factors including daily life functionality, five dimensions of health-related quality of life, the Beck depression inventory, the 6 min walk test (6MWT), the Berg Balance Scale (BBS), and static balance (center of pressure). The Robot-Assisted Gait Therapy (ROB/RAGT) program led to significant improvements across various measures, including a 37% improvement in Barthel Index scores, a 56% increase in 10 m walking speed, and a 68% improvement in 6 min walking distance, as well as notable enhancements in balance and stability. Additionally, the intervention group demonstrated significant gains in all these aspects compared to the control group. In conclusion, the use of robotic therapy can be beneficial in stroke rehabilitation. These devices support the restoration and improvement of movement in various ways and contribute to restoring balance and stability.

Keywords: robotic therapy; stroke rehabilitation; robot-assisted exercise

1. Introduction

In recent years, the use of technology-based neuro-rehabilitation approaches has increased to meet high demand resulting from the rising number of stroke victims [1,2]. Medical robotics nowadays plays a crucial role in preventing, treating, or alleviating numerous severe conditions, assisting in surgeries, hospitals, or rehabilitation [3–6]. Stroke, one of the most frequently occurring diseases worldwide, often leads to permanent disability [7]. The condition is caused by the death of brain cells due to the blockage of a blood vessel supplying the brain (ischemic stroke), or bleeding into or around the brain (hemorrhagic stroke) [8,9]. This interruption results in not receiving fresh oxygenated blood in certain parts of the brain, leading to the death of neurons in that region, which is a primary contributor to long-term disabilities. Following a stroke, the effects are almost immediate and vary depending on the extent of damage within the brain. Common symptoms include sudden numbness, weakness, or paralysis on one side of the body, or more severely, on both sides. These symptoms may manifest as a weakened arm, leg, or eyelid; challenges in speaking or understanding speech; sudden blurred or lost vision; particularly in one eye; dizziness; confusion; instability; and/or severe headaches [7,10]. More than half of stroke survivors experience some degree of lasting hemiparesis or hemiplegia due to damage of the neural tissues, rendering them unable to perform daily activities without assistance [8,10,11].

A large number of lower limb exoskeletons have been developed over the years, usually with the purpose of assisting or augmenting human walking [1,12–28]. Some exoskeletons are stationary, mounted above treadmills and used to provide gait retraining or rehabilitation for persons with disabilities or injuries. Other exoskeletons are mobile, and those can be used either to support the full body weight of an individual or to provide partial assistive forces [29]. Devices in the former category are intended to be used by paralyzed individuals, enabling them to walk in the case where they were previously unable to do so. In the latter category, exoskeletons providing partial gait assistance can be used either by disabled individuals for rehabilitation or gait augmentation, or by healthy individuals to improve strength or endurance [30].

The aim of this research was to assess the importance of robotic technology by comparing Robot-Assisted Gait Therapy (ROB) with standard therapy treatment (STT) in stroke rehabilitation. In the ROB case, we employed robotic devices to aid patients' motor rehabilitation targeting the limbs (Figure 1). In the STT group, we helped rehabilitation with traditional techniques. This research is expected to illuminate the efficacy of robotic treatment in stroke rehabilitation. The results can contribute to faster, more intensive rehabilitation of patients and improve the quality of their life after a stroke.

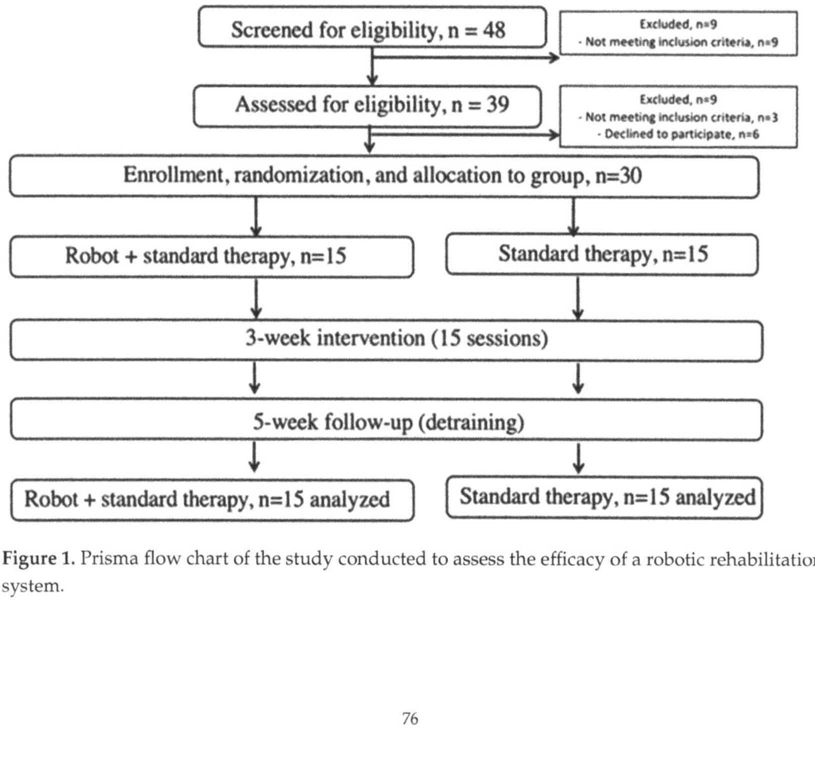

Figure 1. Prisma flow chart of the study conducted to assess the efficacy of a robotic rehabilitation system.

2. Materials and Methods

We performed a multisite, interventional, non-comparative study to evaluate the efficiency of a lower limb robotic device in subjects with hemiplegia/hemiparesis due to ischemic or hemorrhagic stroke. We used the ReStore Soft Exo Suit (Figure 2), an exoskeleton robot designed for the post-stroke rehabilitation of gait (ReWalk, Fototronic Ltd., Budapest, Hungary) [31,32]. The ReStore system has been cleared (CE marked in the EU as a medical device) for functional training, supported by its sensory data-driven force/torque control.

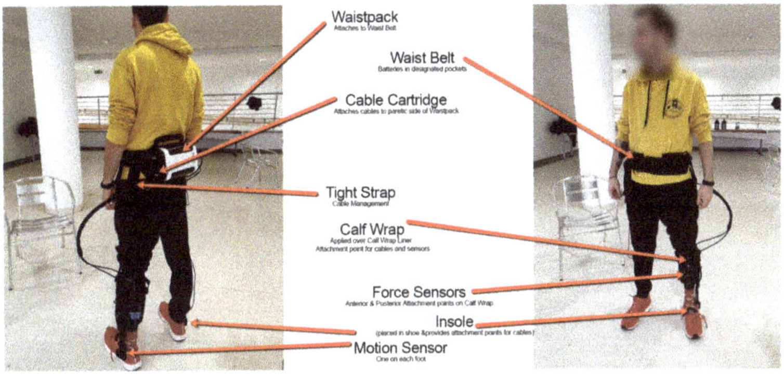

Figure 2. The overview of the ReStore Soft Exo Suit, ReWalk system (Image credit: ReWalk Robotics).

2.1. Participants and Design

Patient inclusion criteria were as follows: first occasion of ischemic stroke diagnosed by a neurologist based on CT or MRI scans; elapsed time after stroke of 2 to 4 weeks; mobility and postural limitation determined by neurologic examination; and a Modified Rankin Scale (mRS) score of 2 or higher. Exclusion criteria included a history of multiple strokes; systolic resting blood pressure (sRBP) less than 120 or greater than 160 mmHg; orthostatic hypotension; carotid artery stenosis; severe heart disease; hemophilia; traumatic brain injury; seizure disorder; uncontrolled diabetes; abnormal electroencephalography; mini Mental State Examination score less than 22; abnormal blood panel; use of sedatives; irregular medication schedule; serious aphasia (Western Aphasia Battery, 25); serious visual or hearing impairments; serious sensory dysfunction; serious orthopedic problems; neurologic conditions affecting motor function (PD, multiple sclerosis, multiple system atrophy, Guillain–Barré syndrome); alcoholism; recreational drug use; smoking after stroke diagnosis; inability to walk a minimum of 100 m with or without a walking aid in 6 min; Berg Balance Scale (BBS) score of 32 or less; Barthel Index (BI) score of 70 or less; inability to understand verbal instructions or prompts from a television screen; or current participation in a self-directed or formal group exercise program other than standard physical therapy. The 30 participants who had previously experienced a stroke were divided into two groups: a Robot-Assisted Gait Therapy (ROB, n = 15) group and a Standard Therapy (STT, n = 15) group. There were no significant differences in demographic and baseline data of the patients. The mean age of the participants was approx. 65 years. Most strokes occurred in the left hemisphere. Participants signed a written informed consent. The Institutional Research Ethics Committee approved the study protocol (IKEB2021/10), which was registered as a clinical trial (NCT05300867). All patients were cared for in the acute part of the neurological department.

We started patient treatment in the subacute state under hospital conditions. All patients remained in the rehabilitation ward until the end of the treatment. This study followed a pre–post–follow-up design. The participants were assessed at three different time points: pre-intervention (baseline), post-intervention (immediately after the intervention), and follow-up (a certain period after the intervention). In the Robot-Assisted Gait

Therapy (ROB), patients received standard therapy with robotic treatment. In the Standard Therapy Treatment (STT), we used only standard therapy. The research was carried out in three stages. The first assessment occurred sub-acutely on the 5th day after the initial treatment. The second examination was scheduled for 15 working days later, followed by a third follow-up evaluation five weeks after the initial treatment.

Notably, all assessments were conducted without the use of the robotic device. For the 6 min walk test, both groups were evaluated, encompassing patients who received robotic treatment as well as those who underwent physiotherapy. The robotic treatment protocol was as follows: before the fitting of the robotic device, there was a 5 min warm-up session that included joint mobilization and passive movements as needed. Following the fitting, there was a 5 min warm-up walk with robotic assistance, designed to encourage patient cooperation with the robot for seamless operation. The main session consisted of a 10 min dimensional walk (along a line), during which the patients maintained a pulse rate between 110 and 130, monitored with a Polar watch. This took place along a 100-meter-long corridor. Subsequently, there were five sets of 2 min obstacle avoidance/slalom walks on a 20-meter-long course. Here, there was one-meter space between each pair of obstacles, and for every 2 min of walking, there was one minute of rest. The aim was to complete the slalom walk as swiftly and accurately as possible.

Finally, there was a 6 min period of weight-bearing exercise on a 100-meter-long track. This entailed 50 m of brisk walking followed by 50 m of relaxed walking. During the rest periods, the robot was dismounted for 5 min, followed by a 10 min stretching session. The physiotherapy treatment protocol mirrored that of the robotic treatment, with the same warm-up and fitting procedures. The main session, too, followed the same structure, including the dimensional walk, obstacle avoidance/slalom walks, and weight-bearing exercise.

2.2. *Outcomes*

2.2.1. Primary Outcomes

The mRS and Barthel Index were employed as the primary outcome measures to assess functional status and activities of daily living in stroke survivors. The mRS demonstrated significant improvement across all intervention groups. Specifically, the Robot-Assisted Gait Therapy (ROB) group exhibited a substantial decrease in mRS scores, indicating enhanced functional independence post-treatment. The Standard Therapy Treatment (STT) group also exhibited notable improvement in mRS scores post-intervention, with a trend towards further amelioration at follow-up. While the effect size was comparatively smaller than in the ROB case, the improvement remained clinically significant. In concurrence with mRS results, the Barthel Index demonstrated substantial improvement across all intervention groups. The ROB group displayed a remarkable increase in Barthel Index scores at post-treatment, indicative of enhanced activities of daily living. This improvement was sustained at follow-up.

2.2.2. Secondary Outcomes

The Berg Balance Scale was employed to assess postural control and balance. The ROB group demonstrated a substantial improvement in Berg Balance Scale scores post-intervention, surpassing the improvements observed in the STT group. These improvements remained stable at follow-up, indicating sustained enhancement in postural control. The 10 m maximal walking speed test provided objective measures of mobility and gait. The ROB group exhibited a substantial improvement in walking speed post-intervention, with a further enhancement observed at follow-up. The ROB group exhibited remarkable improvements in distance walked during the 6 MWT, indicating enhanced endurance levels. These improvements were sustained at follow-up. The STT group exhibited a modest improvement in 6 MWT distance post-intervention, with a trend towards further enhancement at follow-up. The secondary outcome measures corroborated the positive effects observed in the primary outcomes, underscoring the efficacy of the respective interventions in enhancing functional recovery and mobility in stroke survivors.

2.3. Intervention

Patients assessed using the Barthel Index and mRS Scale were randomly assigned to either a non-physical intervention control group (n = 9 out of 39 completed, 30 withdrew before baseline testing), or a high-intensity agility program (15 sessions over 5 weeks, n = 30 completed). Both groups began with joint warm-up exercises and passive stretching as necessary (5 min), followed by slow walking to prepare the muscles and body for the subsequent activity (5 min). Each session concluded with 10 min of stretching for both groups (Figure 1).

2.3.1. Robot-Assisted Gait Therapy (ROB) Group

In the ROB group, the donning/mounting of the robotic device took 5 min. The system recorded the movement pattern of the non-involved (non-paretic) side. Two servo motors generated plantarflexion and dorsiflexion of the involved ankle through connector cables. Patients walked with the wireless control unit affixed to their waist with a belt, which housed two batteries to power the robot. The actuators with motion sensors were strapped to the shank of each leg. Ankle plantarflexion and dorsiflexion would be online (real time with Bluetooth)- configured and the state of walking balance was displayed on the control unit's screen. Based on the patient's gait pattern, the therapist could adjust dorsiflexion and plantarflexion assistances independently. After the proper mounting of the device, the next step was a 5 min warm-up walk with robotic assistance—the goal was to teach the patient to work together with the robot and to be able to work smoothly. Patients, escorted by a therapist, walked for 10 min at a heart rate of 110–130 b $\times$ min^{-1} in a 100-meter-long hallway. They also performed 10 min of slalom walking around obstacles placed ~1 m apart over a 20-meter-long course, with 1 min of rest after each 2 min. The aim was to walk as rapidly and safely as possible. Finally, patients walked for 6 min alternating high- vs. low-intensity walking for 50 m. At the end of the session, patients sat down and the robot was taken off in about 5 min.

2.3.2. Standard Therapy Treatment (STT) Group

In the STT group, participants received standard therapy treatment, which consisted of traditional rehabilitation techniques. This therapy encompassed a range of exercises targeting various aspects of movement recovery, functional ability, and mobility. The objective of the treatment was to enhance the participants' condition and functional abilities to mitigate the effects of the illness or injury. The control (CON) group underwent standard care as prescribed by the government, which entailed 30 min of daily group exercises while seated, and 30 min of individual physical therapy involving walking and balance exercises at local clinics. Seated exercises aimed to strengthen upper extremity and trunk muscles through movements such as lifting, lowering, and rotating medicine balls and weighted sticks. Standing exercises targeted lower extremity function, encompassing various stepping variations (forward, backward, and diagonally while standing on one leg); weight shifting; coordination exercises with arm movements while walking with or without sensory aids; and squatting movements with arm support on a backed chair to reinforce the lower extremity extensor mechanism. Following the exercise sessions, each participant in both groups received a 20 min medical massage of the lower extremities. Participants were instructed to log their symptoms, which were reviewed by therapists daily, and were advised not to modify their diet, medication, or physical activity habits throughout the study period.

2.4. Statistical Analyses

Data were reported as mean $\pm$ SD or median and interquartile ranges. An a priori power analysis using G*Power with the following input parameters was conducted to obtain medium-sized Group $\times$ Time interaction for distance walked over six minutes: effect size of f = 0.25; type I error of 0.05; type II error of 0.80; two groups; three measurements moments; and a correlation of r = 0.50 among groups [1]. These analyses were based on prior data [8,9]. Our analyses revealed a total sample size of ~33, i.e., 16–17 participants per group before an expected dropout of 20%.

The two groups' baseline characteristics were compared with an independent *t*-test. The main analysis was a Group (ROB, STT) by Time (pre-intervention, post-intervention, and follow-up) analysis of variance with repeated measures on Time, followed by Tukey post hoc contrasts. These changes were further characterized via Cohen's effect size (Cohen's d values $\leq$0.49 indicate small, 0.50 $\leq$ d $\leq$ 0.79 medium, and $\geq$0.80 large effect sizes) [10]. Ordinal data or data not normally distributed were analyzed with non-parametric analyses. For these variables, we performed Friedman tests to determine the effects of the interventions on outcome over time. Kendall's W quantified the effect size. A significant Friedman test was followed by a Wilcoxon test as a post hoc analysis to determine whether changes from pre-intervention to post-intervention, and post-intervention to follow-up were significant. The effect size for these within-group changes were computed through the test of probability of superiority for dependent samples (PSdep; a value of 0 or 1 denotes maximal, a value of 0.5 denotes an effect size of zero) [11]. Between-group differences at pre-intervention, post-intervention, and follow-up were assessed using the Mann–Whitney Test and the effect size characterized by η2 (η2 = 0.01: small effects; η2 = 0.06: medium effects; η2 = 0.14: large effects. To determine whether the robotic intervention affected the distance walked with and without wearing the robot in ROB, we performed a Condition of walking (robot, no robot) by Time (pre-intervention, post-intervention, follow-up) analysis of variance with repeated measures on both factors. The level of significance was set for all analyses at $p < 0.05$.

3. Results

3.1. Baseline Characteristics

Table 1 shows the descriptive data for the two groups. There were no differences between the groups in descriptive characteristics at baseline (all $p > 0.05$). Each group had 11 males of the 15 PwST enrolled. Over 70% of strokes occurred in the left hemisphere in each group. Nearly 70% of PwST smoked and 25% reported high levels of alcohol consumption in each group. Hypertension (9/30 PwST), ischemic heart disease (5/30), and diabetes (4/30) were the most frequent co-morbidities.

Table 1. Descriptive characteristics of the two groups of patients.

Variable	ROB		STT	
	Mean	**±SD or n**	**Mean**	**±SD or n**
N (males)	15	11	15	11
Age, y	64.8	5.89	64.7	7.16
Height, m	1.76	0.06	1.75	0.07
Mass, kg	80.7	11.93	82.0	9.23
BMI, kg·m^{-2}	25.9	3.26	26.8	3.15
Days after stroke	5	0.00	5	0.00
Stroke location, n				
Left hemisphere	11		10	
Right hemisphere	3		3	
Cerebellum	1		2	
Smoking, n				
Yes	11		9	
No	4		6	
Alcohol, n				
Yes	4		4	
No	11		11	

Table 1. *Cont.*

Variable	ROB		STT	
	Mean	**±SD or n**	**Mean**	**±SD or n**
Comorbidities, n				
Atherosclerosis	0		1	
Diabetes	2		2	
Fibrillation	1		0	
Gastroenteritis	1		0	
Hyperchol.	1		0	
Hypertension	2		7	
Ischemic HD	3		2	
Rheumatoid a.	1		2	

ROB, Robot-Assisted Gait Therapy group; STT, Standard Therapy Treatment group; BMI, Body Mass Index; Hyperchol., hypercholesterolemia; Ischemic HD, ischemic heart disease; Rheumatoid a., rheumatoid arthritis.

3.2. *Intervention Effects*

Table 2 shows the intervention effects. There were no differences between the two groups in any of the variables at baseline (all $p > 0.05$).

Table 2. Intervention effects on primary and secondary outcomes.

		Pre		Post		Follow-Up	
Variable	**Group**	**Mean**	**±SD**	**Mean**	**±SD**	**Mean**	**±SD**
Primary outcome							
MRS (Md, IQR)	ROB	4.0	1.00	2.0	0.00	1.0	1.00
	STT	3.0	1.00	2.0	1.00	2.0	0.00
Secondary outcomes							
Barthel Index (Md, IQR)	ROB	60.0	0.00	80.0	7.50	80.0	5.00
	STT	60.0	7.50	70.0	10.00	75.0	10.00
Berg Balance Scale	ROB	19.9	2.43	27.1	3.70	28.5	3.40
	STT	20.8	3.14	23.5	2.88	24.3	2.63
10 m walk, m/s	ROB	1.05	0.13	1.61	0.28	1.51	0.24
	STT	1.06	0.12	1.34	0.23	1.40	0.14
6 MWT, m	ROB	148.0	19.71	244.3	29.57	260.7	24.63
	STT	154.0	24.14	185.7	22.75	190.0	11.95
6 MWT with robot, m	ROB	156.3	26.81	337.3	24.32	372.0	32.11
	STT	-	-	-	-	-	-
WEO, cm	ROB	10.07	4.41	6.2	3.69	4.8	2.43
	STT	10.2	3.84	7.6	3.27	6.0	1.89
WEC, cm	ROB	12.4	3.63	8.4	3.74	7.7	2.41
	STT	12.5	4.46	10.5	5.07	10.3	3.32
NEO, cm	ROB	11.1	5.58	9.0	5.46	7.7	3.73
	STT	11.8	3.13	10.2	4.09	10.3	4.40
NEC, cm	ROB	13.0	3.43	11.5	6.21	10.2	3.86
	STT	13.3	4.77	10.7	3.60	11.5	6.22

The text accompanying the table provides the detailed statistical analyses. ROB, Robot-Assisted Gait Therapy (RAGT); STT, Standard Therapy Treatment group; MRS, Modified Rankin Scale; Md, median; IQR, interquartile range; 6 MWT, distance covered during the six-minute walk test; WEO, standing sway measured on a force platform in a wide stance, eyes open; WEC, standing sway measured on a force platform in a wide stance, eyes closed; NEO, standing sway measured on a force platform in a narrow stance, eyes open; NEC, standing sway measured on a force platform in a narrow stance, eyes closed.

3.3. Primary Outcome

The Friedman test revealed that ROB improved the MRS median scores (Table 2, Friedman χ^2 = 27.8, Kendall's W effect size = 0.93). Post hoc analyses showed that the 2-unit pre- to post-intervention improvement by ROB was significant (Wilcoxon post hoc test, p = 0.001, PSdep effect size = 0.99), and the additional 1-unit improvement at follow-up was significant (p = 0.008, PSdep effect size = 0.79). The Friedman test revealed that STT improved the MRS median scores (Table 2, Friedman χ^2 = 25.2, Kendall's W effect size = 0.84). Post hoc analyses revealed that the 1-unit pre- to post-intervention improvement by STT was significant (p = 0.001, PSdep effect size = 0.78), but did not change further by follow-up (p = 0.180, PSdep effect size = 0.50). The Mann–Whitney test did not show between-group differences at post-intervention (U = 67.5, p = 0.061, $\eta 2$ = 0.38). The 1-unit between-group difference at follow-up was significant (U = 39.0, p = 0.002, $\eta 2$ = 0.93).

3.4. Secondary Outcomes

The Friedman test revealed that ROB improved Barthel Index median scores (Table 2, Friedman χ^2 =27.4, Kendall's W effect size = 0.912). Post hoc analyses showed that the 20-point pre- to post-intervention improvement by ROB was significant (Wilcoxon post hoc test, p = 0.001, PSdep effect size = 0.97), and this improved score did not change further at follow-up (p = 0.157, PSdep effect size = 0.48). The Friedman test revealed that STT improved the Barthel Index median scores (Table 2, Friedman χ^2 = 27.1, Kendall's W effect size = 0.90). Post hoc analyses revealed that the 10-point pre- to post-intervention improvement by STT was significant (p = 0.001, PSdep effect size = 0.851), but did not change further during follow-up (p = 0.059, PSdep effect size = 0.44). The Mann–Whitney Test showed that the two groups differed by 10 points at post-intervention (U = 37.0, p = 0.001, effect size $\eta 2$ = 0.78), and ROB was still 5 points higher (improved) than STT at follow-up (U = 22.5, p = 0.001, effect size $\eta 2$ = 0.1.06).

Berg Balance Scale scores revealed a Group by Time interaction (F = 10.5, $p < 0.001$, $\eta 2$ = 0.27, Table 2). ROB improved by 7.2 (±3.86, 37% ±20, d = 2.21) vs. STT which improved by 2.7 points (±2.31, 14% ±13, d = 0.91, both $p < 0.001$), and this 4.5 points (23%) improvement difference was significant (d = 1.16, Tukey post hoc, $p < 0.05$). These improvements did not further change at follow-up ($p > 0.05$), and the 4.2 points between-group difference at follow-up was significant ($p < 0.05$, d = 1.38). The 10-m maximal walking speed data revealed a Group by Time interaction (F = 6.7, $p < 0.002$, $\eta 2$ = 0.20, Table 2). ROB improved 10 m walking speed by 0.57 m/s (±0.30, 56% ±31, d = 2.36). STT improved 10 m walking speed by 0.28 m/s (±0.22, 27% ±22, d = 1.40, both < 0.001). This 0.28 m/s improvement difference was significant ($p < 0.001$, d = 1.12). The 0.11 m/s (d = 0.53) faster gait in ROB vs. STT was still significant at follow-up ($p < 0.05$).

The 6MWT data revealed a Group by Time interaction (F = 34.9, $p < 0.001$, $\eta 2$ = 0.56, Table 2). In the 6MWT, ROB improved by 96 m (±37, 68% ±32, d = 3.69), and STT improved by 32 m (±26, 23% ±20, d = 1.35, both $p < 0.001$); these improvements did not change significantly during follow-up (ROB: 8% ±11; STT: 3% ±10, both $p > 0.05$). Figure 2 shows that the 6MWT distance walked with, vs. without, wearing the robot was 93 m longer at post and 111 m longer at follow-up in ROB (both $p < 0.001$). Sway while standing with a wide stance and eyes open improved similarly in the two groups at post (3.6 cm ±3.99, 28% ±36, Time main effect, F = 24.6, $p < 0.001$, $\eta 2$ = 0.47, Table 2), and these improvements were maintained at follow-up. Sway while standing with a wide stance and eyes closed improved similarly in the two groups at post-intervention (3.0 cm ±5.33, 18% ±45, Time main effect, F = 7.9, $p < 0.001$, $\eta 2$ = 0.22, Table 2), and these improvements did not change at follow-up. Sway while standing with a narrow stance and eyes open improved similarly in the two groups at post-intervention (1.9 cm ±5.12, 9% ±42, Time main effect, F = 4.6, $p < 0.014$, $\eta 2$ = 0.14, Table 2), and these improvements did not change at follow-up. Sway while standing with a narrow stance and eyes closed did not change in any group, neither at post-intervention, nor at follow-up (all $p > 0.05$, Table 2). Figure 2 depicts the effects of standard rehabilitation coupled with robotic training on the distance walked during six minutes with (filled symbols) and without robot (open symbols). The two conditions of walking (robot, no robot) interacted with time (F = 50.4, $p = 0.001$, η2 = 0.79). In the condition of walking with the robot, PwST (n = 15) walked 181 m (±42) or 123% (±50) further ($p < 0.001$) after the robotic intervention (post, d = 7.1). After a 5-week no-intervention follow-up, they walked 35 m (±22) or 10% (±7) further (d = 1.2, $p = 0.011$). When the same PwST were tested for the distance walked without the robot, they also walked 96 m (±37) or 68% (±32) further (post, d = 3.7, $p = 0.001$), and they maintained this gain but did not further increase it at follow-up (d = 0.6, $p = 0.281$). At post-intervention, the difference in distance walked between the two conditions was 93 m (d = 3.4, $p = 0.001$). At follow-up, the between-condition difference in distance walked was 111 m (d = 3.9, $p = 0.001$), as presented in Figure 3.

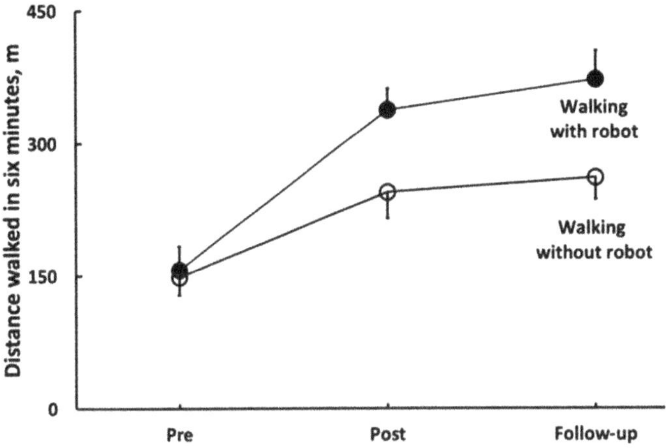

Figure 3. Key outcome of robotic rehabilitation support—the distance patients were able to walk with robot assistance.

4. Discussion

This study compares the effects of incorporating soft exoskeletons in stroke rehabilitation using robotic-assisted therapy (ROB) and standard therapy treatment (STT). The results demonstrate significant improvements in mobility, balance, and overall functional abilities of those stroke patients who underwent ROB. Both ROB and STT led to improvements in the primary outcome measure, as indicated by the significant increase in MRS median scores. However, at follow-up, the improvement in the ROB case was advancing, while STT's improvement remained stagnant.

In addition to the primary outcome, both groups experienced enhancements in secondary outcome measures, including Barthel Index median scores, Berg Balance Scale scores, the 10 m maximal walking speed, 6 MWT distance, and sway. Interestingly, ROB outperformed STT at follow-up, with a sustained 5-point higher improvement in Berg Balance score. Moreover, the 10 m maximal walking speed improvement difference remained significant in favor of ROB both at pre- and post-assessment, and follow-up. Notably, the 6 MWT distance walked with the soft exoskeleton was much greater at both post-assessment and follow-up, showing the potential long-term benefits of incorporating exoskeletons. Sway measures exhibited consistent improvements in both groups at post-assessment, which persisted during the follow-up period. However, Sway NEC showed no change in either group at post-assessment or follow-up. These findings emphasize the value of integrating soft exoskeletons like ROB into comprehensive stroke rehabilitation programs, offering lasting improvements in motor skills and daily activities. Rehabilitation with exoskeletons aimed to improve gait in patients with neurological diseases is a hot topic. Previous research has already proven that robotic exoskeletons are very useful in rehabilitation after stroke [8–10,14]. Contrary to the findings of another study analysis [27], in our study, there was a significant positive outcome using robotic exoskeletons, highlighting the benefits on the 6 MWT.

Based on our research, it can be said that exoskeletons physically strengthen the force and stability of patients, support their joints, and can contribute to restoring or improving their ability to move. Exoskeletons enable intensive and more effective therapy for patients after stroke. The devices allow patients to experience a sense of movement and independence, which can improve their self-confidence. As a result, they can be more motivated in the rehabilitation process and put more effort into relearning and recovery [33–35]. Current research is focused on improving functional ambulation using exoskeletons to improve safe community ambulation [27]. As an aim, our study focused on the use of exoskeletons in neuro-rehabilitation departments. Robotic therapy treatment in these departments is useful, because we can follow the patients' progress better and there is more time to get used to the exoskeleton. Some other studies focused on exoskeletons' long-term effects [36]. We tried to explore exoskeletons in the early rehabilitation after stroke; we obtained similar results as in another study [37], the post-intervention results showed improvements with both standard therapy and robotic therapy, but the latter had a higher impact on the mentioned results. However, considering follow-up results, only the robotic therapy showed a progressive tendency. Similar incremental benefits have been reported in other studies as well [38–40].

These research outcomes are considered significant from the regulatory point of view as well, since the new Medical Device Regulation (MDR) in the EU explicitly makes post-market surveillance and outcome-monitoring compulsory for medical device manufacturers [41–43], and there are similar challenges posed by the U.S. Food and Drug Administration [44].

When using robot treatments in everyday practice, there are many things which need attention. For example, the robot device must fit the patient's body properly to be effective. Because body sizes and types are each unique, there can be challenges in achieving optimal fixation and fit. If the device is not properly fitted or fixed, it cannot adequately support and guide the patient's movement. Robotic devices may sometimes require complex settings or ongoing maintenance to function properly. Device management and maintenance may require additional time and resources from therapists and patients. The aim of this research was to investigate the effectiveness of exoskeletons in the gait rehabilitation of patients after stroke. Nowadays, many new therapies are used in stroke rehabilitations. In the future, it will be an interesting research topic to examine the beneficial effects of these therapies and to compare them.

Moreover, as has been seen with other robotic therapeutic or interventional robotic devices [3,45,46], the overall cost and complexity of maintenance has been an inhibiting factor regarding clinical application. Supporting evidence for clinical outcome significance remains a main goal of treatment solution providers.

5. Limitations

The main limitation of this research is that it was conducted with a relatively small number of patients. With larger groups the level of significance increases, which leads to fewer errors in terms of quantity and quality. For example, it could be stated with greater certainty that the more effective improvement in the robotic rehabilitation therapy group is not just coincidental.

The other limitation is that we examined only a short follow-up period. In addition, we do not have knowledge on the long-term outcomes yet, and do not know the duration of the benefits.

6. Conclusions

The use of robotic therapy treatment can be useful in the rehabilitation of post-stroke patients. Stroke can often cause paralysis or weakness on one side of the body. Robotic treatment can help restore movement in affected limbs. These devices allow patients to begin a range of motion exercises earlier, even if they lack sufficient muscle strength or stability. Robotic therapy contributes to rapid, intensive recovery, while increasing the patients' self-confidence and improving the quality of their everyday life.

7. Suppliers

1. MediTECH Electronic GmbH, 95
2. ReWalk system: Restore, soft exoskeleton
3. Statistical Package for the Social Sciences, SPSS, version 22; IBM.

Author Contributions: Authors contributed equally to the work. All authors have read and agreed to the published version of the manuscript.

Funding: This study was supported in part by the Department of Neurology, Somogy County Kaposi Móricz Teaching University Hospital, and by a "Regional Health Development" award from the Doctoral School of the Faculty of Health Sciences, University of Pécs. The research was supported by the NKFIH from the project 'Research on the health application of artificial intelligence, digital imaging, employment and material technology developments by linking the scientific results of Széchenyi István University and Semmelweis University', under grant number TKP2021-EGA-21.

Institutional Review Board Statement: The study was conducted in accordance with the Declaration of Helsinki, and the protocol was approved by the Ethics Committee of Kaposi Mór Oktató Kórház (IKEB2021/10).

Data Availability Statement: Authors are committed to making the data available upon request.

Acknowledgments: Authors express their sincere gratitude to Zoltán Vadászi for his contributions and engineering support throughout the project. J.T. was supported in part by the János Bolyai Research Scholarship of the Hungarian Academy of Sciences, Hungary. T. Haidegger is a Consolidator Researcher, supported by the Distinguished Researcher program of Óbuda University.

Conflicts of Interest: The authors declare no conflicts of interest. The authors state that the results of the study are presented clearly, honestly, and without fabrication, falsification, or inappropriate data manipulation.

Abbreviations

ROB	Robot-Assisted Gait Therapy
STT	Standard Therapy Treatment
MRS	Modified Rankin Scale
BI	Barthel Index
BBS	Berg Balance Scale
6MWT	6 minute Walk Test
CT	Computed Tomography
MRI	Magnetic Resonance Imaging
rSBP	Resting Systolic Blood Pressure
IT	Inertial Technology
PwST	Patients with Stroke
ReStore Soft Exo Suit	Robotic Exoskeleton Device
ReWalk	Manufacturer of Robotic Exoskeleton
cm	Centimeters
m	Meters
m/s	Meters per Second
min	minutes
SD	Standard Deviation
G*Power	Statistical Power Analysis Software
η2	Eta-squared (Effect Size)
PSdep	Probability of Superiority for Dependent Samples
NEC	Eyes Closed
STT	Soft Exoskeleton

References

1. Esquenazi, A.; Talaty, M.; Packel, A.; Saulino, M. The ReWalk powered exoskeleton to restore ambulatory function to individuals with thoracic-level motor-complete spinal cord injury. *Am. J. Phys. Med. Rehabil.* **2013**, *92*, 617–624. [CrossRef]
2. Shi, D.; Zhang, W.; Zhang, W.; Ding, X. A Review on Lower Limb Rehabilitation Exoskeleton Robots. *Chin. J. Mech. Eng.* **2019**, *32*, 74. [CrossRef]
3. Fichtinger, G.; Troccaz, J.; Haidegger, T. Image-Guided Interventional Robotics: Lost in Translation? *Proc. IEEE* **2022**, *110*, 932–950. [CrossRef]
4. Haidegger, T.; Speidel, S.; Stoyanov, D.; Satava, R.M. Robot-assisted minimally invasive surgery—Surgical robotics in the data age. *Proc. IEEE* **2022**, *110*, 835–846. [CrossRef]
5. Haidegger, T.; Mai, V.; Mörch, C.; Boesl, D.; Jacobs, A.; Rao, R.B.; Khamis, A.; Lach, L.; Vanderborght, B. Robotics: Enabler and inhibitor of the Sustainable Development Goals. *Sustain. Prod. Consum.* **2023**, *43*, 422–434. [CrossRef]
6. Han, S.; Wang, H.; Yu, H. Human–Robot Interaction Evaluation-Based AAN Control for Upper Limb Rehabilitation Robots Driven by Series Elastic Actuators. *IEEE Trans. Robot.* **2023**, *39*, 3437–3451. [CrossRef]
7. Tollár, J.; Vetrovsky, T.; Széphelyi, K.; Csutorás, B.; Prontvai, N.; Ács, P.; Hortobágyi, T. Effects of 2-year-long Maintenance Training and Detraining on 558 Subacute Ischemic Stroke Patients'; Clinical-Motor Symptoms. *Med. Sci. Sports Exerc.* **2022**, *55*, 607–613. [CrossRef]
8. Kim, H.; Lee, S.; Yoon, B. Effects of wearable robot-assisted gait training on walking ability and quality in individuals with stroke: A systematic review and meta-analysis. *Clin. Rehabil.* **2019**, *33*, 1315–1328.
9. Cai, L.; Chen, C.; Chen, Y.; Wu, J. Exoskeleton rehabilitation robot training methods for stroke rehabilitation: A systematic review. *J. Neuroeng. Rehabil.* **2018**, *15*, 1–15.
10. Loureiro, R.C.; Collin, C.A.; Harwin, W.S. Upper limb robot mediated stroke therapy—GENTLE/s approach. *Auton. Robot.* **2019**, *43*, 733–746.
11. Huo, W.; Xia, C.; Wang, J.; Ma, X. A review of wearable lower limb exoskeletons for gait training. *Disabil. Rehabil. Assist. Technol.* **2020**, 1–16.
12. Da Silva Cameirão, M.; Bermúdez IBadia, S.; Duarte, E.; Verschure, P.F. Virtual reality-based rehabilitation speeds up functional recovery of the upper extremities after stroke: A randomized controlled pilot study in the acute phase of stroke using the Rehabilitation Gaming System. *Restor. Neurol. Neurosci.* **2011**, *29*, 287–298. [CrossRef]
13. Kazerooni, H.; Steger, R. (Eds.) *Exoskeletons in Rehabilitation Robotics: Tremor Suppression*; Springer Science & Business Media: Berlin/Heidelberg, Germany, 2014.
14. Gorgey, A.S. Robotic exoskeletons: The current pros and cons. *World J. Orthop.* **2018**, *9*, 112. [CrossRef] [PubMed]
15. Loureiro, R.C.; Harwin, W.S. Exoskeletons and active orthoses: Literature review, design examples and future directions. *Med. Eng. Phys.* **2016**, *38*, 1159–1173.
16. Veneman, J.F.; Kruidhof, R.; Hekman, E.E.; Ekkelenkamp, R.; Van Asseldonk, E.H.; Van der Kooij, H. Design and evaluation of the LOPES exoskeleton robot for interactive gait rehabilitation. *IEEE Trans. Neural Syst. Rehabil. Eng.* **2007**, *15*, 379–386. [CrossRef] [PubMed]
17. Moreno, J.C.; Castermans, T.; Hoellinger, T.; Maciejasz, P.; Dupeyron, A. The CYBERLEGs exoskeleton: An autonomous wearable robot for supporting people with mobility impairments. *IEEE Robot. Autom. Mag.* **2011**, *18*, 37–45.
18. Esquenazi, A.; Talaty, M.; Jayaraman, A. Powered exoskeletons for walking assistance in persons with central nervous system injuries: A narrative review. *PMR* **2016**, *9*, 46–62. [CrossRef]
19. Asbeck, A.T.; De Rossi, S.; Holt, K.G.; Walsh, C.J. A biologically inspired soft exosuit for walking assistance. *Int. J. Robot. Res.* **2015**, *34*, 744–762. [CrossRef]
20. Polygerinos, P.; Galloway, K.C.; Savage, E.; Herman, M.; Walsh, C.J. EMG controlled soft robotic glove for assistance during activities of daily living. *Robot. Auton. Syst.* **2015**, *73*, 171–178.
21. Park, S.; Ha, J.W.; Kim, J. Soft exosuit for hip assistance with a soft posterior module. *Soft Robot.* **2018**, *5*, 700–711.
22. Panizzolo, F.A.; Galiana, I.; Asbeck, A.T.; Siviy, C.; Schmidt, K.; Holt, K.G.; Walsh, C.J. A biologically inspired multi-joint soft exosuit that can reduce the energy cost of loaded walking. *J. Neuroeng. Rehabil.* **2016**, *13*, 43. [CrossRef] [PubMed]
23. Quinlivan, B.T.; Lee, S.; Malcolm, P.; Rossi, D.M.; Grimmer, M.; Siviy, C.; Karavas, N.; Wagner, D.; Asbeck, A.; Galiana, I.; et al. Assistance magnitude versus metabolic cost reductions for a tethered multiarticular soft exosuit. *Sci. Robot.* **2017**, *2*, eaah4416. [CrossRef] [PubMed]
24. Ding, Y.; Panizzolo, F.A.; Siviy, C.; Malcolm, P.; Galiana, I.; Walsh, C.J. Effect of timing of hip extension assistance during loaded walking with a soft exosuit. *J. Neuroeng. Rehabil.* **2018**, *15*, 87. [CrossRef] [PubMed]
25. Faul, F.; Erdfelder, E.; Lang, A.; Buchner, A. G*Power 3: A flexible statistical power analysis program for the social, behavioral, and bio- medical sciences. *Behav. Res. Methods* **2007**, *39*, 175–191. [CrossRef] [PubMed]
26. Cohen, J. *Statistical Power for the Behavioral Sciences*; Erblaum: Hillsdale, NJ, USA, 1988.
27. Karunakaran, K.K.; Gute, S.; Ames, G.R.; Chervin, K.; Dandola, C.M.; Nolan, J.K. Effect of robotic exoskeleton gait training during acute stroke on functional ambulation. *NeuroRehabilitation* **2021**, *48*, 493–503. [CrossRef] [PubMed]
28. Bauer, M.O.; Vizi, M.B.; Galambos, P.; Szalay, T. Direct drive hand exoskeleton for robot-assisted post stroke rehabilitation. *Acta Polytech. Hung.* **2021**, *18*, 37–54. [CrossRef]

29. Di Tommaso, F.; Tamburella, F.; Lorusso, M.; Gastaldi, L.; Molinari, M.; Tagliamonte, N.L. Biomechanics of Exoskeleton-Assisted Treadmill Walking. In Proceedings of the 2023 International Conference on Rehabilitation Robotics (ICORR), Singapore, 24–28 September 2023; pp. 1–6. [CrossRef]
30. Chisholm, A.E.; Alamro, R.A.; Williams, A.M.M.; Lam, T. Overground vs. treadmill-based robotic gait training to improve seated balance in people with motor-complete spinal cord injury: A case report. *J. Neuroeng. Rehabil.* **2017**, *14*, 27. [CrossRef] [PubMed]
31. Awad, L.N.; Esquenazi, A.; Francisco, G.E.; Nolan, K.J.; Jayaraman, A. The ReWalk ReStore™ soft robotic exosuit: A multi-site clinical trial of the safety, reliability, and feasibility of exosuit-augmented post-stroke gait rehabilitation. *J. Neuroeng. Rehabil.* **2020**, *17*, 80. [CrossRef]
32. Awad, L.N.; Bae, J.; O'donnell, K.; De Rossi, S.M.; Hendron, K.; Sloot, L.H.; Kudzia, P.; Allen, S.; Holt, K.G.; Ellis, T.D.; et al. A soft robotic exosuit improves walking in patients after stroke. *Sci. Transl. Med.* **2017**, *9*, eaai9084. [CrossRef]
33. Grissom, R.J.; Kim, J.J. *Effect Sizes for Research: Univariate and Multivariate Applications*, 2nd ed.; Routledge: London, UK, 2012.
34. Tollar, J.; Nagy, F.; Csutoras, B.; Prontvai, N.; Nagy, Z.; Török, K.; Blényesi, E.; Vajda, Z.; Farkas, D.; Tóth, B.E.; et al. High Frequency and Intensity Rehabilitation in 641 Subacute Ischemic Stroke Patients. *Arch. Phys. Med. Rehabil.* **2021**, *102*, 9–18. [CrossRef]
35. Calafiore, D.; Negrini, F.; Tottoli, N.; Ferraro, F.; Ozyemisci-Taskiran, O.; de Sire, A. Efficacy of robotic exoskeleton for gait rehabilitation in patients with subacute stroke: A systematic review. *Eur. J. Phys. Rehabil. Med.* **2021**, *58*, 1–8. [CrossRef]
36. Postol, N.; Grissel, J.; McHugh, C.; Bivard, A.; Spratt, N.J.; Marquez, J. Effects of therapy with a free-standing robotic exoskeleton on motor function and other health indicators in people with severe mobility impairment due to chronic stroke: A quasi-controlled study. *J. Rehabil. Assist. Technol. Eng.* **2021**, *8*, 3–4. [CrossRef]
37. Awad, L.N.; Kudzia, P.; Revi, D.A.; Ellis, T.D.; Walsh, C.J. Walking faster and farther with a soft robotic exosuit: Implications for post-stroke gait assistance and rehabilitation. *IEEE Open J. Eng. Med. Biol.* **2020**, *1*, 108–115. [CrossRef] [PubMed]
38. Zhou, J.; Yang, S.; Xue, Q. Lower limb rehabilitation exoskeleton robot: A review. *Adv. Mech. Eng.* **2021**, *13*, 1–17. [CrossRef]
39. Sarajchi, M.; Sirlantzis, K. Pediatric Robotic Lower-Limb Exoskeleton: An Innovative Design and Kinematic Analysis. *IEEE Access* **2023**, *11*, 115219–115230. [CrossRef]
40. Vassallo, C.; Zinni, G.; Maludrottu, S.; Laffranchi, M.; De Michieli, L. Stairs and ramps ascent and descent: How to design feasible gait patterns for a powered lower-limb exoskeleton. In Proceedings of the 2022 9th IEEE RAS/EMBS International Conference for Biomedical Robotics and Biomechatronics (BioRob), Seoul, Republic of Korea, 21–24 August 2022; pp. 1–6. [CrossRef]
41. Pentek, M.; Zrubka, Z.; Gulacsi, L.; Weszl, M.; Czere, J.T.; Tamás, P. 10 pragmatic points to consider when performing a systematic literature review of clinical evidence on digital medical devices. *Acta Polytech. Hung.* **2023**, *20*, 110–128.
42. Zah, V.; Burrell, A.; Asche, C.; Zrubka, Z. Paying for Digital Health Interventions-What Evidence is Needed? *Acta Polytech. Hung.* **2022**, *19*, 179–199. [CrossRef]
43. Hölgyesi, Á.; Zrubka, Z.; Gulácsi, L.; Baji, P.; Tamás, H.; Kozlovszky, M.; Weszl, M.; Kovács, L.; Péntek, M. Robot-assisted surgery and artificial intelligence-based tumour diag-nostics: Social preferences with a representative cross-sectional survey. *BMC Med. Inform. Decis. Mak.* **2024**, *24*, 1–12, *article in press*.
44. Eguren, D.; Contreras-Vidal, J.L. Navigating the FDA Medical Device Regulatory Pathways for Pediatric Lower Limb Exoskeleton Devices. *IEEE Syst. J.* **2021**, *15*, 2361–2368. [CrossRef]
45. Bhardwaj, S.; Khan, A.A.; Muzammil, M. Lower limb rehabilitation robotics: The current understanding and technology. *Work* **2021**, *69*, 775–793. [CrossRef]
46. Pană, C.F.; Popescu, D.; Rădulescu, V.M. Patent Review of Lower Limb Rehabilitation Robotic Systems by Sensors and Actuation Systems Used. *Sensors* **2023**, *23*, 6237. [CrossRef] [PubMed]

robotics

MDPI

Article

A Framework for Modeling, Optimization, and Musculoskeletal Simulation of an Elbow–Wrist Exosuit †

Ali KhalilianMotamed Bonab, Domenico Chiaradia, Antonio Frisoli and Daniele Leonardis *

Institute of Mechanical Intelligence and Department of Excellence in Robotics & AI, Scuola Superiore Sant'Anna, 56127 Pisa, Italy; ali.khalilianmotamedbonab@santannapisa.it (A.K.B.); domenico.chiaradia@santannapisa.it (D.C.); antonio.frisoli@santannapisa.it (A.F.)

* Correspondence: daniele.leonardis@santannapisa.it

† This paper is an extended version of our paper published in KhalilianMotamed Bonab, A.; Leonardis, D.; Frisoli, A.; Chiaradia, D. Modeling, Optimization, and Musculoskeletal Simulation of Elbow-Wrist Exosuit. In Proceedings of the 2023 21st IEEE International Conference on Advanced Robotics (ICAR), Abu Dhabi, United Arab Emirates, 5–8 December 2023; pp. 460–466.

Abstract: The light weight and compliance of exosuits are valuable benefits not present rigid exoskeleton devices, yet these intriguing features make it challenging to properly model and simulate their interaction with the musculoskeletal system. Tendon-driven exosuits adopt an electrical motor combined with pulleys and cable transmission in the actuation stage. An important aspect of the design of these systems for the load transfer efficacy and comfort of the user is the anchor point positioning. In this paper, we propose a framework, whose first purpose is as a design methodology for the synthesis of an exosuit device, achieved by optimizing the anchor point location. The optimization procedure finds the best 3D position of the anchor points based on the interaction forces between the exosuit and the upper arm. The computation of the forces is based on the combination of a mathematical model of a wrist–elbow exosuit and a dynamic model of the upper arm. Its second purpose is the simulation of the kinematic and physiological effects of the interaction between the arm, the exosuit, and the complex upper limb musculoskeletal system. It offers insights into muscular and exoskeleton loading during operation. The presented experiments involve the development and validation of personalized musculoskeletal models, with kinematic, anthropometric, and electromyographic data measured in a load-lifting task. Simulation of the exosuit operation—coupled with the musculoskeletal model—showed the efficacy of the suit in assisting the wrist and elbow muscles and provided interesting highlights about the impact of the assistance on shoulder muscles. Finally, we provide a possible design of an elbow and wrist exosuit based on the optimized results.

Keywords: soft exosuit; upper limb; musculoskeletal simulation; modeling and optimization; wearable assistive device; physical human–robot interaction (pHRI)

1. Introduction

Assistive exoskeletons, whether soft or rigid in design, offer valuable support for various motor tasks, enhancing users' energy conservation and overall efficiency [1]. Beyond their energy-saving capabilities, these technological solutions serve as a potent tool for therapeutic intervention, particularly for individuals engaged in rehabilitation programs. This motor aid contributes significantly to their recovery journey, ultimately enhancing their overall quality of life [2] and restoring their independence in performing essential activities of daily living (ADLs). Additionally, the utility of exoskeletons extends to labor-intensive occupations and tasks, where they play a pivotal role in assisting workers. For workers engaged in physically demanding roles, such as lifting objects weighing between 3 and 5 kg, exoskeletons can assist as a vital means to mitigate the risks associated with work-related musculoskeletal disorders.

The majority of exoskeletons are typically constructed using inflexible materials, posing a number of challenges. These issues include misalignment with the biological joints, excessive bulkiness, and added weight. However, a promising solution has emerged in the form of soft exoskeletons, commonly known as exosuits. These exosuits are crafted from flexible materials like fabric, webbing, and artificial tendons [3], allowing them to conform comfortably to the wearer's body shape. This flexibility not only inherently resolves alignment problems but also enhances the overall comfort and natural interaction with the exosuit. Furthermore, the use of soft materials significantly reduces the exosuit's bulk, enabling wearers to achieve a greater range of motion and improved agility. This reduction in weight is a crucial advantage, as it minimizes the additional load on the wearer. Consequently, exosuits present a highly adaptable option for enhancing human capabilities.

In particular, within the upper limb exosuit field, shoulder exosuits have gained interest. Studies have consistently demonstrated their effectiveness in reducing muscle activity among healthy individuals [4–6]. Moreover, these exosuits have demonstrated their benefits to subjects with upper limb impairments requiring rehabilitation. Specifically, shoulder exosuits have been proven to enhance usability and alleviate perceived muscle fatigue in wearers [7,8]. These devices have not only been shown to improve passive [4,9] and active [10] ranges of motion but have the ability to extend endurance during static hold [6].

Elbow exosuits, meanwhile, have primarily been developed for preventive and assistive purposes. Several studies have consistently highlighted their effectiveness in reducing muscle activity in healthy subjects [11–13], indicating their potential utility in tasks involving repetitive or demanding elbow movements. Within the scope of wrist exosuits, multiple iterations have been devised to address both assistive and rehabilitative objectives. These wrist exosuits have demonstrated promising outcomes [14,15]. There has also been significant progress in the development of multi-joint upper limb exosuits designed to perform rehabilitation and augmentative functions [7,16,17].

Despite significant advancements in exosuit development, the creation of soft exosuits still heavily relies on approximations and assumptions, as noted by Xiloyannis et al. [3]. Particularly, the determination of both the functional and geometric aspects of these exoskeletons predominantly depends on empirical approaches. Consequently, anchor points may not consistently find their way to the most ergonomic or optimal positions. This oversight could result in discomfort and potential user injury. Moreover, suboptimal anchor point placement can necessitate higher forces from the exosuit to deliver the same level of assistance, leading to larger and heavier systems, particularly for exosuits featuring a Bowden-cable-type transmission, which can suffer from increased frictional losses under substantial forces.

Given the complexity of experiments, achieving accurate exosuit design and optimization through testing alone is challenging. To address this challenge, the integration of precise exosuit modeling with musculoskeletal simulations can complement experimental approaches, offering a more comprehensive understanding of these devices. Such an approach not only saves time and resources but also enhances safety considerations.

While extensive research exists on the design and optimization of lower-limb exoskeletons utilizing musculoskeletal simulations [18–21], limited attention has been given to the development and optimization of exosuits, especially for the upper limbs [22–27]. Currently, there is a notable absence of quantitative models and optimization techniques for the creation of soft upper limb exosuits and their examination concerning human biomechanics via musculoskeletal simulations. Filling this void would result in informative exosuit designs while upholding user safety.

It is worth noting that the studies conducted by Bardi et al. [26] and Sambhav et al. [25] have explored the potential of elbow exosuits through musculoskeletal simulations, but their work has several limitations. Firstly, they employ a simplified two-degree-of-freedom (DOF) model featuring only six muscles, overlooking the complexity of the human arm, potentially leading to unnatural movements. Secondly, the generation of elbow flexion relies on minimum jerk trajectories, neglecting the potential involvement of other joints in load handling. Lastly, the absence of parametric optimizations and strategies for anchor point placement and configuration makes it challenging to generalize their findings to other exosuit designs.

In this paper, we present a design framework for modeling, optimizing, and simulating exosuits, introducing a comprehensive methodology that involves a mathematical model of a wrist–elbow exosuit and a simulation approach that copes with the complex upper limb musculoskeletal system. In more detail, we modeled the human arm dynamics within the interaction forces produced by a tendon-driven exosuit. We proposed a parameterization methodology for the anchor point location and we implemented an optimization procedure that minimizes the integral effect of the tendon force magnitude to reduce the effect of friction losses and excessive tendon tension. From the quantitative analysis, we obtained the optimal parameters for the design of a preliminary wrist–elbow exosuit that we propose in this article. Finally, we implement and evaluate in a simulation framework the dynamic and physiological effect on the human arm of the exosuit with the optimal parameters. Moreover, we extended and deeply elaborated the partial results provided in [28].

2. Materials and Methods

2.1. Musculoskeletal Modeling and Simulation

2.1.1. Experimental Procedure

The experimental data were acquired from three male participants (average age: 30 ± 3 years, height: 179 ± 5.56 cm, weight: 78.34 ± 8.50 kg). All individuals self-reported as right-handed and had no history of upper-extremity musculoskeletal injuries or pathology, neuromuscular impairments, or physical limitations hindering them from performing the required tasks. Ethical approval for the study was granted by the Scuola Superiore Sant'Anna Review Board, and prior to commencing the experiments, written informed consent was obtained from each participant.

The primary objective of this study was to evaluate the effectiveness of the proposed elbow–wrist exosuit and to collect data on muscular activity and arm kinematics during load lifting. To achieve this, we designed the experiments to record arm kinematics and muscular activation of the subjects under two loading conditions. Data were collected through three trials in which participants unimanually lifted their right hand, with and without a 3 kg hand-held weight, based on visual cues. A scheme of the lifting task is shown in Figure 1b. Since the trial durations and overall experiment length were relatively short, the potential impact of fatigue was considered negligible, and therefore, conditions were not randomized to mitigate any fatigue effects.

Arm kinematics were acquired using inertial measurement units (IMUs) provided by Xsens MVN Link (Xsens Technologies B.V., Enschede, The Netherlands). Subjects were equipped with 11 IMUs placed on their hands, forearms, upper arms, scapula, sternum, head, and pelvis, following the guidelines outlined in the Xsens MVN manual. IMU signals were sampled at 240 Hz for all participants, and data were collected using the associated MVN Analyze 2022.0.2 software (Xsens Technologies B.V., Enschede, The Netherlands). A representative subject wearing the sensors is shown in Figure 1c.

Simultaneously, the synchronized activities of targeted muscles were recorded through surface electromyography (sEMG) using a Bagnoli Desktop EMG system (Delsys, Natick, MA, USA). The integration of the IMU-based motion capture system and the EMG recording system was achieved through MVN Analyze software to ensure synchronization between kinematic and muscle activity data.

The specific muscles targeted in this study included the deltoid (anterior, medium, posterior), pectoralis major (sternal), flexor carpi ulnaris (FCU), flexor carpi radialis (FCR), extensor carpi ulnaris (ECU), extensor carpi radialis longus (ECRL), biceps brachii (short head), and triceps brachii (long head). Raw EMG data underwent post-processing, including band-pass filtering (30–450 Hz), full-wave rectification, and low-pass filtering (6 Hz), utilizing a zero-phase second-order Butterworth filter. To enable comparisons of muscle activities across different conditions, subjects, and simulated muscle activities, the post-processed EMG envelopes were normalized based on maximum voluntary contractions.

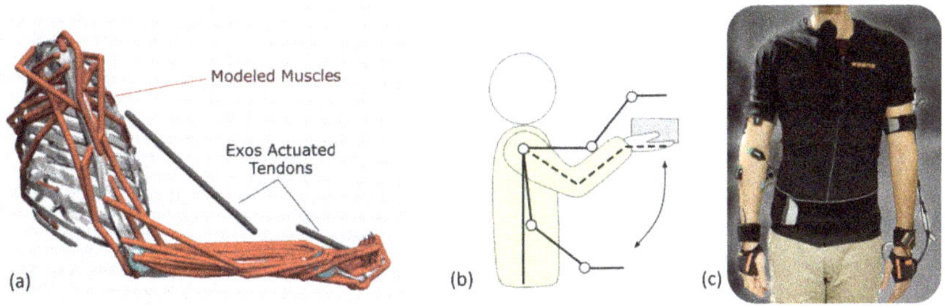

Figure 1. (**a**) The musculoskeletal model, (**b**) the lifting task used for calibration experiments and simulation, (**c**) the experimental setup used for calibration of the model.

2.1.2. Musculoskeletal Model

Musculoskeletal simulations were conducted using OpenSim, a widely adopted open-source software in the realm of movement science [29,30]. In our study, we employed a customized unimanual upper extremity musculoskeletal model [31], implemented within the OpenSim environment [32]. This model [32] incorporates 7 degrees of freedom, encompassing shoulder elevation, elevation plane, shoulder rotation, elbow flexion, forearm rotation, wrist deviation, and wrist flexion. Additionally, it consists of 50 Hill-type muscle–tendon actuators representing the 32 muscles and muscle compartments that traverse the shoulder, elbow, forearm, and wrist joints.

For simulating the unimanual lifting of a hand-held weight, we modeled the load as a disk (height: 62.5 mm, radius: 40 mm) with a uniform density, rigidly attached to the hand within the model. To account for unmodeled passive components and potential muscle weaknesses, we introduced a set of *Coordinate Actuators* to the model's coordinates, serving as *reserve actuators*. These actuators were configured to apply minor joint moments as needed to compensate for these factors.

The musculoskeletal simulations were customized to individual subjects using the experimental data we collected. These simulations encompassed three distinct conditions: simulations of unassisted subjects both with and without a 3 kg weight load (referred to as *loaded* and *noload* subjects, respectively), and simulations of assisted subjects engaged in lifting a 3 kg weight.

2.1.3. Musculoskeletal Simulation Workflow

The simulation process, which is depicted in Figure 2, was initiated with the calculation of inverse kinematics, which relied on the IMU orientation data obtained from the experiments. We executed this step using the OpenSense toolkit [33] within OpenSim 4.4. For each participant and under each condition, we conducted three simulation trials. Within each trial, we utilized the *IMU Placer* and *IMU Inverse Kinematics* tools to produce joint kinematics.

The orientation of each IMU was assigned to its associated rigid body in the model, and then the set of IMU orientations was imported into OpenSense. Due to the unimanual upper extremity model, we only used the sternum and right arm IMU measurements for computation of the inverse kinematics, and the sternum served primarily as the base IMU for our model since the motion of the thorax was not of interest to us.

Using the *IMU Placer* Tool and the IMU calibration data, the fixed orientation of IMU frames in relation to the body segments of the posed model was calibrated. Due to the IMU Placer Tool assumption that the default poses of the model match the pose of the subject during calibration, the model's default posture was manually altered to be aligned with the subject as closely as possible. Additionally, we provided three rotational degrees of freedom on the thorax body to achieve finer results between the experimental IMU orientation and virtual IMUs. The musculoskeletal model of a representative subject with calibrated virtual IMUs is demonstrated in Figure 3.

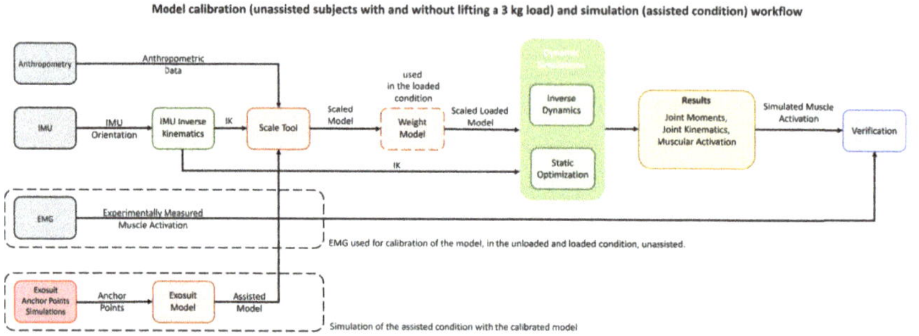

Figure 2. Workflow scheme of the adopted models, summarizing the calibration phase, with the real user and IMU data in the no-load and loaded condition, and the simulation phase, including simulation with exoskeleton co-activation, and verification of the simulations with recorded EMG data.

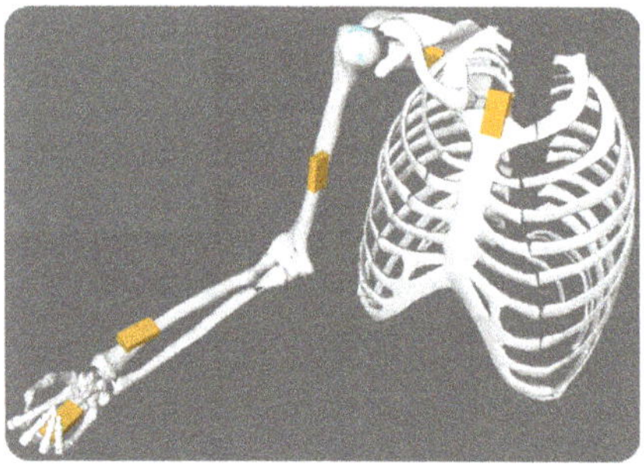

Figure 3. The musculoskeletal model with calibrated virtual IMUs on each body segment.

Once the virtual IMUs' offsets were calibrated, we employed the *IMU Inverse Kinematics* Tool. This tool enables us to determine joint angles that minimize the weighted squared difference between the experimentally measured IMU orientations and the virtual IMU orientations [33]. The weights assigned to each IMU were based on the reliability of their measurements and their significance in determining kinematics. Notably, we down-weighted the sternum IMU because the model did not account for thorax kinematics.

As the rigid body segment length has no influence on IMU-based inverse kinematics [33], the inverse kinematics of joints were computed without scaling the model. However, the inertial and musculotendinous features of the model will directly influence the dynamic simulations; hence, scaling the generic model is required to generate a subject-specific musculoskeletal model and, subsequently, subject-specific dynamic simulation results.

We did not employ optical motion capture equipment during the data-gathering phase; therefore, the standard approach of scaling the model using marker data is not applicable to our simulations. Along these lines, we relied on the manual scaling approach to generate a scaled model.

Given that the segments lengths of the generic model were consistent with the anthropometry data of a 50th percentile male described in [34], scaling of the segments would be possible by taking the same standard measurements from the subjects, as described in Gordon et al. [34]. Consequently, the lengths of the hand, forearm, upper arm, and clavicle bodies of each subject were measured, and then the required scale factor was calculated as a ratio between the length of the segment in the generic model to the measured subject.

These scale factors were incorporated into the OpenSim Scale Tool to scale each segment uniformly and generate the scaled musculoskeletal model. Each segment's mass and inertial characteristics were also scaled by the product of its scale factor. After scaling, the mass of the segments was verified to be comparable to its estimated weight based on the subject mass [35].

Finally, the optimal fiber and tendon slack lengths of the generic model were scaled to retain their ratio across the scaled muscle path length, which concludes our scaling procedure.

We applied the OpenSim Static Optimization (SO) Tool to calculate the muscle activation and, subsequently, the forces required to generate the joint moments of the scaled model that tracked joint kinematics. Even though computed muscle control (CMC) is a common approach for producing muscle-driven simulations [18,20,21,29,32,36], the use of SO was preferred due to the complexity of the musculoskeletal model and, therefore, the time required by CMC for computation of each simulation.

Although the CMC approach takes into account a more realistic muscle model and muscular excitation, it has been shown that both static, CMC and dynamic optimization could provide comparable estimates of muscle forces during typical task performance [37,38]. The CMC would be considered a more appropriate tool to simulate rapid movements when activation and contraction dynamics play a significant role [38,39].

Considering that the objective of this study is to gain qualitative insight into the dynamics of muscle activation and the computational cost of the CMC, it was determined that SO was a more suitable technique to employ in this study.

As indicated in the OpenSim tutorial regarding the Static Optimization Tool, this tool utilizes the inverse kinematics solution of the model to address the equations of motion concerning joint torques, referred to as generalized forces in the model. These joint torques are controlled by the muscle activation-to-force dynamics, which, in turn, are limited by the constraints imposed by the force–length–velocity properties of the muscles, as outlined in Equation (1). This tool effectively solves muscle redundancy by minimizing a weighted sum of squared muscle activations and actuators, as delineated in Equation (2).

$$\sum_{i=1}^{N}[a_i f(F_{i,\max}, l_i, v_i)]r_{i,j} = \tau_j \tag{1}$$

$$J(a,\tau) = \sum_{i=1}^{N}(a_i)^2 + \sum_{r=1}^{R}\left(\frac{\tau_{reserve,r}}{w_r}\right)^2 \tag{2}$$

In these expressions, the variable N signifies the total count of muscles incorporated within the model. Each muscle's activation at a given time step is represented by a_i. Other parameters include $F_{i,\max}$, l_i, v_i, and $f(F_{i,\max}, l_i, v_i)$, which, respectively, denote the maximum isometric force, length, shortening velocity, and the force–length–velocity surface associated with each muscle. Additionally, $r_{i,j}$ represents the moment arm of the muscle relative to the jth joint axis, while τ_j stands for the generalized force acting about the jth joint axis.

In Equation (2), the variable R denotes the count of *reserve actuators* present in the model. The term $\tau_{reserve,r}$ signifies the immediate torque exerted by the rth *reserve actuators*, while w_r stands for the weight factor that scales the penalty associated with activating the rth *reserve actuators* [21]. These actuators are specifically designed to compensate for unaccounted dynamics and muscle weaknesses. Consequently, their weight costs, denoted as "optimal force", were adjusted to significantly increase the cost of their recruitment in comparison to the muscles.

2.1.4. Modeling Exosuits and Simulating Assisted Subjects

The modeling of the wrist–elbow exosuit was achieved through the utilization of the *PathActuator* class, a feature provided by the OpenSim API. This class is specifically designed for the representation of massless actuators capable of applying tension along a specified path. It serves as a practical framework for simulating these actuators within the wrist–elbow exosuit, offering control over tension application and enabling controlled motion along the designated geometry. The geometry path of the actuators is defined by assigning the anchor points as the origin and insertion points of the actuator. The implemented model is depicted in Figure 1a.

Upon incorporating the assistive actuators into the model, the objective function of the static optimization is subjected to a modification, as expressed in Equation (3), wherein the assistive actuators are integrated into the function.

$$J(a,\tau) = \sum_{i=1}^{N} (a_i)^2 + \sum_{r=1}^{R} \left(\frac{\tau_{reserve,r}}{w_r} \right)^2 + \left(\frac{\tau_{exosuit,elbow}}{w_{exosuit,elbow}} \right)^2 + \left(\frac{\tau_{exosuit,wrist}}{w_{exosuit,wrist}} \right)^2 \tag{3}$$

Much like the approach involving *reserve actuators*, the modified equation incorporates additional terms, namely $\tau_{exosuit,wrist}$ and $\tau_{exosuit,elbow}$, which represent the immediate torque applied by the wrist and elbow exosuit actuators, respectively. Correspondingly, $w_{exosuit,wrist}$ and $w_{exosuit,elbow}$ denote the *optimal force* of the wrist and elbow exosuit actuators.

To enable the simulation of an ideal exosuit scenario, the *optimal force* values of both the elbow and wrist actuators were modified to 1000 N. This adjustment aims to significantly reduce the recruitment cost associated with the assistive actuators. This alteration encourages the optimization process to prioritize the utilization of the exosuit over muscular efforts when generating the desired joint moments.

The static optimization in both assisted and unassisted subjects while lifting a load (i.e., *loaded* subjects) employed the same kinematics while unassisted subjects without load (i.e., *noload* subjects) had different kinematics.

3. Exosuit Design

For the design of the exosuit, we considered three sizes of human arm and consequently of the suit. For each size, we computed the dynamics of the human arm and the interaction with the exosuit at the anchor points. From the analytical relation, we optimized the positioning of the anchoring point and we proposed a preliminary design for the elbow–wrist exosuit.

3.1. Modeling of the Arm with the Exosuit

The mass distribution of the human arm was based on [40]; thus, the arm, forearm, and hand masses were evaluated as a percentage of the overall body weight. In particular, the arm mass was 3.25%, the forearm mass was 1.87%, and the hand mass was equal to 0.65%. We chose 75 kg as a reference body weight. The body part lengths were set as in Table 1.

Table 1. Lenght of the arm, forearm, and hand for the three modeled sizes.

Body Link	Small Size Length (m)	Medium Size Length (m)	Large Size Length (m)
Arm	0.30	0.34	0.38
Forearm	0.23	0.26	0.30
Hand	0.05	0.06	0.08

The design and optimization of the wrist–elbow exosuit started from the kinematic and dynamic modeling of the human arm and its interaction with the actuation units. The model takes into account three degrees of freedom (DoFs) for the shoulder, one DoF for the elbow, and two DoFs (flexion/extension and prono/supination) for the wrist. The modeled kinematic chain of the arm is shown in Figure 4a.

The dynamic equation describing the arm motion is recalled in Equation (4).

$$B(q)\ddot{q} + C(q,\dot{q})\dot{q} + G(q) + J(q)^T \gamma_e = \tau \tag{4}$$

where $q, \dot{q}$, and $\ddot{q}$ are the vector of the joint angles, speed, and acceleration, respectively, $B(q)\ddot{q}$ are the linear inertial terms, $C(q, \dot{q})\dot{q}$ are the centripetal and Coriolis terms, $G(q)$ are the gravitational terms, $J(q)^T \gamma_e$ is the effect of the external wrench on the joints, and τ is the joint torque vector.

For the actuation stage, we considered assisting only the flexion/extension of the three districts—shoulder, elbow, and wrist—and thus we considered the use of one motor per joint. Torque was applied to the human via Bowden cables from the motor pulley to an anchor point at the assisted body segment. For each actuator, we can identify a center of rotation and two anchor points:

- The first anchor point on the proximal segment where the actuator and the sheath of the Bowden cable are fixed.
- The second anchor point on the distal segment where the cable ends.

To optimize the tendon forces as a function of the anchor point locations, we determined the geometrical relation between them and the joint torques.

Figure 4b shows the geometric variables we used to derive the parametric equation of the forces exerted from the exosuit on the arm. The actuation force vector is constrained on the line connecting the two anchor points, identified by p_{iu} and p_{id}, respectively.

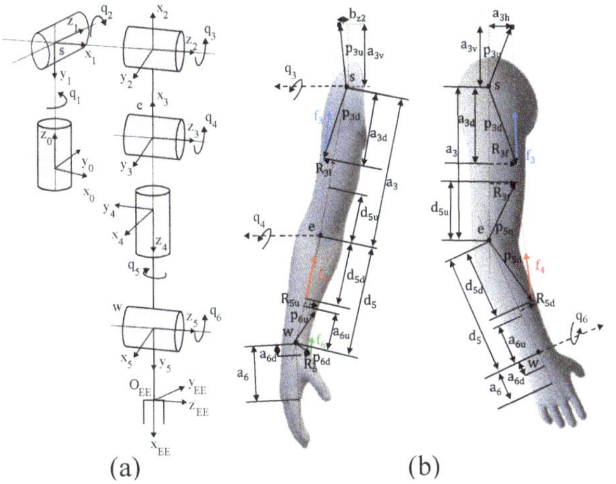

Figure 4. Modeling of the human arm and its interaction with the exosuit. The kinematic chain used for the model (**a**), the geometrical parameters used for the generalized forces computation (**b**).

The relation between the generalized forces τ that generate work on the Lagrangian coordinates and the actuator forces on the tendons is expressed by Equation (5)

$$\tau = J_{act}^T(q) f_{tend} \quad (5)$$

where the vector components are related to the three chosen flexion/extension movements

$$\tau = [\tau_3 \quad \tau_4 \quad \tau_6]^T; \; f_{tend} = [f_3 \quad f_4 \quad f_6]^T \quad (6)$$

where $\tau, f_{tend} \in R^{3\times1}$, the terms f_i are scalars and represent the magnitude of the forces, $[.]^T$ represents transpose, and $J_{act}(q) \in R^{3\times3}$ is the Jacobian matrix that relates the joint torque vector with the tendon forces applied by the actuators.

The matrix $J^T{}_{act}(q)$ is obtained from the equation:

$$\tau_i = \sum_{j=1}^{N_F} \frac{\partial p_j}{\partial q_i}^T \cdot f_j \quad (7)$$

where τ_i is the generalized force that acts on the generalized coordinate q_i; $\boldsymbol{p}_j$ is the application point of the force $\boldsymbol{f}_j$, that is, the j-th actuator force that makes work on the i-th generalized coordinate. $\boldsymbol{f}_j$ is computed as:

$$\boldsymbol{f}_i = f_i \frac{\left(\boldsymbol{p}^0_{\mathrm{j\,u}}(t) - \boldsymbol{p}^0_{\mathrm{j\,d}}(t)\right)}{\left\|\boldsymbol{p}^0_{\mathrm{j\,u}}(t) - \boldsymbol{p}^0_{\mathrm{j\,d}}(t)\right\|} \quad (i,j) \in \{(3,3),(4,5),(6,6)\} \tag{8}$$

where $\boldsymbol{p}^0_{\mathrm{j\,u}}$ and $\boldsymbol{p}^0_{\mathrm{j\,d}} \in R^{3\times1}$ are the position vectors represented in the Newtonian reference frame as shown in Figure 4. For the shoulder, elbow, and wrist flexion/extension case, the generalized forces become (for i $\in \{3,4,6\}$):

$$\tau_i = \frac{\partial \boldsymbol{p}^0_{\mathbf{3d}}(t)}{\partial q_i}^T \cdot \boldsymbol{f}_3 + \frac{\partial \boldsymbol{p}^0_{\mathbf{4d}}(t)}{\partial q_i}^T \cdot \boldsymbol{f}_4 + \frac{\partial \boldsymbol{p}^0_{\mathbf{6d}}(t)}{\partial q_i}^T \cdot \boldsymbol{f}_6 \tag{9}$$

We want to study the dependency of the value of the generalized forces on varying the parameters a_{3d}, a_{3h}, a_{3v}, a_{4d}, a_{4u}, a_{6d} and a_{6u}. The values of f_3, f_4 and f_6 are obtained by inverting the Jacobian matrix $\boldsymbol{J}_{act}(\boldsymbol{q})$ that is determined by using Equations (5), (7) and (9).

3.2. Exosuit Anchor Point Location Optimization

With the relation between the three tendon forces and the geometrical parameters of the anchor points, we built an optimization procedure to minimize the cost index defined in (10) for a human-like minimum jerk trajectory — as implemented in [11] — to simulate a smooth, human movement. We designed a cost index as one of the possible functions to minimize the amplitude of the tendons' pulling force and to take into account its integral effect. We assumed that the efficiency of the transmission system remains constant throughout the exercise and that the friction losses are solely proportional to the cable tension.

$$J = \int_0^t \sum_i f_i^2 dt \ , \ i = 4,6 \tag{10}$$

We used genetic algorithms to find an optimal/sub-optimal solution due to the non-linearity and high complexity of the problem. For the genetic algorithm, we set the initial population of 50 individuals. Each one is characterized by its genes, which refer to optimization parameters. Moreover, each individual of the generation is evaluated by the cost function (Equation (10)), and then the next population is generated by using the *tournament selection* operator. The *elite count* and the *crossover fraction* were set to 40% and 0.5, respectively. We set the maximum number of iterations equal to $100\times(number\ of\ variables)$, whereas the *function tolerance* between two iterations was set to 10^{-6}. As a crossover function, we used the *intermediate* with the *ratio* parameter equal to 0.5. Finally, the mutation strategy adopted was the *adaptive feasible* due to the presence of constraints and the possibility of exploring the solution space with a random direction of the mutation process.

Before starting the optimization procedure, we set the values of the known parameters to $R_{3f} = 0.075$ m, $R_{5d} = 0.045$ m, $a_{3d} = \frac{a_3}{2}$, $a_{3h} = \frac{a_3}{8}$, $a_{3v} = \frac{a_3}{2}$. Moreover, the physical limit of the parameters became a constraint for the optimization variable. The optimization converged by proving the parameters in Table 2.

As a result, the effect of decreasing parameter R_6 results in an increase in force f_3 and a decrease in f_2. Moreover, the parameter a_{6d} tends to be equal to the upper limit, i.e., the distance between the wrist and the center of the hand. The parameter a_{6u} tends to be as small as possible and thus as close as possible to the wrist, while parameters R_6 and R_{5u} coincide with their own upper limits.

Lastly, it is convenient to have R_{3f}, R_{5d}, d_{5d}, and d_{5u} as large as possible.

The exosuit modeled and simulated in the following subsections was set up by using the results of the presented optimization procedure for a medium size suit.

Table 2. Optimized parameters for the elbow and wrist for the three selected sizes.

Parameter Name	Small Size (m)	Medium Size (m)	Large Size (m)
a_{6d}	0.05	0.06	0.08
R_6	0.035	0.035	0.035
a_{6u}	0.01	0.01	0.01
R_{5u}	0.05	0.05	0.05
d_{5d}	0.23	0.26	0.3
R_{5d}	0.05	0.05	0.05
d_{5u}	0.3	0.3	0.38
R_{3f}	0.075	0.075	0.075

3.3. Exosuit Design

The design of the exosuit was conceived to merge soft and flexible materials—fabrics and plastic—to wrap around the human arm and transmit forces to its wearer's skeletal structure. The proposed design comprises three main modules: the shoulder harness, the forearm module, and the hand glove (see Figure 5a). Each proximal module transmits forces to its next distal one through a tendon transmission; thus, when the tendons are tensioned, an assistive torque is delivered to the joint between the two modules. To efficiently apply the forces to the forearm and the hand, we stiffened the two fabric modules with a flexible 3D-printed ABS structure. This solution has already been proven to be effective for the wrist soft exosuit in [14]. In more detail, the forearm module (see Figure 5b) comprises a forearm band made of fabric with a plastic shell sewn on to it. The shell has an ergonomic shape that matches the 3D scan of the forearm of a mannequin with a height of 1.75 m The shell has a threefold purpose: it distributes the pressure due to interaction forces on a larger zone of the forearm, it makes the transmission of forces effective, and it hosts the anchor points and the compact embedded electronics for the local sensors. The anchor points on the forearm are located on a small 3D-printed arch that connects the two sides of the shell. The arch is sewn on to a band that can be tightened around the user's forearm. The hand module (see Figure 5c) is composed of a glove with flexible and local reinforcements. The 3D-printed shell of the hand was conceived to be ergonomic and to not hinder hand closing/opening. An IMU is installed on the hand dorsum, from which data are retrieved via the embedded board on the forearm. The interaction forces between the exosuit and the user are collected by the compact load cells installed between the distal anchor points and the tendons. The proximal anchor point of the elbow joint is located on the shoulder harness at the level of the arm. Each tendon is wrapped around a pulley and is then routed in a Bowden sheath that is firmly connected between the proximal and distal anchor points.

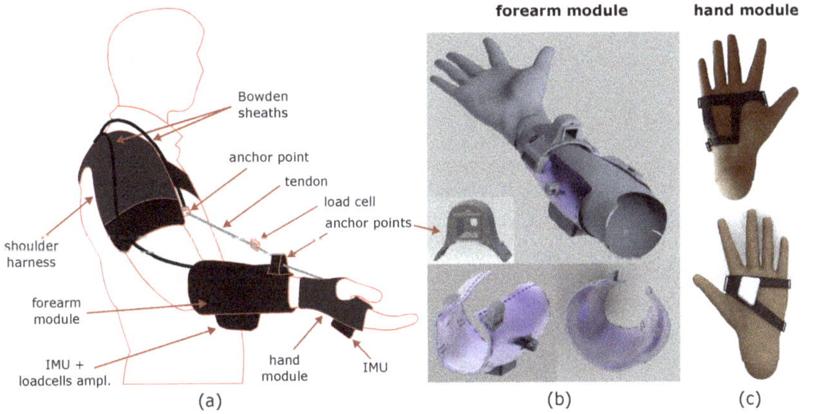

Figure 5. Proposed design of the exosuit. Sketch of the whole exosuit (**a**), views of the 3D-printed forearm module (**b**), and views of the 3D-printed hand module (**c**).

4. Results and Discussion

4.1. Validation of Simulations

The OpenSim model adopted in this study underwent prior verification conducted by Holzbaur et al. [31] and Saul et al. [32]. Considering that no significant changes were made to the model for these simulations, it was not necessary to perform any further verification to support its use in our experiments.

The virtual IMUs tracked the orientation of the experimental IMUs, with the root mean square errors detailed in Table 3 for both the unloaded and loaded conditions. It is noteworthy that an error associated with the thorax IMU was anticipated and, accordingly, its impact on the inverse kinematics was significantly reduced through down-weighting. Given the reliance on IMU-based measurements and inverse kinematic calculations, as described in [33], we maintain that the computed kinematics remain sufficiently dependable, particularly considering that the primary findings of this study are of a qualitative nature.

Table 3. Median and interquartile range (IQR) of the root mean square of the virtual and experimental IMUs' orientation error.

IMU Name	*noload* Condition (Median $\pm$ IQR)	*loaded* Condition (Median $\pm$ IQR)
Thorax IMU	0.498 ± 0.14	0.460 ± 0.15 rad
Scapula IMU	0.034 ± 0.01	0.032 ± 0.00 rad
Humerus IMU	0.085 ± 0.02	0.040 ± 0.02 rad
Radius IMU	0.170 ± 0.13	0.226 ± 0.17 rad
Hand IMU	0.156 ± 0.16	0.229 ± 0.18 rad

The alignment between the recorded electromyography (EMG) data of the specified muscles and the simulated muscle activities exhibits a satisfactory timing consistency for the majority of the targeted muscles, as depicted in Figures A1–A3. Additionally, shifts in simulated muscle activities during the lifting of a load resemble analogous patterns observed in the majority of EMG measurements taken during the load-lifting task. This correspondence indicates the consistency between the simulated and observed muscle responses during load-related activities.

As both simulated muscle activities and EMG measurements of the muscles are prone to different errors [32,41,42], they should be compared in light of these error sources. First of all, it should be noted that recorded EMG signals are subject to delay, and this must be taken into account when comparing electromyography data with simulated activity data [42]. Second, since the EMG measurements were normalized using the voluntary maximum contractions of each subject, it was not expected that the amplitudes would be similar between simulation and EMG due to the inherent variability that is associated with this normalization. Instead, we expected to observe similar trends in the amplitude of muscle activities when comparing *noload* to *loaded* conditions. Further, the static optimization method computes the muscle activation under the assumption of inextensible tendons and does not take into account the contribution of the parallel elastic elements of the muscles, which can result in differences between simulation-based muscle activities and measured EMG data. Lastly, the kinematic tracking error results in arm motions that are slightly different to the motions of the arm during the experiments, which may also be a reason for the difference between the simulations and experiments.

The ratios of RMS and peak torque provided by reserve actuators to the net joint moment across degrees of freedom and simulations were 17.74% and 5.84%, respectively, for the *noload* condition, while the ratios were 2.54% and 9.71% for the *loaded* condition. These ratios for the assisted subjects were 0.075% and 0.28%, which is expected, as exosuit actuators provide the required torques to the joints of interest with a lower penalization cost.

Although most of these values are higher than the ratio recommended by Hicks et al. [42], the reserve actuators do not exceed the recommended torques by OpenSim. Although the ratio of the reserve actuator to the joint moment was high in the hand and wrist, a comparison of the muscle activities to EMG measurements demonstrated a similar onset and offset timing; additionally, further analyses of these reserve torques show that most of these torques are injected to satisfy the imposed constraints in the model. The kinematic uncertainty was another cause of the high ratio between the reserve torque and joint moments (e.g., a high wrist deviation would result in a small constraint violation and an injection of force via the wrist deviation ligament, which was compensated for by the torque provided by the reserve actuator of the wrist deviation coordinate). Considering the good agreement of timings between simulated muscular activities and EMG measurements, it was concluded that the contribution of the reserve actuators would not significantly affect the conclusions of this study.

4.2. Exosuit Performance

Through an evaluation of the cumulative energy expended by the muscles, it became evident that the elbow–wrist exosuit effectively reduces the overall energy expenditure of the arm during lifting activities. Further analysis of the muscular energy expenditure within each joint demonstrates the exosuit's indirect support for shoulder joints while assisting the elbow and wrist. Moreover, the analysis reveals an increase in energy consumption for the muscles encircling the wrist joint due to the assistance torque provided to this joint, as visually presented in Figure 6. To optimize muscle energy expenditure across the entire arm muscle group, it may be advantageous to enhance the activity of select muscles, as the optimization process encompasses a set of muscles and actuators. Consequently, an increase in the activity of certain muscles and the associated higher energy expenditure within the wrist-contributing muscles can yield favorable optimization outcomes by reducing the overall energy consumption of the arm's muscles. This behavior aligns with findings from simulation-based investigations involving assistive devices [18,20,21].

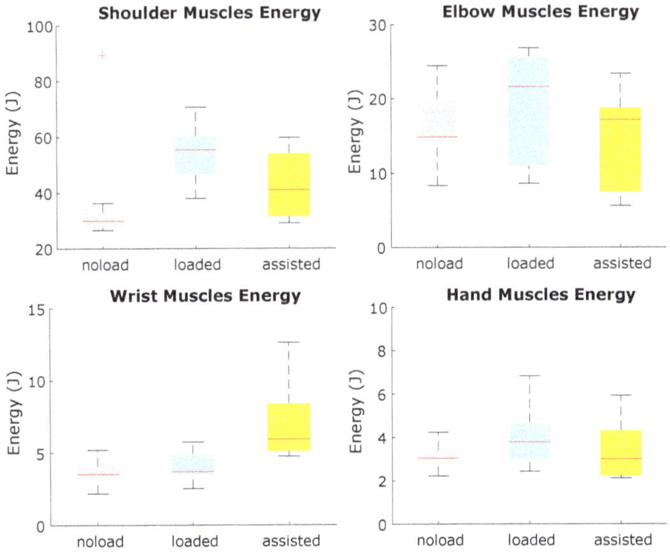

Figure 6. Energy consumption of muscles contributing to joint motions during *noload*, *loaded*, and assisted conditions.

Although the elbow and wrist actuators exert a similar range of force with 266.50 ± 74.59 and 155.91 ± 68.06 N, the actuating speed range of the elbow actuator (0.17 ± 0.06 rad/s) is relatively higher than that of wrist actuator (0.09 ± 0.02 rad/s). In turn, this results in increased mechanical work on the elbow actuator and an enhanced level of assistance to the elbow joint. Quantitatively, the mean range of power delivered by the elbow actuator is 7.18 ± 4.66 W, while the wrist actuator delivers power with a mean range of 3.13 ± 1.41 W throughout arm motion. As can be seen from the representative profiles of the exosuit in Figure 7, the qualitative force, speed, and power profiles are in accordance with the quantitative analysis of the performance of the exosuit.

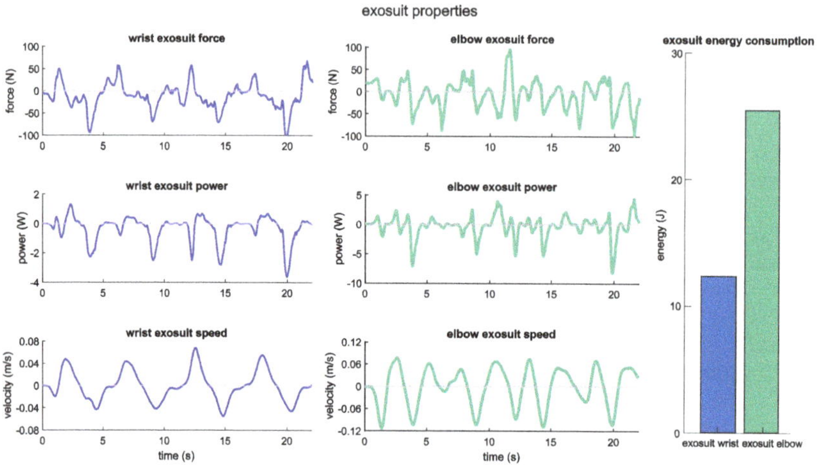

Figure 7. Exosuit force, speed, and power profiles for a representative subject.

4.3. Lifting Load Effect on Arm Kinematics and Dynamics

Since subjects were instructed to follow the visual cues during the experiments for both *noload* and *loaded* conditions, the range of motion of coordinates and the kinematics of the joints were similar during arm lifting with and without a load. While the joints are expected to have similar kinematics, the speeds of the joints differ considerably. Comparing the speed of joints indicates that shoulder elevation and rotation coordinates have slowed down by 0.49 ± 0.38 and 0.45 ± 1.07 rad/s. Furthermore, the wrist joint speed has been reduced by 0.39 ± 0.42 and 0.27 ± 0.26 rad/s in wrist flexion and deviation, respectively. Lastly, the elbow flexion and radioulnar pronation/supination speed reduced less than other joints by 0.25 ± 0.48 and 0.17 ± 0.20 rad/s, respectively. The root mean square of joint kinematics is shown in Figure 8 for lifting with and without a hand-held load which confirms the discussed results on the effect of lifting a load on the kinematics and speed of the arm. Additionally, the kinematic and speed profiles of joints are shown in Figures A4 and A5 for a representative subject.

It should be noted that there is significant within-subject variation while performing the task; as we only provided some visual landmarks during the experiments, this variation within the subjects while reaching the visual cues was expected.

It would be intuitively expected that lifting a load, which is carried out primarily in the sagittal plane, would result in greater joint moments in both the elevation and flexion degrees of freedom. The comparison of the joint moments of subjects under two experimental conditions confirms that the results are consistent with expectations, as represented in Figure 9.

The shoulder joint moment was the most affected, with the highest effect on the shoulder elevation coordinate. The median moment for the elevation moment increased from 8.43 (IQR, 4.50) to 18.22 (IQR, 9.2) N-m. The moment of the elbow flexion was also significantly increased from a median of 2.39 (IQR, 0.68) to 8.11 (IQR, 1.2) N-m. Moreover, the moment of wrist flexion, which performed virtually no work during lifting without a load, was significantly increased from 0.26 (IQR, 0.19) to 1.78 (IQR, 0.60) N-m.

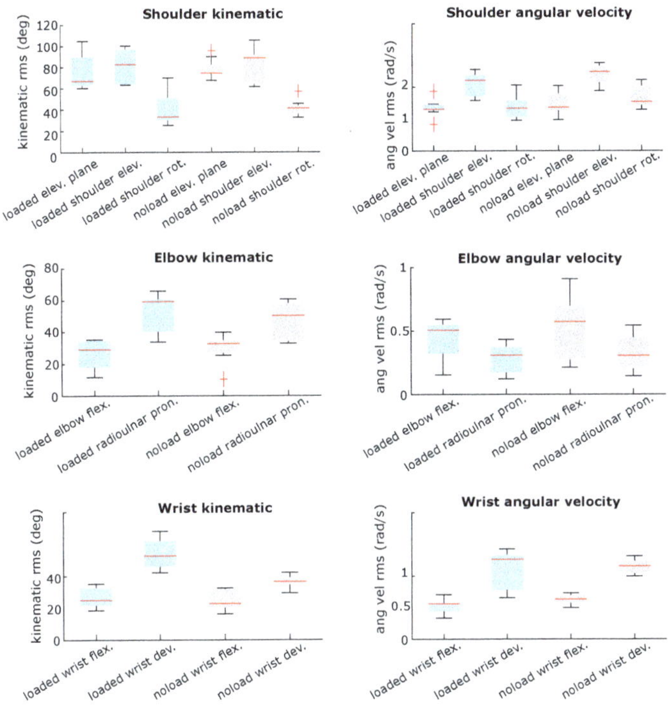

Figure 8. Effect of load lifting on the kinematics of an arm.

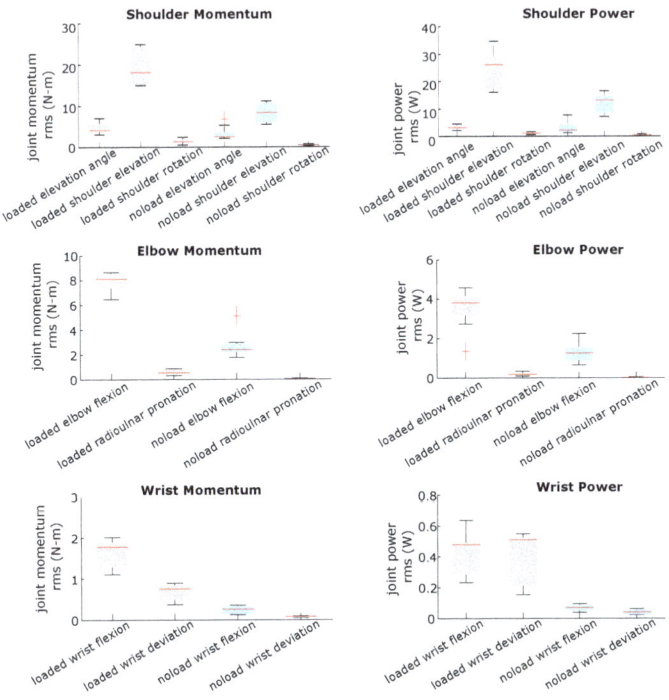

Figure 9. Effect of load lifting on the arm joint momentum and power.

As a result of analyzing the kinematics of the task under two different loading conditions, along with the joint moments, it appears that the joints are required to perform significantly more mechanical work to lift a load than lifting an arm without the additional load, with the greatest increase in mechanical work occurring in the sagittal plane. Based on the results of the kinematics and dynamics of these joints, it can be concluded that effective assistance for the elbow and wrist joints can reduce the work that is required to be performed by muscles in these joints.

4.4. Exosuit and Lifting Load's Effects on Muscle Activities

The elbow–wrist exosuit had a substantial impact on the muscle activity across various arm muscles. It is interesting to note that this effect extended beyond the muscles directly involved in elbow and wrist movements, affecting those associated with shoulder joint movements as well. Figure 10 visually depicts the muscle activation levels in selected arm muscles, with the data normalized as a percentage of their maximum activity (i.e., normalized to 1). These muscles were chosen based on their ability to generate force during the lifting task and their significant contribution to arm motion. Upon analysis of Figure 10, it is evident that lifting a load significantly alters the activation levels of these representative muscles throughout the arm. These findings suggest that shoulder muscles play a crucial role in compensating for the additional load during arm lifting.

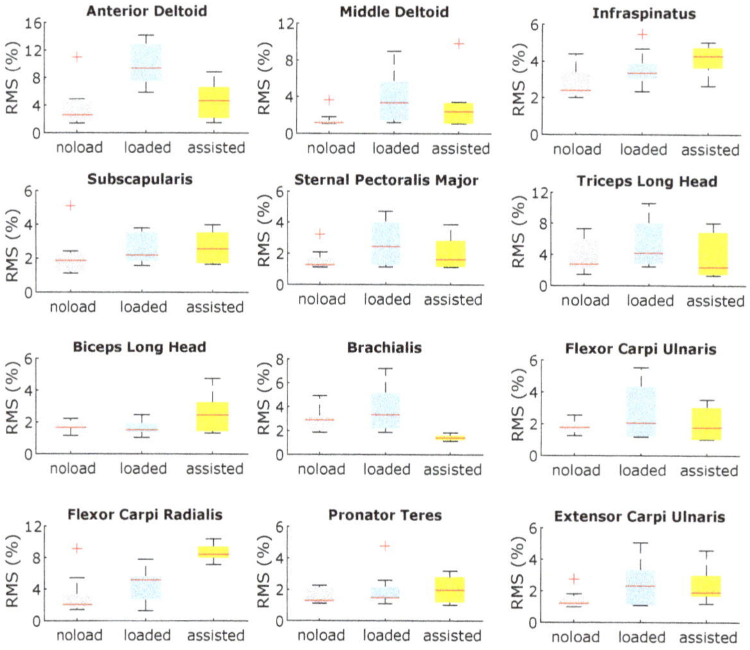

Figure 10. Effect of load lifting and assistance from the wrist–elbow exosuit on the magnitude of activation of arm representative muscles.

The exosuit primarily impacts muscle activities related to the elbow and shoulder joints by reducing their activation levels, while simultaneously increasing the activities of muscles associated with the wrist joint. In particular, the flexor carpi radialis muscle, a major contributor to wrist movement, experiences a significant increase in activity. This heightened activity of the flexor carpi radialis, coupled with the relatively minor effect of assistance on other wrist muscles, results in an overall increase in energy consumption among the muscles responsible for wrist motion.

Furthermore, the assistance provided by the exosuit to the arm alters the coordination of muscles involved in shoulder movements, leading to a more economical recruitment of shoulder muscles during the task. Upon closer examination, it is evident that the activity of the deltoid muscle notably decreases, with the required force being compensated by heightened activity in more energy-efficient muscles such as the infraspinatus and subscapularis.

4.5. Discussion

An evaluation of the exosuit's performance in providing assistance to the arm has shown that anchor points and therefore the moment arm available to the exosuit to provide moment play a significant role in the device's effectiveness. It could be inferred from the results that although the anchor points were optimized for a model of the arm, an optimization framework in which both the exosuit and musculoskeletal model are integrated, as proposed in [18], could possibly lead to better results than optimizing the anchor points on the dynamic model of the arm. Specifically, under the constraints of the design, we believe that the anchor point for the wrist may need to be selected with greater care in order to provide more mechanical activity to the joint.

In accordance with our results, the exosuit has the potential to affect the activity of muscles that do not span the assisted degree of freedom, as shown in studies using assistive devices on lower limbs [18,20,21]. It is important, however, to carefully examine this behavior in a study based on experimental data relating to the upper limb.

According to the simulations, the shoulder is also responsible for bearing an important portion of the added load during arm lifting. There is, however, a significant challenge in designing a portable and lightweight shoulder exosuit for assistance, as discussed in [43]. The results of our study, however, suggest that we may be able to reduce the load related to muscles spanning the shoulder during load handling by using an elbow exosuit which, due to its nature, is easier to design and control.

4.6. Study Limitation

The results of simulation-based studies of exosuits need to be interpreted in light of their limitations. As one of the major limitations of this method, the kinematics of the assisted subjects are assumed to remain unchanged from the experimental data. During musculoskeletal simulations, static optimization cannot account for kinematic adaptation due to provided assistance; thus, it is assumed that unassisted and assisted subjects have the same joint moment and kinematics. Similarly, as OpenSim cannot support changes in the dynamic properties of subjects, the exosuit considered for musculoskeletal simulations is assumed to be massless.

It is important to note that the musculoskeletal model and simulation methods in general have certain inherent limitations, as discussed in [32,42], which should be taken into account when interpreting the conclusions drawn from this study.

In addition to the limitations of the musculoskeletal simulations, the experimental method employed in this study is also prone to errors that could impact the outcome of the simulations. As it was discussed earlier, the motion data of subjects were collected using an IMU-based motion capture system, and the kinematics were estimated based on OpenSense. Both IMU-based motion capture systems and estimations of the kinematics are prone to drift and error, which has already been acknowledged.

Although EMG recordings of the muscles that have been used to validate the musculoketal simulation are considered the ground truth for the validity of simulations, these measurements are highly sensitive to the placement of the sensor and other environmental effects and therefore, there is a high within-subject variation while measuring them.

Another point to be considered when interpreting the specific results of this work is the small size of the dataset used for calibrating the muscular activation model. Here, the focus of the study was to provide a comprehensive methodology for modeling and simulating the effect of an upper limb exosuit, and hence guiding its design parameters. To validate the specific results obtained in the simulation, a larger dataset is needed to meet the statistical power requirements [44]. Therefore, we used the obtained simulation results to qualitatively evaluate the effect of the exosuit on the musculoskeletal model of the arm and still showed interesting trends in the adopted design solution that were not obvious before.

5. Conclusions

This work presented a framework for the design and simulation of upper limb exosuits, covering all the developmental steps from modeling to optimization and simulation. Although focused on the design of an elbow–wrist exosuit, this framework represents a comprehensive methodology suitable for the design and simulation of other upper-limb-actuated exosuits. The complexity of the upper limb musculoskeletal system is here addressed both through a kinematic model, developed to design and optimize the exosuit layout, and through a complex musculoskeletal model of the upper limbs, developed to simulate device operation and its impact on the muscular activation of the user. Taking into account such a higher level of complexity of the upper limbs is the main advantage of this method with respect to other works adopting a simplified model depending on the actuated DOFs of the developed device.

The proposed framework can be generalized to other soft exoskeleton designs, even though we studied a wrist–elbow exosuit as a case study to contextualize the design process. Different designs can involve other segments (i.e., the shoulder) and in particular other assisted tasks, therefore changing the optimization and the load simulation results. In the developed method, the first step is the implementation of the analytical kinematic model of the arm, which can be transferred to the design of other upper limb exoskeletons, and the definition of the actuated joints and target trajectories. With the proposed approach, optimized anchor points of the soft exoskeleton were found. In the scope of the presented load-lifting task, the minimum jerk trajectory was adopted as the cost function criterion. Then, a musculoskeletal model was developed to simulate the effects of the exosuit on the user, considering all the different muscle units affecting the shoulder, elbow, and wrist. The purpose of this method is to obtain a well-calibrated and comprehensive musculoskeletal model of the user for the given task and then to simulate the effect of the exoskeleton before its actual implementation. The calibration experimental procedure has to be performed based on the desired task, although it is usable for different exoskeleton designs and anchor point optimization procedures. In order to better simulate real muscular activation, the calibration procedure uses experimental EMG and IMU data. Then, the final simulations with the musculoskeletal model can evaluate the effects of the exosuit activation at the level of the different muscle units, and the results can be compared with the unassisted condition. Interestingly, it emerges that not only obvious body segments and muscle units are affected by the exoskeleton activation, but also muscle units in other body districts (i.e., the shoulder) and on other dimensional axes than the planar task trajectories. These effects would not emerge through a simplified simulation reduced to the spatial and joint dimensions of the task. While on the one hand, the obtained model provides interesting insights into the effect of exoskeleton assistance and allows for evaluations at the design stage before prototype implementation, on the other hand, the results have to be considered from a qualitative perspective. Due to the complexity of the model, calibration, and other estimated factors, it is not expected that the model will resemble the precise quantitative behavior of the final prototype.

Together with the optimized layout of the anchor points, we provide a possible implementation of an exosuit at the level of CAD design in order to contextualize the approach within a real use case and its possible implementation. Further development in this direction includes testing a working prototype in order to compare experimental data with simulations. While it is unreasonable to expect a close matching between the results of musculoskeletal simulations and data collected from human-in-the-loop evaluations due to a number of limitations intrinsic to a complex simulation process as discussed above, the use of a more refined model and calibration can reduce this gap. The presented musculoskeletal simulation method has the considerable advantages of providing design guidelines and capturing trends, allowing for a systematic analysis of the consequences of various design decisions before their real-world implementation.

Author Contributions: Conceptualization, A.K.B., D.C., A.F. and D.L.; methodology, A.K.B., D.C., A.F. and D.L.; software, A.K.B. and D.C.; validation, A.K.B. and D.C.; formal analysis, A.K.B., D.C. and D.L.; investigation, A.K.B., D.C., A.F. and D.L.; resources A.F. and D.L.; data curation, A.K.B., D.C. and D.L.; writing—original draft preparation, A.K.B., D.C. and D.L.; writing—review and editing, A.K.B., D.C., A.F. and D.L.; visualization, A.K.B., D.C. and D.L.; supervision, D.C. and A.F.; project administration A.F.; funding acquisition, A.F. All authors have read and agreed to the published version of the manuscript.

Funding: This research was funded by project SUN, funded from the European Union's Horizon Europe research and innovation program under grant agreement No 101092612

Institutional Review Board Statement: This study was approved by the Board of Ethics of the Scuola Superiore Sant'Anna of Pisa, Italy on 26 March 2021 https://www.santannapisa.it/en/university/board-ethics, ID 152021.

Informed Consent Statement: Informed consent was obtained from all subjects involved in the study.

Data Availability Statement: The raw data supporting the conclusion of this article can be made available by the authors upon request.

Acknowledgments: We thank Edoardo Corsi for their precious help in the modeling of the human arm and for the design of the anchor point optimization procedure.

Conflicts of Interest: The authors declare that the research was conducted in the absence of any commercial or financial relationships that could be construed as potential conflicts of interest.

Appendix A. Simulated Muscle Activities and Measured Electromyography of a Representative Subject under *noload* and *loaded* Conditions

The figures presented herein illustrate a comparative analysis between the simulated muscle activities and the electromyographic (EMG) data obtained experimentally for the targeted muscles. These figures aim to compare the timing of muscle activations between the measured EMG data and the simulated muscles. Additionally, the figures compare the changes in muscular activities between no-load and loaded conditions for both EMG and simulated muscle activities.

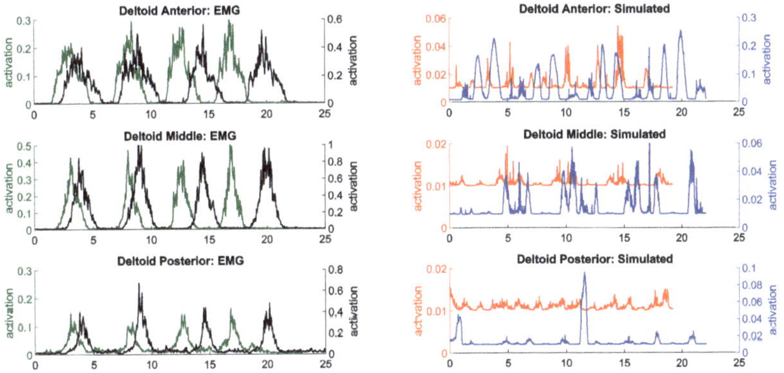

Figure A1. *Cont.*

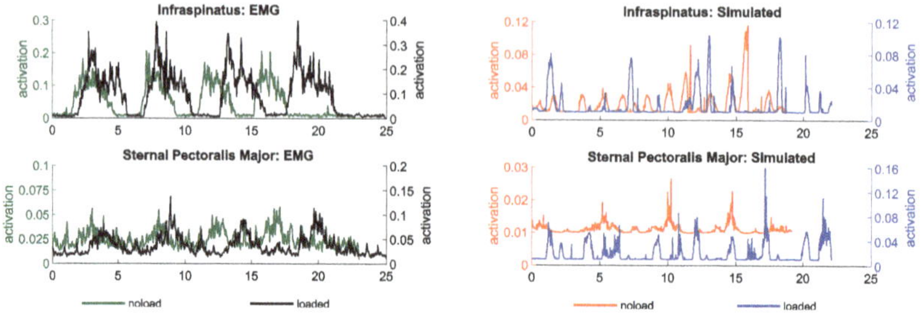

Figure A1. Simulated muscle activities and measured electromyography of muscles contributing to shoulder motion in *noload* and *loaded* conditions.

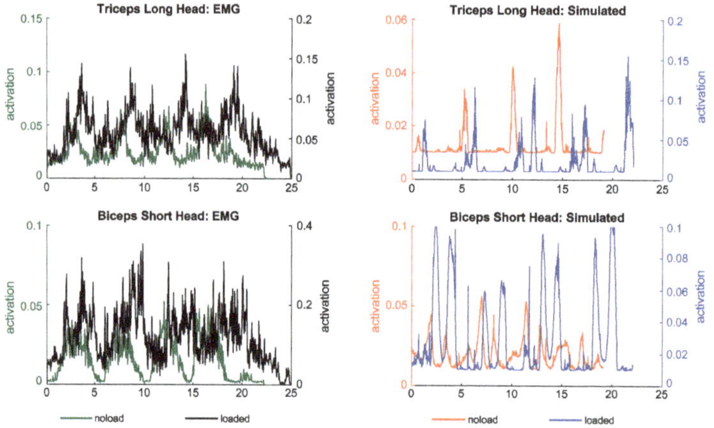

Figure A2. Simulated muscle activities and measured electromyography of muscles contributing to elbow and radioulnar motions in *noload* and *loaded* conditions.

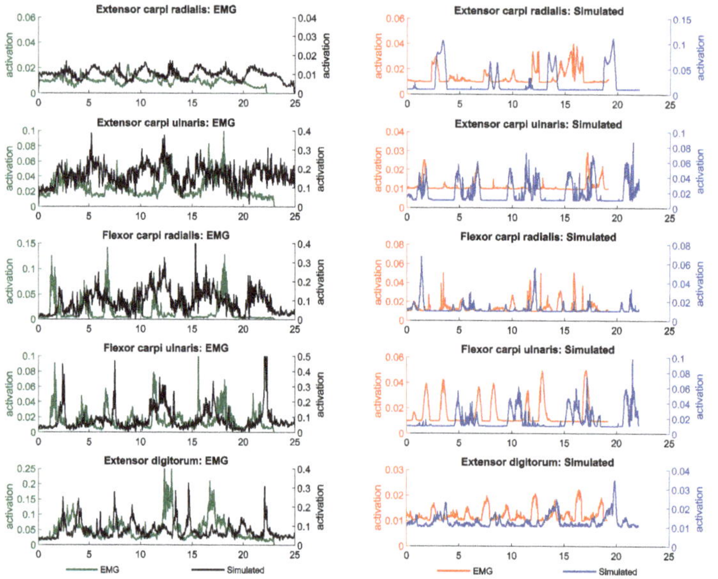

Figure A3. Simulated muscle activities and measured electromyography of muscles contributing to wrist motion in *noload* and *loaded* conditions.

Appendix B. Kinematic and Speed Profiles of a Representative Subject's Joints under *noload* and *loaded* Conditions

The following figures illustrate the kinematic and speed profiles of upper limb joints for a representative subject during arm lifting, with and without the additional load of holding a weight in their hand. These figures aim to offer insight into the kinematic variations during arm lifting under different load conditions. Specifically, they demonstrate how the kinematics of a representative subject differ between the two loading conditions.

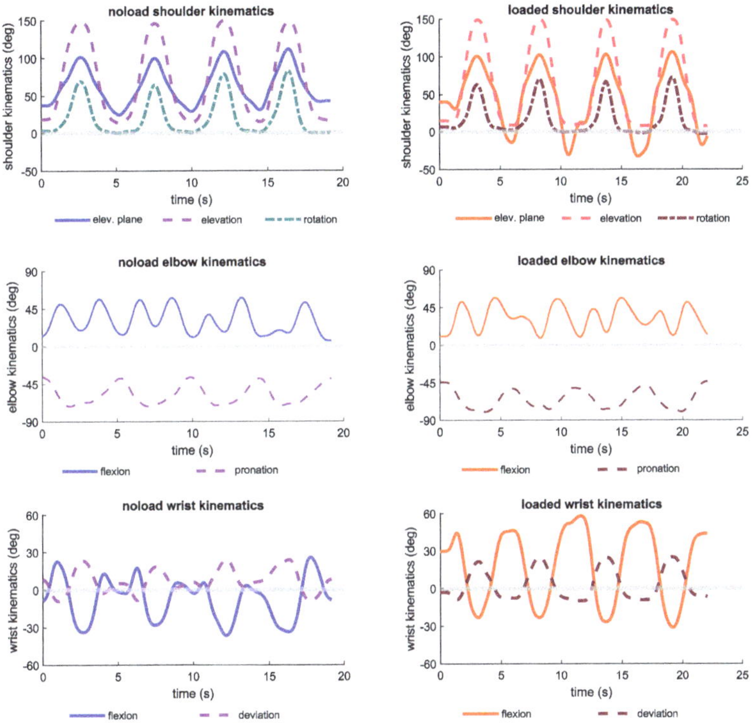

Figure A4. Kinematic profiles of shoulder, elbow, and wrist joints during *noload* and *loaded* conditions.

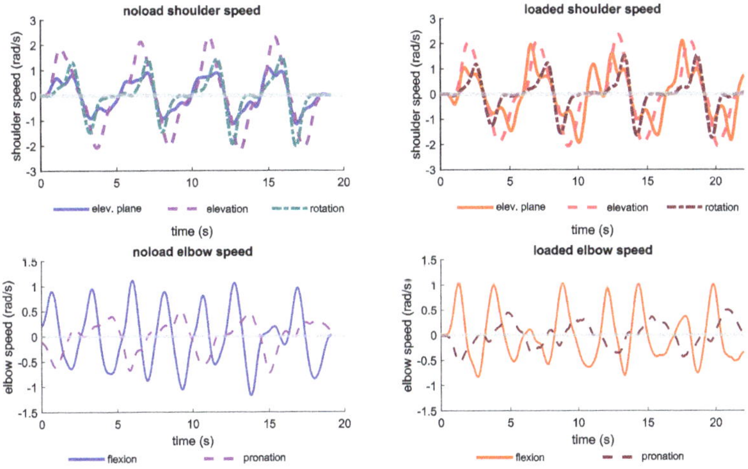

Figure A5. *Cont.*

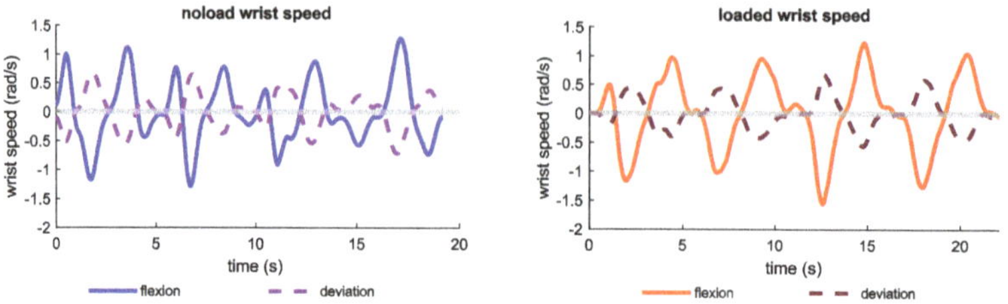

Figure A5. Speed profiles of shoulder, elbow, and wrist joints during *noload* and *loaded* conditions.

References

1. Gull, M.A.; Bai, S.; Bak, T. A review on design of upper limb exoskeletons. *Robotics* **2020**, *9*, 16. [CrossRef]
2. van Ommeren, A.L.; Smulders, L.C.; Prange-Lasonder, G.B.; Buurke, J.H.; Veltink, P.H.; Rietman, J.S. Assistive technology for the upper extremities after stroke: Systematic review of users' needs. *JMIR Rehabil. Assist. Technol.* **2018**, *5*, e10510. [CrossRef] [PubMed]
3. Xiloyannis, M.; Alicea, R.; Georgarakis, A.M.; Haufe, F.L.; Wolf, P.; Masia, L.; Riener, R. Soft robotic suits: State of the art, core technologies, and open challenges. *IEEE Trans. Robot.* **2021**, *38*, 1343–1362. [CrossRef]
4. Simpson, C.; Huerta, B.; Sketch, S.; Lansberg, M.; Hawkes, E.; Okamura, A. Upper extremity exomuscle for shoulder abduction support. *IEEE Trans. Med. Robot. Bionics* **2020**, *2*, 474–484. [CrossRef]
5. O'Neill, C.T.; Phipps, N.S.; Cappello, L.; Paganoni, S.; Walsh, C.J. A soft wearable robot for the shoulder: Design, characterization, and preliminary testing. In Proceedings of the 2017 International Conference on Rehabilitation Robotics (ICORR), London, UK, 17–20 July 2017; IEEE: Piscataway, NJ, USA, 2017; pp. 1672–1678.
6. Georgarakis, A.M.; Xiloyannis, M.; Wolf, P.; Riener, R. A textile exomuscle that assists the shoulder during functional movements for everyday life. *Nat. Mach. Intell.* **2022**, *4*, 574–582. [CrossRef]
7. Lessard, S.; Pansodtee, P.; Robbins, A.; Trombadore, J.M.; Kurniawan, S.; Teodorescu, M. A soft exosuit for flexible upper-extremity rehabilitation. *IEEE Trans. Neural Syst. Rehabil. Eng.* **2018**, *26*, 1604–1617. [CrossRef] [PubMed]
8. O'Neill, C.; Proietti, T.; Nuckols, K.; Clarke, M.E.; Hohimer, C.J.; Cloutier, A.; Lin, D.J.; Walsh, C.J. Inflatable soft wearable robot for reducing therapist fatigue during upper extremity rehabilitation in severe stroke. *IEEE Robot. Autom. Lett.* **2020**, *5*, 3899–3906. [CrossRef]
9. Li, N.; Yang, T.; Yu, P.; Chang, J.; Zhao, L.; Zhao, X.; Elhajj, I.H.; Xi, N.; Liu, L. Bio-inspired upper limb soft exoskeleton to reduce stroke-induced complications. *Bioinspiration Biomim.* **2018**, *13*, 066001. [CrossRef]
10. Proietti, T.; O'Neill, C.; Gerez, L.; Cole, T.; Mendelowitz, S.; Nuckols, K.; Hohimer, C.; Lin, D.; Paganoni, S.; Walsh, C. Restoring arm function with a soft robotic wearable for individuals with amyotrophic lateral sclerosis. *Sci. Transl. Med.* **2023**, *15*, eadd1504. [CrossRef] [PubMed]
11. Xiloyannis, M.; Chiaradia, D.; Frisoli, A.; Masia, L. Physiological and kinematic effects of a soft exosuit on arm movements. *J. Neuroeng. Rehabil.* **2019**, *16*, 1–15. [CrossRef]
12. Thalman, C.M.; Lam, Q.P.; Nguyen, P.H.; Sridar, S.; Polygerinos, P. A novel soft elbow exosuit to supplement bicep lifting capacity. In Proceedings of the 2018 IEEE/RSJ International Conference on Intelligent Robots and Systems (IROS), Madrid, Spain, 1–5 October 2018; IEEE: Piscataway, NJ, USA, 2018; pp. 6965–6971.
13. Nassour, J.; Zhao, G.; Grimmer, M. Soft pneumatic elbow exoskeleton reduces the muscle activity, metabolic cost and fatigue during holding and carrying of loads. *Sci. Rep.* **2021**, *11*, 12556. [CrossRef] [PubMed]
14. Chiaradia, D.; Tiseni, L.; Xiloyannis, M.; Solazzi, M.; Masia, L.; Frisoli, A. An assistive soft wrist exosuit for flexion movements with an ergonomic reinforced glove. *Front. Robot. AI* **2021**, *7*, 595862. [CrossRef] [PubMed]
15. Choi, H.; Kang, B.B.; Jung, B.K.; Cho, K.J. Exo-wrist: A soft tendon-driven wrist-wearable robot with active anchor for dart-throwing motion in hemiplegic patients. *IEEE Robot. Autom. Lett.* **2019**, *4*, 4499–4506. [CrossRef]
16. Nam, C.; Rong, W.; Li, W.; Cheung, C.; Ngai, W.; Cheung, T.; Pang, M.; Li, L.; Hu, J.; Wai, H.; et al. An exoneuromusculoskeleton for self-help upper limb rehabilitation after stroke. *Soft Robot.* **2022**, *9*, 14–35. [CrossRef] [PubMed]
17. Proietti, T.; O'Neill, C.; Hohimer, C.J.; Nuckols, K.; Clarke, M.E.; Zhou, Y.M.; Lin, D.J.; Walsh, C.J. Sensing and control of a multi-joint soft wearable robot for upper-limb assistance and rehabilitation. *IEEE Robot. Autom. Lett.* **2021**, *6*, 2381–2388. [CrossRef]
18. KhalilianMotamed Bonab, A. Simulation Based Optimal Design of Exoskeletons to Reduce Metabolic Cost and Improve Energy Efficiency. Master's Thesis, Sabanci University, Istanbul, Turkiye, 2021.
19. Aftabi, H.; Nasiri, R.; Ahmadabadi, M.N. Simulation-based biomechanical assessment of unpowered exoskeletons for running. *Sci. Rep.* **2021**, *11*, 11846. [CrossRef] [PubMed]
20. Dembia, C.L.; Silder, A.; Uchida, T.K.; Hicks, J.L.; Delp, S.L. Simulating ideal assistive devices to reduce the metabolic cost of walking with heavy loads. *PLoS ONE* **2017**, *12*, e0180320. [CrossRef] [PubMed]
21. Uchida, T.K.; Seth, A.; Pouya, S.; Dembia, C.L.; Hicks, J.L.; Delp, S.L. Simulating ideal assistive devices to reduce the metabolic cost of running. *PLoS ONE* **2016**, *11*, e0163417. [CrossRef] [PubMed]

22. Joshi, S.; Beck, I.; Seth, A.; Della Santina, C. Minimalistic Soft Exosuit for Assisting the Shoulder via Biomechanics-Aware Optimization. In Proceedings of the 2022 IEEE-RAS 21st International Conference on Humanoid Robots (Humanoids), Ginowan, Japan, 28–30 November 2022; IEEE: Piscataway, NJ, USA, 2022; pp. 667–673.
23. Vo, T.E.; Jhangiani, R.; Robbins, A.; Elor, A. Designing user-specific soft robotic wearable muscular interfaces with iterative simulation. In Proceedings of the 2020 IEEE International Conference on Smart Computing (SMARTCOMP), Bologna, Italy, 14–17 September 2020; IEEE: Piscataway, NJ, USA, 2020; pp. 253–255.
24. Lamers, E.P.; Zelik, K.E. Design, modeling, and demonstration of a new dual-mode back-assist exosuit with extension mechanism. *Wearable Technol.* **2021**, *2*, e1. [CrossRef]
25. Sambhav, R.; Jena, S.; Chatterjee, A.; Bhasin, S.; Santapuri, S.; Kumar, L.; Muthukrishnan, S.P.; Roy, S. An integrated dynamic closed loop simulation platform for elbow flexion augmentation using an upper limb exosuit model. *Front. Robot. AI* **2022**, *9*, 768841. [CrossRef]
26. Bardi, E.; Ambrosini, E.; Pirelli, A.; Pedrocchi, A.; Braghin, F.; Covarrubias, M.; Gandolla, M. Upper limb exosuit cable routing optimization. In Proceedings of the 2022 International Conference on Rehabilitation Robotics (ICORR), Rotterdam, The Netherlands, 25–29 July 2022; IEEE: Piscataway, NJ, USA, 2022; pp. 1–6.
27. Noei, V.; Lakany, H. Analysis of movement of an elbow joint with a wearable robotic exoskeleton Using OpenSim software. In Proceedings of the 2022 44th Annual International Conference of the IEEE Engineering in Medicine & Biology Society (EMBC), Glasgow, UK, 11–15 July 2022; pp. 4342–4345. [CrossRef]
28. Bonab, A.K.; Leonardis, D.; Frisoli, A.; Chiaradia, D. Modeling, Optimization, and Musculoskeletal Simulation of Elbow-Wrist Exosuit. In Proceedings of the 2023 21st International Conference on Advanced Robotics (ICAR), Abu Dhabi, United Arab Emirates, 5–8 December 2023; pp. 460–466. [CrossRef]
29. Seth, A.; Hicks, J.L.; Uchida, T.K.; Habib, A.; Dembia, C.L.; Dunne, J.J.; Ong, C.F.; DeMers, M.S.; Rajagopal, A.; Millard, M.; et al. OpenSim: Simulating musculoskeletal dynamics and neuromuscular control to study human and animal movement. *PLoS Comput. Biol.* **2018**, *14*, e1006223. [CrossRef] [PubMed]
30. Delp, S.L.; Anderson, F.C.; Arnold, A.S.; Loan, P.; Habib, A.; John, C.T.; Guendelman, E.; Thelen, D.G. OpenSim: Open-source software to create and analyze dynamic simulations of movement. *IEEE Trans. Biomed. Eng.* **2007**, *54*, 1940–1950. [CrossRef] [PubMed]
31. Holzbaur, K.R.; Murray, W.M.; Delp, S.L. A model of the upper extremity for simulating musculoskeletal surgery and analyzing neuromuscular control. *Ann. Biomed. Eng.* **2005**, *33*, 829–840. [CrossRef] [PubMed]
32. Saul, K.R.; Hu, X.; Goehler, C.M.; Vidt, M.E.; Daly, M.; Velisar, A.; Murray, W.M. Benchmarking of dynamic simulation predictions in two software platforms using an upper limb musculoskeletal model. *Comput. Methods Biomech. Biomed. Eng.* **2015**, *18*, 1445–1458. [CrossRef] [PubMed]
33. Al Borno, M.; O'Day, J.; Ibarra, V.; Dunne, J.; Seth, A.; Habib, A.; Ong, C.; Hicks, J.; Uhlrich, S.; Delp, S. OpenSense: An open-source toolbox for inertial-measurement-unit-based measurement of lower extremity kinematics over long durations. *J. Neuroeng. Rehabil.* **2022**, *19*, 22 . [CrossRef] [PubMed]
34. Gordon, C.C.; Churchill, T.; Clauser, C.E.; Bradtmiller, B.; McConville, J.T. Anthropometric Survey of US Army Personnel: Methods and Summary Statistics 1988. Technical Report; Anthropology Research Project Inc.: Yellow Springs, OH, USA, 1989.
35. Winter, D.A. *Biomechanics and Motor Control of Human Movement*; John Wiley & Sons: Hoboken, NJ, USA, 2009.
36. McFarland, D.C.; McCain, E.M.; Poppo, M.N.; Saul, K.R. Spatial dependency of glenohumeral joint stability during dynamic unimanual and bimanual pushing and pulling. *J. Biomech. Eng.* **2019**, *141*, 051006. [CrossRef] [PubMed]
37. Lin, Y.C.; Dorn, T.W.; Schache, A.G.; Pandy, M.G. Comparison of different methods for estimating muscle forces in human movement. *Proc. Inst. Mech. Eng. Part H J. Eng. Med.* **2012**, *226*, 103–112. [CrossRef] [PubMed]
38. Anderson, F.C.; Pandy, M.G. Static and dynamic optimization solutions for gait are practically equivalent. *J. Biomech.* **2001**, *34*, 153–161. [CrossRef] [PubMed]
39. Thelen, D.G.; Anderson, F.C.; Delp, S.L. Generating dynamic simulations of movement using computed muscle control. *J. Biomech.* **2003**, *36*, 321–328. [CrossRef]
40. Dempster, W.T.; Gaughran, G.R. Properties of body segments based on size and weight. *Am. J. Anat.* **1967**, *120*, 33–54. [CrossRef]
41. Clancy, E.A.; Morin, E.L.; Merletti, R. Sampling, noise-reduction and amplitude estimation issues in surface electromyography. *J. Electromyogr. Kinesiol.* **2002**, *12*, 1–16. [CrossRef] [PubMed]
42. Hicks, J.L.; Uchida, T.K.; Seth, A.; Rajagopal, A.; Delp, S.L. Is my model good enough? Best practices for verification and validation of musculoskeletal models and simulations of movement. *J. Biomech. Eng.* **2015**, *137*, 020905. [CrossRef] [PubMed]
43. Rinaldi, G., Tiseni, L.; Xiloyannis, M.; Masia, L.; Frisoli, A.; Chiaradia, D. Flexos: A Portable, SEA Based Shoulder Exoskeleton with Hyper-redundant Kinematics for Weight Lifting Assistance. In Proceedings of the 2023 IEEE World Haptics Conference (WHC), Delft, The Netherlands, 10–13 July 2023; pp. 252–258. [CrossRef]
44. Button, K.S.; Ioannidis, J.; Mokrysz, C.; Nosek, B.A.; Flint, J.; Robinson, E.S.; Munafò, M.R. Power failure: Why small sample size undermines the reliability of neuroscience. *Nat. Rev. Neurosci.* **2013**, *14*, 365–376. [CrossRef] [PubMed]

robotics

MDPI

Article

Reducing Hand Kinematics by Introducing Grasp-Oriented Intra-Finger Dependencies

Tomislav Bazina [1,2,3], Goran Mauša [1,3], Saša Zelenika [1,2,3] and Ervin Kamenar [1,2,3,*]

[1] University of Rijeka, Faculty of Engineering, Vukovarska 58, 51000 Rijeka, Croatia; tomislav.bazina@uniri.hr (T.B.); goran.mausa@uniri.hr (G.M.); szelenika@uniri.hr (S.Z.)
[2] University of Rijeka, Centre for Micro- and Nanosciences and Technologies, Radmile Matejčić 2, 51000 Rijeka, Croatia
[3] University of Rijeka, Center for Artificial Intelligence and Cybersecurity, Radmile Matejčić 2, 51000 Rijeka, Croatia
* Correspondence: ekamenar@uniri.hr; Tel.: +385-51-651-585

Abstract: Loss of hand functions, often manifesting in the form of weakness or spasticity from conditions like stroke or multiple sclerosis, poses challenges in performing activities of daily living (ADLs). The broad area of rehabilitation robotics provides the tools and knowledge necessary for implementing efficient restorative therapies. These therapies aim to improve hand functionality with minimal therapist intervention. However, the human hand evolved for various precision and power gripping tasks, with its intricate anatomy featuring a large number of degrees of freedom—up to 31—which hinder its modeling in many rehabilitation scenarios. In the process of designing prosthetic devices, instrumented gloves, and rehabilitation devices, there is a clear need to obtain simplified rehabilitation-oriented hand models without compromising their representativeness across the population. This is where the concept of kinematic reduction, focusing on specific grasps, becomes essential. Thus, the objective of this study is to uncover the intra-finger dependencies during finger flexion/extension by analyzing a comprehensive database containing recorded trajectories for 23 different functional movements related to ADLs, involving 77 test subjects. The initial phase involves data wrangling, followed by correlation analysis aimed at selecting 116 dependency-movement relationships across all grasps. A regularized generalized linear model is then applied to select uncorrelated predictors, while a linear mixed-effect model, with reductions based on both predictor significance and effect size, is used for modeling the dependencies. As a final step, agglomerative clustering of models is performed to further facilitate flexibility in tradeoffs in hand model accuracy/reduction, allowing the modeling of finger flexion extensions using 5–15 degrees of freedom only.

Keywords: robotic rehabilitation; grasp-oriented hand kinematics reduction; activities of daily living; dependency-movement relationship; hierarchical clustering

1. Introduction

The worldwide increasing occurrence of the hindrance of hand functions, often caused by conditions such as stroke or multiple sclerosis, poses challenges in performing activities of daily living (ADLs) and represents a growing societal challenge. Ensuring timely, frequent, and intensive administration of physical therapy, crucial for effective recovery, is challenging [1]. The recent literature suggests that utilizing robotic-assisted rehabilitation emerges as a viable solution to this issue, with minimal therapist interventions [2]. The human hand, characterized by its intricate anatomy featuring up to 31 degrees of freedom (DOFs) [3], evolved to perform various precision and power gripping tasks. However, designing prosthetic devices, instrumented gloves, and rehabilitation devices to mimic anthropomorphic hand features entirely is not feasible due to the high dimensionality of the kinematic problems, spatial constraints, and hand dexterity. Therefore, one of the primary challenges in designing hand robotic rehabilitation devices involves selecting appropriate movement subsets or grasp typologies to optimize the recovery of ADL. Kinematic models should incorporate the minimal possible number of DOFs while fully satisfying the intended functionality and possessing the capability to accurately predict grasping types essential for performing ADLs, such as opening a bottle, using a knife, or holding a pen [4].

To develop reduced and representative kinematic models, conducting research and comprehending hand kinematics through experimentally recorded hand movements is imperative [5]. In [6], the authors implemented a musculoskeletal model of the upper extremity, including the wrist, index finger, and thumb, while the authors in [7] extended the research to include other fingers, both using OpenSim [8]. Authors in [3] utilized the AnyBody Modeling System™ to implement a comprehensive model. The intention of the mentioned studies was primarily to present detailed hand models for comprehensive musculoskeletal research, rather than focusing on reducing the DOFs. In the studies [8,9], reduced kinematic models were presented. Still, they were based on a limited number of subjects, usually less than 10, while the considered grasps were divided into prismatic and circular types only. In [10], the authors developed a pneumatically driven soft robotic hand based on a kinematic model derived from experiments conducted on only six subjects. They relate proximal interphalangeal (PIP) and distal interphalangeal (DIP) joints linearly. In [11], the authors characterized fingertip trajectories during reach-and-grasp studies on 10 healthy subjects performing five different grasps. Using correlation analysis, they found the approximate linearity in the relationship between PIP and metacarpophalangeal (MCP), as well as DIP and PIP joint angles. However, they obtained a relatively low PIP–DIP slope of 0.3, compared to [9,10], which suggested a higher PIP–DIP slope of 2/3. In [12], the authors focused on hand model kinematic reductions using principal component analysis (PCA), but with six subjects grasping cylinder shapes only. The study conducted by [13] involved 22 subjects, which facilitated grouping 26 grasps with similar kinematics related to ADLs, and identifying five sparse hand synergies using PCA. In [14], 24 subjects participated in 24 ADLs, utilizing PCA with Varimax rotation to minimize the number of DOFs in each synergy, resulting in truly sparse synergies. Two core synergies associated with PIP and MCP finger joint flexions were identified. Conversely, Ref. [15] argues, based on data from six subjects grasping nine objects, that the commonly used PCA method in synergy detection fails to reveal sparse synergies, instead utilizing a combination of all available DOFs. Consequently, alternative methods such as l_1 regularization and sparse dictionary learning have been proposed.

The focus of this study is to present grasp-oriented intra-finger dependencies, aiming to obtain relatively accurate yet simple and applicable sparse models of human hand movements. If successfully developed, these models would enable the development of far more versatile and anthropomorphic robotic rehabilitation devices and prosthetic hands. For modeling joint dependencies during grasping, we utilized the largest known database of human hand movements [16], comprising synchronously collected values of joint angles in degrees [4]. These data encompass 77 test subjects performing 23 different functional movements (grasps) related to ADLs. Due to the variety of subjects and grasps present in the database, authors analyzing synergies using the same dataset and PCA approach [17] obtained 12 synergies to account for only 80% of the variability, a much higher number than presented in the recent literature. However, since each synergy is a linear combination of all available DOFs, implementing all 12 synergies for prosthetic or rehabilitation device design or control is a complex task. Thus, we attempted to complement the synergy-based approach by introducing simpler 1-to-1 joint dependency relations.

The first step of the approach involved decoupling each grasp into its constituent joint movements and focusing only on 16 finger joints performing flexion/extension. Due to the hand anatomy, these joints cover most of the hand's ranges of motion (ROM) [18]. Then, the dataset was prepared using summary statistics and joint anatomical ROM. We grouped the prepared constituent joint movements into pairwise intra-finger joint dependencies, followed by computing correlation matrices between the pairs belonging to each finger, to achieve an insight into possible relationships. Based on correlations, we identified 116 highly to very highly correlated dependency-movement relationships for modeling (i.e., motions belonging to certain grasps). Each relationship is modeled using a regularized and relaxed generalized linear model (GLM) [19] for uncorrelated predictor selection. The selected predictors are then used in a weighted linear mixed-effects model to include both subject random-effects and dependency fixed-effects. The models are further reduced using both predictor significance and effect size. Subsequently, we conducted agglomerative model clustering based on similarity to reduce the number of necessary models for kinematic reduction from 116 to the proposed 30. Finally, we synthesized the results by presenting the remaining independent DOFs for finger flexions/extensions during each of the 23 grasps.

Following the described approach, our study achieved several key contributions:

- We introduced refined procedures for data wrangling, generating a meticulously curated dataset for the comprehensive modeling and analysis of human hand movements.
- Our novel approach to modeling intra-finger dependency-movement relationships enabled the establishment of motion patterns for each dependency across all subjects. It generated interpretable and sparse, yet accurate, integrated models. Additionally, it significantly reduced the total number of DOFs involved in grasping for all investigated functional movements.
- Applying hierarchical model clustering enabled flexibility in reducing the number of models capable of describing all 116 identified dependencies with a desired error margin. Based on the similarity in coefficients, we proposed 30 such model clusters.

2. Materials and Methods

The analysis in the performed study is based on the publicly available NinaPro multimodal database [16], which comprises a large dataset of human hand movements [4]. It includes kinematic data from 77 healthy subjects acquired with a Cyberglove-II fitted with 22 resistive sensors. A linear relationship is assumed between the output and the measured angle for all the sensors. The experiment comprises two exercises: (1) basic movements of the fingers and (2) grasping and functional movements. In this chapter, we outline data wrangling procedures to curate the dataset, modeling methodology, and error metrics.

2.1. Data Relabeling

The dataset was released as part of three multimodal datasets, each with different sampling rates (DB1: 100 Hz, DB2: 2 kHz, and DB5: 200 Hz), including calibrated kinematic data from 27, 40, and 10 subjects, respectively [4]. It should be noted that both hand configurations and functional movements in the DB1 database needed to be relabeled ($2 \rightarrow 1$ and $3 \rightarrow 2$, respectively) due to incorrect numbering. Additionally, since several databases have been stitched together, the subject numbering does not coincide with that in DB9_Index [16], so it has also been relabeled. Forty different hand movements have been recorded, along with an additional rest position. Two exercises from [4] are included: Exercise B, labeled (1), and Exercise C, labeled (2).

Exercise B(1):

- 8 isometric and isotonic hand configurations;
- 9 basic movements of the wrist.

Exercise C(2):

- 23 grasping and functional movements (everyday objects).

In the original DB2 dataset, with subjects numbered 28 to 67, the movements for Exercise 2 (referred to as restimulus in the original dataset) had to be renumbered from 1. This was achieved by subtracting 17 from each exercise ID number. The cleaned data is saved for each subject and exercise in a separate *.parquet* file format (see Table 1 for identifiers).

Table 1. Identifier table for the cleaned dataset.

Subject	Laterality	Gender	Age	Height	Weight	Exercise	Movement	Repetition
1–77	Right Handed, Left Handed	Male, Female	22–45	150–192	44–105	1, 2	1–23	1–6

The cleaned data is then concatenated by rows into one file (*s1-77_e1-2.parquet*), consisting of 183,773,343 data points and 22 features containing joint angle values (joint names: Carpometacarpal (CMC), Metacarpophalangeal (MCP), Interphalangeal (IP), Proximal Interphalangeal (PIP), Distal Interphalangeal Joint (DIP), WRIST; finger numbers: 1...5; the notation "f" for flexion/extension, "a" for abduction), along with 9 identifier column, as shown in Table 1.

2.2. Data Preprocessing

The dataset is analyzed using Apache Spark 3.1 in conjunction with the tidyverse package [20] and its R interface, *sparklyr* [21]. It is important to note that the data preprocessing step is crucial, particularly given the inherent errors in this type of experimental data acquisition, which can result in certain data points representing anatomically impossible movements. In the first step, all not available (NA) values in the dataset are isolated, which leads to the conclusion that the abduction/adduction difference between the index and middle finger contains only NA values. In [4], it is mentioned that those measurements were not included due to sensor noise. Therefore, the MCP2_a column is also omitted in this study. In the resulting dataset, only distinct rows are retained. This decision is made due to the data being sampled over time without timestamps, where certain points were likely duplicated multiple times.

In the second step, only Exercise 2(C) is isolated because it contains grasps and functional movements. All abduction/adduction movements are dropped because they contain angle differences between two adjacent fingers, rather than an absolute finger deviation from the reference point. The rest position is also dropped, reducing the dataset to 25 columns and 50,866,742 rows.

The dataset is further grouped based on subject motion and joint angle. Boxplot data is then generated, including the number of observations (n), as well as the minimum, maximum, mean, median, 1st (Q1), and 3rd (Q3) quartiles. Additionally, the interquartile range (IQR) is calculated as the difference between the cutoff values for the lowest 25% (Q1) and the highest 75% (Q3). The boxplot data is presented at the subject level, disregarding different repetitions, but separately for each joint angle associated with a certain movement. The boxplot data for Exercise 2 are detailed in Table 2. Each subject's median joint angle is used to construct the boxplots in Figure 1a,b.

Table 2. Exercise 2 boxplot data explanation.

Movement	Joint Angles	Subject	Boxplot Data	
1	CMC1_f	1	n, min, max, mean, median, Q1, Q3, IQR	mean IQR, median of medians
1	CMC1_f	2	n, min, max, mean, median, Q1, Q3, IQR	
1	...	...	...	
1	MCP1	1	n, min, max, mean, median, Q1, Q3, IQR	mean IQR, median of medians
1	MCP1	2	n, min, max, mean, median, Q1, Q3, IQR	
1	...	...	...	
2	CMC1_f	1	n, min, max, mean, median, Q1, Q3, IQR	
...	...	...	...	

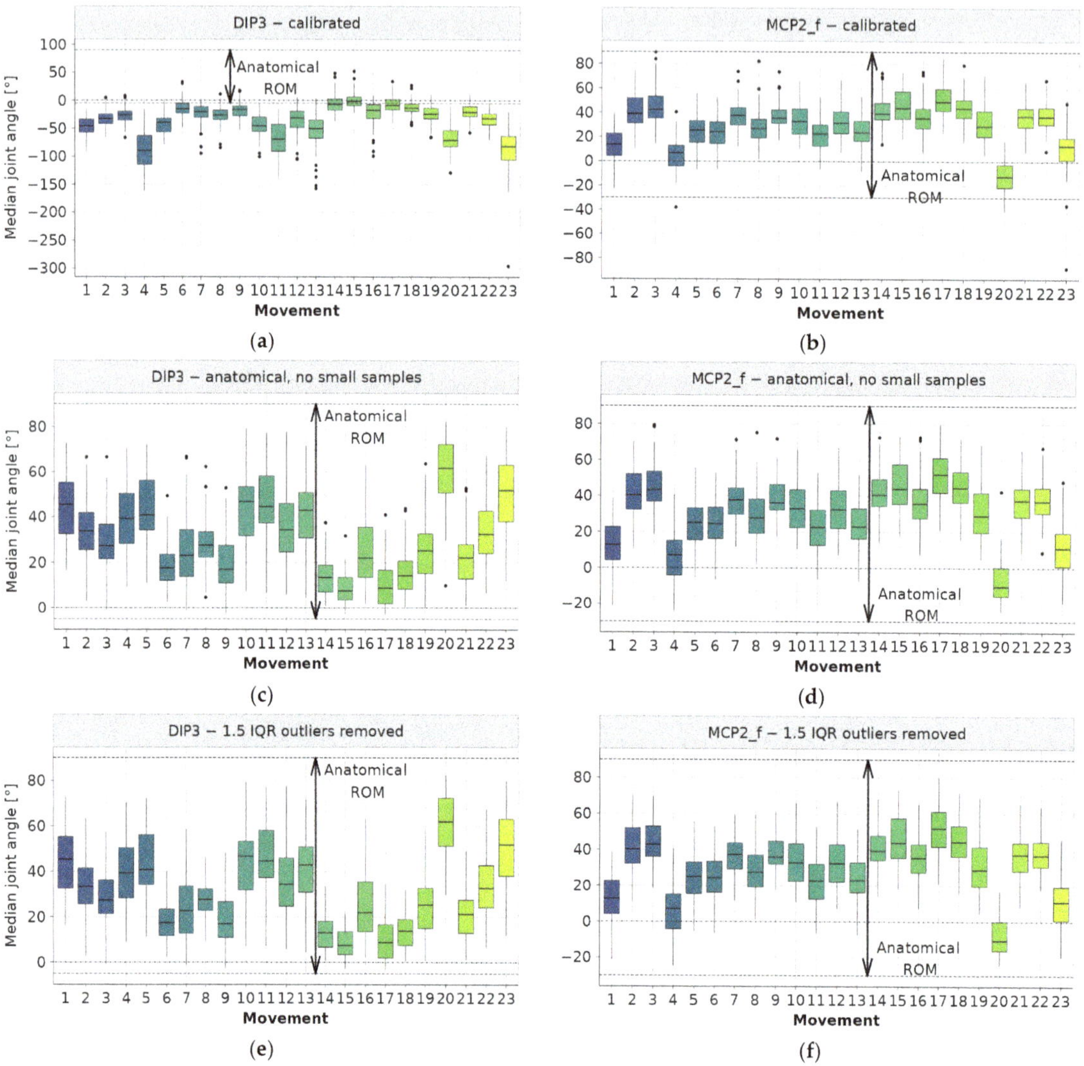

Figure 1. Example steps for joint angle data preprocessing (colors correspond to movements): (**a**) DIP3—calibrated data, (**b**) MCP2_f—calibrated data, (**c**) DIP3—filtered to anatomical ROM and small samples removed, (**d**) MCP2_f—filtered to anatomical ROM and small samples removed, (**e**) DIP3—outliers removed using iterative 1.5 IQR rule, (**f**) MCP2_f—outliers removed using iterative 1.5 IQR rule.

Only examples containing DIP3 and MCP2_f data are shown, while complete boxplots can be found in the main authors' GitHub repository [22]. From Figure 1a, it is evident that nearly all median joint angle values fall outside the anatomical angle range. Therefore, it can be concluded that a negative sign has been used for the DIP3 flexion angle. The same observation applies to CMC5, DIP4, and DIP5. The authors of the database [4] also stated that:

> *"DIP sensors provide reliable angles when a subject's hand size is large (i.e., when the glove properly fits the hand). They may provide partial results when the hand of the subject is small. Therefore, attention needs to be taken when using the information."*

The same restriction applies to this work. The range of median values for the other joint angles typically aligns with the anatomical range, as demonstrated by the MCP2_f example in Figure 1b. Upon examination of the diagram depicting median joint values for PIP3 and PIP4, it is observed that many measurements fall outside the anatomical range. However, this phenomenon is most likely attributed to sensor noise and hand anthropometrics [4].

The next preprocessing step is to obtain only "valid" data, that is, the data located inside the anatomical range. Therefore, in Figure 1c,d, the sign of the previously mentioned joint angles data is reversed, and all invalid values (i.e., those outside of anatomical ROM according to Table 3) are filled with NA values. The rationale behind filling invalid data with NA, instead of dropping the entire row (observation), is to conserve the data as much as possible for later inferences, since one noisy sensor reading does not imply that all other readings were noisy too.

Table 3. Anatomical ROM of digits [2,6,9].

Thumb—Finger 1 [°]			Fingers 2–4 [°]			Finger 5 [°]			
CMC1_f	MCP1	IP1	MCP_f	PIP	DIP	CMC5	MCP5_f	PIP5	DIP5
$-15 \div 50$	$-40 \div 45$	$-5 \div 75$	$-30 \div 90$	$-5 \div 120$	$-5 \div 90$	$0 \div 15$	$-30 \div 90$	$-5 \div 135$	$-5 \div 90$

The data for each joint angle is aggregated next, per joint type and motion, and the boxplot data are calculated. Then, the mean IQR, averaging all subject IQRs, is calculated to determine the angular range in which 50% of each joint movement is expected to occur (see Figure 1). Data filtering is performed due to the lack of diversification for proper modeling using the following criteria:

- If the sample size is too small ($n < 100$), fill with NA values;
- If a too-small part of the entire motion is captured ($IQR\ share = \frac{subject\ IQR}{mean\ IQR} < 0.5$), fill with NA values.

The first phase of filtering resulted in the removal of a large number of outlier values, as evident by comparing the example diagrams in Figure 1a–d. However, a significant number of outlier values still remain in the data, prompting the incorporation of a second elimination phase. This phase involves an iterative procedure, where the 1.5 IQR rule [23] for outlier detection is applied. Joint angle data is once again aggregated per joint type and movement, and medians per subject are used to calculate grouped IQR, as well as the 1st (Q1) and 3rd (Q3) quartiles. Subsequently, all subject median angles falling outside the range between Q1 − 1.5 IQR and Q3 + 1.5 IQR are deemed outliers and removed from the dataset. Data is processed through 6 iterations to remove all outliers, as shown in the examples in Figure 1e,f.

2.3. Data Analysis and Sampling

The representativeness of each subject in the entire dataset is also investigated using subject–movement contingency tables for each finger. A condensed table showing the distribution of observations across fingers and subjects is presented in Figure 2. The shape size represents the remaining number of movements (1–23) per subject and for each finger, while the shape fills denote the average number of observations per each movement. It is evident that a clear imbalance exists in the dataset. Specifically, the first 27 subjects, as well as subjects numbered 68–77, typically have up to 3000 observations per movement (including repetitions). In contrast, subjects 28–67, belonging to the second database, usually have between 20,000 and 60,000 observations per movement. This imbalance could pose challenges when using models based on the entire dataset without appropriate sampling strategies.

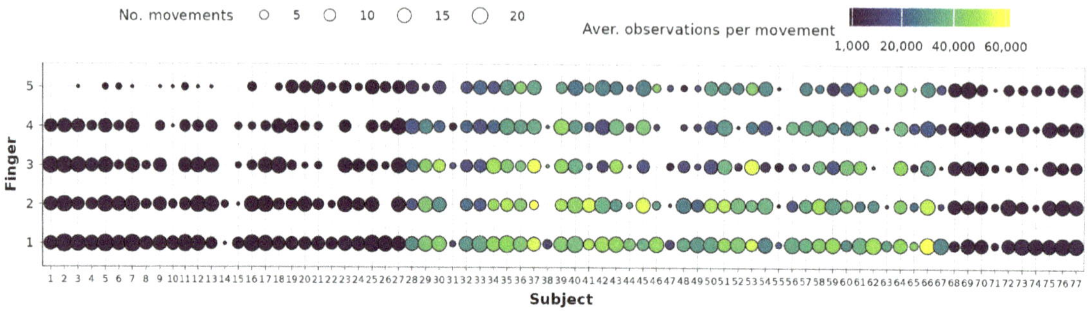

Figure 2. Subject–fingers contingency tables after data preprocessing.

Examining Figure 2 further, it is evident that in the case of certain subjects (e.g., subjects 14 and 38), a notable portion of the data was eliminated during earlier preprocessing stages. Additionally, due to the same reason, subjects 1–15 will have minimal impact on little-digit joint dependency modeling. To minimize the effect of unbalanced data and retain variability and generalization ability, it is therefore decided that dependencies will be observed on a repetition level, and each subject repetition will be used as a self-sufficient unit for data analyses.

For further analysis and modeling, a total of 18 intra-finger dependencies are identified, taking into account only 16 finger joints performing flexion/extension, as presented in Table 4. The dependencies are obtained as a combination of all joints comprising a single finger. For the movement basis, a joint closer to the root of the kinematic chain is always selected.

Table 4. Investigated inter-finger dependencies.

Thumb—Digit 1	Index—Digit 2	Middle—Digit 3	Ring—Digit 4	Little—Digit 5
MCP1—IP1 CMC1_f—MCP1 CMC1_f—IP1	MCP2_f—PIP2 MCP2_f—DIP2 PIP2—DIP2	MCP3_f—DIP3 MCP3_f—PIP3 PIP3—DIP3	MCP4_f—DIP4 MCP4_f—PIP4 PIP4—DIP4	CMC5—MCP5_f CMC5—DIP5 CMC5—PIP5 MCP5_f—DIP5 MCP5_f—PIP5 PIP5—DIP5

Correlation matrices, which serve as indicators of linearity, are generated for all flexion/extension joints belonging to the same finger, as well as for each motion, subject, and repetition separately, using the procedure outlined in Figure 3. It should be noted that 71,328 correlation coefficients (r) are obtained, ranging between -1 and 1, with between 56 and 358 coefficients present for each joint dependency. This provides, in the authors' opinion, sufficient statistical power to conclude the nature of the dependency. The significance level for the correlation coefficients was set to 5%.

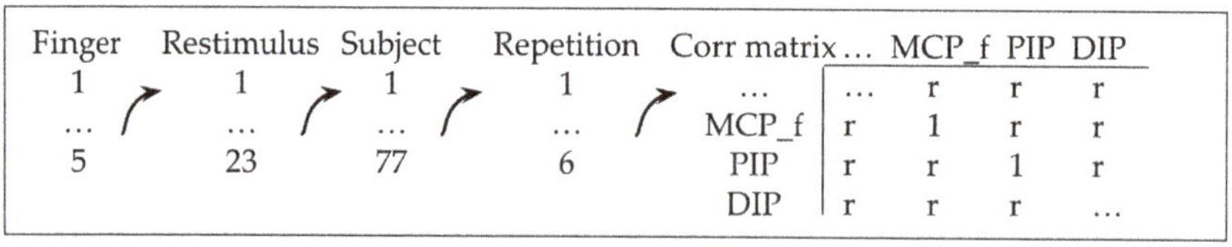

Figure 3. The procedure of obtaining correlation matrices.

Two examples of investigated intra-finger dependencies for the third and fifth digits are presented in Figure 4a,b. All obtained correlation coefficients related to a single finger dependency and a single movement are summarized using boxplots, and their median values are calculated. Only highly correlated dependencies (absolute median $r \geq 0.7$), identified using the recommendations from [24], are highlighted using a color map. The right diagram in Figure 4a,b shows boxplot examples with outliers removed using the iterative IQR rule, resulting in the removal of 4037 outlier values, while leaving 67,291 correlation coefficients. Complete diagrams for all fingers and movements can be found in the main authors' GitHub repository [22].

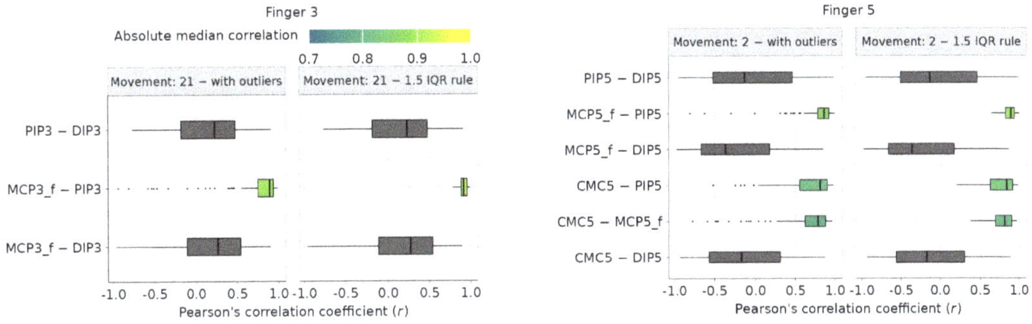

(**a**) (**b**)

Figure 4. Example of intra-finger correlation dependencies before and after 1.5 IQR outlier removal: (**a**) finger 3 dependencies during movement 21, (**b**) finger 5 dependencies during movement 2.

Next, only dependencies with an absolute median correlation coefficient greater than or equal to 0.7, highly and very highly correlated, per [24], are investigated. After visually inspecting the scatter plots, it is concluded that some repetitions only partially describe motion, lacking completeness. Two additional sampling methods, previously mentioned, are applied, but this time at the repetition level rather than the subject level:

- Repetitions with too-small ROM, compared to median dependency-movement, are discarded: $IQR\ share = \frac{repetition\ IQR}{median\ dependency - movement\ IQR} < 0.5$;
- Newly generated outlier values are removed using the iterative 1.5 IQR rule based on correlation coefficients.

The sampling yields 11,643 usable correlation coefficients. In Figure 5, the dependency-movement diagram assigns each point a median correlation coefficient, illustrating the grouping of highly correlated intra-finger dependencies per movement.

Out of 18 defined dependencies, 16 are correlated in at least 1 of the 23 movements. This leads to the conclusion that flexions PIP5—DIP5 and PIP4—DIP4 are not kinematically associated during any of the grasping movements present in the dataset. During movements 2 and 3, respectively, 10 and 11 dependencies are highly correlated. On the other hand, during movement 15, a high correlation is present only for the PIP2—DIP2 dependency. It can also be concluded that MCP flexion/extension is very frequently correlated with PIP flexion/extension for digits 3, 4, and 5, occurring in 18 to 20 out of 23 different movements. For the index finger, the same dependency is highly correlated in only 7 movements. Additionally, second-digit PIP2 and DIP2 flexion/extension are highly correlated in 19 movements. Also, it can be concluded that during thumb movement the incidence of intra-finger relationships is very rare, as indicated by their grouping at the bottom of the diagram in Figure 5. Only 5 relationships are revealed across 5 movements, making the thumb the most independent digit, agreeing with [11]. Overall, 116 dependency-movement relationships are therefore identified for further investigation.

Examples of frequency distributions for one highly correlated (MCP3_f—PIP3) and most often occurring dependency, as well as one (CMC5—MCP5_f) with $r = 0.76$ occurring less frequently, are presented in Figure 6.

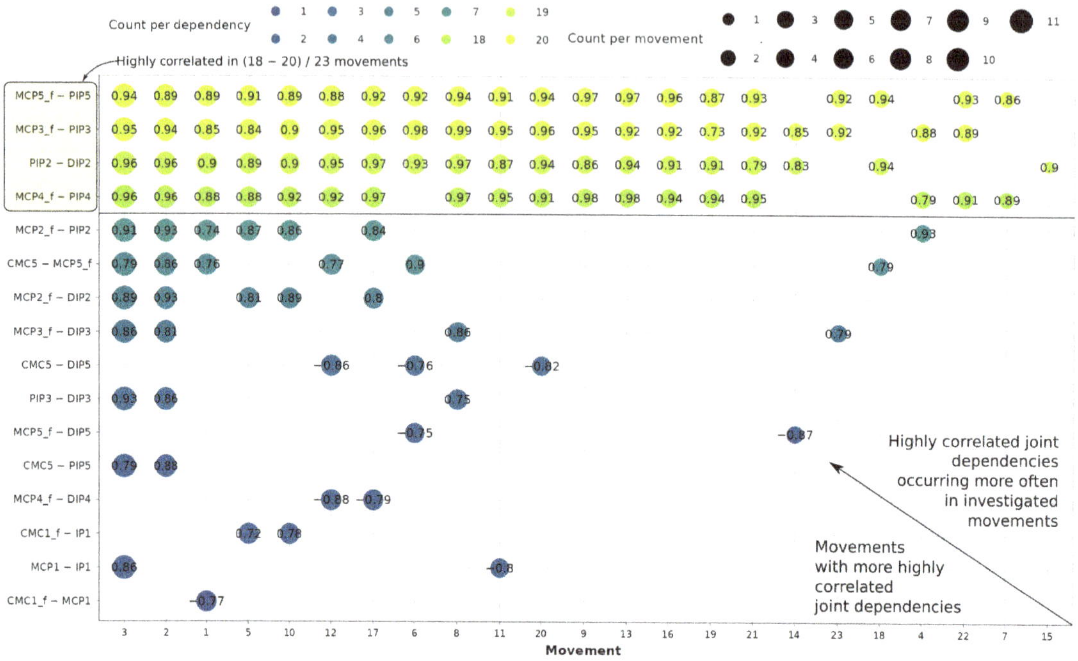

Figure 5. Correlation analysis of joint dependencies and movements where they occur most often.

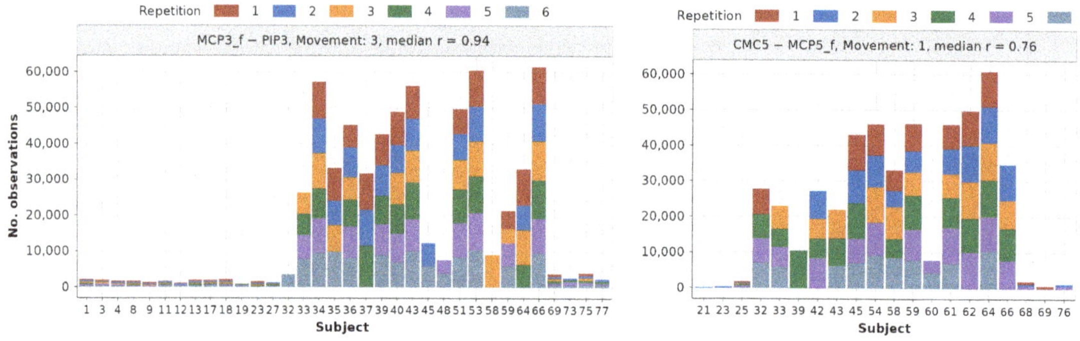

(**a**) (**b**)

Figure 6. Data distribution example for dependencies across subjects and repetitions after 1.5 IQR outlier removal: (**a**) MCP3_f—PIP3 dependency for movement 3, (**b**) CMC5—MCP5_f dependency for movement 1.

Distributions for all dependencies can be found in the main authors' GitHub repository [22]. Due to the previously described data preservation techniques, for modeling the MCP3_f—PIP3 relationship during movement 3, there are as many as 34 subjects, 155 repetitions, and 634,050 observations. On the other hand, for modeling the CMC5—MCP5_f relationship during movement 1, 20 different subjects, 75 repetitions, and 485,267 observations are available. It can also be observed that in the first example, there is a balanced number of subjects from DB1 and DB2, and only 4 subjects from DB3 are available. In the second example, subjects from DB2 constitute a large majority, but this claim cannot be generalized to the rest of the dependencies.

To validate the captured variation, a summary of the remaining data per dependency-movement is shown in Figure 7. The minimum number of subjects in the subsequent modeling part is 9 per single dependency-movement relationship, although, in the middle 50% of cases, it spans 19 and 33. The number of repetitions, which will be observed as a single enclosed data unit, ranges between 25 and 274 per dependency-movement. The midspread of repetitions per subject is between 3 and 4.5.

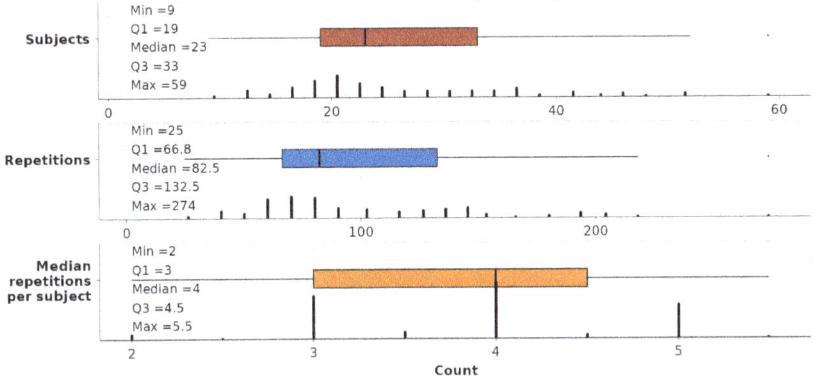

Figure 7. Summary statistics on the number of subjects (red), repetitions (blue), and median number of repetitions per subject (orange) across all 116 dependency-movement relationships.

2.4. Machine Learning-Based Intra-Finger Dependency-Movement Relationship Modeling

Traditional machine learning principles are applied to dependency-movement modeling, with a larger portion of the data allocated for training models (~80% of repetitions) and the remaining reserved for testing purposes (~20% of repetitions). Additionally, an assumption is made that both the movement reaching phase and the "returning to the rest position" phase follow the same trajectory. Due to the previously mentioned imbalance in the data, since each of the three dataset parts is sampled using significantly different sampling rates, the data is sampled for each dependency-movement relationship in a way that entire repetitions are set aside, ensuring they belong to different subjects to increase the representativeness of the models. Additionally, a customized version of stratified sampling is utilized to split the training data into k folds for hyperparameter tuning through cross-validation. To determine the appropriate number of folds, we consider the minimum number of different subjects (9) and repetitions (25) from Figure 7. A minimum of 5 different repetitions per stratum is deemed sufficient to ensure the necessary set variability. The data describing a certain dependency-movement is then split into 5 folds, with 1 fold (20% of repetitions) used as a test set and the rest for 4-fold cross-validation and hyperparameter tuning. In the authors' opinion, the highest representativeness is introduced in each fold by maximizing the number of different subjects (diversifying repetitions from the same subject) in each fold, so the stratified sampling is performed using subjects (1–77) and repetitions (1–6) for each dependency-movement relationship, rather than using observations directly. The customized version of stratified sampling is performed in the following way:

1. A vector of fold IDs is generated for each relationship, containing repeating sequences in the 1–5 range, with a length equal to the number of repetitions.
2. The vector of subjects is randomly shuffled, followed by the random shuffling of repetitions belonging to each subject, resulting in a random list of repetitions.
3. Randomly listed repetitions are assigned to folds sequentially.

Using the described procedure, more unique subjects are present in each fold, resulting in more consistent 4-fold cross-validation compared to simple random repetition folds' assignments. Each fold contains, therefore, an uneven number of observations and an approximately even number of repetitions.

As elaborated above and illustrated in Figure 6, the dataset exhibits imbalances. However, each repetition must hold equal weight when modeling a certain relationship. A simple approach that could be applied involves the repetition of observations. However, this approach would add additional data points to an already very large dataset and is hence not utilized in this study. Instead, observation weighting is introduced. The process begins by counting the total number of observations and repetitions per dependency-movement relationship. By dividing these figures, the total weight coefficient for each repetition is determined. Then, the number of observations within each repetition is counted, and each observation is assigned the proper weight w_i by dividing the total repetition weight coefficient by the number of observations counted. The weighting procedure ensures that each repetition equally contributes to the model-building process for the dependency.

Three predicting variables are chosen for the modeling process. For each dependency, in addition to the dependee joint, the subject height and weight are also selected. All variables are transformed using polynomial (second order) and exponential transformations and fed to the model matrix consisting of all mentioned variables, their first order interactions, and intercept, totaling 46 terms. The entire model matrix is then standardized (centered and scaled) by first subtracting the mean from each explanatory variable and dividing it by its standard deviation to conclude both the variable significance and effect size. It is important to note that the standardization procedure is performed separately for each of the 116 modeled dependencies. Also, the dependent variables are standardized before model fitting.

Two different modeling approaches are employed, the first serving as a baseline and a variable selection model and the second as a main model for inferring about the modeled dependencies. For variable selection, a regularized generalized linear model (GLM), implemented in the R library *glmnet* [19], is used as an extension of ordinary linear regression (OLS). The GLM model consists of three parts: a linear combination of predictors, probability distribution of the dependent variable, and a link function enabling the transformation of the predictor. For a probability distribution, a normal distribution is used, with the identity function as a link function, yielding a model in the following standardized form:

$$E\left(\frac{y-\overline{y}}{\sigma_y}\right) = \beta_{s0} + \beta_{s1}\frac{x_1-\overline{x}_1}{\sigma_{x1}} + \cdots + \beta_{si}\frac{x_i-\overline{x}_i}{\sigma_{xi}} + \cdots, \quad y \sim N(\overline{y}, \sigma_y), \tag{1}$$

where $E(\cdot)$ denotes expectation of a random variable, y the dependent joint, x_i all previously described predictors, $\overline{\cdot}$ variable mean, σ variable standard deviation, and β_{si} the standardized model coefficients.

A previously set goal is to obtain sparse models, so lasso regression [19] is used to tackle the correlations between variables and promote sparsity in selecting predictors. A coefficient approximation is implemented as a minimization problem with a negative log-likelihood term, as well as a regularization term using the hyperparameter λ and the l_1 norm of the sum of the coefficients [19]:

$$\lambda \|\beta_{s0} + \beta_{s1} + \cdots + \beta_{si} + \cdots \|_1 \tag{2}$$

Another employed strategy, i.e., relaxation of coefficients during GLM fitting, involves fitting both regularized lasso and ordinary least-square (OLS) regression (without regularization), using the same subset of predictors selected by the lasso. Subsequently, a convex combination of coefficients is utilized to obtain the relaxed coefficients:

$$\beta_s^{relax}(\lambda, \gamma) = \gamma\beta_s^{\gamma} + (1-\gamma)\beta_s^{OLS}, \tag{3}$$

where β_s^{relax} represents the relaxed coefficient, γ the mixing parameter, β_s^{γ} the regularized coefficient, and β_s^{OLS} the coefficient obtained through OLS fitting. By applying this strategy, some of the parameter shrinking due to lasso is undone (relaxed) and better estimates for the coefficients are explored. A final GLM strategy involves penalizing specific predictors to ensure their consistent retention in the final output.

The second model, utilized as the final one for inferring dependencies, is a linear mixed-effect (LME) model, implemented in the R library *lme4* [25]. It is selected due to the natural grouping of the data by subjects, as observed during visual inspection, and by incorporating previous knowledge from experiments (involving one glove size but different subject hand sizes) conducted in [4]. The respective modeling procedure involves initially grouping the data to account for random effects and then conducting linear regression with fixed effects to address the remaining residual variance. The selected type of the LME model is a random intercept with fixed slopes, where each subject represents a single level in the multilevel modeling or a random effect. Therefore, for each subject (denoted as a set S), we compute its intercept term, while the slopes are computed as an estimate for the entire population. The relation describing the used LME model is:

$$\frac{y-\overline{y}}{\sigma_y} = \beta_{s0j} + \beta_{s1}\frac{x_1-\overline{x}_1}{\sigma_{x1}} + \cdots + \beta_{si}\frac{x_i-\overline{x}_i}{\sigma_{xi}} + \cdots, j \in S, \quad (4)$$

where the same nomenclature as in (1) applies, with the alteration in standardized intercept terms β_{s0j} referring to the j-th subject. Considering subjects as a random effect, and assuming the underlying data is representative of the population, we can estimate the mean and variance across the subject intercept terms. This information enables us to make reasonable predictions about the subjects who were not part of this study.

After detailing data splitting, stratified sampling, cross-validation, weighting, standardization, and modeling strategies, the comprehensive procedure for obtaining sparse and representative models is elaborated next. The following comprehensive modeling procedure is applied to each dependency-movement relationship. Due to the inclusion of randomized stratified sampling in the modeling process, the entire process is repeated in 10 runs to assess the degree of variation in the selected predictors and the obtained coefficients in the LME model. The variation in the obtained coefficients and the selected predictors is extremely small, and the resulting models are selected using:

- Primary criteria: selecting a model with similar coefficient values consistently occurring across different runs,
- Secondary criteria: selecting a model with the lowest error metrics (as described in the Results and Discussion sections).

During GLM modeling, a regularization tuning parameter λ is varied in a grid of 100 values ranging between 0.05 and 0.1. For tuning the hyperparameter γ, five values spanning between 0 (complete relaxation) and 1 (no relaxation) are selected. During the 4-fold cross-validation, the resulting model is not chosen as the one with the minimum mean cross-validated error but rather as the most regularized (sparse) model for which the cross-validated mean error is within one standard deviation from the minimum mean error. Additionally, observation weights are supplied to GLM models. The GLM model fitting is conducted by using maximal likelihood estimation, with linear, polynomial, and exponential transformations of the dependee joint being penalized to ensure they are always retained in the resulting model for consistency. Large sample sizes (ranging from 84,000 to 740,000 observations in the training dataset, as shown in Table S1 in the Supplementary Materials) and the introduction of variable standardization help reduce the problem of multicollinearity by decreasing standard errors.

After identifying the influential predictors and establishing a baseline GLM model, the LME model is constructed using initially the same predictors, along with the same 4 folds utilized during GLM cross-validation. Typically, a prerequisite for LME modeling is to have at least five distinct levels for random effects, which is fulfilled by a minimum of 9 different subjects present in each subset of the training dataset (the median value is 23 subjects, whereas the maximum is 58). To align with one of the key objectives of the paper, which is to introduce reduced and simplified models, reductions in the LME model are determined by both the effect size and its statistical significance. Given that regression coefficients are standardized, the model can be simplified, as one standardized regression coefficient often has a significantly smaller magnitude compared to another. Standardized coefficients can therefore be compared similarly to correlations, where higher values imply stronger practical relationships between variables. The cutoff level for effect size, based on Cohen's guidelines [26], is set to retain only medium (0.30–0.49) and large (>0.50) effect size predictors in the reduced model, while the significance level is set to retain only highly significant predictors (p-value < 0.001).

By interchangeably selecting the highly significant subset of predictors and the subset with a medium to high effect size, three iterations are required during the model reduction process to obtain the final model. After obtaining the final reduced LME models and reporting them according to [27], the rationale for grouping data by subjects is validated by computing the intraclass correlation coefficient (ICC). The latter compares the variance of the random effect (subject intercept) σ_s^2 to the total variance (the sum of the random effect σ_s^2 and the residual variance σ_r^2) within the model as

$$ICC = \frac{\sigma_s^2}{\sigma_s^2 + \sigma_r^2}. \quad (5)$$

Thus, the ICC coefficients inform about a percentage of variance that can be explained using random effects (subject-to-subject variations), which implies the reliability of the modeling approach. Guidelines according to [28] can be adopted, where values

- <0.5 indicate poor reliability,
- 0.5–0.75 indicate moderate reliability,
- 0.75–0.9 indicate good reliability,
- >0.9 indicate excellent reliability.

2.5. Error Metrics

To validate the models, two error metrics are used, both weighted to balance the dataset. Since the data contained outliers, as an absolute error metric for evaluating the models, the weighted mean absolute error (WMAE) is selected:

$$WMAE = \frac{1}{\sum_{i=1}^{n} w_i} \sum_{i=1}^{n} w_i |y_i - \hat{y}_i|, \quad (6)$$

where n represents the length of the train or test dataset, w_i the previously computed observation weight, y_i the observation of the dependent joint, and $\hat{y}_i$ the predicted dependent joint value. Another, relative metric, called double-weighted mean absolute percentage error (WWMAPE) is used:

$$WWMAPE = \frac{\sum_{i=1}^{n} w_i |y_i - \hat{y}_i|}{\sum_{i=1}^{n} w_i |y_i|}, \quad (7)$$

with the same nomenclature as in (6). WWMPAE is chosen since the metric behaves well for smaller, larger, and close-to-zero joint angle values.

3. Results

Here we present summary statistics for random and fixed effect predictors, error analyses, clustering of LME models, and standardized coefficient analyses.

3.1. Random and Fixed Effect Predictors

The summary statistics on the obtained ICCs and the variance of the random effects are shown in Figure 8. The median value across all 116 models is 0.78, suggesting good approach reliability. A total of 4 models have ICCs < 0.5 (poor), 46 are in the range of 0.5–0.75 (moderate), 51 are in the range of 0.75–0.9 (good), and 15 have ICCs > 0.9 (excellent). Although the inclusion of random effects in 4 models (23:MCP3_f—DIP3, 4:MCP4_f—PIP4, 17:MCP4_f—DIP4, 2:MCP2_f—PIP2) is questionable with ICCs < 0.5, the selection of dependencies for the modeling is performed via mean correlations (see Figure 5), and they will be kept. The variance of the random effects (subject intercepts) is also represented as a summary statistic across all 116 obtained LME models. It ranges from 0.16–2.9, with IQR values between 0.6–1.13. Detailed information is in Table S2.

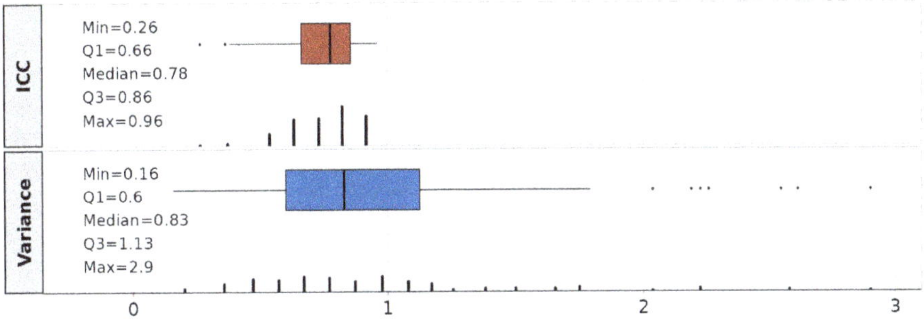

Figure 8. Intraclass correlation coefficients (ICC, red) and variance (blue) of random effects related to linear mixed-effect (LME) models.

A summary statistic on selected predictors in the final LME models, both significant and with medium to strong effect, is provided in Figure 9. Four standardized predictors are identified: linear (lin), polynomial (poly), and exponential (exp) transformations of the dependee, as well as subject height. Additionally, five standardized interactions (denoted with ":") are identified:

- polynomial and exponential transformation of height (poly:height_exp),
- polynomial and exponential transformation of weight (poly:weight_exp),
- exponential and exponential transformation of height (exp:height_exp),
- linear and polynomial transformation of height (lin:height_poly),
- exponential and exponential transformation of weight (exp:weight_exp).

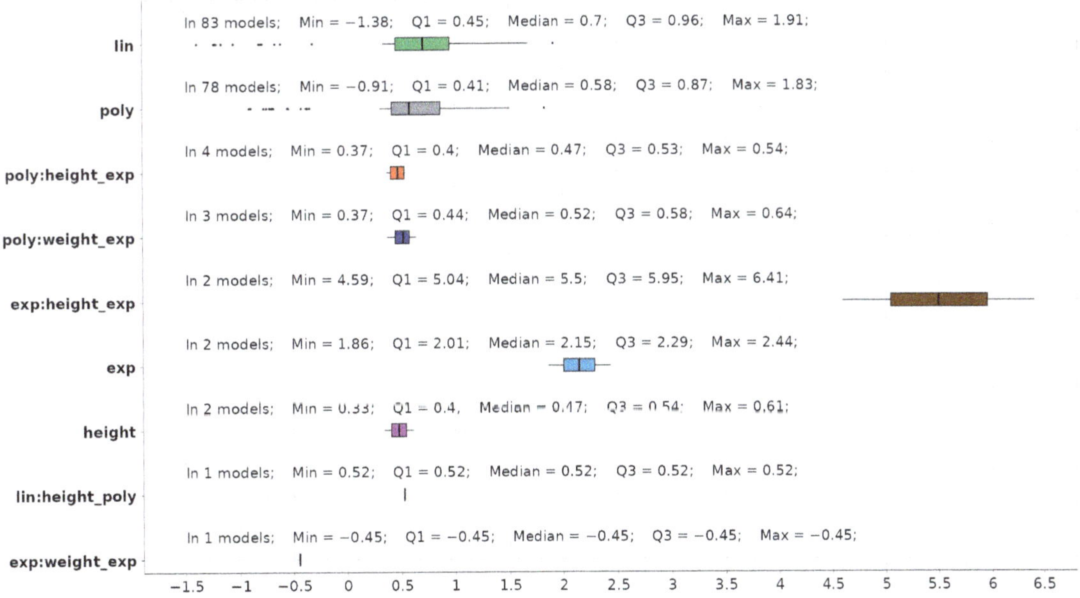

Figure 9. Summary statistics on selected predictors (colored differently) in the final LME models.

If random subject intercept is counted, the average number of predictors per model is 2.5. Out of the 116 provided models, 83 contain linear, 78 contain polynomial, and 45 contain both types of coefficients. Additionally, 11 models incorporate other predictors or interactions besides linear or polynomial terms. The comprehensive model coefficient analysis is presented in Appendix A (Figures A1 and A2). After presenting the fixed effect coefficients for each model, the best approach for dealing with the random (subject) effect is to present the intercept means across all subjects used for modeling. Those intercepts can be further generalized and used as an unbiased estimator for the entire population; they are also represented in Figure A2.

In Figure 10, we present two distinct dependency-movement relationships across a subset of subjects and repetitions, used for both training and testing data to visually validate the LME modeling approach: one with a higher correlation coefficient (3:MCP3_f—PIP3) and the other with a lower one (12:MCPF4_f—DIP4). A clear, natural grouping of the data based on subjects is evident. Scatter plots for all modeled dependencies and subjects can be found in the authors' GitHub repository [22].

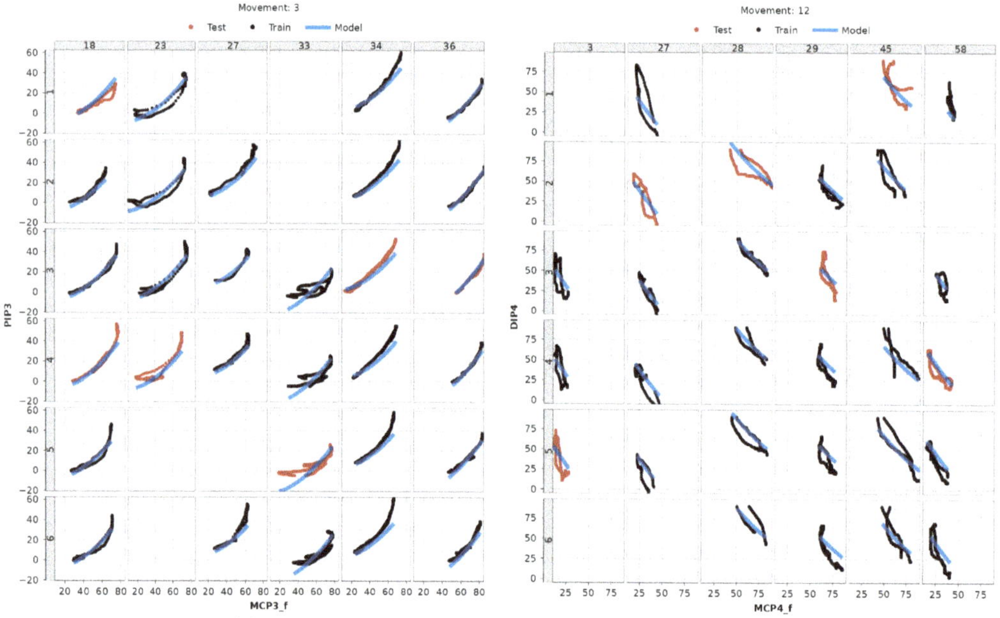

(a) (b)

Figure 10. Examples of LME model fitted to data (blue) with repetitions belonging to train data (black) and test data (red). Numeration at the top represents the subject ID, and numeration to the left the repetition ID: (**a**) MCP3_f—PIP3 dependency for movement 3 (fixed hook grasp), (**b**) MCP4—DIP4 dependency for movement 12 (precision sphere grasp).

3.2. Model Error Metric Analysis

A summary of the statistics on the error metrics is depicted in Figure 11. It is evident that, when compared to GLM models, the LME models fit the data with much smaller absolute and relative errors. The absolute WMAE for the LME approach across models ranges from 2.4° to 16° (median 7.5°) on the test dataset and from 1.8° to 15.2° (median 7.2°) on the train dataset. The relative WWMAPE for the same approach ranges from 11% to 56.1% (median 27.9%) on the test dataset, and from 8.2% to 57.9% (median 28.7%) on the training dataset. The detailed graphical results of the error metric analyses are provided in Appendix A (Figure A3 for WMAE and Figure A4 for WWMAPE), while a detailed table representation for readers' reference can be found in Table S1.

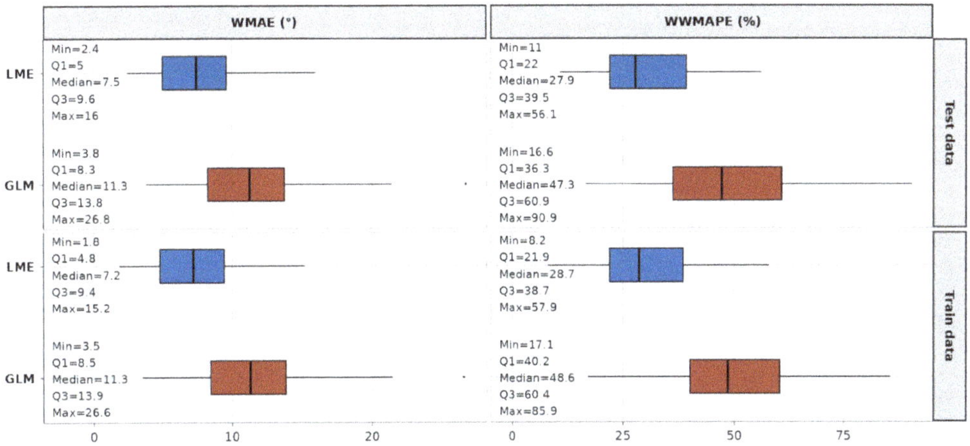

Figure 11. Summary statistics on WMAE and WWMAPE error metrics for LME (blue) and GLM (red) models.

3.3. Clustering Based on Model Coefficient Analysis

Lastly, we perform agglomerative clustering based on standardized coefficients. The goal is to identify similarities between dependencies across different motions. The clustering is performed using both fixed and random effects from the LME models and by substituting the missing coefficients with zeros. The distance matrix with pairwise distances between each of the 116 identified models is computed using Euclidean distance as a metric for similarities between model coefficients. Then, clustering is performed using "complete" linkage, where the metric for joining existing clusters is the largest distance between two dependencies (one from each cluster). The method is also called "farthest neighbor clustering". The resulting dendrogram is depicted in Figure 12. The authors estimate that 30 color-coded clusters, obtained by cutting the tree at a distance of 0.52, are appropriate for reducing the number of models. This number was obtained by visually inspecting the dendrogram in Figure 12, as well as by ensuring that the average absolute difference between standardized coefficients, when taking into account an average of 2.5 coefficients per model, remained below 0.33. The clustering method not only reduces the number of models required to describe all kinematic reductions from 116 to 30 but also the number of models used for the kinematic characterization of each grasp type (see Table 5). The investigation of the finger flexion/extension during all functional movements, initially involving 16 DOFs, can therefore be reduced by up to 11 DOFs, with a median of 4. Thus, the remaining flexion/extension grasp models comprise between 5 and 15 independent DOFs, with a median of 12. Considering model clustering, the number of reduction models per grasp ranges from one to nine, with a median of four.

When the models are grouped into 30 clusters, the coefficients for each cluster can be estimated as the mean values of the standardized coefficients (refer also to Figures A1 and A2) belonging to the clustered models, as depicted in Figure 13. In the figure, the minimum and maximum coefficient values per cluster are also presented, as are the singular clusters containing only one model.

The results of the LME modeling, performed in this work, still show that the major factor in explaining the variance during the kinematic modeling and the model reduction of flexion/extension angles is the subject-to-subject variation (modeled as a random effect), with a median value of 78% variance explained by such "per subject" grouping structure. This finding could potentially be attributed to the calibration protocol for the database, which involved a post-processing procedure performed according to [29]. This procedure utilized 10 subjects and 65 guided movements as the basis for computing sensor gain values, as referenced in [4], which were used by all subjects. It is also very interesting to note that the only selected coefficient for "per subject" grouping was intercept, which allows shifting the data by a constant. So, for each of the 116 developed models in this paper, all subjects used during the modeling process exhibited a similar pattern during the grasping motion but shifted by a subject-specific constant.

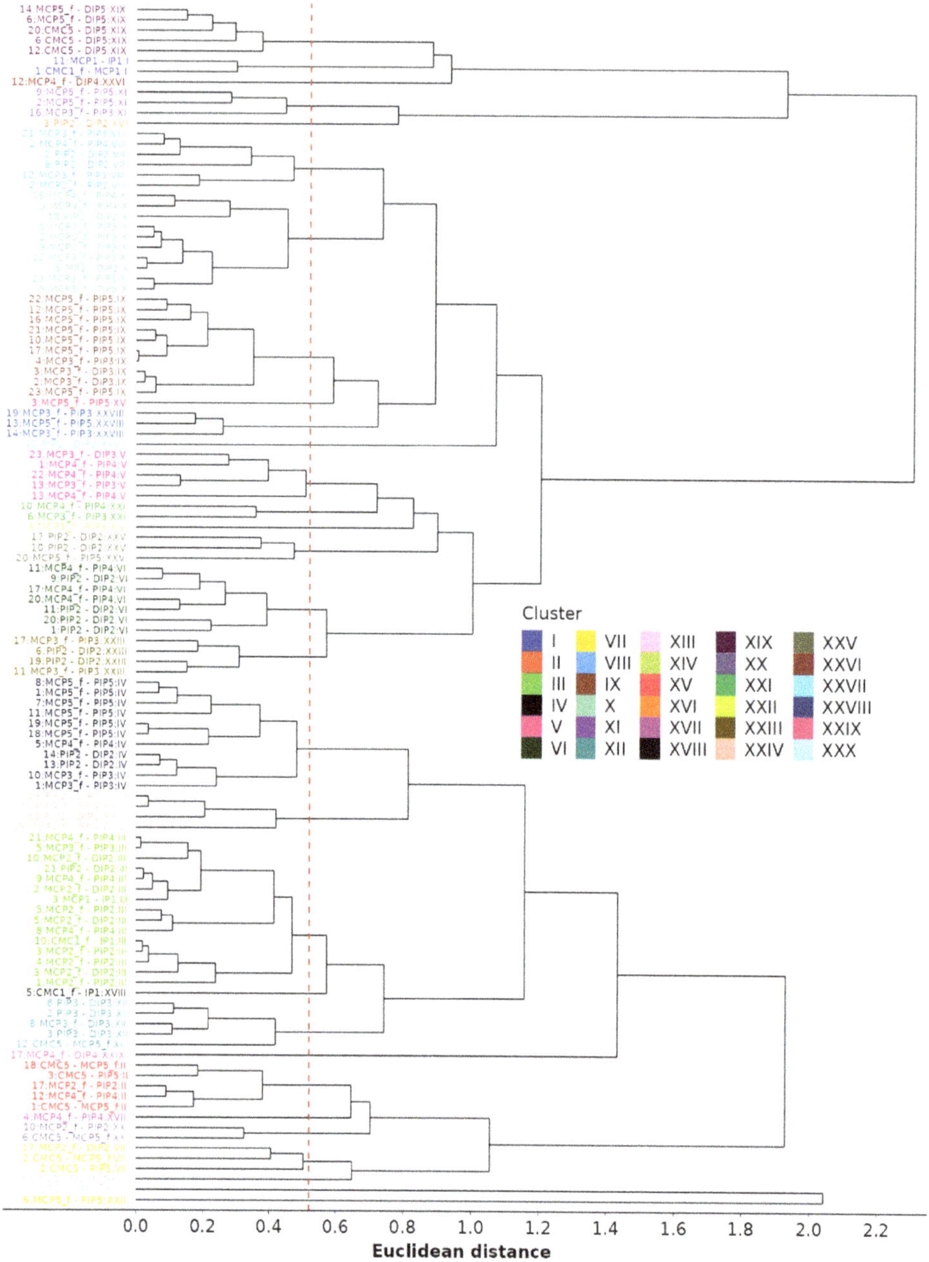

Figure 12. Agglomerative (hierarchical) clustering of models based on the similarity of standardized coefficients, including a proposed cutoff line (dotted red).

Table 5. Remaining movement DOFs and reduction models after reductions.

Movement	3	2	1	5	10	12	17	6	8	11	20	9	13	16	19	21	14	23	18	4	22	7	15
DOFs reduction	11	10	7	7	7	7	7	6	6	5	5	4	4	4	4	4	3	3	3	3	3	2	1
# models per cluster	III × 3	VII × 2 VIII × 2	IV × 2	III × 3 X × 2	III × 2	-	-	XIX × 2	XII × 2	VI × 2	VI × 2	-	V × 2	-	-	III × 2	-	-	-	-	-	-	-
# reduction models	9	8	6	4	6	7	7	5	5	4	4	4	3	4	4	3	3	3	3	3	3	2	1
DOFs remaining	5	6	9	9	9	9	9	10	10	11	11	12	12	12	12	12	13	13	13	13	13	14	15

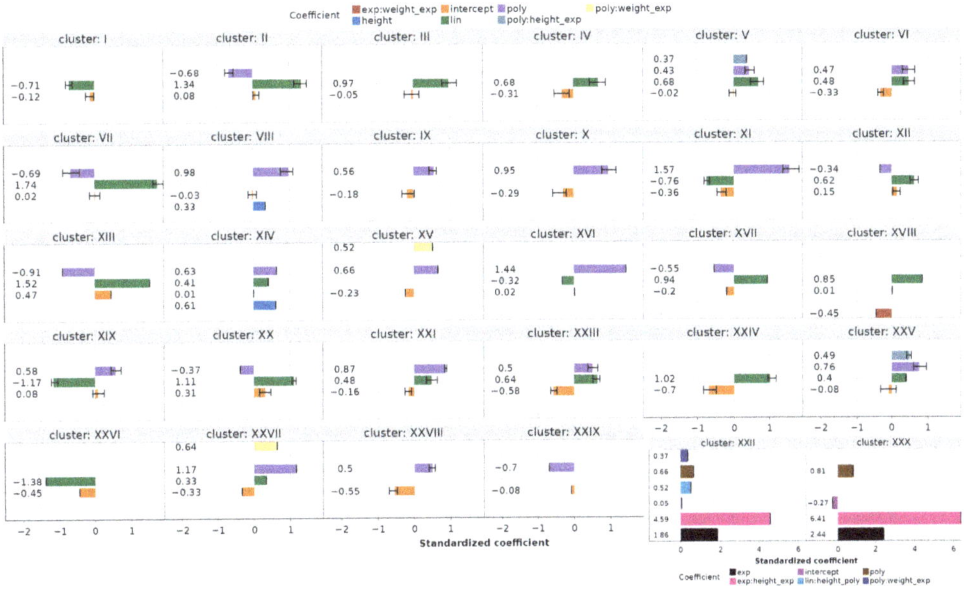

Figure 13. Clustered models with mean, minimum, and maximum coefficient values.

4. Discussion

The study described in this work presents a comprehensive investigation of grasp-oriented intra-finger dependencies, intending to develop accurate yet simple and applicable sparse kinematically reduced models of human hand movements. It is based on the large open-source database comprising synchronized joint angle values from 77 test subjects performing 23 different functional movements related to ADLs.

The method serves as a supplement to the extensively researched synergy-based PCA methods [11–14,17], intending to further alleviate control challenges and reduce the number of required actuation mechanisms. Since only intra-finger dependencies have been investigated in the paper, the proposed method views joint dependencies from a different perspective in terms of simpler and easier-to-implement 1-to-1 joint relationships, considering only joints located physically close to each other. Authors analyzing the same large dataset using a PCA-based approach [17] obtained a large number of 12 synergies to account for only 80% of the variance during grasping. Designing devices based on all of those synergies would be extremely challenging since existing devices typically utilize only 1–3 synergies [30,31]. Furthermore, there is a downside to the mechanical aspect of implementing PCA-obtained synergies. Devices based on synergistic control typically retain all degrees of freedom (DOFs) while reducing only the control aspect, leading to challenges in complex device design and necessitating trade-offs due to limited space for actuator placement. For instance, in [30], the authors omitted five joint actuators (all DIP + IP) and fixed the joints due to this constraint. Conversely, in [31], only the first postural synergy was used during device design, explaining 60% of the movement variance, resulting in evident reductions in DOFs. However, significant residual variance remained during the investigated activities of daily living (ADL) grasps. The mechanical design of the synergy was implemented as a multichannel pulley, with some compliance added to the transmission. The anthropomorphism of both designs could be further enhanced for certain grasps by introducing customized transmission elements using relationships proposed in this paper. Our methodology also enables the design of single-finger actuators as independent units, in contrast to synergies that involve multiple finger joints.

We initially introduced data wrangling techniques to curate the dataset. By focusing on finger flexion/extension movements and employing rigorous data preparation techniques, we identified 116 highly to very highly correlated dependency-movement relationships across all grasps. Subsequently, each relationship was modeled using a regularized and relaxed GLM for uncorrelated predictor selection. This was followed by further refinement by employing, as the final modeling technique, a weighted LME, where model reductions were based on both predictor significance and effect size. Both models were validated using the WMAE and WWMAPE metrics. For the final reduced LME models on the test datasets, the absolute WMAE ranged from 2.4° to 16° (median 7.5°), while the relative WWMAPE ranged from 11% to 56.1% (median 27.9%).

Through the use of hierarchical model clustering, we attained flexibility in reducing the number of models capable of describing the identified dependencies. This was achieved while maintaining the error margin, quantified by the Euclidean distance between standardized coefficients, to a lower value than 0.52. That is, starting from 116 models, the approach allowed a reduction down to 30 models. While all the data preparation and processing steps must be conducted offline, the resulting models are suitable for real-time implementation in rehabilitation devices and prosthetic hands. We synthesized the results by presenting the remaining independent DOFs for the fingers' flexions/extensions during each of the 23 ADL grasps. Notably, the trajectories involved in different functional movements exhibited numerous correlations, allowing for a significant reduction in the total number of DOFs, with certain grasps requiring 5–15 DOFs (median 12) for kinematic characterization. This validation aligns well with the authors' initial assumption regarding the application of grasp-oriented models during the rehabilitation procedures.

While the authors aimed to concisely present both the methodology and results for reducing grasp-oriented hand kinematic models, the complexity of the underlying problem and the wide variety of 21 ADL grasps led to the identification of as many as 30 clustered reduction relations. Some grasp models, including holding and cutting with a knife, turning a screwdriver, prismatic and tip pinching, prismatic four-finger grasp, and parallel extension grasp, posed greater challenges for reduction. The reduction in DOFs for these grasps ranged between 1 and 3. Thus, alternative approaches may be necessary to simplify the design of rehabilitation devices or prosthetic hands for such grasping types. Although the study analyzed a large number of subjects and grasps, the identified dependencies may not fully represent the diversity of hand movements across the entire population, as hand coordination can vary among individuals.

The direction for further research, along with an additional limitation, involves exploring inter-finger joint dependencies. The intention is to present these dependencies using the devised methodology and prepared dataset in this paper. Such a study could offer additional assistance in the development of anthropomorphic devices, leading to further reductions in the DOFs and simplification of design and control complexity.

Overall, this study lays the groundwork for future research in the field of prosthesis design and hand rehabilitation. It offers in-depth insights and structured methodologies that can contribute to the advancement of robotic rehabilitation devices.

Supplementary Materials: The following supporting information can be downloaded at: https://www.mdpi.com/article/10.3390/robotics13060082/s1, Table S1: Modelling information and error metrics; Table S2: Random effects; Table S3: Means and standard deviations for variable standardization.

Author Contributions: Conceptualization, T.B. and E.K.; methodology, T.B.; software, T.B.; validation, T.B., E.K., G.M. and S.Z.; formal analysis, T.B.; investigation, T.B.; resources, E.K. and S.Z.; data curation, T.B.; writing—original draft preparation, T.B. and E.K.; writing—review and editing, T.B., E.K., G.M. and S.Z.; visualization, T.B.; supervision, E.K.; funding acquisition, E.K. and S.Z. All authors have read and agreed to the published version of the manuscript.

Funding: This research was funded by the University of Rijeka; grant numbers: UNIRI-INOVA-1-22-10, uniri-iskusni-tehnic-23-47, and uniri-tehnic-18-32.

Institutional Review Board Statement: Not applicable.

Informed Consent Statement: Not applicable.

Data Availability Statement: The primary author, T.B., made the code available at https://github.com/tbazina/kinematic-database, accessed on 2 April 2024.

Acknowledgments: The research was conducted as part of the following projects: Rehabilitation devices based on the principles of soft robotics and biomechatronic sensors, Developing advanced rehabilitation devices using machine learning methods, and Innovative mechatronic structures for smart technological solutions.

Conflicts of Interest: The authors declare no conflicts of interest.

Appendix A. LME Model Coefficients' Detailed Analysis and Model Error Metric Analyses

Figures A1 and A2 provide standardized values of obtained LME model coefficients across all 116 dependency-movement relationships. Combining the same modeled dependency-movements in Figures A1 and A2 gives a complete picture of the coefficients.

Figure A2 separates only linear (lin) and polynomial (poly) coefficients, with the inclusion of the mean subject intercept as a random effect for all 116 models. Dependencies in Figure A1, besides lin and/or poly, include up to seven additional model coefficients. The following predictors proved both significant and with medium-to-high effect:

- Subject height or its transformed interaction with other predictors in 9/116 models,
- Transformed subject weight in interaction with other predictors in 4/116 models.

For potential model coefficient users, the authors recommend standardizing the variables before using the coefficients and then back-transforming the scaling and centering on the dependent variable y using either the self-acquired means and standard deviations or Table S3 in the Supplementary Materials.

Figure A3 depicts the detailed analysis of the weighted mean absolute error (WMAE), while Figure A4 shows the overall results of the weighted mean absolute percentage error (WMAPE) on the train and the test datasets for all 116 identified models using both GLM and LME methods. The error metric is calculated according to Equations (6) and (7) provided in the main text. For readers' convenience, a table representation of these results is provided in Table S1 within the Supplementary Materials.

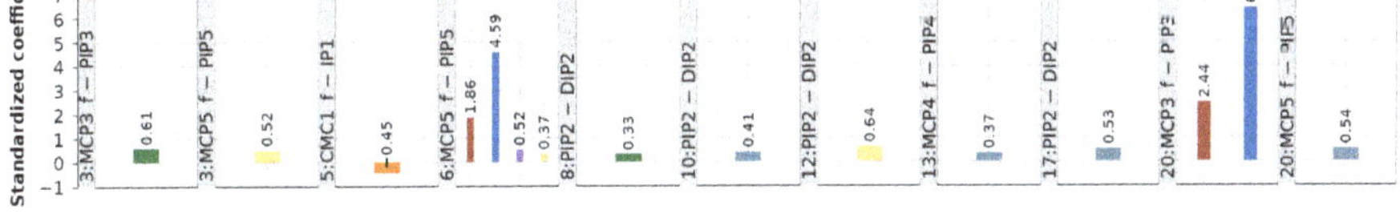

Figure A1. Standardized coefficient values for modeled dependencies that comprise linear (lin) and/or polynomial (poly) and other predictors and interactions: exponential (exp), height, and weight (":" denotes interaction).

Figure A2. Standardized coefficient values for all modeled dependencies that consist of random effects—subject intercept (subj_inte) and fixed effects—linear (lin) and polynomial (poly).

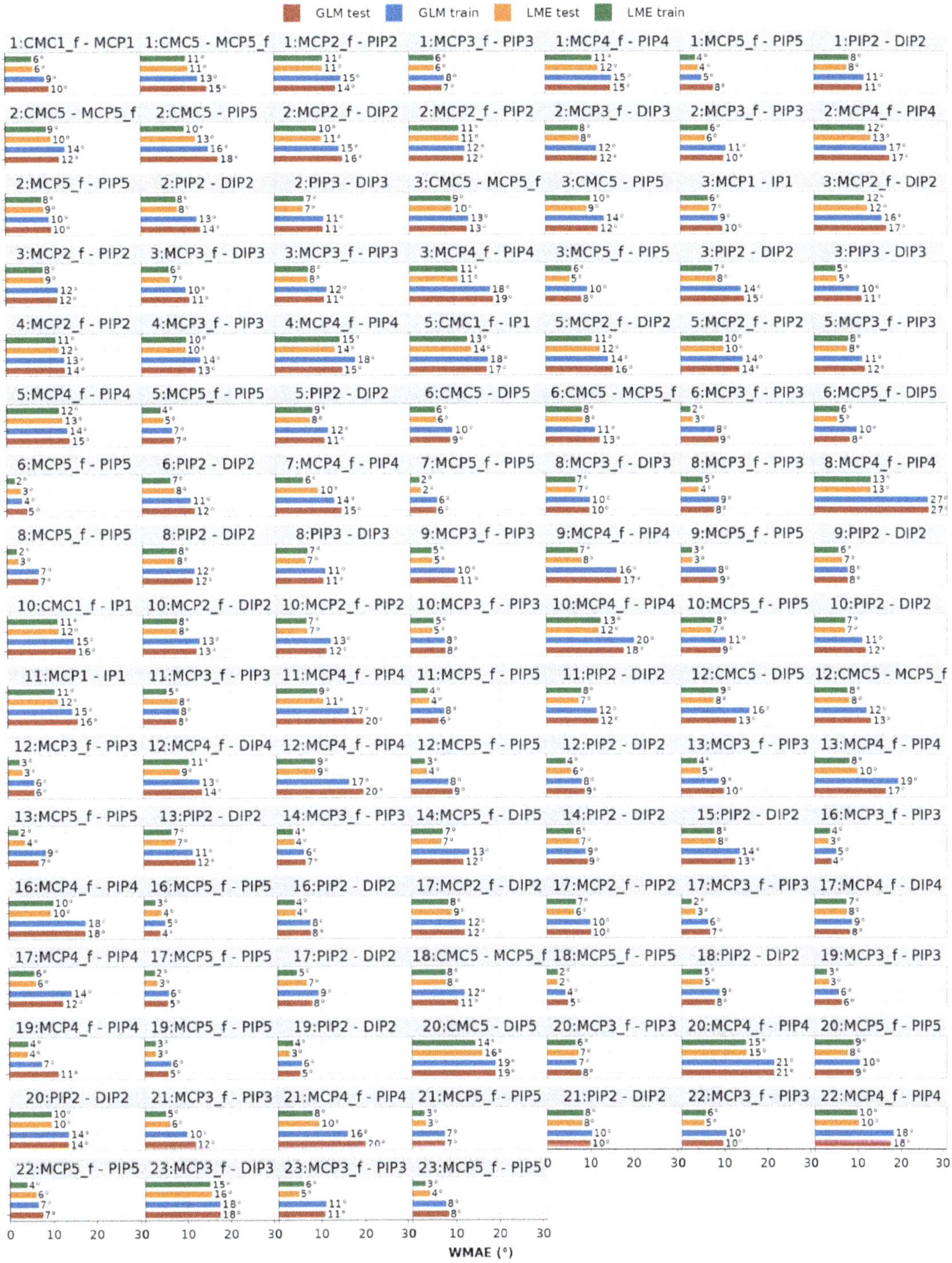

Figure A3. Weighted mean absolute error (WMAE) on train and test datasets across all 116 modeled dependencies for both GLM and LME models.

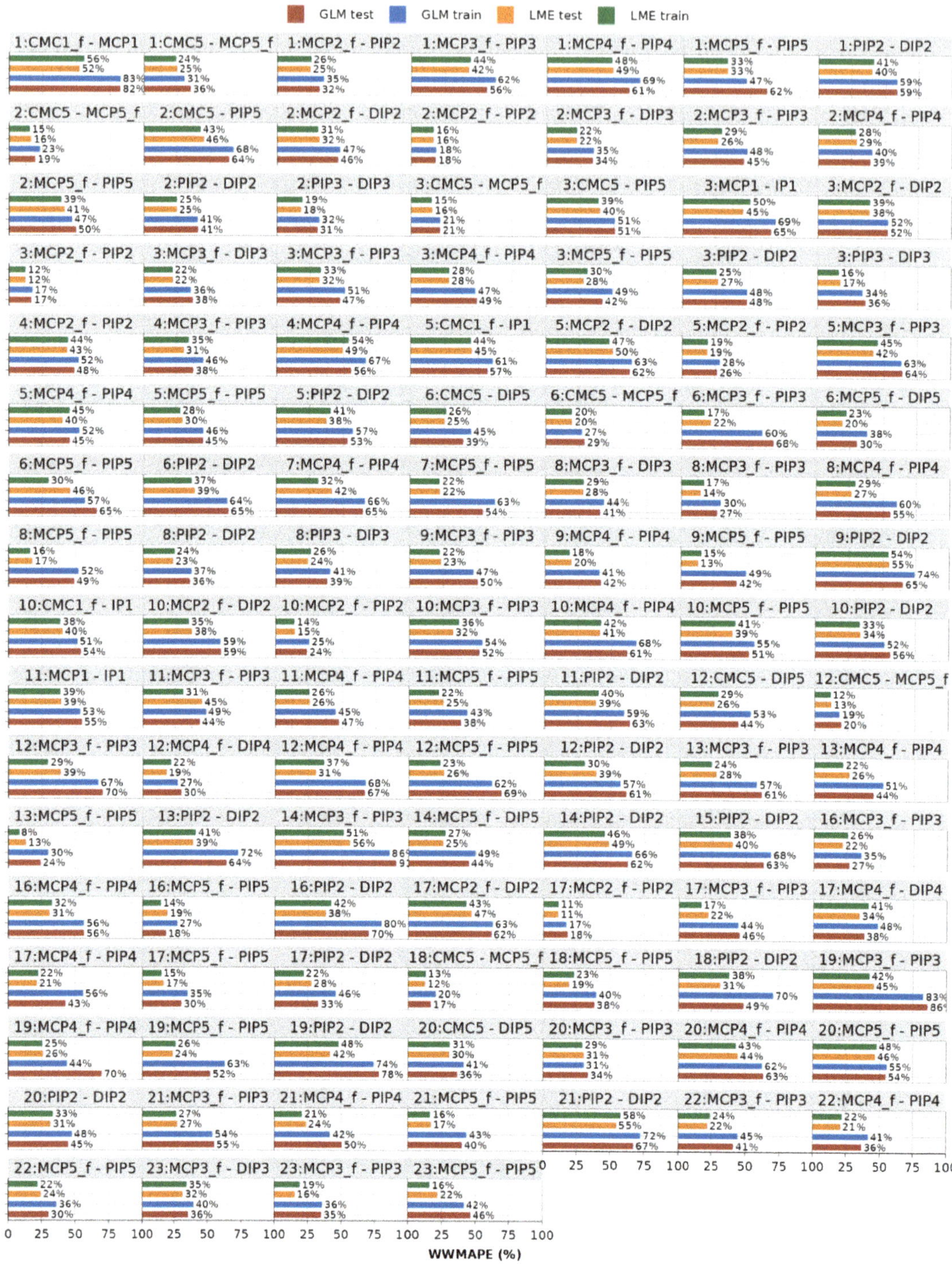

Figure A4. Double-weighted mean absolute percentage error (WWMAPE) on train and test datasets across all 116 modeled dependencies for both GLM and LME models.

References

1. Lang, C.E.; Lohse, K.R.; Birkenmeier, R.L. Dose and timing in neurorehabilitation: Prescribing motor therapy after stroke. *Curr. Opin. Neurol.* **2015**, *28*, 549–555. [CrossRef]
2. Colombo, R.; Sanguineti, V. *Rehabilitation Robotics: Technology and Application*; Academic Press: London, UK, 2018.
3. Engelhardt, L.; Melzner, M.; Havelkova, L.; Fiala, P.; Christen, P.; Dendorfer, S.; Simon, U. A new musculoskeletal AnyBody™ detailed hand model. *Comput. Methods Biomech. Biomed. Engin* **2020**, *24*, 777–787. [CrossRef] [PubMed]
4. Jarque-Bou, N.J.; Atzori, M.; Müller, H. A large calibrated database of hand movements and grasps kinematics. *Sci. Data* **2020**, *7*, 12. [CrossRef] [PubMed]
5. Li, R.; Wang, H.; Liu, Z. Survey on Mapping Human Hand Motion to Robotic Hands for Teleoperation. *IEEE Trans. Circuits Syst. Video Technol.* **2022**, *32*, 2647–2665. [CrossRef]
6. Holzbaur, K.R.; Murray, W.M.; Delp, S.L. A model of the upper extremity for simulating musculoskeletal surgery and analyzing neuromuscular control. *Ann. Biomed. Eng.* **2005**, *33*, 829–840. [CrossRef] [PubMed]
7. Ma'touq, J.; Hu, T.; Haddadin, S. A validated combined musculotendon path and muscle-joint kinematics model for the human hand. *Comput. Methods Biomech. Biomed. Engin* **2019**, *22*, 727–739. [CrossRef] [PubMed]
8. Delp, S.L.; Anderson, F.C.; Arnold, A.S.; Loan, P.; Habib, A.; John, C.T.; Guendelman, E.; Thelen, D.G. OpenSim: Open-Source Software to Create and Analyze Dynamic Simulations of Movement. *IEEE Trans. Biomed. Eng.* **2007**, *54*, 1940–1950. [CrossRef] [PubMed]
9. Cobos, S.; Ferre, M.; Ángel Sánchez-Urán, M.; Ortego, J.; Aracil, R. Human hand descriptions and gesture recognition for object manipulation. *Comput. Method. Biomec.* **2010**, *13*, 305–317. [CrossRef] [PubMed]
10. Zhang, N.; Zhao, Y.; Gu, G.; Zhu, X. Synergistic control of soft robotic hands for human-like grasp postures. *Sci. China Technol. Sci.* **2022**, *65*, 553–568. [CrossRef]
11. Kamper, D.G.; Cruz, E.G.; Siegel, M.P. Stereotypical Fingertip Trajectories During Grasp. *J. Neurophysiol.* **2003**, *90*, 3702–3710. [CrossRef]
12. Jarque-Bou, N.; Gracia-Ibáñez, V.; Sancho-Bru, J.; Vergara, M.; Pérez-González, A.; Andrés, F. Using kinematic reduction for studying grasping postures. An application to power and precision grasp of cylinders. *Appl. Ergon.* **2016**, *56*, 52–61. [CrossRef] [PubMed]
13. Jarque-Bou, N.J.; Vergara, M.; Sancho-Bru, J.L.; Gracia-Ibáñez, V.; Roda-Sales, A. Hand Kinematics Characterization While Performing Activities of Daily Living Through Kinematics Reduction. *IEEE Trans. Neural Syst. Rehabil. Eng.* **2020**, *28*, 1556–1565. [CrossRef] [PubMed]
14. Gracia-Ibáñez, V.; Sancho-Bru, J.L.; Vergara, M.; Jarque-Bou, N.J.; Roda-Sales, A. Sharing of hand kinematic synergies across subjects in daily living activities. *Sci. Rep.* **2020**, *10*, 6116. [CrossRef] [PubMed]
15. Prevete, R.; Donnarumma, F.; d'Avella, A.; Pezzulo, G. Evidence for sparse synergies in grasping actions. *Sci. Rep.* **2018**, *8*, 616. [CrossRef] [PubMed]
16. Ninapro. Available online: https://ninapro.hevs.ch/ (accessed on 26 March 2024).
17. Jarque-Bou, N.J.; Scano, A.; Atzori, M.; Müller, H. Kinematic synergies of hand grasps: A comprehensive study on a large publicly available dataset. *J. Neuroeng. Rehabil.* **2019**, *16*, 63. [CrossRef] [PubMed]
18. Bazina, T.; Kamenar, E.; Zelenika, S.; Črnjarić-Žic, N.; Schnurrer-Luke-Vrbanić, T. Hand model with dependency constrained joints for applications in rehabilitation robotics. *Med. Flum.* **2022**, *58*, 385–398. [CrossRef]
19. Tay, J.K.; Narasimhan, B.; Hastie, T. Elastic Net Regularization Paths for All Generalized Linear Models. *J. Stat. Softw.* **2023**, *106*, 1–31. [CrossRef] [PubMed]
20. Wickham, H.; Averick, M.; Bryan, J.; Chang, W.; McGowan, L.D.A.; François, R.; Grolemund, G.; Hayes, A.; Henry, L.; Hester, J.; et al. Welcome to the Tidyverse. *J. Open Source Softw.* **2019**, *4*, 1686. [CrossRef]
21. Luraschi, J.; Kuo, K.; Ruiz, E. *Mastering Spark with R: The Complete Guide to Large-Scale Analysis and Modeling*; O'Reilly Media: Newton, MA, USA, 2019.
22. GitHub. Available online: https://github.com/tbazina/kinematic-database (accessed on 2 April 2024).
23. Rousseeuw, P.J.; Hubert, M. Robust statistics for outlier detection. *Wires Data Min. Knowl.* **2011**, *1*, 73–79. [CrossRef]
24. Mukaka, M.M. Statistics corner: A guide to appropriate use of correlation coefficient in medical research. *Malawi Med. J.* **2012**, *24*, 69–71.
25. Bates, D.; Mächler, M.; Bolker, B.; Walker, S. Fitting Linear Mixed-Effects Models Using lme4. *J. Stat. Softw.* **2015**, *67*, 1–48. [CrossRef]
26. Nieminen, P. Application of Standardized Regression Coefficient in Meta-Analysis. *BioMedInformatics* **2022**, *2*, 434–458. [CrossRef]
27. Meteyard, L.; Davies, R.A. Best practice guidance for linear mixed-effects models in psychological science. *J. Mem. Lang.* **2020**, *112*, 104092. [CrossRef]
28. Koo, T.K.; Li, M.Y. A Guideline of Selecting and Reporting Intraclass Correlation Coefficients for Reliability Research. *J. Chiropr. Med.* **2016**, *15*, 155–163. [CrossRef] [PubMed]
29. Gracia-Ibáñez, V.; Vergara, M.; Buffi, J.H.; Murray, W.M.; Sancho-Bru, J.L. Across-subject calibration of an instrumented glove to measure hand movement for clinical purposes. *Comput. Methods Biomech. Biomed. Eng.* **2016**, *20*, 587–597. [CrossRef]

30. Laffranchi, M.; Boccardo, N.; Traverso, S.; Lombardi, L.; Canepa, M.; Lince, A.; Semprini, M.; Saglia, J.A.; Naceri, A.; Sacchetti, R.; et al. The Hannes hand prosthesis replicates the key biological properties of the human hand. *Sci. Robot.* **2020**, *5*, eabb0467. [CrossRef]
31. Alicea, R.; Xiloyannis, M.; Chiaradia, D.; Barsotti, M.; Frisoli, A.; Masia, L. A soft, synergy-based robotic glove for grasping assistance. *Wearable Technol.* **2021**, *2*, e4. [CrossRef]

robotics

MDPI

Article

Towards Prosthesis Control: Identification of Locomotion Activities through EEG-Based Measurements

Saqib Zafar [1,2,*], Hafiz Farhan Maqbool [2,3], Muhammad Imran Ashraf [2], Danial Javaid Malik [2], Zain ul Abdeen [2], Wahab Ali [2], Juri Taborri [1] and Stefano Rossi [1,*]

[1] Department of Economics, Engineering, Society and Business Organization, University of Tuscia, 01100 Viterbo, Italy; juri.taborri@unitus.it
[2] Department of Mechanical, Mechatronics, and Manufacturing Engineering, University of Engineering and Technology, Lahore 38000, Pakistan; farhan.maqbool@uet.edu.pk (H.F.M.); imranashraf111112525@gmail.com (M.I.A.); danialjmalik@gmail.com (D.J.M.); mughalz330@gmail.com (Z.u.A.); wahabali485@gmail.com (W.A.)
[3] Human-Centered Robotics Lab, National Centre of Robotics and Automation, Lahore 45200, Pakistan
* Correspondence: saqib.zafar@unitus.it (S.Z.); stefano.rossi@unitus.it (S.R.)

Abstract: The integration of advanced control systems in prostheses necessitates the accurate identification of human locomotion activities, a task that can significantly benefit from EEG-based measurements combined with machine learning techniques. The main contribution of this study is the development of a novel framework for the recognition and classification of locomotion activities using electroencephalography (EEG) data by comparing the performance of different machine learning algorithms. Data of the lower limb movements during level ground walking as well as going up stairs, down stairs, up ramps, and down ramps were collected from 10 healthy volunteers. Time- and frequency-domain features were extracted by applying independent component analysis (ICA). Successively, they were used to train and test random forest and k-nearest neighbors (kNN) algorithms. For the classification, random forest revealed itself as the best-performing one, achieving an overall accuracy up to 92%. The findings of this study contribute to the field of assistive robotics by confirming that EEG-based measurements, when combined with appropriate machine learning models, can serve as robust inputs for prosthesis control systems.

Keywords: prosthesis control; machine learning; EEG; activity recognition; independent component analysis

1. Introduction

The loss of limbs, often resulting from trauma, illness, or congenital conditions, significantly impacts an individual's mobility and quality of life [1,2]. Advances in prosthetic technology have significantly improved the functional capabilities and comfort of amputees, facilitating greater independence and participation in daily activities [3].

Among these innovations, the utilization of electroencephalography (EEG) signals to control prosthetic devices represents the leading edge of innovative research [4,5]. EEG, a non-invasive technique that records electrical activity along the scalp, provides a direct window into the brain's activity, offering insights into a user's intentions [6]. Harnessing these signals, research has been dedicated to design innovative systems able to measure neural activities and convert them into prosthetic devices' movements, enabling individuals with limb impairments to interact with the world in unprecedented ways [7]. EEG-based approaches have overcome the traditional methods based on residual muscle activity gathered from surface electromyography or external switches, which are often characterized by poor movement accuracy and a restricted range of motion [8,9]. Several studies have shown a significant incidence of issues that amputees face when using conventional control methods, with up to 70% reporting difficulties, such as comfort and stability [10]. Instead,

EEG-based prosthetic control systems are directly fed with signals associated with motor intentions. Through signal processing algorithms and machine learning techniques, these systems decode neural patterns, discerning commands for various movements such as walking, running, or even fine tasks associated with the upper limbs [11]. This not only enhances the naturalness and fluidity of prosthetic movements but also empowers users with greater autonomy and functionality in their daily life. Moreover, the versatility of EEG-based prosthetic control extends beyond mere movement execution.

Thus, it is clear how the EEG signal identification and classification of lower-limb activities has gained significant attraction during the last two decades [12,13]. Thus, several studies have been published to understand the feasibility of classifying gait-related parameters through the analysis of EEG signals. Among others, Liu et al. [14] explored the use of BCI to decode lower-limb movement intention from EEG signals, aiming to promote motor recovery and brain plasticity. The study focused on continuous classification and asynchronous detection of movement-related cortical potentials during self-initiated ankle plantar flexion tasks. In comparison to current online detection techniques, the suggested framework showed a greater true-positive rate, fewer false positives, and comparable latencies [14]. Chai et al. [15] attempted to identify gait-related movements in subjects walking with and without an exoskeleton by analyzing the EEG signals. By using features related to mu- and beta-frequency bands, an average classification accuracy of 74% was obtained for the testing sets [15]. A comparison among different neural network algorithms fed with EEG-based features was proposed in [16], revealing the support vector machine model as the best one, achieving accuracy greater than 98% in the recognition of gait phases. A similar approach was proposed by Bodda et al. for the identification of the stance and swing phase utilizing the analysis of EEG activity [17]. The intention of walking movement has been discriminated by using a support vector machine with RBF kernel, achieving an overall accuracy of 73% when the algorithm was fed with features extracted from EEG signals gathered from six healthy subjects and two amputees [18]. To automatically identify unstable gait patterns, Soangra and colleagues [19] applied both machine learning and deep learning algorithms to implement a BCI able to prevent falls, finding the recurrent network as the best solution with an accuracy greater than 80% [19]. A support vector machine classifier combined with a directed acyclic graph was validated to move a prosthetic leg according to specific gait trajectories [20]. By testing the method on three healthy subjects, it was observed that all of them were able to smoothly walk on floors and stairs. It is clear that all the previously reported articles are focused on specific parameters of the gait, such as gait phases or stability, rather than the discrimination of different walking activities. In addition, no studies have been published to understand the performance of EEG-based algorithms when walking on irregular terrains; in fact, all the papers only evaluated the performance in controlled environments.

Despite the plethora of studies and the advantages of using EEG for developing control systems of prostheses, challenges persist in guaranteeing the widespread adoption of EEG-controlled prosthetics, ranging from signal variability to the need to test the methodology in uncontrolled environments over irregular terrains. To the best of the authors' knowledge, the comparison among different machine learning algorithms to identify the best method for the identification of different locomotion tasks in different walking terrains outdoors is still lacking, since all the studies focused on level walking in a laboratory. Therefore, the contribution of this study is to fill this gap by comparing the performance of different machine learning algorithms, particularly random forest and k-nearest neighbors, in classifying locomotion activities based on EEG data. The findings of this study are expected to advance the field by providing insights into the most effective algorithms for implementing EEG-based prosthetic control systems.

2. Materials and Methods

2.1. Participants

Ten healthy male young adults aged from 18 to 22 years old were enrolled in the study. The participants were selected while avoiding subjects with physical and/or neurological disorders. The whole content of the experiment was explained, and a written informed consent was obtained from all the subjects. The protocol was compliant with the ethical standards outlined in the Declaration of Helsinki and it was approved by the BioEtichs Committee of the University of Engineering and Technology, Lahore—Pakistan with n. 4138 (29 October 2019).

2.2. Experimental Setup and Procedure

To measure the EEG signals, the commercially available 14-channel Emotiv EPOC headset was used [21]. The device is able to track the electrical impulses produced by the brain using 14 electrodes placed at AF3, F7, F3, FC5, T7, P7, O1, O2, P8, T8, FC6, F4, F8, and AF4 positions, according to the international 10–20 system [22]. According to the system, the left hemisphere brain signals are acquired through odd numbers, whereas even numbers are used for the right side. Two additional electrodes, which are CMS and DRL on the left and right side, respectively, were used to reduce the noise. Table 1 indicates the area covered by the used electrodes and the specific information gathered from each electrode.

Table 1. Areas of the brain covered by all the electrodes.

Electrodes	Brain Area	Role
AF3, AF4, F3, F4, F7, F8	lobus frontalis	Detect cognitive function related to decision-making and motor planning
FC5, FC6, T7, T8	lobus temporalis	Detect brain activities associated with complex motor coordination
P7, P8	lobus parietalis	Integrate sensory information and managing spatial navigation
O1, O2	lobus occipitalis	Capture visual processing signals that influence balance and movements

Figure 1 reports the sensor system and the location of the electrodes on the scalp.

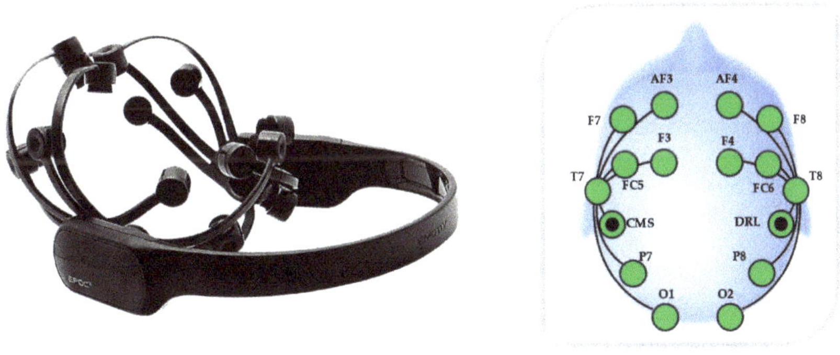

(**a**) (**b**)

Figure 1. (**a**) The hardware of EMOTIV Epoc headset, (**b**) the position of the 14 electrodes.

The device provides a 14-bit resolution for each EEG channel, ensuring precise data capture. The sampling frequency of the Emotiv EPOC can be configured to either 128 Hz or 256 Hz, with the latter used in this study. This frequency is sufficient for capturing the relevant brainwave activity, particularly in the alpha- and beta-frequency bands, which are commonly analyzed in EEG studies. For data transmission, the Emotiv EPOC uses a wireless Bluetooth connection. The data is transmitted in real time to a USB dongle connected to a computer, allowing for live monitoring and analysis of EEG signals. The device is powered by an internal rechargeable battery, which provides approximately 12 h of continuous operation. This device works with a software package that features a user-friendly interface that not only shows the user the contact quality of the electrodes with the scalp but also show the EEG quality of the brain activities. The Emotiv Epoc headset has been already validated for brain–computer interface applications [23].

A skilled operator placed the Emotiv Epoc headset on the scalp of each participant, adjusting it to ensure the correct placement of each electrode on the relative area. It is worth noting that the proper positioning of the headset over the scalp yields the desired quality of the acquired signals. The hair and the skin of the user act as a damper for the detection of electrical activity; thus, a conductive gel is used to reduce the mismatch of the impedance. Before starting the experimental procedure, the EEG quality was tested using the dedicated software, assuring the achievement of quality equal to 100%, which corresponds to full contact between the headset and the scalp. During this preliminary test, participants were instructed to remain relaxed and avoid excessive movement during data collection.

After that, participants were involved in the actual experimental procedure during which raw EEG data were acquired. Specifically, each participant was asked to perform a variety of locomotion activities: (i) walking on level ground (W); (ii) ascending stairs (AS); (iii) descending stairs (DS); (iv) ascending a ramp (AR); and (v) descending a ramp (DR). Each task was repeated three times. The participants wore their normal daily shoes and performed the movements on their self-selected speed. Rest periods were considered between each task to minimize fatigue and check EEG data quality. To avoid bias in the results due to the protocol sequence, the order of tasks was randomized across participants.

2.3. *Data Processing and Analysis*

Figure 2 depicts the flowchart starting from the data acquisition to the machine learning application. As observed, the flowchart also includes: (i) pre-processing and (ii) feature extraction and artifact removal. All the analyses were conducted in Matlab (R2022a, The MathWorks Inc., Natick, MA, USA) using the EEGLAB toolbox (version 14.1.0) [24].

2.3.1. Pre-Processing

The first step of the data analysis involved the removal of certain frequencies. Although different types of filters were initially considered, the Butterworth band-pass filter was consistently selected for all subsequent analyses due to its superior performance, as illustrated in Figure 3. Specifically, a 6th-order Butterworth band-pass filter, which is known for its smooth frequency response and lack of ripples, was applied to isolate and analyze alpha (8–13 Hz) and beta (13–30 Hz) waves. This filtering enhances the signal-to-noise ratio, making it particularly suitable for detecting brain activity patterns relevant to locomotion, according to the literature [12]. In addition, it has been demonstrated that the filtering allows enhancing of the signal-to-noise ratio, permitting a more reliable and robust detection of brain activity patterns, a fundamental aspect for the application of machine learning algorithms [19].

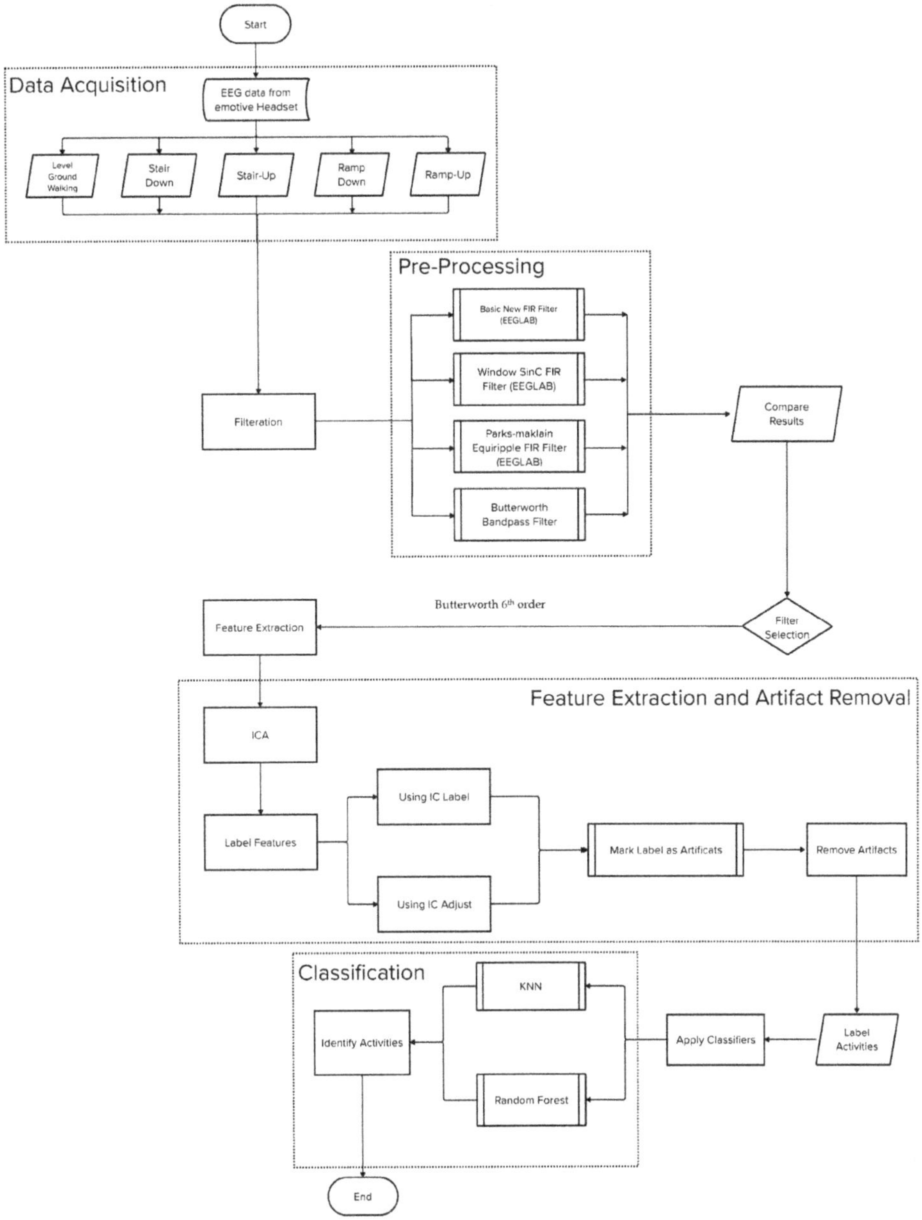

Figure 2. Flowchart of the data processing and analysis.

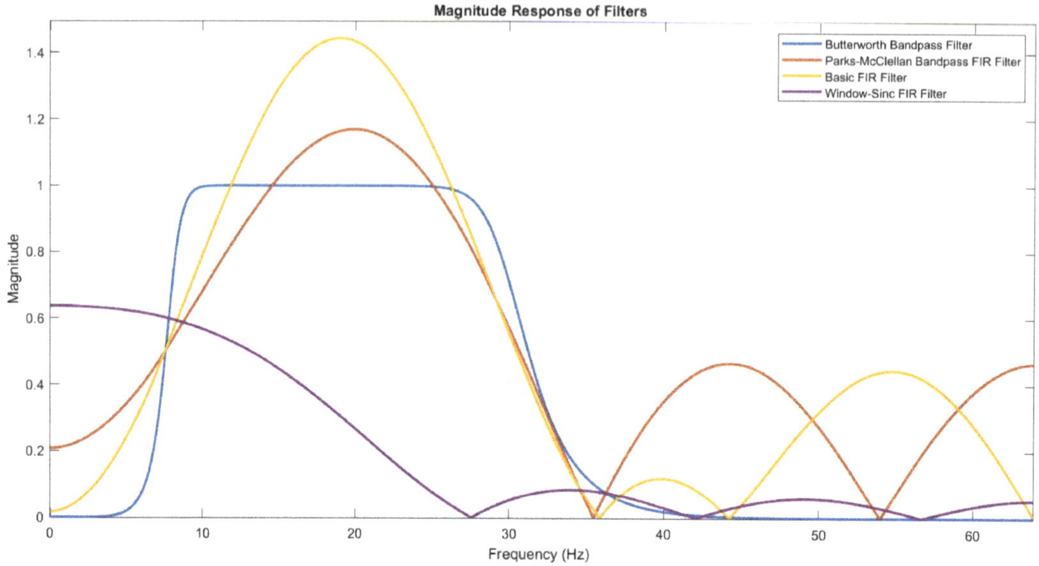

Figure 3. Frequency response of different filters in the EEGLAB toolbox.

2.3.2. Feature Extraction and Artifact Removal

After filtering, data were analyzed to extract the features for the application of the machine learning algorithms. Feature extraction has been carried out by applying the independent component analysis (ICA). The data-driven method known as ICA is effective for blind source separation and signal decomposition. The idea is to separate these sources by taking advantage of their statistical independence, and the observed data are assumed to be a linear combination of unknown-source signals [25]. ICA is frequently used in the context of EEG (electroencephalography) to separate the recorded EEG data into independent components, each of which represents a different brain source or activity [26]. Specifically, the acquired EEG signal for each subject and each locomotion task is organized into a matrix where rows represent different channels and columns represent time points. Given a 14-channel EEG signal $\mathbf{X} \in \mathbb{R}^{14\times T}$ where T is the number of time points, we applied the information maximization (informax) algorithm [26,27] to decompose it into 14 independent components $\mathbf{S} \in \mathbb{R}^{14\times T}$. The decomposition of the matrix followed Equation (1):

$$\mathbf{W}\cdot\mathbf{X} = \mathbf{S} \quad (1)$$

where **X** is the matrix acquired through the EEG system, **W** represents the unmixing matrix, and **S** the sources, also called independent components—ICs. Thus, the 14-channel signals were decomposed into 14 ICs, ordering them in accordance to decreasing variances [28].

An example of the decomposition is reported in Figure 4.

After the decomposition, the EEGLAB toolbox allowed for the automatic labelling of the independent components. Specifically, eye blinks, eye movements, muscle activity, electrocardiographic artifacts, and other brain-related elements can be distinguished by using a statistical approach [26].

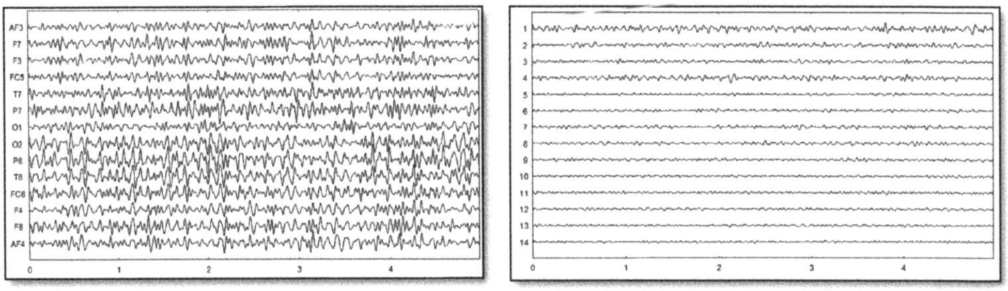

Figure 4. EEG signals (**Left**) and independent components (**Right**) (x-axis represents the time in seconds, while the y-axis represents the micro voltage measured by each electrode and ICs).

A further artifact removal method was applied by using the ADJUST algorithm of the ICA. While ICA is used for breaking down EEG signals into independent components, ADJUST focuses on automatic artifact detection and removal. Thus, informax ICA is typically used as initial step to break down the EEG signals, whereas ADJUST is applied to further clean the data. The ADJUST algorithm, proposed in [29], computed a set of spatial and temporal features for each IC extracted by informax ICA. In particular, the algorithm used six features:

- Spatial Average Difference (SAD)—A measure of the spatial distribution of ICs in terms of the difference between central and peripheral electrodes. It measures the average difference in voltage between the front and back parts of the scalp.
- Variance Time Course (VTC)—A measure of the temporal variance in ICs. It measures rapid fluctuation in the EEG signals.
- Range of Time Course (RTC)—A measure of the range of the IC time course. It measures the difference between the maximum and minimum values of the time course of an independent component.
- Spatial Variance of the Average (SVA)—A measure of the spatial variance of the average activity of ICs. It calculates the variance in the scalp map averaged across all electrodes, helping to identify components where the distribution of activity deviates significantly from the typical spatial patterns observed in neural signals.
- Kurtosis of Time Course (KTC)—A measure of the tailedness of the IC time course distribution, assessing the temporal characteristics of the EEG signal. A higher kurtosis value indicates a more peaked and potentially spiky distribution.
- Spatial Entropy (SE)—A measure of the spatial distribution entropy of ICs. It quantifies how uniformly the signal energy is distributed over the scalp.

Table 2 reported the selected threshold for each feature.

Table 2. Temporal and spatial features computed through ADJUST and related threshold value T.

Feature	Threshold Value (T)
Spatial Average Difference (SAD)	15 μV
Variance of the Time Course (VTC)	0.1
Range of the Time Course (RTC)	3
Spatial Variance of the Average (SVA)	2
Kurtosis of the Time Course (KTC)	3
Spatial Entropy (SE)	2

The predefined threshold was, then, applied to the extracted features to classify each IC as either artifact or non-artifact. After that, decision rules based on the combinations of features were used for the final classification according to Table 3, where T indicates the threshold value previously reported.

Table 3. Artifact classification rules.

Artifact	Features
Eye blink	SAD > T, KTC > T, SE < T
Vertical eye movements	VTC > T
Horizontal eye movements	RTC > T
General discontinuities (muscle activity)	VTC > T, RCT > T

Following the rules, the ICs classified as artifacts were removed, and the cleaned EEG data were reconstructed by back-projecting the remaining ICs.

2.3.3. Activity Recognition through Machine Learning

To automatically identify the locomotion activities from the EEG data, a comparison between two supervised machine learning algorithms was performed. In particular, random forest (RF) and k-nearest neighbor (kNN) were compared.

RF is a commonly used supervised machine learning algorithm belonging to the binary classifier category [30,31]. The algorithm works by combining the outputs of multiple uncorrelated decision trees to produce a single classification. Specifically, each individual tree classifies a specific class, and the one with the most votes is considered the final prediction. Thanks to the bootstrap aggregating method, RF allows us to improve the performance of a single decision tree algorithm [32]. When designing the model, one main hyperparameter must be selected, which is the number of trees, also known as the number e of estimators. In our application, we selected e equal to 100 after conducting preliminary tests with various values (e.g., 50, 100, 150, and 200). The selection of 100 estimators was based on achieving a balance between classification accuracy and computational efficiency. Our tests revealed that increasing the number of estimators beyond 100 provided only marginal improvements in accuracy, with diminishing returns in performance. For instance, while using 150 or 200 estimators slightly improved the accuracy, the gains were not significant enough to justify the additional computational cost, particularly in real-time applications such as prosthesis control, where processing speed is crucial.

k-NN is one of the most widespread supervised machine learning algorithms for physical activity recognition, belonging to the geometric classifiers [33]. The algorithm works by considering each combination of features as a point in an n-dimensional space, where n indicates the number of classes to be classified. The classification is based on understanding which is the most common class among the k-nearest neighbors with the general aim to maximize the distance with respect to the other classes. When designing the model, two main hyperparameters must be selected, which are the type of computed distance and the number k of neighbors considered for the computation. In our application, we selected k equal to 5, and the Euclidean distance is considered for the computation of the distance between neighbors.

The selected algorithm was compared by using two different datasets, with the former composed of independent components extracted by the informax ICA and the latter composed of the independent components extracted by the ADJUST algorithm. Hereinafter, the first dataset is referred to as ICs and the second one as adj_ICs. The performance of the algorithm was determined by applying a cross-validation, dividing the dataset into 80% for training and 20% for the test. To apply the supervised methodology, each datapoint was manually labelled with the related class, as in Table 4.

Table 4. Classes associated with each locomotion activity. W stands for level ground walking, AS for ascending stairs, DS for descending stairs, AR for ascending ramp, and DR for descending ramp.

	W	AS	DS	AR	DR
Class	0	1	2	3	4

The performance of each classifier, independently per each tested dataset, was computed by using common metrics, which involved the computation of the confusion matrix. A 5 × 5 confusion matrix, where 5 indicates the number of classes to be classified, was obtained for each classifier, independently per each dataset and each algorithm. Starting from the confusion matrix, the following synthetic indices were computed:

- Accuracy A—being the ratio between the correctly predicted locomotion activities and the total data. Accuracy is an overall index that takes into account all the five classes together. The computation of the accuracy follows Equation (2):

$$A = \frac{TP + TN}{TP + FP + TN + FN} \tag{2}$$

where TP, TN, FP, and FN are the true positive, true negative, false positive, and false negative, respectively.

- Recall R—being the ratio between the TP and the sum of TP and FN, specific per each class, according to Equation (3):

$$R = \frac{TP}{TP + FN} \tag{3}$$

- Precision P—being the ratio between the TP and the sum of TP and FP, specific per each class, according to Equation (4):

$$P = \frac{TP}{TP + FP} \tag{4}$$

- F1-score—being the harmonic of R and P, thus specific for each class, according to Equation (5):

$$\text{F1-score} = 2 \cdot \frac{R \cdot P}{R + P} \tag{5}$$

A classifier is considered optimum when it is associated with all the above-mentioned indexes by greater than 0.80 [33]. In addition, it is worth noting that by using the reported indices, the robustness of the algorithm to both type I and type II errors was considered. Specifically, accuracy and recall take into account type II, i.e., avoiding false negatives; whereas precision takes into account type I, i.e., avoiding false positives [34].

3. Results and Discussion

An example of the graph obtained by the application of infomax ICA and ADJUST is reported in Figure 5, where it is possible to see the statistical approach revealing the probability that each IC belongs to brain-related activity.

For the sake of completeness, Table 5 reports the number of brain-related features for each activity extracted by the two tested ICA's algorithms.

Table 5. Number of independent components related to brain activity for each locomotion task. W stands for level ground walking, AS for ascending stairs, DS for descending stairs, AR for ascending ramp, and DR for descending ramp.

	W	AS	DS	AR	DR
ICs	13	12	13	11	10
adj_ICs	10	11	11	7	3

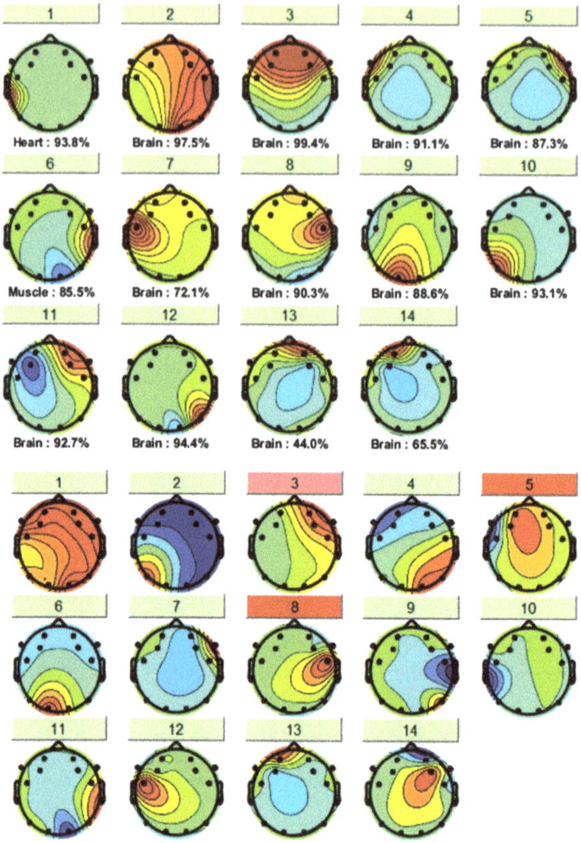

Figure 5. (**a**) Example of informax ICA results related to ascending stairs, (**b**) example of ADJUST results related to descending stairs. The number on the scalp stands for the specific components found by the independent component analysis, whereas the percentage indicates the confidence associated with the type of identified component. The colors on the scalp represent different levels of voltage, with warmer colors indicating higher levels of electrical potential, whereas blue and green indicate lower levels of activity. Black curves indicate isopotential lines, closer lines indicate steeper gradients of electrical potential, whereas widely spaced lines indicate more gradual changes.

Moving to the machine learning algorithms, the results of the performance analysis are depicted in Table 6.

In the case of the random forest (RF) algorithm, the ICs dataset demonstrates an overall accuracy of 0.73, which is lower than the threshold for the optimum classifier [33]. Within this dataset, R is notably high for indices W and DR, achieving values of 0.96 and 0.92, respectively. However, R is lower for DS and AS, with values of 0.25 and 0.47, whereas the AR index exhibits a moderate R of 0.61. The precision values vary, ranging from 0.70 for W to 0.89 for AR, with DS achieving the highest P at 0.79. Finally, the F1-score is highest for DR at 0.87 and lowest for DS at 0.38. When analyzing the adj_ICs dataset with the RF algorithm, there is a marked improvement in overall accuracy, which rises to 0.93, falling in the optimal range [33]. Recall remains very high across all indices, particularly for W (0.99) and DR (0.98), while DS, despite having the lowest R among the indices, still records a substantial 0.80, which is in line with the above-mentioned threshold. P is consistently high across all indices, with values exceeding 0.90. Correspondingly, the F1-score also shows high values, particularly for DR (0.98) and W (0.95). Conversely, the k-nearest neighbors (kNN) algorithm exhibits a lower overall accuracy of 0.64 on the ICs dataset. For this dataset, the R is highest for W (0.84) and DR (0.83), but it is quite low for DS (0.24). Precision for kNN varies moderately, with values ranging from 0.53 for AS to 0.79 for DS. The F1-score is highest for DR at 0.76 and lowest for DS at 0.34. The performance of the kNN algorithm improves when applied to the adj_ICs dataset, achieving an overall accuracy of 0.80. R is highest for DR (0.99) and W (0.91) but remains low for DS (0.27). P is, instead, highest for DS at 0.93 and lowest for DR at 0.67. The F1-score ranges from 0.42 for DS to 0.87 for W.

Table 6. Performance indices for the machine learning algorithms with both training datasets. W stands for level ground walking, AS for ascending stairs, DS for descending stairs, AR for ascending ramp, and DR for descending ramp. THe overall accuracy is reported in bold for reading convenience.

Algorithm	Dataset	Index	W	AS	DS	AR	DR	Overall
RF	ICs	Accuracy	-	-	-	-	-	**0.73**
		Recall	0.96	0.47	0.25	0.61	0.92	-
		Precision	0.70	0.74	0.79	0.89	0.83	-
		F1-score	0.81	0.58	0.38	0.73	0.87	-
	adj_ICs	Accuracy	-	-	-	-	-	**0.93**
		Recall	0.99	0.94	0.80	0.80	0.98	-
		Precision	0.91	0.93	0.93	0.90	0.98	-
		F1-score	0.95	0.93	0.86	0.85	0.98	-
kNN	ICs	Accuracy	-	-	-	-	-	**0.64**
		Recall	0.84	0.35	0.24	0.71	0.83	-
		Precision	0.68	0.53	0.61	0.54	0.70	-
		F1-score	0.75	0.43	0.34	0.61	0.76	-
	adj_ICs	Accuracy	-	-	-	-	-	**0.80**
		Recall	0.91	0.93	0.27	0.55	0.99	-
		Precision	0.83	0.74	0.93	0.84	0.67	-
		F1-score	0.87	0.82	0.42	0.67	0.80	-

By comparing the results, the random forest algorithm consistently outperforms kNN in terms of overall accuracy for both datasets. By considering all the metrics together, it is clear that only the RF algorithm on the adj_ICs dataset revealed itself as optimum for all the indices, whereas the kNN algorithm implemented on the adj_ICs dataset does not meet all the performance criteria, although it is characterized by an optimal overall accuracy. In fact, even if high accuracy indicates that the classifier is generally making correct predictions, a lower value of precision does not allow us to exclude a large number of false positives [34]. Considering the final aim of the classifier, which is to be implemented into a control system for prostheses, it is clear how a classifier with a high rate of false positives can severely affect the user experience by causing safety risks, increased cognitive load, and reduced performance [35]. Moreover, the RF algorithm must be preferred to kNN for other theoretical reasons. One of the primary benefits of RF is its robustness and ability to handle a wide variety of data types and structures [31]. Unlike kNN, which relies on the notion of distance metrics and can struggle with high-dimensional data, RF constructs multiple decision trees and merges their results to improve accuracy and control overfitting. This ensemble approach allows RF to manage complex datasets, as EEG data, more effectively and produce more reliable predictions. Another significant advantage of RF is its robustness to noise and overfitting, which is fundamental in the case of the EEG dataset. This is why each tree in the forest is built from a random subset of the data, which helps to mitigate the impact of anomalies and noise, leading to more generalized and stable predictions [31]. Speed and scalability are other areas where RF outperforms kNN. Once a random forest model is trained, making predictions is relatively fast because it involves threshold-based classification rather than computing distances to every training example, as required by kNN. This efficiency makes random forest more suitable for large-scale applications where rapid predictions are necessary, for example, in the real-time control of prostheses [36]. Concerning the comparison between the two ICA algorithms, it is clear that the use of the ADJUST algorithm for the extraction of the independent components allows continuous increase of the performance. This finding is in line with the literature, where it has been proved that ADJUST provides a more robust and reliable method for artifact removal [29]. As a consequence, it has been already proven that by removing artifacts and enhancing the signal-to-noise ratio, data are better suited for training and testing supervised learning models [37]. Finally, the achieved performance of the best-performing algorithm is comparable with the one reported in the literature for the discrimination of other gait-related activities, such as the risk of falls [19], gait phases, [15,16] and gait initiation [18], even if the results have been obtained with different machine learning algorithms. This finding could suggest the development of a control system based on different machine learning algorithms, each tailored to a specific task.

By focusing on the specific errors made by each classification algorithm, in RF based on the ICs dataset, RF struggles notably with detecting ascending stairs and descending stairs movements. This is reflected in its low recall values for these activities, indicating that the algorithm often fails to identify these movements when they occur. This low recall suggests a high rate of false negatives, where actual instances of these movements are missed by the model. The precision of RF across the various movements also highlights its classification errors; for ascending stairs and descending stairs movements, the algorithm shows moderate-to-low precision, meaning that while it identifies some instances correctly, it also misclassifies a significant number of non-relevant instances as these movements. This is evident from the precision scores, where ascending stairs and descending stairs movements have lower values compared to other activities. The adjustment of ICs improves both recall and precision across the board, reducing the occurrence of these false negatives and false positives and resulting in a more balanced performance. kNN, instead, exhibits a different error profile. With the ICs dataset, kNN's recall is particularly low for ascending stairs and descending stairs movements, similar to that of RF, which suggests that the algorithm frequently misses these movements. This indicates that kNN has a high false-negative rate, where true instances of these movements are not detected. Additionally, kNN shows lower precision for ascending stairs and descending stairs movements, implying that when the algorithm does predict these movements, it often does so incorrectly, leading to a high rate of false positives. With the adjusted ICs dataset, kNN shows improvements in recall for most movements, especially for ascending stairs and descending ramps. This suggests that the adjustments help the algorithm better identify these activities, though challenges remain. Precision also improves, but not uniformly across all movements. Despite these improvements, kNN still exhibits variability in its performance, reflecting a continued presence of classification errors in certain movements. These error patterns highlight the need for further refinement in both algorithms to achieve more reliable and accurate movement detection.

By summarizing, we can affirm that the RF fed with EEG-based features extracted through the ADJUST algorithm for the independent component analysis could be a suitable solution for implementing a control system for the real-time movement of prosthetic limbs also in uncontrolled environments, such as the daily activities involving locomotion on irregular terrains.

Limitations

Although the results are promising, the study presents some limitations that must be addressed to fully validate and generalize the findings. To build on this work, it is crucial to conduct additional research that encompasses a larger and more diverse sample. Expanding the pool of enrolled participants to include individuals with different demographic characteristics will enhance the representativeness of the results and ensure that the findings are broadly applicable. Furthermore, it is important to apply the algorithm by including participants who are actual users of prosthetic devices. This practical testing will provide valuable insights into the algorithm's effectiveness and usability in everyday scenarios, including various distractions and obstacles and also considering possible optimization for the computational time required by the signal process. Moreover, further machine and deep learning algorithms will be compared. By addressing these aspects, future research can offer a more comprehensive understanding and confirm the algorithm's practical utility across different contexts and populations.

Finally, due to the spread of flexible electronic sensors in several applications for biological healthy data collection [38–41], their applicability for EEG acquisition could be tested.

4. Conclusions

Aiming to understand if it is possible to use EEG-based machine learning algorithms to automatically distinguish locomotion tasks, we comparatively examined the random forest and k-nearest neighbors methods trained with brain activity features extracted through two different independent component analyses' algorithms. The findings demonstrated that the RF algorithm, especially when applied to datasets processed using the ADJUST algorithm for independent component analysis (ICA), consistently outperformed kNN in terms of overall accuracy, recall, precision, and F1-score. In addition, all the metrics overcame the optimal threshold, up to an overall accuracy of 92%, promoting the use of electroencephalography signals combined with machine learning algorithm for controlling prosthetic devices. Future research should focus on testing and refining these algorithms in real-world conditions to ensure the reliability of these systems in uncontrolled environments, as well as to increase the amount of data for realizing a standard training of the model.

Author Contributions: Conceptualization, S.Z., H.F.M., M.I.A., D.J.M., Z.u.A., W.A. and S.R.; Data curation, H.F.M., J.T. and S.R.; Formal analysis, S.Z., H.F.M., M.I.A., D.J.M., Z.u.A., W.A. and S.R.; Methodology, S.Z., H.F.M., M.I.A., D.J.M., Z.u.A., W.A., J.T. and S.R.; Software, J.T.; Supervision, S.Z., H.F.M., J.T. and S.R.; Validation, J.T. and S.R.; Writing—original draft, S.Z., H.F.M., M.I.A., D.J.M., W.A. and J.T.; Writing—review and editing, S.Z., H.F.M., Z.u.A. and S.R. All authors have read and agreed to the published version of the manuscript.

Funding: This research received no external funding.

Data Availability Statement: Data are available under request to the corresponding authors.

Conflicts of Interest: The authors declare no conflicts of interest.

References

1. Sarroca, N.; Valero, J.; Deus, J.; Casanova, J.; Luesma, M.J.; Lahoz, M. Quality of Life, Body Image and Self-Esteem in Patients with Unilateral Transtibial Amputations. *Sci. Rep.* **2021**, *11*, 12559. [CrossRef]
2. Sinha, R.; van den Heuvel, W.J.; Arokiasamy, P. Factors Affecting Quality of Life in Lower Limb Amputees. *Prosthet Orthot. Int.* **2011**, *35*, 90–96. [CrossRef] [PubMed]
3. Morgan, S.J.; Liljenquist, K.S.; Kajlich, A.; Gailey, R.S.; Amtmann, D.; Hafner, B.J. Mobility with a Lower Limb Prosthesis: Experiences of Users with High Levels of Functional Ability. *Disabil. Rehabil.* **2022**, *44*, 3236–3244. [CrossRef]
4. Jamil, N.; Belkacem, A.N.; Ouhbi, S.; Lakas, A. Noninvasive Electroencephalography Equipment for Assistive, Adaptive, and Rehabilitative Brain–Computer Interfaces: A Systematic Literature Review. *Sensors* **2021**, *21*, 4754. [CrossRef]
5. Ahmed, F.; Iqbal, H.; Nouman, A.; Maqbool, H.F.; Zafar, S.; Saleem, M.K. A Non Invasive Brain-Computer-Interface for Service Robotics. In Proceedings of the 2023 3rd International Conference on Artificial Intelligence (ICAI), Islamabad, Pakistan, 22–23 February 2023; IEEE: Piscataway, NJ, USA; pp. 142–147.

6. Castiblanco Jimenez, I.A.; Gomez Acevedo, J.S.; Marcolin, F.; Vezzetti, E.; Moos, S. Towards an Integrated Framework to Measure User Engagement with Interactive or Physical Products. *Int. J. Interact. Des. Manuf. (IJIDeM)* **2023**, *17*, 45–67. [CrossRef]
7. Li, P.; Qian, Y.; Si, N. Electroencephalogram and Electrocardiogram in Human-Computer Interaction. In Proceedings of the 2022 IEEE 2nd International Conference on Data Science and Computer Application (ICDSCA), Dalian, China, 28 October 2022; IEEE: Piscataway, NJ, USA; pp. 646–654.
8. Gehlhar, R.; Tucker, M.; Young, A.J.; Ames, A.D. A Review of Current State-of-the-Art Control Methods for Lower-Limb Powered Prostheses. *Annu. Rev. Control* **2023**, *55*, 142–164. [CrossRef]
9. Fleming, A.; Stafford, N.; Huang, S.; Hu, X.; Ferris, D.P.; Huang, H. Myoelectric Control of Robotic Lower Limb Prostheses: A Review of Electromyography Interfaces, Control Paradigms, Challenges and Future Directions. *J. Neural Eng.* **2021**, *18*, 041004. [CrossRef]
10. Gomez-Vargas, D.; Ballen-Moreno, F.; Barria, P.; Aguilar, R.; Azorín, J.M.; Munera, M.; Cifuentes, C.A. The Actuation System of the Ankle Exoskeleton T-FLEX: First Use Experimental Validation in People with Stroke. *Brain Sci.* **2021**, *11*, 412. [CrossRef] [PubMed]
11. Orban, M.; Elsamanty, M.; Guo, K.; Zhang, S.; Yang, H. A Review of Brain Activity and EEG-Based Brain–Computer Interfaces for Rehabilitation Application. *Bioengineering* **2022**, *9*, 768. [CrossRef]
12. Tariq, M.; Trivailo, P.M.; Simic, M. EEG-Based BCI Control Schemes for Lower-Limb Assistive-Robots. *Front. Hum. Neurosci.* **2018**, *12*, 312. [CrossRef]
13. Kline, A.; Forkert, N.D.; Felfeliyan, B.; Pittman, D.; Goodyear, B.; Ronsky, J. FMRI-Informed EEG for Brain Mapping of Imagined Lower Limb Movement: Feasibility of a Brain Computer Interface. *J. Neurosci. Methods* **2021**, *363*, 109339. [CrossRef]
14. Liu, D.; Chen, W.; Lee, K.; Chavarriaga, R.; Iwane, F.; Bouri, M.; Pei, Z.; Millan, J. del R. EEG-Based Lower-Limb Movement Onset Decoding: Continuous Classification and Asynchronous Detection. *IEEE Trans. Neural Syst. Rehabil. Eng.* **2018**, *26*, 1626–1635. [CrossRef]
15. Chai, J.; Chen, G.; Thangavel, P.; Dimitrakopoulos, G.N.; Kakkos, I.; Sun, Y.; Dai, Z.; Yu, H.; Thakor, N.; Bezerianos, A.; et al. Identification of Gait-Related Brain Activity Using Electroencephalographic Signals. In Proceedings of the 2017 8th International IEEE/EMBS Conference on Neural Engineering (NER), Shanghai, China, 25–28 May 2017; IEEE: Piscataway, NJ, USA; pp. 548–551.
16. Wei, P.; Zhang, J.; Tian, F.; Hong, J. A Comparison of Neural Networks Algorithms for EEG and SEMG Features Based Gait Phases Recognition. *Biomed. Signal Process. Control* **2021**, *68*, 102587. [CrossRef]
17. Bodda, S.; Maya, S.; Em Potti, M.N.; Sohan, U.; Bhuvaneshwari, Y.; Mathiyoth, R.; Diwakar, S. Computational Analysis of EEG Activity during Stance and Swing Gait Phases. *Procedia Comput. Sci.* **2020**, *171*, 1591–1597. [CrossRef]
18. Hasan, S.M.S.; Siddiquee, M.R.; Atri, R.; Ramon, R.; Marquez, J.S.; Bai, O. Prediction of Gait Intention from Pre-Movement EEG Signals: A Feasibility Study. *J. NeuroEng. Rehabil.* **2020**, *17*, 50. [CrossRef] [PubMed]
19. Soangra, R.; Smith, J.A.; Rajagopal, S.; Yedavalli, S.V.R.; Anirudh, E.R. Classifying Unstable and Stable Walking Patterns Using Electroencephalography Signals and Machine Learning Algorithms. *Sensors* **2023**, *23*, 6005. [CrossRef] [PubMed]
20. Gao, H.; Luo, L.; Pi, M.; Li, Z.; Li, Q.; Zhao, K.; Huang, J. EEG-Based Volitional Control of Prosthetic Legs for Walking in Different Terrains. *IEEE Trans. Autom. Sci. Eng.* **2021**, *18*, 530–540. [CrossRef]
21. Vokorokos, L.; Madoš, B.; Ádám, N.; Baláž, A. Data Acquisition in Non-Invasive Brain-Computer Interface Using Emotiv Epoc Neuroheadset. *Acta Electrotech. Inform.* **2012**, *12*, 5. [CrossRef]
22. Homan, R.W.; Herman, J.; Purdy, P. Cerebral Location of International 10–20 System Electrode Placement. *Electroencephalogr. Clin. Neurophysiol.* **1987**, *66*, 376–382. [CrossRef]
23. LaRocco, J.; Le, M.D.; Paeng, D.-G. A Systemic Review of Available Low-Cost EEG Headsets Used for Drowsiness Detection. *Front. Neuroinform.* **2020**, *14*, 553352. [CrossRef] [PubMed]
24. Brunner, C.; Delorme, A.; Makeig, S. Eeglab–an Open Source Matlab Toolbox for Electrophysiological Research. *Biomed. Eng./Biomed. Tech.* **2013**, *58*, 000010151520134182. [CrossRef]
25. Hyvärinen, A.; Oja, E. Independent Component Analysis: Algorithms and Applications. *Neural Netw.* **2000**, *13*, 411–430. [CrossRef] [PubMed]
26. Delorme, A.; Makeig, S. EEGLAB: An Open Source Toolbox for Analysis of Single-Trial EEG Dynamics Including Independent Component Analysis. *J. Neurosci. Methods* **2004**, *134*, 9–21. [CrossRef] [PubMed]
27. Sai, C.Y.; Mokhtar, N.; Arof, H.; Cumming, P.; Iwahashi, M. Automated Classification and Removal of EEG Artifacts with SVM and Wavelet-ICA. *IEEE J. Biomed. Health Inform.* **2018**, *22*, 664–670. [CrossRef]
28. Malik, A.N.; Iqbal, J.; Tiwana, M.I. EEG Signals Classification and Determination of Optimal Feature-Classifier Combination for Predicting the Movement Intent of Lower Limb. In Proceedings of the 2016 2nd International Conference on Robotics and Artificial Intelligence (ICRAI), 1–2 November 2016; IEEE: Piscataway, NJ, USA; pp. 45–49.
29. Mognon, A.; Jovicich, J.; Bruzzone, L.; Buiatti, M. ADJUST: An Automatic EEG Artifact Detector Based on the Joint Use of Spatial and Temporal Features. *Psychophysiology* **2011**, *48*, 229–240. [CrossRef] [PubMed]
30. Mannini, A.; Sabatini, A.M. Machine Learning Methods for Classifying Human Physical Activity from On-Body Accelerometers. *Sensors* **2010**, *10*, 1154–1175. [CrossRef] [PubMed]
31. Ho, T.K. Random Decision Forests. In Proceedings of the 3rd International Conference on Document Analysis and Recognition, Montreal, QC, Canada, 14–16 August 1995; pp. 278–282.

32. Attal, F.; Mohammed, S.; Dedabrishvili, M.; Chamroukhi, F.; Oukhellou, L.; Amirat, Y. Physical Human Activity Recognition Using Wearable Sensors. *Sensors* **2015**, *15*, 31314–31338. [CrossRef]
33. Taborri, J.; Palermo, E.; Rossi, S. Automatic Detection of Faults in Race Walking: A Comparative Analysis of Machine-Learning Algorithms Fed with Inertial Sensor Data. *Sensors* **2019**, *19*, 1461. [CrossRef] [PubMed]
34. Neyman, J.; Pearson, E.S.; Yule, G.U. The Testing of Statistical Hypotheses in Relation to Probabilities a Priori. *Math. Proc. Camb. Philos. Soc.* **1933**, *29*, 492. [CrossRef]
35. Bai, O.; Kelly, G.; Fei, D.-Y.; Murphy, D.; Fox, J.; Burkhardt, B.; Lovegreen, W.; Soars, J. A Wireless, Smart EEG System for Volitional Control of Lower-Limb Prosthesis. In Proceedings of the TENCON 2015-2015 IEEE Region 10 Conference, Macao, China, 1–4 November 2015; IEEE: Piscataway, NJ, USA; pp. 1–6.
36. Maqbool, H.F.; Husman, M.A.B.; Awad, M.I.; Abouhossein, A.; Iqbal, N.; Dehghani-Sanij, A.A. A Real-Time Gait Event Detection for Lower Limb Prosthesis Control and Evaluation. *IEEE Trans. Neural Syst. Rehabil. Eng.* **2017**, *25*, 1500–1509. [CrossRef]
37. Stalin, S.; Roy, V.; Shukla, P.K.; Zaguia, A.; Khan, M.M.; Shukla, P.K.; Jain, A. A Machine Learning-Based Big EEG Data Artifact Detection and Wavelet-Based Removal: An Empirical Approach. *Math. Probl. Eng.* **2021**, *2021*, 2942808. [CrossRef]
38. Ma, B.; Huang, K.; Chen, G.; Tian, Y.; Jiang, N.; Zhao, C.; Liu, H. A Dual-Mode Wearable Sensor with Coupled Ion and Pressure Sensing. *Soft Sci.* **2024**, *4*, 1–9. [CrossRef]
39. Kim, K.H.; Kim, J.H.; Ko, Y.J.; Lee, H.E. Body-Attachable Multifunctional Electronic Skins for Bio-Signal Monitoring and Therapeutic Applications. *Soft Sci.* **2024**, *4*, 24. [CrossRef]
40. Jan, A.A.; Kim, S.; Kim, S. A Skin-Wearable and Self-Powered Laminated Pressure Sensor Based on Triboelectric Nanogenerator for Monitoring Human Motion. *Soft Sci.* **2024**, *4*, 10. [CrossRef]
41. Dong, W.; Yang, L.; Gravina, R.; Fortino, G. Soft Wrist-Worn Multi-Functional Sensor Array for Real-Time Hand Gesture Recognition. *IEEE Sens. J.* **2022**, *22*, 17505–17514. [CrossRef]

robotics

MDPI

Article

Design and Experimental Evaluation of Multiple 3D-Printed Reduction Gearboxes for Wearable Exoskeletons

Riccardo Bezzini [1,2], Giulia Bassani [1,2], Carlo Alberto Avizzano [1,2], and Alessandro Filippeschi [1,2,*]

[1] Institute of Mechanical Intelligence, Scuola Superiore Sant'Anna, 56127 Pisa, Italy; riccardo.bezzini@santannapisa.it (R.B.); g.bassani@santannapisa.it (G.B.); c.avizzano@santannapisa.it (C.A.A.)
[2] Department of Excellence in Robotics and AI, Scuola Superiore Sant'Anna, 56127 Pisa, Italy
* Correspondence: alessandro.filippeschi@santannapisa.it

Abstract: The recent advancements in wearable exoskeletons have highlighted their effectiveness in assisting humans for both rehabilitation and augmentation purposes. These devices interact with the user; therefore, their actuators and power transmission mechanisms are crucial for enhancing physical human–robot interaction (pHRI). The advanced progression of 3D printing technology as a valuable method for creating lightweight and efficient gearboxes enables the exploration of multiple reducer designs. However, to the authors' knowledge, only sporadic implementations with relatively low reduction ratios have been reported, and the respective experimental validations usually vary, preventing a comprehensive evaluation of different design and implementation choices. In this paper, we design, develop, and examine experimentally multiple 3D-printed gearboxes conceived for wearable assistive devices. Two relevant transmission ratios (1:30 and 1:80) and multiple designs, which include single- and double-stage compact cam cycloidal drives, compound planetary gearboxes, and cycloidal and planetary architectures, are compared to assess the worth of 3D-printed reducers in human–robot interaction applications. The resulting prototypes were examined by evaluating their weight, cost, backdrivability, friction, regularity of the reduction ratio, gear play, and stiffness. The results show that the developed gearboxes represent valuable alternatives for actuating wearable exoskeletons in multiple applications.

Keywords: wearable exoskeletons actuator; pHRI; 3D-printed reducers; cycloidal reducer; planetary gearbox

1. Introduction

In recent years, the development of wearable exoskeletons has seen significant growth, driven by their potential in a wide range of applications. Indeed, these devices can be used for assistance [1], rehabilitation [2], and augmentation [3]. Several research efforts aimed at enhancing wearable exoskeletons focus on mechanical [4] and control [5] solutions to improve performance in terms of physical human–robot interaction (pHRI), leading to increasingly safe and ergonomic devices that ensure efficient modulation of interaction forces tailored to specific applications.

High-performance actuators, comprising motors and power transmission mechanisms, are crucial for enhancing pHRI [6,7]. Therefore, the actuation modules of exoskeletons must be efficient while ensuring low costs and weights to maintain the affordability and usability of the device [8]. Among the diverse methods for actuating wearable exoskeletons, electric motors with high torque density, paired with suitable gearing systems, stand out as valuable and common solutions [9]. The literature contains multiple implementations of geared electric-motor-driven exoskeletons, such as Refs. [10–13], exhibiting a wide range of reducer designs and transmission ratios tailored to the specific requirements of different applications.

Despite the undeniable value of current 'geared' exoskeletons, the use of transmission mechanisms introduces challenges such as increased complexity, weight, and cost. Since reducing weight and cost is desirable for exoskeletons, some studies have explored using 3D-printed components to develop lighter wearable robots [14,15]. However, given the recent advancements in additive manufacturing (AM), 3D-printed components also emerge as a promising option for developing efficient, lightweight, and cost-effective reducers, and are also capable of enhancing pHRI in robotic exoskeletons, thus addressing the issues of rising costs and weights associated with traditional reduction gearboxes.

Several studies have assessed the value of using polymeric materials for building gears. For example, Ref. [16] investigated materials for lightweight reduction gears aimed at reducing robot weight by using composite materials and resins. Weight reduction tends to decrease stiffness, resulting in a drop in speed and precision performance. The authors evaluated the applicability of replacing metal parts with plastic materials produced by a fused deposition modeling 3D printer. In other works, such as Refs. [17–19], the authors evaluated the influences of multiple printing parameters such as the printing nozzle temperature, speed, printing bed temperature, and infill percentage, while assessing fatigue life and the failure types of 3D-printed gears made of polylactic acid (PLA). In [20], the authors carried out experimental determinations to generate new insights regarding the capability of 3D-printed gears to function in mechanisms without lubrication, considering factors like sliding speed, material hardness, surface finish, and geometry. Moreover, some studies focused on evaluating dimensional accuracy, form errors, and surface quality regarding FFF (fused filament fabrication) [21,22].

However, to the authors' knowledge, only a few recent studies explored the possibility of exploiting 3D-printed-geared transmission in wearable devices [23–25]. Other works presented scattered implementations with isolated experimental investigations of 3D-printed reducers, which do not allow for comparisons between different gearbox designs and reduction ratios. For example, in [26,27], the authors presented 3D-printed actuators, but they limited the study to low reduction ratios (from 1:7.5 to 1:15), only considering the classic planetary design and its compound variation. Other studies focused on 3D-printed cycloidal reducers, such as Refs. [23,28,29], where the authors presented design details and experimental results, focusing on single low-ratio (1:11 and 1:30) cycloidal reducers.

Notwithstanding the merits of the mentioned works, the literature lacks a more extensive and comprehensive evaluation of 3D-printed reducers. Therefore, the goal of this work is to investigate and compare multiple 3D-printed reducers to examine the possibility of using such mechanisms in wearable exoskeletons and enhance proper pHRI.

This study presents a fairly wide-ranging comparison of 3D-printed reducers, exposing lightweight and low-cost implementations of three different transmission solutions, i.e., single- and double-stage cycloidal reducers, planetary compound transmissions, and the combination of cycloidal and planetary gearboxes in a double-stage reducer. These designs are examined by inspecting the respective performances of two reduction ratios, i.e., 1:30 and 1:80, which are plausible for rehabilitative devices, as well as for exoskeletons conceived for assistance and augmentation. Overall, eight reducers are compared. Their 3D models (STL files) are available upon request to the authors, together with the list of off-the-shelf components (bearings, screws, and nuts) exploited for the assembly.

In summary, the main contributions of this paper are as follows:

- The design and realization of eight different 3D-printed reduction gearboxes, for a comprehensive evaluation of their features.
- A comparison of multiple transmission designs and reduction ratios, which, to the authors' knowledge, have not been previously examined in the field of 3D-printed actuators (e.g., compact double stage cycloidal reducers, high transmission ratios above 1:50, and combinations of cycloidal and planetary gearboxes).
- An experimental evaluation of multiple performance indexes (e.g., backdrive torque, friction, gear play, stiffness, etc.) for each reducer that concurrently allows for a comprehensive assessment of several transmission designs implementing different reduction ratios.

The remainder of this paper is organized as follows:Section 2 presents a brief presentation of the reduction designs exploited in this work; Section 3 presents a brief presentation of the reduction designs exploited in this work, followed by more detailed descriptions of the presented 3D-printed mechanisms. Section 4 presents the experimental setup, metrics, and test procedures. Section 5 presents some evaluative considerations on the results of the experimental analysis, discusses the different features of the investigated reduction mechanisms, focuses on the current limitations of the proposed approach, and presents the expected future works. Finally, Section 6 presents a summary of the proposed work, along with the most relevant inferences.

2. Background

2.1. Transmissions Architectures

2.1.1. Single-Stage Cycloidal Reducer

The working principle of the cycloidal reducers involves four main components: an eccentric shaft that serves as the input motion, a cycloid disk mounted on the eccentric shaft that engages with the pins (or rollers) forming the fixed cycloidal base, and a set of output pins fixed to the carrier, representing the transmission's output. The reduction mechanisms are named after the profile of the disk, which is indeed derived from a *cycloid* [30]. A simplified illustration is reported in Figure 1.

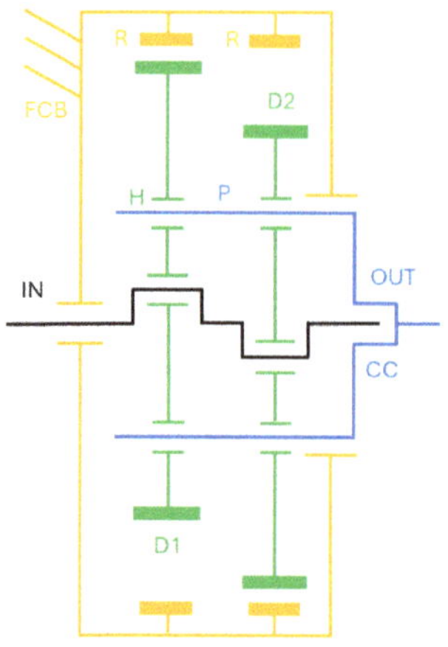

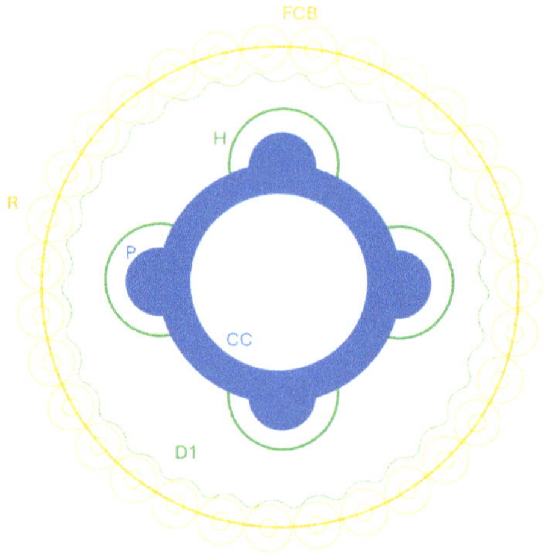

Figure 1. Schematic illustrations of the structure of the single-stage cycloidal reducer. Both the lateral (**a**) and frontal (**b**) views are reported for clarity. The acronyms used represent parts that are the same color. **IN** refers to the input shaft (in black) with eccentric sections. **FCB** refers to the fixed cycloidal base (in yellow), to which the rollers (**R**, still in yellow) are connected. **D1** and **D2** are the two cycloidal disks, in green. **CC** refers to the cycloidal carrier (in blue), which is composed of a certain number of pins (**P**) that are driven by interacting with the holes (**H**). The carrier represents the output of this reducer.

The rotation of the eccentric shaft causes the roto-translation of the cycloid disk, which engages with the cycloid base's rollers (in this case, bearings). The rotation of the disk generates the movement of the output pins in the holes in the cycloid disc. This bore–pin coupling allows the output shaft to rotate non-eccentrically. The output shaft's rotational speed can be deduced by the gear ratio, as follows:

$$i = \frac{n_l}{n_l - N_p}, \quad (1)$$

where n_l denotes the number of lobes of the cycloidal disk and N_p denotes the number of rollers connected to the fixed cycloidal base. The cycloidal base can be composed of pins or rollers (usually bearings or bushings); the main differences between these two architectures are studied in [29]. Two cycloid disks were used (each engaging with a different set of rollers), with a difference in phase of 180°, ensuring that the unbalanced forces compensate each other, resulting in smoother operation at high speeds and reduced vibrations. The two sets of rollers that engage with the disks are identical.

The cycloidal systems allow us to obtain high reduction ratios simply with a difference of only one tooth between the number of rollers and the number of lobes on the disk. These reducers also ensure lower frictions and smoother contact forces, with respect to the classic geared wheels, between the disk and the cycloidal base, composed of bearings as rollers (a *pin-wheel configuration*), allowing for more efficient contact dynamics between the disk and base (creeping contacts are prevented).

2.1.2. Double-Stage Cycloidal Reducer

As can be deduced from the previous explanation of the cycloidal reducer's architecture (especially considering Figure 1b), for high reduction ratios, the cycloidal architecture demands a high number of rollers. These rollers must be distributed along a sufficiently large circumference, which increases the reducer's width. To avoid this issue, the design proposed in [31] can be used. This architecture is illustrated in Figure 2a.

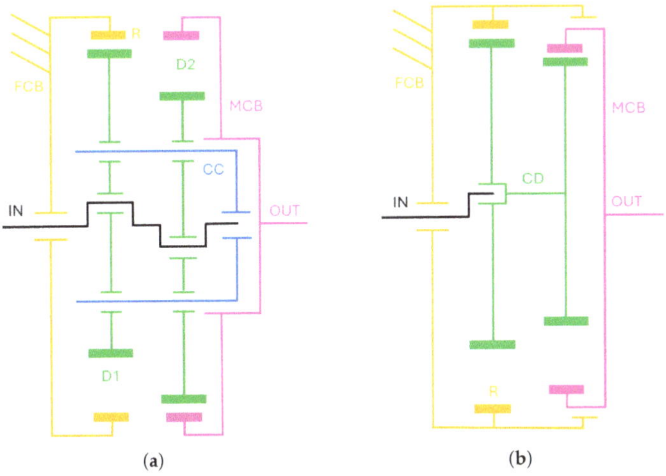

Figure 2. Schematic illustrations of the structure of the double-stage cycloidal reducer. On the left, the dual-stage double-disk architecture is presented (**a**), while on the right side, a scheme of the compact disk double-stage cycloidal reducer (**b**) is presented. The acronyms used represent parts that are the same color. **IN** refers to the input shaft (in black) with eccentric sections. **FCB** refers to the fixed cycloidal base (in yellow), to which the rollers (R, still in yellow) are connected. **D1** and **D2** are the two different cycloidal disks, which are connected to the same shaft and carrier but are in contact with two different groups of rollers. **CC** refers to the cycloidal carrier (in blue). **CD** refers to the compact disk, a part that includes two joint cycloidal disks moved by the same shaft but engaged with different sets of rollers. **MCB** refers to the moving cycloidal base, another part connected to a set of rollers (in purple), which obtains its motion from the interaction with the second disk **D2** and corresponds to the output of this reducer.

This design allows for high reduction ratios while maintaining reasonable encumbrance since the reduction ratio is computed as follows:

$$i = \frac{n_1}{N_2}, \quad (2)$$

where n_1 denotes the number of lobes of the disk of the first cycloidal stage, while N_2 denotes the number of rollers that compose the moving cycloidal base, which is the base of the second cycloidal stage.

However, this design maintains the presence of a carrier, which inevitably leads to the presence of screws (used to increase the resistance of the pins) and bearings, which are mounted in the holes of the cycloidal disks to improve the contact dynamics between output pins and disk holes.

To avoid these problems, some works (e.g., [32,33]) exploit an alternative version of a double-stage cycloidal drive, with a compact disk (composed of two joint disks) that avoids the presence of a carrier, allowing for a significant decrease in weight and cost. This architecture's reduction ratio is computed as follows:

$$i = \frac{n_1 N_2}{n_1 N_2 - n_2 N_1}, \quad (3)$$

where n_1 denotes the number of lobes of the disk of the first cycloidal stage, N_2 denotes the number of rollers that compose the moving cycloidal base (the base of the second cycloidal stage), and n_2 denotes the number of lobes of the second-stage cycloidal disk.

2.1.3. Cycloidal–Planetary (CP) Series Reducer

Planetary transmissions have four main components: the sun gear, planetary gears, the carrier, and the ring gear, which is the only internally toothed component of the reducer. This kind of mechanism comprehends several modes of operation, determined by which parts are fixed and which parts rotate. Typically, only two of the three sets of gears will rotate. Concerning the implementations presented in this work, the planetary configuration consists of a fixed ring gear, a rotating sun gear as the input, and a rotating carrier (connected to the planet gears) as the output.

The gear ratio in a planetary transmission is determined by the difference in the number of teeth on the ring gear and the sun gear. Given the following equations, which represent the sun–planet and planet–ring interactions, respectively, the overall gear ratio of a planetary gearbox can be deduced in the generic case, which involves the rotation of the gears:

$$N_s\omega_s + N_p\omega_p - (N_s + N_p)\omega_c = 0 \quad (4)$$

$$N_r\omega_r + N_p\omega_p - (N_r + N_p)\omega_c = 0 \quad (5)$$

where N stands for the number of teeth, ω represents the rotating velocity, and the subscripts s, p, r, and c denote *sun*, *planet*, *ring*, and *carrier*, respectively. Concerning the planetary gearsets presented in this work, we consider the relation between the number of teeth:

$$N_r = N_s + 2N_p. \quad (6)$$

Moreover, as mentioned previously, the ring gear is fixed in the designed gearboxes, so $omega = 0$. Finally, the transmission ratio considered here for the single-stage planetary transmissions is as follows:

$$\frac{\omega_c}{\omega_s} = \frac{N_s}{N_s + N_r}. \quad (7)$$

Usually, simple epicyclic planetary stages used with a stationary ring gear are used for implementing gear ratios that vary from 1:3 to 1:9.

The **CP** reducers are designed as a series combination of cycloidal and planetary reducers. The output of the cycloidal stage (the carrier) serves as the input for the subsequent planetary stage, the sun. This configuration optimizes the unique advantages of each type: cycloidal reducers with lower ratios provide manageable radial dimensions, and planetary stages, as mentioned previously, are limited to reduction ratios up to 1:9 [34]. The resulting gear ratio can be deduced by combining 1 and 7, obtaining Equation (8):

$$i = i_{cycloidal}\, i_{planetary} = \frac{N_s}{N_s + N_r}\, \frac{n_l}{n_l - N_p}. \tag{8}$$

In Figure 3, a schematic representation of the cycloidal–planetary reducer is reported.

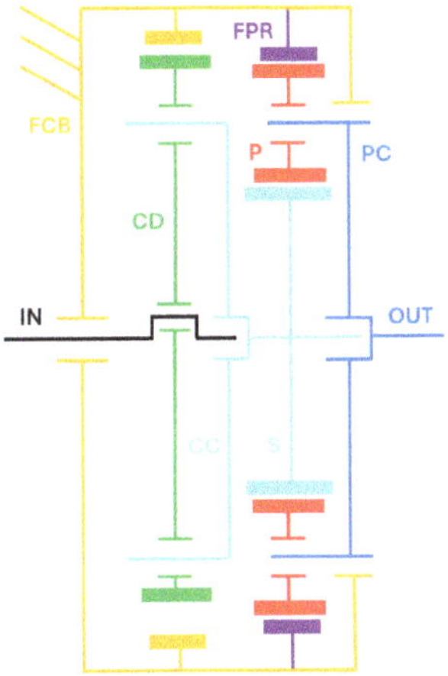

Figure 3. Schematic illustration of the structure of the cycloidal–planetary (**CP**) series reducer. The acronyms reported are abbreviations for parts of the same color. **IN** refers to the input shaft (in black) with a single eccentric section. **FCB** refers to the fixed cycloidal base (in yellow), to which the rollers (R, still in yellow) are connected. **CD** refers to the cycloidal disk. **CC** refers to the cycloidal carrier (in light blue), which is composed of another consequent section (the planetary Sun **S** joined to the first one. **P** stands for planet (in red), while **FPR** refers to the fixed planetary ring, which is rigidly connected to the cycloidal base. **PC** refers to the planetary carrier that corresponds to the output of this reducer.

2.1.4. Compound Planetary Reducer

Given the limitations of standard planetary gearboxes in achieving the high reduction ratios required for this study, the design detailed in [34] represents a suitable and compact architecture. In that work, the author analyzed and designed epicyclic gear arrangements to achieve higher gear ratios.

Due to the possibility of implementing high ratios, compound-stepped planetary gear (CSPG) drives are suitable for applications with size restrictions, e.g., gear reducers for actuators in wearable robots. The design of the reducers, shown in Figure 4 and selected from those proposed in [34], is a combination of two stages (addressed as A and B) of planetary reducers. Unlike the traditional planetary architecture, this compound transmission utilizes two ring gears: the first one (Stage A) is fixed to the stator of the motor while the second ring gear (Stage B) is the output of the reducer. The input shaft moves the sun of Stage A. Stage B does not include a sun gear. The compound planets are composed of two different base planets rigidly connected to form a single component. The reduction ratio of this reducer can be computed according to the following equation:

$$i = \frac{1 + \dfrac{z_{3a}}{z_{1a}}}{1 - \dfrac{z_{2b}z_{3a}}{z_{2a}z_{3b}}}, \tag{9}$$

where z_{ij} denotes the number of teeth of a general gear and the subscripts consist of $i \in \{1, 2, 3\}$ (these numbers denote the Sun, planet, and ring, respectively), and $j \in \{a, b\}$ (these letters denote the first and second planetary stages, respectively).

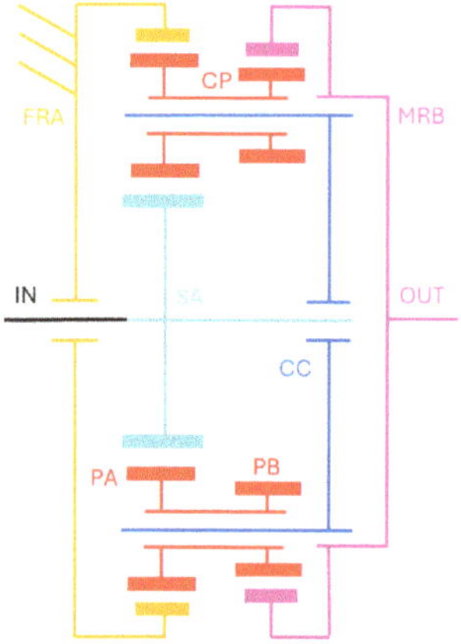

Figure 4. Schematic illustration of the structure of the planetary compound (**CO**) reducer. The acronyms used represent parts that are the same color. **IN** refers to the input shaft (in black), which corresponds to the planetary Sun **SA** of Stage A of the compound reducer. **FRA** refers to the planetary fixed ring of Stage A (in yellow). **CP** refers to the compound planet (in red), composed of two joint planets (**PA** and **PB**, respectively, the planet of Stage A and the planet of Stage B). **CC** refers to the compound carrier (in blue) to which the compound planets are connected. **MRB** refers to the planetary moving ring of Stage B, which corresponds to the output of this reducer.

3. Materials and Methods

3.1. Design Assumptions and Constraints

The first design constraint is the transmission ratio, whose selected values are 1:30 and 1:80. These values were selected because lower ratios would demand high-torque expensive motors, which is in contrast with the goal of cost-effective and wearable actuators. Instead, higher ratios may produce excessive reflected inertia and higher backdrive torques [13], which is undesirable in pHRI. To set encumbrance constraints, as references, we considered 3D-printed reducers from valuable works such as Refs. [26,28,29] (with the maximum reduction ratio of 1:15). The diameter and height constraints used in designing the target reducers were slightly reduced from the dimensions reported in previous studies. The goal was to maintain reasonable dimensions while achieving higher reduction ratios; therefore, the maximum diameter and height were set, respectively, to 100 mm and 55 mm.

3.2. Proposed Reducers

This section presents the structures of the proposed reducers. In the following, the proposed reducers will be addressed with acronyms that refer to the gearbox designs: **CY** stands for *cycloidal*, **CO** symbolizes the *compound planetary* design, and **CP** stands for the *cycloidal–planetary series*. For example, **CY30** refers to the cycloidal reducer with a ratio of 1:30, while **CO80** stands for the compound planetary gearbox with a reduction ratio equal to 1:80. Regarding the **CY80** reducers, since three versions were explored to assess the characteristics of this design, each reducer will be referred to using **CY80vx**, where $x \in \{1, 2, 3\}$.

3.2.1. CY30

For the design of this reducer and the other reducers, including the cycloidal stages, the roller choice was fundamental, since it affected the other dimensions once the reduction ratio was set. A low roller radius allows for reduced encumbrances, but it may reduce the torque transmission capability of the reducer.

On the other hand, large rollers may lead to better torque performances. However, given the target ratio (1:30) and the constraint on the maximum diameter (100 mm), an excessively high roller diameter would not fit the design goal. Moreover, larger rollers (bearings) would cause an excessive increase in the cost and weight of the reducer. The chosen roller radius of 4 mm represents a valid compromise, balancing reducer dimensions, weight, and costs. Moreover, its internal diameter of 3 mm allows fixing the rollers to the cycloidal base using M3 screws, which is important for guaranteeing a stable and resistant connection between the base and the rollers.

Once the roller dimensions were established, the minimum possible cycloidal base radius was computed to ensure that the rollers would not interfere with each other's motion. The choice of the cycloidal base radius is also correlated with the eccentricity. Indeed, an excessively small base radius would limit the eccentricity. Given a specific roller dimension and cycloidal base radius, an increase in eccentricity could cause the cycloidal disk to have an increasingly discontinuous lateral surface, thereby resulting in severely irregular output motion. The same reasoning regarding the parameters' values was applied in the design of other cycloidal stages presented later and will not be repeated. Table 1 displays the chosen values for the design parameters of the **CY30** reducer.

Table 1. Design parameters of the CY30 reducer.

Parameter	Value
Fixed cycloidal base radius (location of rollers)	41 mm
Number of rollers	31
Roller radius	4 mm
Eccentricity	1 mm
Number of carrier output pins	6
Output pin radius	4 mm
Carrier radius	24 mm

Figure 5 represents a CAD model of the exploded view of the **CY30** reducer, without including bearings (except for the rollers) and screws. The input shaft features two opposing eccentric sections, each coupled through bearings to the disks, with one disk phased 180° opposite the other. These disks engage with two sets of rollers, separated by a row of printed spacers. Both the spacers and the rollers are connected to the cycloidal base (the lower and upper white parts) using screws and nuts. Also, screws of varying lengths are used to reinforce the pins that make up the cycloidal carrier.

3.2.2. CY80

According to the reduction ratio Formula (3), the chosen **CY80** architecture allows for multiple combinations regarding the number of rollers of the fixed and moving cycloidal bases. Apart from the number of rollers, eccentricity is the other parameter that directly influences the dimensions of the reducer.

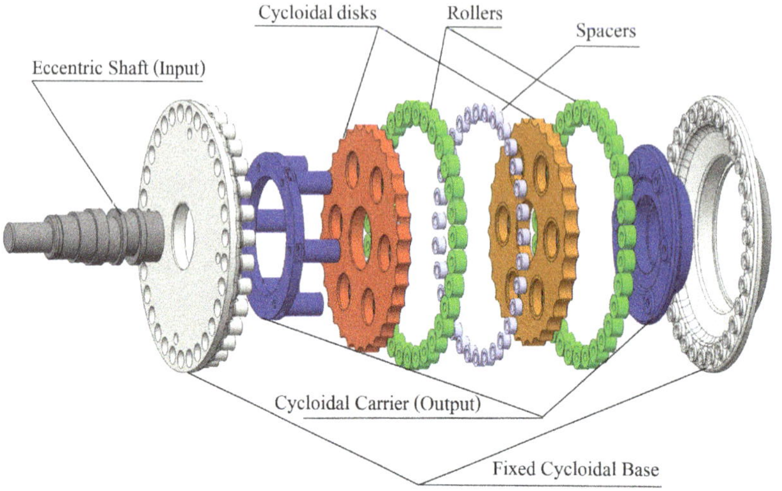

Figure 5. Exploded view of the CAD model of the cycloidal (**CY30**) reducer. Bearings, nuts, and screws were hidden for better comprehensibility of the Figure. The distinct elements illustrated with the same color (the upper and lower parts of the fixed cycloidal base, as well as the two parts of the cycloidal carrier) are rigidly connected through screws in the final assembly.

Since this reduction mechanism is not widespread (to the authors' knowledge, it was never implemented in a 3D-printed version), we designed and tested different alternatives for the number of rollers and eccentricity. This contributes to this work's goal of exploring different architectures for 3D-printed reducers. The design parameters reported in Table 2 describe the three presented design arrangements:

- **CY80v1** implements a solution with minimum dimensions. Both the number of rollers at the fixed and moving cycloidal bases are the minimum required to achieve the 1:80 ratio. Also, the eccentricity is limited to 1 mm.
- **CY80v2** implements a version with the maximum number of rollers that allows respecting the maximum diameter constraint (considering the rollers with a 4 mm radius), combined with an eccentricity that is set to 0.8 mm.
- **CY80v3** implements the reducer version with the minimum number of rollers (the same as the first version). However, the dimensions have been pushed almost to the maximum limit. Indeed, as can be noted by comparing the values from Table 2, the diameters of the cycloidal bases are the same, thus using the same number of rollers as in **CY80v1** allows for a pronounced eccentricity (2.5 mm).

Variants with both a high number of rollers and high eccentricity were avoided in order to not exceed the encumbrance constraints.

The CAD models in Figure 6 display the exploded views of the three CY80 reducers. The input shafts feature a single eccentric section, which connects to the double-stage compact disk via two ball bearings, not shown in the images. The separate stages of rollers are attached to their respective bases (either fixed or moving). The upper part of the fixed cycloidal base encloses the entire reducer and also serves as a support for the Moving Base, which is connected to it through another bearing.

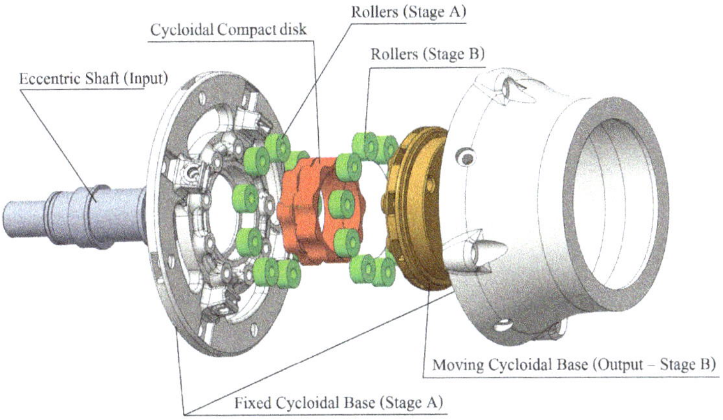

(**a**) CY80v1

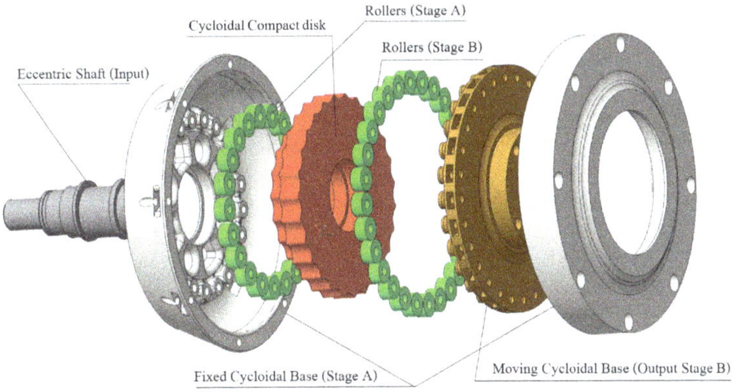

(**b**) CY80v2

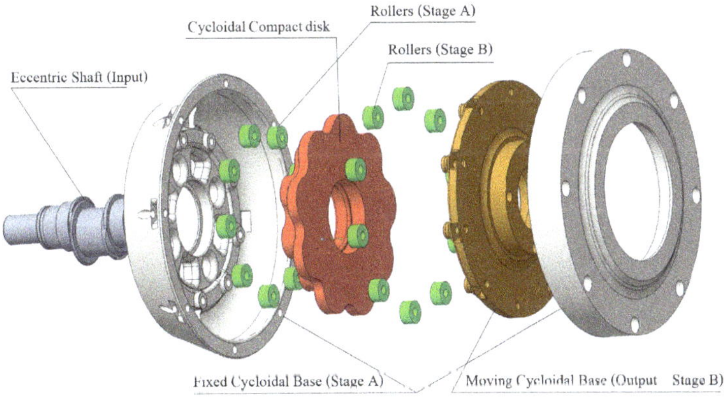

(**c**) CY80v3

Figure 6. Exploded views of the CAD models of the three cycloidal double-stage compact disk reducers (**CY80v1**, **CY80v2**, and **CY80v3**). Bearings, nuts, and screws are not shown for a better comprehensibility of the Figure. The distinct elements illustrated with the same color (the upper and lower parts of the fixed cycloidal base) are rigidly connected through screws in the final assembly.

Table 2. Design parameters of the three versions of the CY80 reducer.

Parameter	CY80v1	CY80v2	CY80v3
Fixed cycloidal base radius A (location of rollers)	18.1 mm	28.5 mm	28.5 mm
Number of rollers A	9	21	9
Moving cycloidal base radius B (location of rollers)	18.1 mm	37 mm	37 mm
Number of rollers B	10	28	10
Roller radius	4 mm	4 mm	4 mm
Eccentricity	1 mm	0.8 mm	2.5 mm

3.2.3. CP30 and CP80

For the design of the cycloidal-planetary reducers, the series combination of these architectures has necessitated joint considerations regarding dimensional compatibility for proper integration. First of all, the respective reduction ratios to be combined were selected to maximize the efficiency of the two architectures.

Since classical single-stage planetary reducers are used to implement low transmission ratios [35], we opted for 1:3 and 1:4 ratios for the total targets of 1:30 and 1:80, respectively. This led to the selection of 1:10 and 1:20 transmission ratios for the respective cycloidal stages. Since these values are lower than the 1:30 presented earlier, this design approach reduces radial encumbrances in both the **CP** reducers with respect to the **CY30**.

However, it is clear from the basic structure of a cycloidal reducer that the presence of the carrier sets an inferior limit to the reducer's diameter. A valid compromise was found with a 35 mm fixed cycloidal base radius and a 21 mm carrier radius. As noted in Table 3, these values were utilized for both the **CP** reducers as well as other design parameters.

Table 3. Design parameters of the CP30 and CP80 reducers.

Parameter	CP30	CP80
Fixed cycloidal base radius (roller location)	35 mm	35 mm
Number of rollers	11	21
Roller radius	4 mm	4 mm
Eccentricity	1.2 mm	1.2 mm
Number of cycloidal carrier output pins	6	6
Output pin radius	3.8 mm	3.8 mm
Cycloidal carrier radius	21 mm	21 mm
Number of teeth (Ring)	52	51
Number of teeth (Planets)	13	17
Number of teeth (Sun)	26	17
Number of planets	6	4
Teeth Module	1 mm	1 mm
Teeth Pressure angle	25°	25°
Planetary Carrier Radius	19.5 mm	17 mm

Once the dimensions of the cycloidal stage were set, we designed the planetary stages to keep their encumbrance smaller than the cycloidal one. The number of teeth of the external ring (together with the teeth module) determines the maximum diameter of the planetary stage. We used gears with a module of 1 mm, a practical compromise between excessively small teeth, which resulted in modest resistance and difficulties in accurately printing the gear profile, and larger modules that led to unacceptable encumbrance. The equations below detail the relationships between the teeth module, radial encumbrance, and teeth height.

$$H_t = 2.25\,\mathrm{m}, \tag{10}$$

$$P_g = Z_g\,\mathrm{m}, \tag{11}$$

where H_t represents the height of the teeth (function of the module m) and P_g denotes the primitive circumference of the gear, which gives an approximate idea of the gear's encumbrance, and which is computed as the product of the module and the number of teeth Z_g. Once the correct ring's teeth number was set, the rest of the parameters can be deduced from Equation (7). Table 3 presents the whole set of parameters for the CP30 and CP80 reducers. The CAD models reported in Figure 7 present the exploded views of the **CP** reducers.

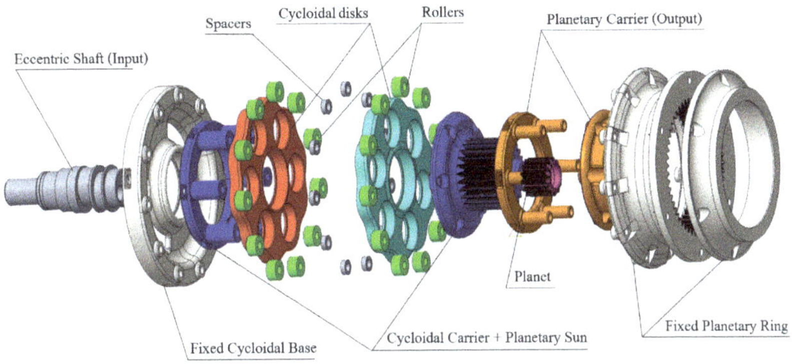

(**a**) CP30

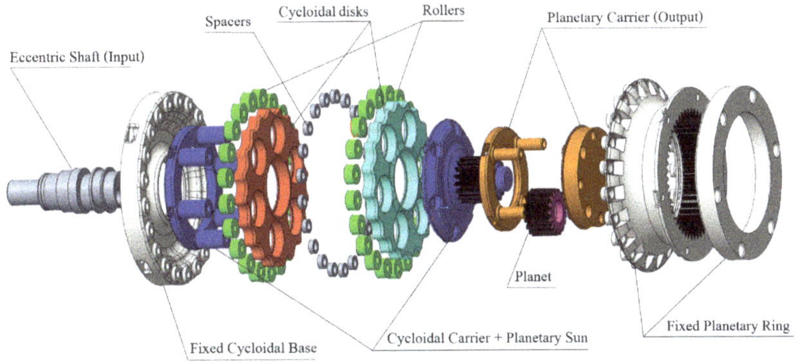

(**b**) CP80

Figure 7. Exploded views of the CAD models of both the cycloidal–planetary reducers (**CP30** and **CP80**). Bearings, nuts, and screws are not shown for a better comprehensibility of the Figure. For the same reason, not the planets are represented. The distinct elements illustrated with the same color (the fixed cycloidal base with the fixed planetary ring, the two parts of the cycloidal carrier, and the two parts of the planetary carrier) are rigidly connected through screws in the final assembly.

3.2.4. CO30 and CO80

From Equation (9), a target reduction ratio can be achieved with multiple combinations of teeth numbers. At the same time, compound reducers are not subject to the encumbrance constraints of the cycloidal stage that limited our target dimensions in the CP reducers. Therefore, we were able to increase the module to 1.2 mm, up from 1 mm in CP reducers.

The increase in the teeth module leaves room for the selection of teeth numbers, and we set the minimum number of teeth for the gears (both sun and planets) of the two stages at 16, to enable the design of carrier pins with a sufficiently large diameter. This size is crucial to accommodate two bearings for each planet for proper assembly on the carrier pin. Given these conditions, we managed to implement the minimum teeth choices that met the mentioned constraints for both **CO30** and **CO80**. As can be noticed from Table 4, the two designs presented have an equal carrier radius and almost identical dimensions.

The CAD models reported in Figure 8 present the exploded views of the **CO** reducers. The sun of the first stage (i.e., the input) engages with the Stage A planets inside the Stage A fixed ring. Given that the compound planets are composed of two different gears rigidly connected, the motion of the sun induces the common carrier to rotate; thus, the Stage B planets engage with the Stage B ring, which is the output of the reducer.

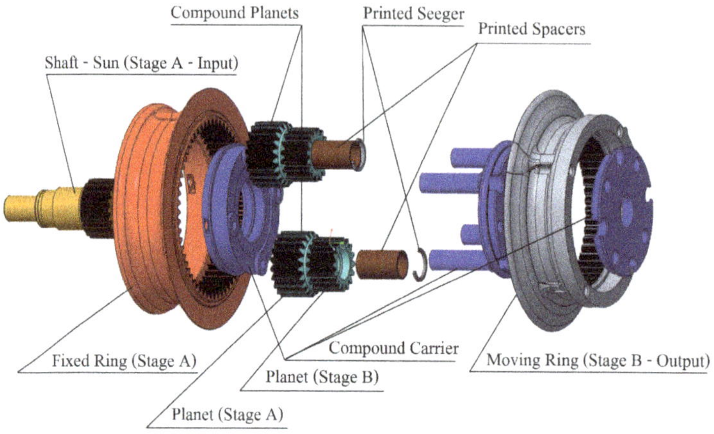

(**a**) CO30

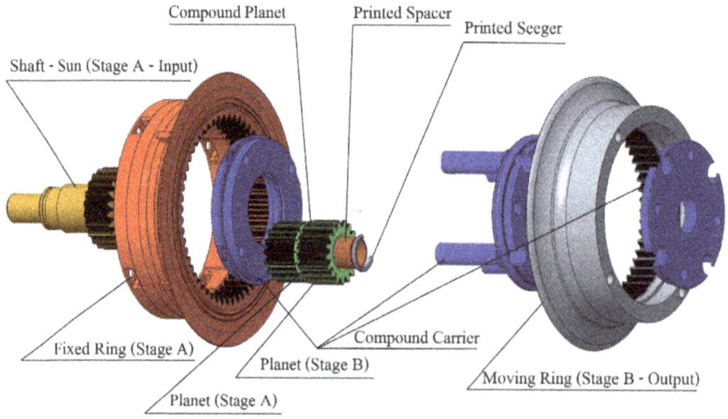

(**b**) CO80

Figure 8. Exploded view of the CAD model of both planetary compound reducers (**CO30** and **CO80**). Bearings, nuts, and screws were hidden for better comprehensibility of the figure. For the same reason, not all four planets are represented. The distinct elements illustrated with the same color (the three parts of the compound carrier) are rigidly connected through screws in the final assembly.

Table 4. Design parameters of the CO30 and CO80 reducers.

Parameter	CO30	CO80
Number of teeth Ring A	58	54
Number of teeth Planets A	20	16
Rotation angle Planets A	81°	123.75°
Number of teeth Sun A	18	22
Number of teeth Ring B	54	55
Number of teeth Planets B	16	17
Rotation angle Planets B	123.75°	111.176°
Number of planets	4	4
Teeth Module	1.2 mm	1.2 mm
Teeth Pressure angle	25°	25°
Carrier Radius	22.8 mm	22.8 mm

3.3. Materials, Printers, and Off-the-Shelf Components

To develop the presented reducers, PLA was used since it combines reasonably low costs and valuable mechanical properties [21]. The printers used were the Ultimaker S7 Pro Bundle and the Ultimaker S3-Extended, with Ultimaker Cura used as a slicer. The parts that were not produced through 3D printing were the bearings, screws, and nuts. Indeed, apart from the mentioned components, spacers and Seeger rings were produced through printing procedures.

The lists of necessary non-printed components for each reducer are presented in the tables in Appendix A. Apart from the bearings, which are clearly essentials in the reducers' structures, off-the-shelf components (especially the screws) were fundamental in strengthening some highly loaded structural components, such as the carrier pins in the exploited designs, and linking the rollers to the cycloidal bases.

3.4. Evaluation Metrics

To evaluate the features of the proposed reducers and compare different reduction ratios implemented through multiple designs, the following metrics were taken into consideration when designing the experimental protocols described in the next section:

Speed regularity: This parameter describes the oscillating deviation between the actual output speed of a reducer (given a specific motor speed) and its expected value. It is calculated as the product of the motor's speed and the reduction ratio, according to the following formula:

$$R = 100\left(1 - \frac{\Delta\omega_r}{i\,\omega_m}\right), \tag{12}$$

where R denotes the regularity (expressed as a percentage value), ω_r denotes the reducer's speed, i denotes the transmission ratio, and ω_m denotes the motor's velocity.

It is important to evaluate the regularity of a reducer to assess the precision and stability of the actuator's ability to maintain a specific velocity

Friction: This refers to the torque that the motor must generate to overcome the static (Coulomb) and dynamic (viscous) forces that resist the reducer's motion. Understanding the actuator's internal friction is essential for implementing friction compensation, which significantly enhances transparency in pHRI.

Gear play: The range of motion of the reducer's output (in the locked-input condition) that can be observed without sensing resisting torques from the actuator. Lower gear play corresponds to a more precise motion of the actuator.

Gear stiffness: The relation between the torque applied to the output of the reducer (in the locked-input condition) and the consequent motion monitored at the output itself. This parameter has preferred values, depending on the application of the actuator itself. For example, a stiffer actuator increases precision in trajectory following control, while a more compliant system can be preferred for a smoother pHRI.

Backdrive torque: The static torque that has to be applied to the output link of the reducer to initiate the motor's motion. This feature is essential in wearable devices that should function without obstructing the user's voluntary motions.

Size, weight, and cost: Ultimaker PLA (polylactic acid) was used for the development of the reducer components, meaning that the transmission masses, encumbrances, and costs are primarily influenced by the bearings and screws used, depending on their quantities. Wearable devices should be as lightweight and compact as possible to enhance user acceptance and usability. Moreover, ensuring cost-effective actuators while maintaining valuable performance is crucial for broadening the use of assistive wearable devices in both work-related environments and everyday-life applications.

4. Experimental Assessment

This section first describes two configurations of the experimental setup used to identify the investigated features. Then, the experimental procedures for each test are presented.

4.1. Experimental Setup

Figure 9 presents the setup with photos and CAD models of the two possible experimental arrangements, addressed as **C1** and **C2**, reported, respectively, in Figure 9a,b. Figure 9c highlights the main hardware components.

The experimental setup is composed of the brushless motor (EC 90 flat, 360 W, ϕ 90 mm, Maxon, Bad Homburg, Germany) with an integrated 2-channel encoder (MILE 512–6400 CPT, Maxon) coupled to the reducer's input through the motor support. The reducer's output is coupled to the incremental magnetic encoder (H2 Series, Phoenix America, Fort Wayne, IN, USA) through the encoder support, the output link, and the output shaft. These components are fixed to a vertical beam with a 3D-printed support structure.

The motor-encoder assembly is controlled by the three-phase brushless DC motor driver (STEVAL-SPIN3201, STMicroelectronics, Geneva, Switzerland). The magnetic encoder and the two load cells (CZL635, Phidgets Inc.), placed in a case on the output arm, are connected to the STM32 Nucleo-144 development board (NUCLEO-F767ZI, STMicroelectronics). Both boards are connected to the central unit (Intel NUC 11 Pro, i7-1165G7) running Windows 11 and Simulink (MATLAB, Mathworks Inc., Natick, MA, USA), where a PID (*discrete PID controller,* Simulink block) controls the speed, and a Kalman filter estimates the motor speed.

4.2. Experimental Protocols and Metrics Examination

The experimental apparatus allows testing the reducers and comparing their characteristics through the evaluation of their performances via multiple procedures. Before testing the reducers' performances, we identified the motor's torque constant as well as the motor's static and viscous internal friction. To identify the torque constant, we operated the motor at a constant velocity while it exerted constant torques to move known loads. We determined the motor's internal friction by driving the motor to follow multiple low-frequency speed sine references. The registered current data were used to implement the motor's friction compensation.

(**a**) C1 configuration.

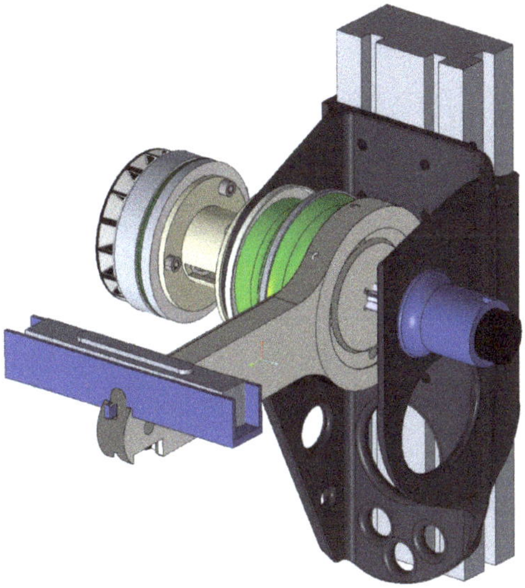

(**b**) C2 configuration.

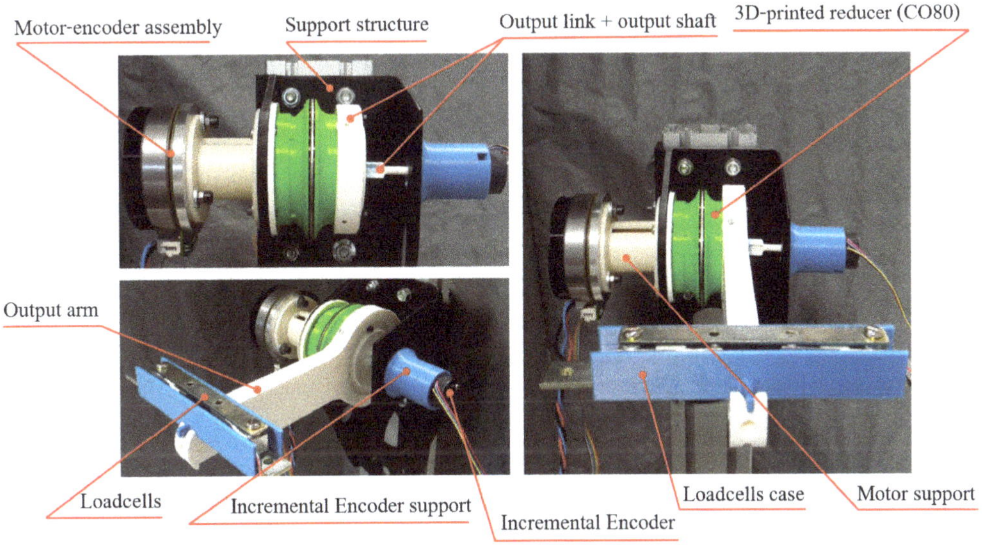

(**c**) Photos of the two experimental arrangements.

Figure 9. Experimental apparatus for testing the reducers. In Figures (**a**,**b**), the CAD models of the **C1** and **C2** arrangements of the experimental setup are presented for a clearer view. (**c**) Photos and notes to clarify the composition of the experimental setup (the reducer is the **CO80**) both in the configuration with and without the output arm and the load cells.

4.2.1. Speed Regularity

This test required using the **C1** experimental setup. To evaluate the speed regularity, the PID speed control was used to control the motor velocity, setting a sequence of step references from 20 rad/s to 120 rad/s, with 20 rad/s increments. The same test was repeated three times for each reducer with positive speed references, and three times with negative velocities. For each speed step, the mean oscillation of the reducers' output velocity around the target value is monitored and divided by the actual target speed, as specified in Equation (12).

4.2.2. Friction

This test required the **C1** experimental setup. Transmission friction was estimated by imposing motor speed sinusoidal references in the range of ± 100 rad/s with a frequency of 0.005 Hz. The *Sine Wave* Simulink block was used to generate the reference signal. For this procedure, we followed the methodologies described in references [28,36]. Each reference signal was followed by the motor for at least three different periods, i.e., more than 6 min. The same experiment was repeated three times for each reducer, Velocity and current were registered during this procedure. Subsequently, the following friction model was fit for each reducer:

$$\tau_{fr} = \begin{cases} S_c + D_v\,\dot{q} & \text{if } \dot{q} \geq 0 \\ -S_c + D_v\,\dot{q} & \text{if } \dot{q} \leq 0 \end{cases} \tag{13}$$

where τ_{fr} denotes the friction torque, S_c denotes the static Coulomb friction component, D_v denotes the dynamic viscous factor, and $\dot{q}$ denotes the motor velocity. The current information was reported to torque data by multiplying them by the motor's current constant.

4.2.3. Gear Play

This test required the **C2** experimental setup. Gearing play was estimated by measuring the maximum possible output motion (variation in the output magnetic encoder data) without motion of the motor axis, which was detected using the motor-integrated encoder data. This experiment involved manually moving the output arm to different positions over a full output turn without applying significant torque, to prevent joint stiffness from influencing the measured output shaft motion and leading to inaccurate gear play estimates. For each reducer, these tests were conducted during three separate experimental sessions.

4.2.4. Gear Stiffness

This test required the **C2** experimental setup. Transmission stiffness was estimated by manually applying a series of loads to the load cell assembly, mounted on the arm (with a 0.2 m lever) while monitoring the current load cell force signal. This was repeated six times for each reducer, around different output positions with 60° increments, to account for position dependence. We sampled the applied torque values by multiples of 5, then we evaluated a possible linear fit that produced a valuable estimated reducer's stiffness, i.e., the torque-displacement ratio.

4.2.5. Backdrive Torque

This test required the **C2** experimental setup. To obtain information about the backdrivability of the full actuator, i.e., the motor connected to each of the reducers, we exploited the combination of arm and load cells. The motor was initially positioned to make the output arm horizontal, providing a reference for adjusting the torque due to the weight of the arm and the load cells, which varies with the analyzed angular position. Gradually increasing forces were manually applied to the load cells until the motor began to move. This procedure was repeated at least five times during each of the three different experimental sessions.

The value of the backdrive torque was estimated by detecting motor movement and evaluating the corresponding applied torque. To accurately sample the torque value required to initiate the backdrive motion, we selected an angular displacement threshold of 0.175°, which is twice the encoder resolution, to detect the onset of motor movement. The corresponding torque value was identified for each experiment.

As mentioned before, The considered torque is the sum of the forces manually applied to the load cells, as well as the weight of the 3D-printed arm and the load cells themselves. This torque is then adjusted based on the output angle relative to the horizontal position.

4.2.6. Encumbrance, Weight, and Cost

Regarding the sizes of the reducers, their maximum height and diameter were obtained from the model and verified through the measurements. To evaluate the cost, the sum of the prices of the non-printed components (bearings, screws, and nuts) was added to the cost of the printed parts. The values of the PLA elements were estimated based on their weights by considering the price of the used material as the sum of the material cost, the amortization of the printer estimated on the printer's whole life, and the energy supply cost.

The prices of the non-printed components (reported from the webpage of the same dealer) were considered based on the quantities necessary for each reducer: for example, when buying a certain quantity of the same bearing, the cost per unit decreases. Therefore, the cost of each reducer depends on the number of units of the same components that constitute it. The weights of the reducers were simply measured through a scale.

5. Results and Discussion

The experimental data gathered through the previously mentioned procedures allowed for a fair comparison of the reducers' performances and characteristics in relation to the described metrics.

5.1. Speed Regularity

In Figure 10, one of the sequences of the speed steps performed by the motor-reducers system is represented by the reference signal and both the motor and the output velocities.

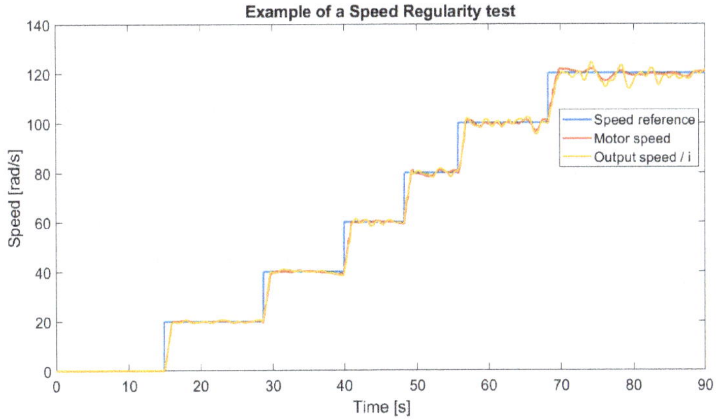

Figure 10. Representation of the data from one of the performed speed regularity tests. The reference signal (in blue) consists of a series of speed steps (from 0 rad/s to 120 rad/s, with steps of 20 rad/s). The other signals represent the motor and the reducer's output velocities (the latter was corrected through the reduction ratio, i.e., i, to plot it together with the motor's speed).

The latter was multiplied for the specific ratio to clarify the comparison with the motor velocity. It has to be noted that, for the regularity evaluations, the data from the velocity transient phases were ignored. Table 5 presents the reducers' regularity values for the evaluated velocities. The best values for each velocity step are presented in bold characters. The mean and standard deviation values for each reducer are reported in the first column of Table 6.

Table 5. Regularity of the reducers at the investigated motor velocities.

Motor Speed [rad/s]	**20**	**40**	**60**	**80**	**100**	**120**
CY30 Regularity [%]	96.05	95.29	95.65	97.37	96.4	95.9
CO30 Regularity [%]	**97.86**	96.55	**95.88**	**96.75**	**97.09**	**96.41**
CP30 Regularity [%]	95.5	94.8	95.77	95.85	94.87	96.25
CP80 Regularity [%]	95.9	**96.88**	94.9	94.35	95.51	95.68
CO80 Regularity [%]	94.4	94.89	95.33	96.51	95.07	95.84
CY80v1 Regularity [%]	91.29	92.3	92.73	92.12	93.87	93.43
CY80v2 Regularity [%]	93.85	93.1	95.69	95.97	94.55	95.28
CY80v3 Regularity [%]	88.58	89.41	90.82	89.32	88.87	90.36

Table 6. Table of the results from the tests carried out with the **C1** experimental setup.

ID	**Regularity [%]**	**Static Friction [mNm]**	**Viscous Friction [mNms/rad]**
CY30	96.11 ± 0.72	20.3 ± 0.64	$1.78 \pm 0.11 \cdot 10^{-1}$
CY80v1	93.12 ± 1.70	14.2 ± 0.42	$1.22 \pm 0.09 \cdot 10^{-1}$
CY80v2	94.76 ± 1.1	14.6 ± 0.48	$1.34 \pm 0.12 \cdot 10^{-1}$
CY80v3	89.56 ± 0.86	23.4 ± 0.65	$1.49 \pm 0.08 \cdot 10^{-1}$
CO30	$\mathbf{96.96 \pm 0.59}$	22.3 ± 0.71	$0.91 \pm 0.11 \cdot 10^{-1}$
CO80	95.34 ± 0.75	28.5 ± 0.93	$\mathbf{0.82} \pm 0.07 \cdot 10^{-1}$
CP30	95.51 ± 0.57	$\mathbf{13.4} \pm 0.39$	$1.16 \pm 0.09 \cdot 10^{-1}$
CP80	95.54 ± 0.87	13.7 ± 0.75	$1.59 \pm 0.10 \cdot 10^{-1}$

By comparing the regularity values across different monitored motor speeds, we demonstrated that regularity does not deteriorate with the evaluated speeds. Therefore, the performance of the reducers remains consistent at higher speeds, which is a beneficial feature for transmission.

From Table 5, it is clear that—for most of the considered motor speed values—the best regularity was achieved by the **CO30** reducer. Valuable performances were verified for the **CY30** reducer. Regarding the other presented gearboxes, from Table 5, it can be seen that the worst results were registered for **CY80v1** and **CY80v3**, which showed remarkably higher oscillations during the speed regularity tests. Concerning the contribution of the cycloidal profiles' parameters, the measured regularities suggest that an increment in the eccentricity leads to an increment of the speed fluctuations' amplitude. Indeed, **CY80v3** (which features the highest eccentricity among the cycloidal stages reported in this work) presents the highest oscillations for the tested velocities. The regularity difference between **CY80v1** and **CY80v2** can be attributed to the difference in the number of lobes. A higher number of rollers in both cycloidal stages ensures smoother motion of the cycloidal disk, as it maintains contact with more rollers during rotation. For a similar reason (considering the standard cycloidal gearbox used in **CY30**) we can justify the high regularity of the 1:30 cycloidal reducer. Lastly, the **CP** reducers exhibit reasonable regularities, considering both the 1:30 and 1:80 reducers. Indeed, these reducers were designed with relatively low eccentricity, which, combined with the planetary stage, resulted in acceptably regular reducers.

To summarize, the proposed **CY80** architecture exhibited the greatest velocity deviations, while **CP80** demonstrated the highest regularity among the 1:80 reducers.

It should be noted that features such as regularity are strongly influenced by the lack of reproducibility and tolerance limitations linked to the process of fused filament fabrication. These characteristics depend on multiple settings and factors, such as the printer, the slicer, and the printing environment.

5.2. Friction

During the experimental session carried out to estimate speed regularity, we recorded motor current, which was used to estimate the torque needed to move the actuator through the motor torque constant.

The sampled motor torque and speed were used to identify the adopted friction model by computing the static and viscous friction parameters of Equation (13). An example of this process is presented in Figure 11. In Figure 12, the resulting friction models for the reducers are reported. We separately present the results regarding the two different ratios (1:30 in Figure 12a and 1:80 in Figure 12b) to avoid ambiguous superimposition of the functions.

The mean and standard deviation values for both the static and viscous friction factors of the reducers are reported in Table 6. The best values are marked in bold text.

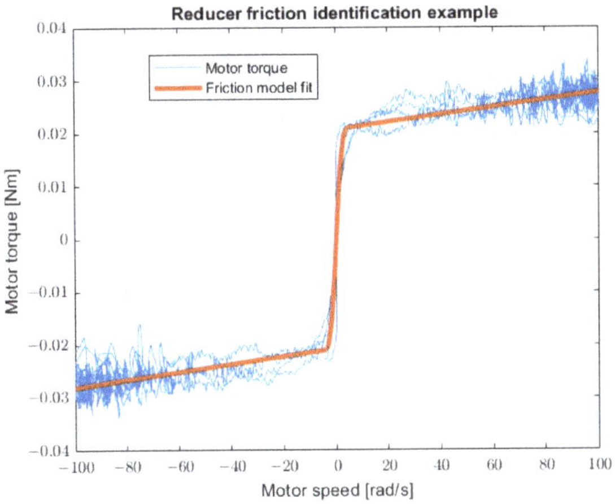

Figure 11. Example of the friction model identification of a reducer. The motor torque signal (in blue) was derived by multiplying the registered motor current by the motor's torque constant. Then, the resulting torque values were used to find the friction model's parameters and plot the fitting function (in red).

Based on the plots in Figure 12 and the values reported in Table 6, it can be noted that the architectures that incorporate a cycloidal stage (**CP** and **CY** reducers) display lower static frictions, unfortunately exhibiting higher viscous components at the same time. The opposite statements describe the **CO** models. The highest and lowest registered static friction torques are, respectively, the ones reported for the **CO80** and **CP30** reducers. Concerning the viscous component, the lowest (and, thus, the best) results were achieved by the **CO80** reducers, while the highest value is the one monitored for the **CY30**, confirming that the cycloidal reducers show higher dynamic frictions that become more prevailing with the increment of used rollers. Nonetheless, we can state that the presented reducers demonstrated valuable performances regarding their internal friction factors.

It is noteworthy that the reducers presented in this work display significantly lower frictions than the 1:11 transmissions from [28,29], regarding both the static and the viscous components, despite implementing higher reduction ratios.

Considering the potential applications of the proposed reducers in wearable exoskeletons, different requirements can be identified depending on the device's purpose. For instance, in a device where the joints frequently reverse direction, low static friction is essential. On the other hand, some applications may require high joint velocities, necessitating transmissions with low viscous friction. Based on the device's requirements, the friction model can be used to determine the torque needed by the motor to compensate for resisting forces.

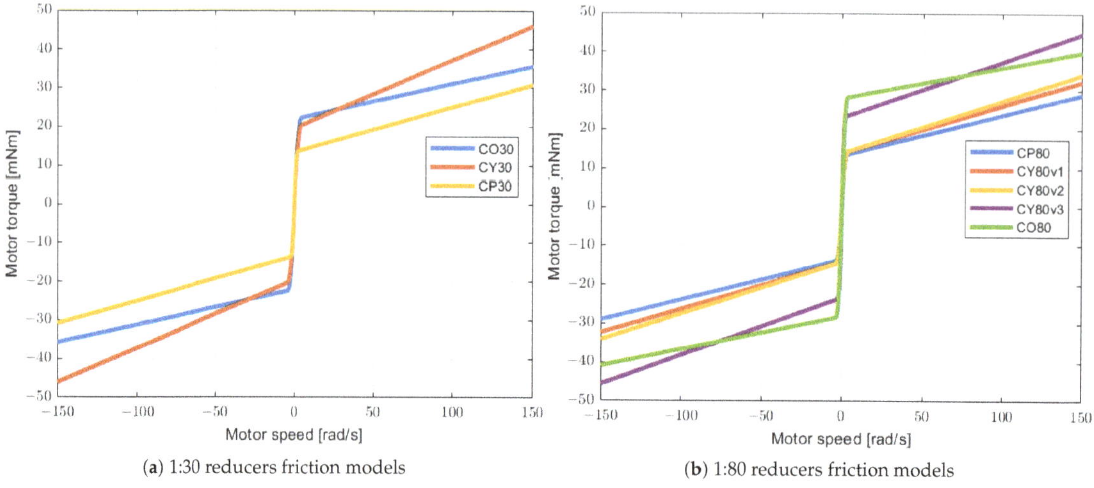

Figure 12. The identified friction torques for the presented reducers: (**a**) the results regarding the 1:30 reducers and (**b**) the models regarding the 1:80 reducers.

5.3. Gear Play

Gear play was estimated according to the procedure reported in Section 4.2.3. The mean and standard deviations of measured play are reported in Table 7, with the best values marked in bold text. By evaluating the gear play results reported in Table 7, the **CY** reducers display the highest range of angular motion. Concerning the **CY30** reducer, both the dimensions of the carrier pins and the surfaces of the disks affect the gear play. In the case of the **CY80** reducers, the dimensions of the disk relative to the cycloidal base rollers influence the gear play, as does the contact interface between the two components of the double compact disk.

The impact of 3D-printing constraints on dimensional tolerances, combined with repeatability issues, is particularly evident for cycloidal architectures. Indeed, the best gear play results are those presented for the **CO** reducers. Despite the underperforming CO reducers, the **CP** models display valuable gear play compared to off-the-shelf planetary gearboxes with similar transmission ratios.

Table 7. Table of the results from the tests carried out with the **C2** experimental setup.

ID	Backdrive Torque [Nm]	Gear Play [°]	Gear Stiffness [Nm/rad]
CY30	0.66 ± 0.032	1.85 ± 0.39	641.4 ± 72.73
CY80v1	>35	8.41 ± 0.58	278.1 ± 33.62
CY80v2	>35	2.69 ± 0.34	659.5 ± 52.54
CY80v3	4.89 ± 0.385	1.89 ± 0.41	344.7 ± 36.54
CO30	0.67 ± 0.040	0.53 ± 0.21	723.2 ± 71.05
CO80	>35	$\mathbf{0.23 \pm 0.11}$	821.7 ± 57.72
CP30	$\mathbf{0.59 \pm 0.030}$	1.1 ± 0.14	573.6 ± 59.52
CP80	0.70 ± 0.044	0.89 ± 0.23	472.5 ± 43.15

5.4. Gear Stiffness

The linear fitting of the motor torque-angular displacement profiles enabled the estimation of each gear stiffness. An example (for the **CO30** reducer) of the linear fit of experimental stiffness data is presented in Figure 13. The overall plot of the torque-displacement mean values for each sampled torque and linear fits for the reducers are reported in Figure 14.

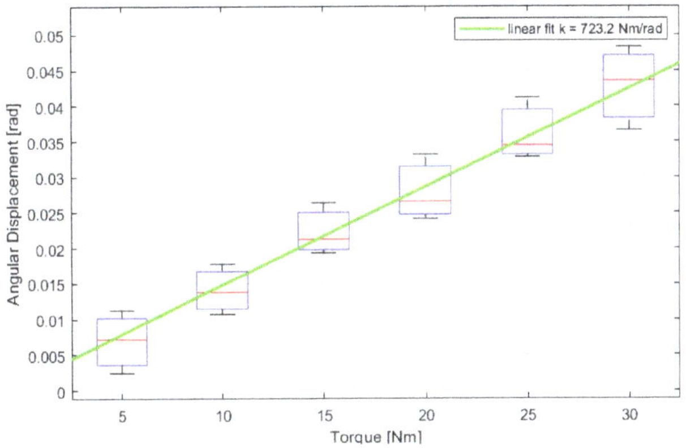

Figure 13. Instance from an experimental stiffness identification procedure. The reducer's output angular displacements are reported based on the respective torque value. Each box plot represents the distribution of the displacement data for each torque sample. The linear function describes the stiffness approximation for the **CO30** reducer.

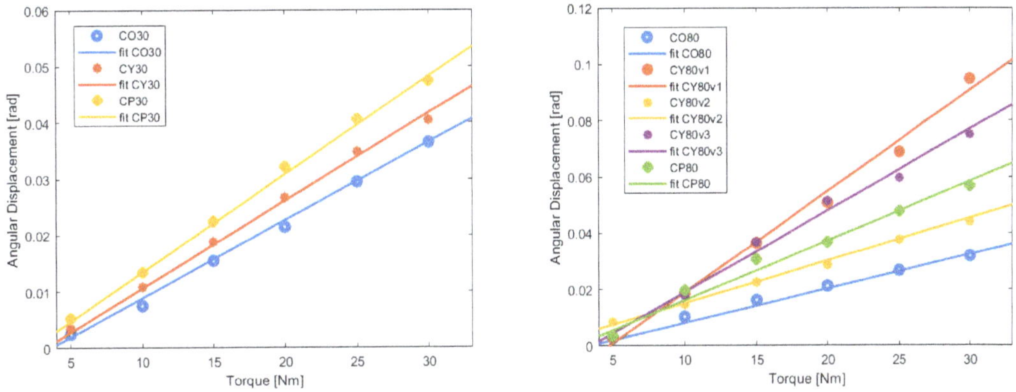

(**a**) 1:30 reducers stiffness models (**b**) 1:80 reducers stiffness models

Figure 14. Comprehensive illustration of the linear fitted functions that approximate the reducers' stiffness based on the experimental displacement-torque data. The two reported plots present the torque-displacement mean values for each of the examined torques (displayed through different shapes and based on the reducers' architecture) and linear fit functions. Figure (**a**) presents the results regarding the 1:30 reducers and figure (**b**) reports the plot concerning the 1:80 reducers.

The stiffness mean values and standard variations are computed for each reducer by using the resulting stiffness for each of the analyzed starting positions. Considering the values reported in Table 7, the highest stiffness estimations are those related to the **CO** reducers. As mentioned before (during the evaluation of gear play, friction, and regularity) the presence of the cycloidal stage influences also the reducers' stiffness, given the nature of the contact between the rollers and the 3D-printed disks. Moreover, compared to the **CP** models, the **CO** reducers use teeth with a module of 1.2 mm, which appears to provide greater stiffness. The estimated stiffness values are 4–10 times lower than those of commercial off-the-shelf planetary gearboxes. However, these differences are still negligible when it comes to the control of wearable exoskeletons.

Apart from the **CO** and **CP** models, the **CY30** and **CY80v2** cycloidal reducers stand out for their significant stiffness. The two remaining models, **CY80v1** and **CY80v3**, have a reduced number of rollers, resulting in limited disk-roller contact points and a smaller contact area. This feature can cause the printed disks to buckle under high torques, although it does not necessarily compromise the reducers' performances.

5.5. Backdrive Torque

The mean values and standard deviations of the computed backdrive torques (measured at the reducers' output) are reported in Table 7. The best value, that is, the one regarding the **CP30** reducers, is marked in bold text. As can be stated by the presented results, the 1:30 reducers present extremely valuable backdrive torques, such that these transmissions could be certainly used in wearable devices for assistance or augmentation.

On the contrary, **CO80**, **CY80v1**, and **CY80v2** are non-backdrivable. Thus, their uses are restricted to cases where the user's motions should not deviate from the robot's trajectory, such as in several rehabilitative devices, or in complex designs that include force sensors at the human–robot interfaces. **CY80v3** is the only CY80 model that can be backdriven. Even if the necessary torque is quite high, this result was achieved by combining the minimum number of rollers with a high eccentricity. The roller configuration used in **CY80v2** would have resulted in a backdrivable design if paired with high eccentricity, but—as discussed previously—this solution would have led to an unacceptable increase in the reducer's width.

The **CP** architecture demonstrated the lowest backdrive torque for both the 1:30 and 1:80 reducers. The **CP80** reducer stands out as the only 1:80 model that is reasonably backdrivable. Moreover, it exhibits such a low backdrive torque that it is comparable to the values obtained from the other 1:30 transmissions.

5.6. Encumbrance, Weight, and Cost

Table 8 reports the empirical data regarding encumbrances (via maximum heights and widths), weights, and costs for the presented reducers. The best values are marked in bold text. Regarding the maximum width, the best reducers are **CP30** and **CP80**. It should be noted that the **CO** reducers could have had a reduced width, but their radial encumbrance is limited by the axial bearing (as shown in the photos in Figure 15 and the CAD models 8).

Table 8. Table of the encumbrance, weight, and cost of the presented reducers.

ID	Diameter [mm]	Height [mm]	Weight [g]	Cost [€]
CY30	92	**33.5**	304	133.05
CY80v1	80	40	**184**	**51.34**
CY80v2	99	36.5	308	101.71
CY80v3	99	36.5	257	66.95
CO30	100	53.6	364	83.17
CO80	100	53.6	358	83.71
CP30	**78**	52	272	116.26
CP80	**78**	52	302	131.42

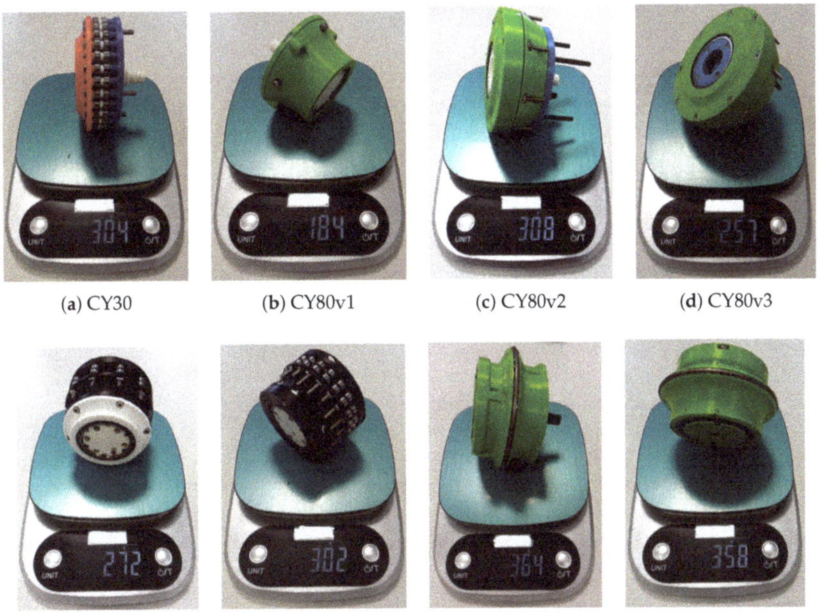

(a) CY30 (b) CY80v1 (c) CY80v2 (d) CY80v3

(e) CP30 (f) CP80 (g) CO30 (h) CO80

Figure 15. Photos of the designed reducers regarding the balance used to verify their weights.

Considering the reducers' heights, despite the double stage, the **CO** and **CP** reducers meet the design constraints, but the **CY** transmissions achieve the best results. In particular, **CY30** has the lowest axial encumbrance. The chosen compact disk cycloidal architecture for **CY80** guarantees optimal values since it excludes the carrier, thus reducing the reducers' height. The absence of the carrier also impacts the weight and cost of the **CY80** reducers, since without the carrier, the presence of multiple bearings, screws, and 3D-printed pins can be avoided.

The **CY30** reducer has a relatively high weight and cost, primarily due to the presence of the rollers. A similar observation applies to the **CP** reducers. However, the heaviest reducers are **CO30** and **CO80**, which—at the same time—exhibit particularly low prices, given the limited number of non-printed components.

Beyond the previous statements, which were provided to offer a clear comparison of the weights and costs of the reducers developed in this work, it is important to note that some of these transmission mechanisms have lower (or comparable) costs and weights than other 3D-printed reducers described in the literature (e.g., [27–29,37]), which nevertheless implement lower reduction ratios.

Concerning the reducers' weights, the models presented in this study display significantly lower masses with respect to the printed transmissions from other works [27–29,37], despite implementing considerably higher transmission ratios. Indeed, the mentioned works present low-reduction gearboxes (from 1:8 to 1:11), achieving masses that vary between 360 g and 780 g. The differences in the implemented reduction ratios lead to inevitable cost discrepancies. In [28,29], the authors presented cycloidal reducers with a 1:11 ratio, costing between EUR 65 and 98, resulting in more cost-effective solutions compared to some of our models. However, as discussed before, since the cycloidal architecture's cost strongly depends on the number of rollers–bearings, which increase directly with the ratio, the cost of a printed gearbox necessarily rises as the reduction ratio increases. Moreover, the lower cost achieved in [29] was realized for a reducer where the fixed outer cycloidal ring does not consist of rollers and bearings but is entirely printed, thus explaining the significantly lower price. Nevertheless, considering the other architectures we presented, the production costs we have reported represent a noteworthy achievement given the higher transmission ratios.

Regarding the reducers' encumbrance, only the 1:10 device from [37] presented a lower diameter, while with the transmission heights, the 1:11 reducers presented in [28,29] displayed a notably lower axial encumbrance with respect to our models.

5.7. Overall Comparative Examination

In Figure 16, the spider plots of the examined features for each reducer are presented, allowing a straightforward and comprehensive assessment of the mechanisms. Different colormaps are used for each of the three main architectures presented in this work (**CY**, **CP**, **CO**). Each characteristic is displayed on a scale with maximum and minimum values specified under the metrics' names. These ranges were selected to facilitate effective visual interpretation and comparison of the reducers. The optimal value in the considered range for each feature, i.e., low backdrive torque, low cost, and low friction, is placed on the outer circumference. Consequently, the larger the area inside the spider plot, the better the performance of the reducer.

Nonetheless, it should be noted that since the ranges were specifically chosen for comparison among these reducers, a smaller area does not necessarily indicate a poor model, but rather a reducer whose performance is inferior compared to the best one obtained in this study. Indeed, the experimental results showed that each designed reducer has both benefits and drawbacks. For example, concerning the cycloidal reducers, significant differences can be observed between **CY30** and **CY80**—due to the distinct architectures used for the 1:30 and 1:80 gearboxes—and among the different implementations of the compact-double-disk design. These differences are strongly influenced by factors such as the number of rollers, the eccentricity, and the target dimensions.

Looking at Figure 16, it is clear that the **CP** architecture maintains similar attributes despite considerable differences in the transmission ratios. Indeed, the spider plots in Figure 16e,f show analogous shapes. The main differences concern the viscous friction and cost, resulting from the differing number of rollers between the two reducers.

A similar consideration can be applied to the compound reducers. In this case, however, significant differences can be found in the backdrive torque and static friction values (the **CO80** reducer was found to be non-backdrivable in our experiments).

Considering the implemented reduction ratios, the obtained weights, encumbrances, and prices turn out to be highly valuable for the developed mechanisms. Even if some of the presented models have proven themselves to be non-backdrivable, the other reducers showed significant performances regarding this feature. Concerning the identified friction components, it is clear that all proposed models exhibit considerable properties.

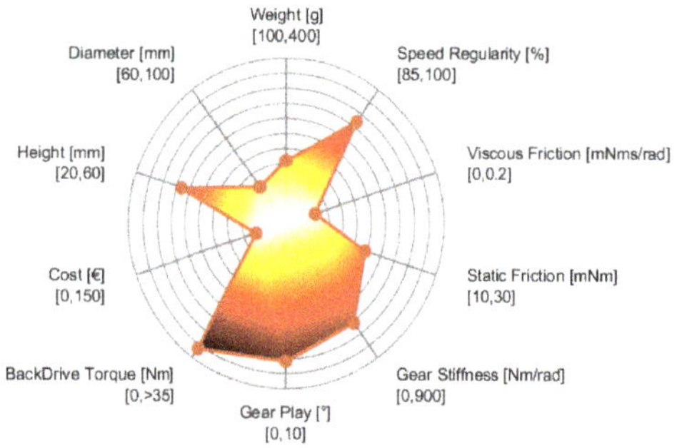

(**a**) CY30

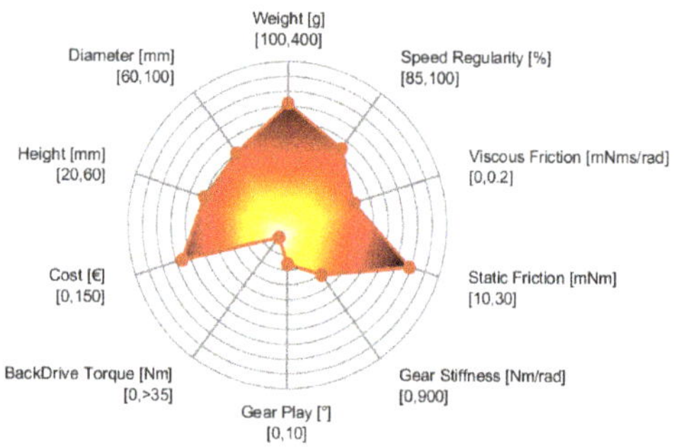

(**b**) CY80v1

Figure 16. *Cont.*

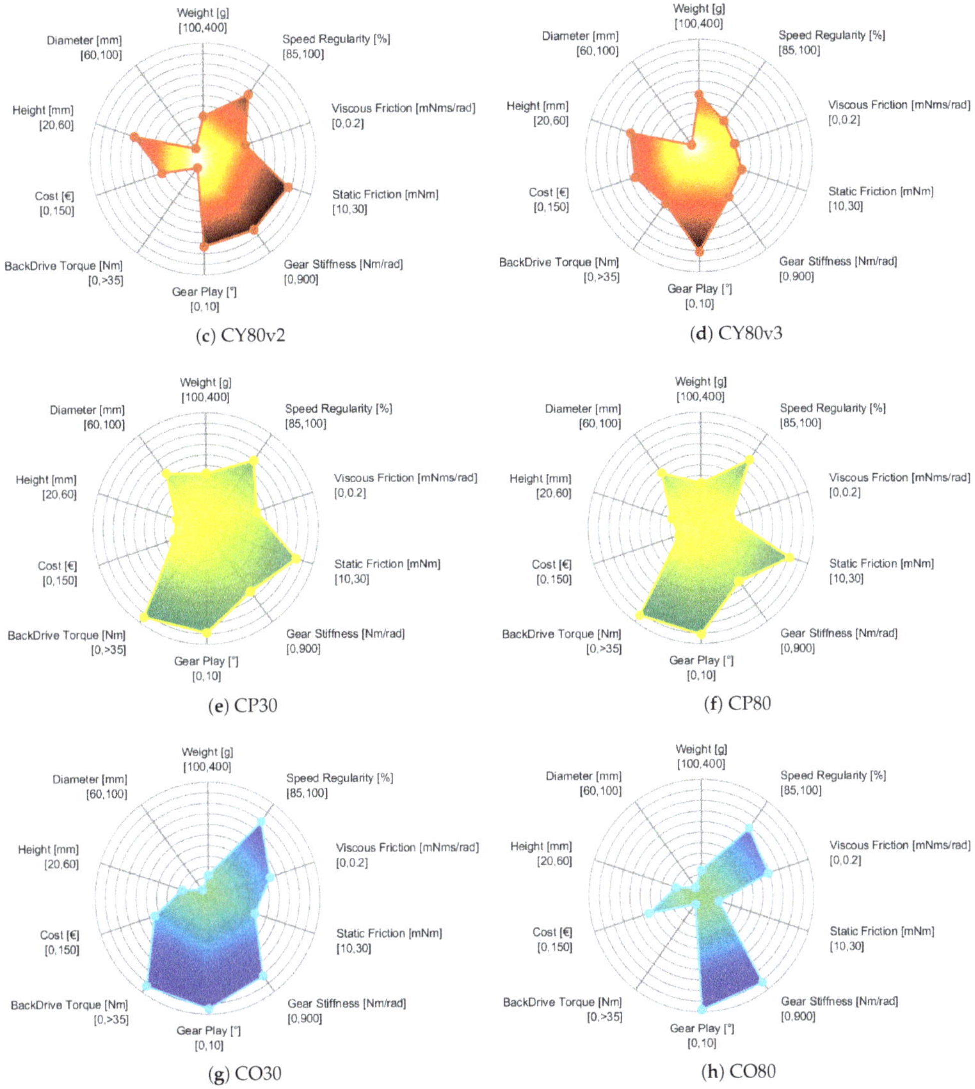

Figure 16. Spider plots that summarize the reducers' performances regarding the considered metrics. For each feature, the unit of measurement is specified together with the minimum and maximum values that can be reached in the plot. The best value for each metric is set on the outer circumference, which means that the larger the area inside the plot, the better the reducer. Different color maps have been adopted to distinguish different architectures.

6. Conclusions and Future Works

In this study, we designed, developed, and compared multiple 3D-printed reducers conceived for wearable assistive devices.

To provide a comprehensive evaluation of various features, we analyzed different transmission architectures. These included lightweight and low-cost implementations of single- and double-stage cycloidal reducers, planetary compound transmissions, and combinations of cycloidal and planetary gearboxes in double-stage reducers.

The general goal of our work was to investigate the prospect of using 3D-printed reducers in wearable exoskeletons, an approach that would lead to cost-effective and lightweight solutions. We examined different reducers' properties (i.e., backdrive torque, static and viscous friction, speed regularity, gear play, gear stiffness, encumbrance, weight, and cost) to inspect the different characteristics of each design and implementation and to inspect the relevance of the uses of these reducers for wearable devices. Indeed, the BOM and .stl files for reproducing the presented transmissions are available upon request from the corresponding author.

The evaluation we carried out and the subsequent considerations are meant to clarify the strengths and limitations of each reducer's 3D-printed implementation, helping to target the right architecture based on the selected task requirements. To summarize, multiple reducers showed highly valuable performances across the selected metrics, while others, notwithstanding their merits with respect to some of the analyzed features, require some improvements.

Comparing the numerical results shows that the proposed series composition of cycloidal and planetary architectures is valuable from multiple perspectives. Thus, future work will aim to perfect this design by improving its regularity while simultaneously reducing its cost and height. The planetary compound reducers mainly need enhancements in terms of encumbrance and weight. For the 1:30 cycloidal reducer, testing a smaller diameter implementation could be beneficial (also aiming to reduce costs and viscous friction). Further exploration will be carried out to model a **CY80** reducer that hopefully could combine the best features of the three implementations presented in this study.

Finally, as pointed out during the discussion of the results, the reducers evaluated in this work present significantly enhanced characteristics with respect to the mentioned state-of-the-art 3D-printed reducers, especially regarding weight, encumbrance, and friction torque.

A noteworthy limitation in our work is related to the use of the same material (PLA) for all printed components of the reducers. Clearly, different designs—such as the teeth for gears or the lobes of the cycloidal disks—could benefit from the use of various materials available for FFF. Thus, future efforts will aim to investigate the influence of different materials on the metrics considered in this work, to enhance the composition of each element in relation to its structural function. Once optimal materials are selected, we aim to optimize the design parameters to minimize encumbrance, weight, and cost of the presented reducers and improve their performance, to better suit them for use in a wearable exoskeleton.

Moreover, this work does not include an evaluation of the durability and resistance of the proposed reducers. The reason is that our primary goal and focus in this paper was to compare promising architectures for printed reducers using parameters that are typically considered when selecting a reducer for an actuator. However, structural and wear analyses represent further directions to assess and compare the proposed reducers.

Author Contributions: Conceptualization, R.B., A.F.; methodology, R.B., C.A.A. and A.F.; software, R.B., G.B., C.A.A. and A.F.; validation, R.B., G.B. and A.F.; formal analysis, R.B., A.F.; investigation, R.B.; resources, R.B., G.B., C.A.A. and A.F.; data curation, R.B.; writing—original draft preparation, R.B., G.B. and A.F.; writing—review and editing, R.B., G.B., C.A.A. and A.F.; visualization, R.B., A.F.; supervision, R.B., G.B. and A.F.; project administration, A.F.; funding acquisition, R.B., C.A.A. and A.F. All authors have read and agreed to the published version of the manuscript.

Funding: This research was funded by the Department of Excellence in Robotics and AI, Scuola Superiore Sant'Anna, 56127 Pisa, Italy.

Data Availability Statement: The data presented in this study (BOM and .stl files of the reducers' components) are available on request from the corresponding author due to privacy.

Conflicts of Interest: The authors declare no conflicts of interest.

Appendix A. Non-Printed Components

In this appendix, the non-3D-printed components used for the developed reducers are reported in the following tables.

Table A1. CY30 non-3D-printed components.

Bearings	Number of Units	Screws and Nuts	Number of Units
693	62	M3X30	2
61,700	12	M3X25	31
6802	2	M3X16	6
6803	3	M3 nuts	37
6808	1		

Table A2. CY80v1 non-3D-printed components.

Bearings	Number of Units	Screws and Nuts	Number of Units
693	19	M3X25	2
6802	3	M3X12	19
6803	1	M3X8	4
6808	1	M3 nuts	23

Table A3. CY80v2 non-3D-printed components.

Bearings	Number of Units	Screws and Nuts	Number of Units
693	49	M3X25	2
6803	4	M3X12	49
6808	1	M3X16	8
		M3 nuts	57

Table A4. CY80v3 non-3D-printed components.

Bearings	Number of Units	Screws and Nuts	Number of Units
693	19	M3X25	2
6803	4	M3X12	19
6808	1	M3X16	8
		M3 nuts	27

Table A5. CP30 non-3D-printed components.

Bearings	Number of Units	Screws and Nuts	Number of Units
693	22	M3X25	2
MR95	12	M3X20	17
61,700	13	M3X16	6
6802	3	M3 nuts	23
6808	1		

Table A6. CP80 non-3D-printed components.

Bearings	Number of Units	Screws and Nuts	Number of Units
693	42	M3X25	2
MR95	8	M3X20	27
61,700	13	M3X16	4
6802	3	M3 nuts	31
6808	1		

Table A7. CO30 non-3D-printed components.

Bearings	Number of Units	Screws and Nuts	Number of Units
MR128	8	M3X30	1
61,700	1	M4X40	4
6803	1	M4 nuts	4
6810	2		
AX 75,100	1		

Table A8. CO80 non-3D-printed components.

Bearings	Number of Units	Screws and Nuts	Number of Units
MR128	8	M3X30	1
61,700	1	M4X40	4
6803	1	M4 nuts	4
6810	2		
AX 75,100	1		

References

1. Farris, D.; Harris, D.; Rice, H.; Campbell, J.; Weare, A.; Risius, D.; Armstrong, N.; Rayson, M. A systematic literature review of evidence for the use of assistive exoskeletons in defence and security use cases. *Ergonomics* **2023**, *66*, 61–87. [CrossRef] [PubMed]
2. Zhao, C.; Liu, Z.; Zhu, L.; Wang, Y. Design and Research of Series Actuator Structure and Control System Based on Lower Limb Exoskeleton Rehabilitation Robot. *Actuators* **2024**, *13*, 20. [CrossRef]
3. Zhang, X.; Chen, X.; Huo, B.; Liu, C.; Zhu, X.; Zu, Y.; Wang, X.; Chen, X.; Sun, Q. An integrated evaluation approach of wearable lower limb exoskeletons for human performance augmentation. *Sci. Rep.* **2023**, *13*, 4251. [CrossRef] [PubMed]
4. Stroppa, F.; Soylemez, A.; Yuksel, H.; Akbas, B.; Sarac, M. Optimizing Exoskeleton Design with Evolutionary Computation: An Intensive Survey. *Robotics* **2023**, *12*, 106. [CrossRef]
5. Baud, R.; Manzoori, A.; Ijspeert, A.; Bouri, M. Review of control strategies for lower-limb exoskeletons to assist gait. *J. Neuroeng. Rehabil.* **2021**, *18*, 1–34. [CrossRef]
6. Calanca, A.; Toxiri, S.; Costanzi, D.; Sartori, E.; Vicario, R.; Poliero, T.; Di Natali, C.; Caldwell, D.; Fiorini, P.; Ortiz, J. Actuation selection for assistive exoskeletons: Matching capabilities to task requirements. *IEEE Trans. Neural Syst. Rehabil. Eng.* **2020**, *28*, 2053–2062. [CrossRef]
7. Barjuei, E.; Ardakani, M.; Caldwell, D.; Sanguineti, M.; Ortiz, J. Optimal selection of motors and transmissions in back-support exoskeleton applications. *IEEE Trans. Med. Robot. Bionics* **2020**, *2*, 320–330. [CrossRef]
8. Yu, S.; Huang, T.; Yang, X.; Jiao, C.; Yang, J.; Chen, Y.; Yi, J.; Su, H. Quasi-direct drive actuation for a lightweight hip exoskeleton with high backdrivability and high bandwidth. *IEEE/ASME Trans. Mechatron.* **2020**, *25*, 1794–1802. [CrossRef]
9. Tiboni, M.; Borboni, A.; Vérité, F.; Bregoli, C.; Amici, C. Sensors and Actuation Technologies in Exoskeletons: A Review. *Sensors* **2022**, *22*, 884. [CrossRef]
10. Ko, H.; Lee, S.; Koo, D.; Lee, I.; Hyun, D. Waist-assistive exoskeleton powered by a singular actuation mechanism for prevention of back-injury. *Robot. Auton. Syst.* **2018**, *107*, 1–9. [CrossRef]
11. Li, Y.; Guan, X.; Han, X.; Tang, Z.; Meng, K.; Shi, Z.; Penzlin, B.; Yang, Y.; Ren, J.; Yang, Z.; et al. Design and preliminary validation of a lower limb exoskeleton with compact and modular actuation. *IEEE Access* **2020**, *8*, 66338–66352. [CrossRef]
12. Mori, K.; Fujimoto, Y. Implementation of Motion Intention Prediction to Highly Back-Drivable Exoskeleton. In Proceedings of the IECON 2023-49th Annual Conference Of The IEEE Industrial Electronics Society, Singapore, 16–19 October 2023; pp. 1–6.

13. Zhu, H.; Nesler, C.; Divekar, N.; Peddinti, V.; Gregg, R. Design principles for compact, backdrivable actuation in partial-assist powered knee orthoses. *IEEE/ASME Trans. Mechatron.* **2021**, *26*, 3104–3115. [CrossRef] [PubMed]
14. Mian, S.; Abouel Nasr, E.; Moiduddin, K.; Saleh, M.; Alkhalefah, H. An Insight into the Characteristics of 3D Printed Polymer Materials for Orthoses Applications: Experimental Study. *Polymers* **2024**, *16*, 403. [CrossRef] [PubMed]
15. Roveda, L.; Pesenti, M.; Rossi, M.; Rodriguez, M.; Pedrocchi, A.; Braghin, F.; Gandolla, M. User-centered back-support exoskeleton: Design and prototyping. *Procedia CIRP* **2022**, *107*, 522–527. [CrossRef]
16. Iizuka, K.; Takesue, N. Comparison of Characteristics of Internal Planetary Gear Reducer with Epitrochoid Curve using Metal and 3D Printed Parts. In Proceedings of the 2023 IEEE/SICE International Symposium On System Integration (SII), Atlanta, GA, USA, 17–20 January 2023; pp. 1–6.
17. Tunalioglu, M.; Agca, B. Wear and service life of 3-D printed polymeric gears. *Polymers* **2022**, *14*, 2064. [CrossRef]
18. Zhang, Y.; Mao, K.; Leigh, S.; Shah, A.; Chao, Z.; Ma, G. A parametric study of 3D printed polymer gears. *Int. J. Adv. Manuf. Technol.* **2020**, *107*, 4481–4492. [CrossRef]
19. Muminović, A.; Braut, S.; Božić, Ž.; Pervan, N.; Skoblar, A. Experimental failure analysis of polylactic acid gears made by additive manufacturing. *Procedia Struct. Integr.* **2023**, *46*, 125–130. [CrossRef]
20. Ciobanu, R.; Rizescu, C.; Rizescu, D.; Gramescu, B. Surface Durability of 3D-Printed Polymer Gears. *Appl. Sci.* **2024**, *14*, 2531. [CrossRef]
21. Buj-Corral, I.; Zayas-Figueras, E. Comparative study about dimensional accuracy and form errors of FFF printed spur gears using PLA and Nylon. *Polym. Test.* **2023**, *117*, 107862. [CrossRef]
22. Jiang, S.; Hu, K.; Zhan, Y.; Zhao, C.; Li, X. Theoretical and experimental investigation on the 3D surface roughness of material extrusion additive manufacturing products. *Polymers* **2022**, *14*, 293. [CrossRef]
23. Barsomian, C.; Eswaran, N.; Pesenti, M.; Gandolla, M.; Braghin, F.; Carpanzano, E.; Roveda, L. Dynamic characterization and control of a back-support exoskeleton 3D-printed cycloidal actuator. *CIRP Ann.* **2024**, *73*, 29–32. [CrossRef]
24. Sanchez, A.; Rossos, T.; Mihailidis, A.; Laschowski, B. Preliminary Development of a Robotic Hip-Knee Exoskeleton With 3D-Printed Backdrivable Actuators. In Proceedings of the International Design Engineering Technical Conferences And Computers And Information In Engineering Conference, Washington, DC, USA, 25–28 August 2024; Volume 87363, p. V008T08A072.
25. Liu, Y.; Zhang, L.; Wang, R.; Smith, C.; Gutierrez-Farewik, E. Weight distribution of a knee exoskeleton influences muscle activities during movements. *IEEE Access* **2021**, *9*, 91614–91624. [CrossRef]
26. Urs, K.; Adu, C.; Rouse, E.; Moore, T. Design and characterization of 3d printed, open-source actuators for legged locomotion. In Proceedings of the 2022 IEEE/RSJ International Conference On Intelligent Robots And Systems (IROS), Kyoto, Japan, 23–27 October 2022; pp. 1957–1964.
27. Yoshida, T.; Endo, G.; Okubo, A.; Nabae, H. Experimental Evaluation of a Quasi-direct-drive Actuator with a 3D-printed Planetary Gear Reducer. In Proceedings of the 2023 IEEE/SICE International Symposium On System Integration (SII), Atlanta, GA, USA, 17–20 January 2023; pp. 1–6.
28. Roozing, W.; Roozing, G. 3D-printable low-reduction cycloidal gearing for robotics. In Proceedings of the 2022 IEEE/RSJ International Conference On Intelligent Robots And Systems (IROS), Kyoto, Japan, 23–27 October 2022; pp. 1929–1935.
29. Roozing, W.; Roozing, G. Experimental comparison of pinwheel and non-pinwheel designs of 3D-printed cycloidal gearing for robotics. In Proceedings of the 2024 IEEE International Conference On Robotics And Automation (ICRA), Yokohama, Japan, 13–17 May 2024; pp. 7091–7098.
30. Chen, B.; Fang, T.; Li, C.; Wang, S. Gear geometry of cycloid drives. *SCience China Ser. Technol. Sci.* **2008**, *51*, 598–610. [CrossRef]
31. Blagojevic, M.; Marjanovic, N.; Djordjevic, Z.; Stojanovic, B.; Disic, A. A new design of a two-stage cycloidal speed reducer. *J. Mech. Des.* **2011**, *133*, 085001-1. [CrossRef]
32. Lin, T.; Schabacker, M.; Ho, Y.; Kuo, T.; Tsay, D. Geometric Design and Dynamic Analysis of a Compact Cam Reducer. *Machines* **2022**, *10*, 955. [CrossRef]
33. Lin, W.; Shih, Y.; Lee, J. Design of a two-stage cycloidal gear reducer with tooth modifications. *Mech. Mach. Theory* **2014**, *79*, 184–197. [CrossRef]
34. Kapelevich, A.; AKGears, L. High gear ratio epicyclic drives analysis. *Ratio* **2013**, *3*, 62–67.
35. Matsuki, H.; Nagano, K.; Fujimoto, Y. Bilateral drive gear—A highly backdrivable reduction gearbox for robotic actuators. *IEEE/Asme Trans. Mechatron.* **2019**, *24*, 2661–2673. [CrossRef]
36. Huang, X.; Rui, Y.; Wang, C.; Huang, H.; Zhang, Z.; Fan, C.; Yang, Y. Gravity Compensation Based Control for Lower-Limb Load-Bearing Exoskeleton. In Proceedings of the 2021 6th International Conference On Control, Robotics And Cybernetics (CRC), Shanghai, China, 9–11 October 2021; pp. 230–234.
37. Satake, H.; Takesue, N. Comparison of Characteristics of Cycloidal Gear Reducer Using Metal, Plastic and 3D Printed Parts. In Proceedings of the 2024 IEEE/SICE International Symposium On System Integration (SII), Ha Long, Vietnam, 8–11 January 2024; pp. 1531–1536.

robotics

MDPI

Article

Hybrid LDA-CNN Framework for Robust End-to-End Myoelectric Hand Gesture Recognition Under Dynamic Conditions

Hongquan Le [1], Marc in het Panhuis [2]perscript1,*

[1] School of Mechanical, Materials, Mechatronic and Biomedical Engineering, University of Wollongong, Wollongong, NSW 2500, Australia; hql471@uowmail.edu.au (H.L.); gspinks@uow.edu.au (G.M.S.)
[2] School of Science, University of Wollongong, Wollongong, NSW 2500, Australia; panhuis@uow.edu.au
* Correspondence: gursel@uow.edu.au

Abstract: Gesture recognition based on conventional machine learning is the main control approach for advanced prosthetic hand systems. Its primary limitation is the need for feature extraction, which must meet real-time control requirements. On the other hand, deep learning models could potentially overfit when trained on small datasets. For these reasons, we propose a hybrid Linear Discriminant Analysis–convolutional neural network (LDA-CNN) framework to improve the gesture recognition performance of sEMG-based prosthetic hand control systems. Within this framework, 1D-CNN filters are trained to generate latent representation that closely approximates Fisher's (LDA's) discriminant subspace, constructed from handcrafted features. Under the train-one-test-all evaluation scheme, our proposed hybrid framework consistently outperformed the 1D-CNN trained with cross-entropy loss only, showing improvements from 4% to 11% across two public datasets featuring hand gestures recorded under various limb positions and arm muscle contraction levels. Furthermore, our framework exhibited advantages in terms of induced spectral regularization, which led to a state-of-the-art recognition error of 22.79% with the extended 23 feature set when tested on the multi-limb position dataset. The main novelty of our hybrid framework is that it decouples feature extraction in regard to the inference time, enabling the future incorporation of a more extensive set of features, while keeping the inference computation time minimal.

Keywords: human-computer interface; muscle-computer interface; surface electromyography; prosthetic hand control; rehabilitation robotics

1. Introduction

Myoelectric gesture recognition translates sEMG signals into a limited set of discrete hand gestures that fulfill most daily user's needs and is featured in various commercial prosthetic hands [1–3]. Hand gesture recognition systems are typically based on classical machine learning and deep learning. Classical machine learning models, such as Linear Discriminant Analysis (LDA) [4], Quadratic Discriminant Analysis (QDA) [5], and Support Vector Machine (SVM) [6,7], are the predominant approaches for sEMG-based hand gesture recognition, due to their computational efficiency and intuitive interpretations, making them suitable for use in prosthetic systems [1,8]. Manual feature extraction is essential for identifying discriminative information in sEMG signals [2]. Advancements in deep learning have enabled the ability to recognize hand gestures from raw sEMG signals by directly extracting discriminative features. Over the years, a variety of deep learning architectures have been proposed for sEMG-based gesture recognition, including 1D-CNN [9], 2D-CNN [10], an LSTM-CNN hybrid [11], multi-stream 1D-CNNs [9,12], multi-stream 1D-CNN-LSTM [9], and Transformer-based models [13,14].

While early research on sEMG hand gesture recognition showed promising results [4,10,12], a significant limitation was that the recognition performance was evaluated in limited settings. As sEMG gesture classifiers only perform effectively in conditions where the signals' characteristic are closely similar [15], there has been a shift toward addressing the non-stationarities of sEMG signals, particularly for conditions not encountered during training. The most straightforward approach is to gather more data across diverse conditions [6]. Other potential solutions include incorporating additional modalities, such as inertial measurement units (IMUs) [16], pressure-based force myography (pFMG) [17], and RGB [18,19], or depth cameras [20]. Another approach is the use of feature engineering to enhance the robustness of myoelectric hand gesture classifiers [6,7,21]. However, such solutions can increase the user training burden or system complexity, further reducing prosthesis user acceptance.

Notably, previous studies have consistently shown that LDA improves recognition performance in the presence of sEMG non-stationarity. Vidovic, Hwang, Amsüss, Hahne, Farina, and Müller [5] found that over five days, LDA provided up to 10% more stable performance than QDA. Similarly, Phinyomark, et al. [22] observed that over 21 days, LDA reduced the recognition errors by 8% to 20% compared to QDA and the random forest algorithm. Lorrain et al. [23] found that LDA improved the recognition performance by 8% to 35% compared to a Gaussian Kernel SVM in the presence of transient sEMG signals. Al-Timemy, Khushaba, Bugmann, and Escudero [6] reported that LDA consistently achieved the lowest recognition error compared to random forest, Naive Bayes, and kNN across all feature sets, under varying contraction forces.

Despite progress in the field, sEMG-based hand gesture recognition still faces many challenges, especially when dealing with the non-stationary nature of sEMG signals. The performance of classical machine learning methods, while being the default approach in regard to commercial products due to their proven robustness [24], is heavily dependent on the choice of the input feature set [22,25]. Feature engineering often leads to complex and non-parallelizable computations, making their deployment on wearable devices for prosthetic control more difficult. Deep learning, on the other hand, is often regarded as a universal approximator that relies on a small number of standardized, parallelizable operations [26]. However, the robustness of deep learning for myoelectric hand gesture recognition under dynamic conditions has not been clinically validated. In our previous work, we found no significant performance difference between LDA and deep CNNs when evaluating gestures recorded under unseen conditions [27]. Since LDA is not only a classification method, but also a dimensionality reduction technique, and given its demonstrated robustness in previous studies [5,22,27], we hypothesize that LDA's discriminant subspace (or Fisher's representation) serves as a highly compressed and rich form of representation. We further hypothesize that a deep CNN can approximate this representation, thereby bypassing the need for explicit temporal feature extraction during inference.

In light of this observation, we propose a hybrid CNN-LDA framework in this study. In regard to this framework, a 1D-CNN is used to extract the temporal features, so that the model's latent representation approximates Fisher's discriminant subspace of the LDA classifier. The novelty of our framework is that the feature extraction occurs only during the training stage, while, during inference, the model predicts hand gestures directly from raw sEMG signals.

Our proposed LDA-CNN framework can be viewed as a form of feature-level knowledge distillation, which is considered richer than conventional class probability-based (response based) knowledge distillation [28]. Zeng et al. [29] introduced a cross-modality, response-based knowledge distillation approach that transfers information from ultrasound to the sEMG modality. They first trained a hand gesture recognition model using only ultrasound data, which was then used as the teacher model. The student model for the sEMG modality was subsequently trained jointly with the ultrasound teacher model to capture cross-modal knowledge. In another study, Wei et al. [30] proposed using a generative adversarial network (GAN) to distill the relationship between sEMG and IMU modalities. During inference, the pseudo-IMU data generated by the GAN are combined with sEMG signals to enhance recognition performance. Unlike most prior work that distills knowledge from a teacher deep neural network [28–30], our method distills knowledge from Fisher's discriminant subspace. Traditionally, Fisher's discriminant subspaces are computed analytically using methods such as Singular Value Decomposition or Eigenvalue Decomposition [31], which are prone to numerical instability. In contrast, deep learning models are typically trained using mini-batch optimization frameworks [32]. By leveraging deep learning to approximate Fisher's representation, our method introduces a spectral regularization effect that mitigates the numerical instability associated with the direct computation of Fisher's subspace.

Our proposed framework is tested on two public datasets: one with hand gestures recorded for five different upper limb positions [7] and one with hand gestures recorded under three different levels of contraction force [6]. Our investigation focuses on the 'train-one-test-all' validation scheme. In regard to this scheme, only three repetitions recorded under a single condition (either one limb position or one contraction force) are used for training. The testing dataset includes both the training conditions and novel conditions that were not used during training, better aligning with real-world operating conditions of prosthetic hand systems. The contributions from our proposed framework include:

1. Highlighting the robustness of Fisher's representation for sEMG gesture recognition under dynamic conditions (multi-limb positions and contraction forces);
2. Highlighting the problem of overfitting in regard to deep CNNs trained with cross-entropy on a limited dataset;
3. Improving sEMG hand gesture recognition under dynamic conditions through the knowledge distillation of manual sEMG features in Fisher's discriminative subspace as deep convolutional weights;
4. Applying gradient-based optimization of the CNN optimization framework to address the numerical instability of LDA Rayleigh–Ritz quotient for large feature sets;
5. Ensuring the system's real-time robustness to avoid perceptible user delays by utilizing fast GPU computation.

2. Materials and Methods

2.1. Benchmark Datasets

2.1.1. Multiple Limb Position Hand Gesture Dataset

The Multiple Limb-Position Dataset (Limb.Pos. dataset [7], Figure 1) comprises recordings of eight hand gestures, performed under five distinct limb positions, namely P1 through P5, by 11 intact subjects (9 males and 2 females). The gestures include four wrist movements, flexion, extension, pronation, and supination, and three active hand movements, pinch grip, power grip, and open hand, plus one inactive gesture of resting. However, this investigation excluded the resting hand gesture for two reasons: (1) it can be detected via changes in the sEMG amplitude [33], and (2) to further analyze the impact of the covariate shift on the detection rate of active gestures. The sEMG signals were captured using seven Delsys DE 2.x electrodes and amplified by a Delsys Bagnoli amplifier, with a gain of 1000. These signals were then converted to a digital format, at 4 kHz, using the

BNC-2090 ADC module. The dataset was preprocessed by the dataset recording author, using a bandpass filter ranging from 20 to 450 Hz and a 50 Hz notch filter to eliminate power line interference. To further reduce the processing time, we also downsampled the sEMG signal to 2 kHz.

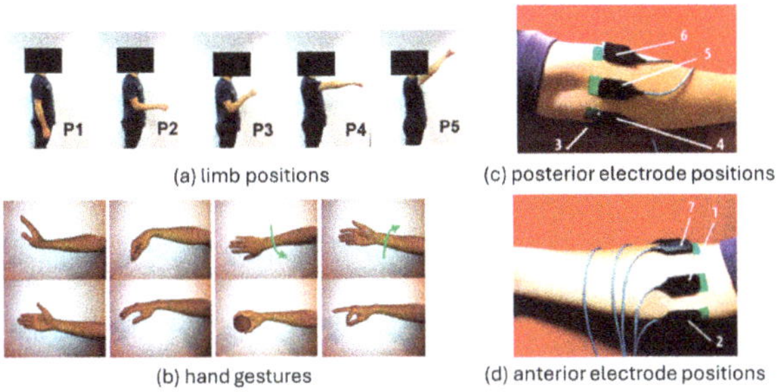

Figure 1. (**a**) Five limb positions (P1–P5), (**b**) eight hand gestures, and (**c**,**d**) electrode placements from Limb.Pos. dataset [7].

2.1.2. Amputee sEMG Multi-Contraction Forces Dataset

The Amputee sEMG Multi-Contraction Force Dataset (Amp.Force. dataset [6], Figure 2) includes sEMG recordings from nine unilateral transradial volunteers, each with varying types of amputation and different familiarity with prosthetic systems. The primary objective of the use of this dataset is to explore the impact of covariate shifts in the response to changes in the contraction force. This is of significant practical importance, as many commercial prosthetic systems employ proportional control based on muscle force [34]. The sEMG signals were recorded using eight pairs of Ag/AgCl sEMG electrodes, positioned on the stump of the amputated upper limb. The sEMG signal was recorded at 2 kHz, then preprocessed using a 4th order Butterworth filter, with cutoff frequencies set at 20 Hz and 500 Hz. The participants performed six hand gestures, thumb flexion, index flexion, fine pinch, tripod grip, hook grip, and spherical grip, with each gesture repeated 5 to 8 times. The contraction forces were categorized into three levels, low, moderate, and high, and maintained for 8 to 12 s, during each gesture repetition. Additionally, the participants received feedback on the sEMG amplitude to ensure accurate perception of the invoked muscle force.

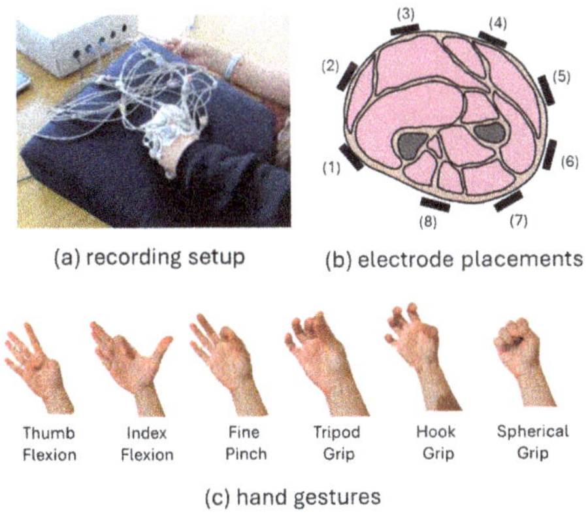

Figure 2. (**a**) Recording setup, (**b**) electrode placements and (**c**) recorded hand gestures from Amp.Force. dataset [6].

2.2. sEMG Feature Extraction

Figure 3 illustrates the forward generation process of an sEMG signal. The surface EMG (sEMG) signal represents the summation of the electrical activity from all the active muscle fiber action potentials (MFAPs) within the detection volume of the electrodes [35]. These MFAPs are generated by motor neuron activation and propagate through biological tissues, where they are subject to distortion caused by tissue impedance and noise, before reaching the skin surface [2,36]. The level of muscle force generated is regulated by the central nervous system through two primary mechanisms: the number of recruited motor units and the firing rate of these motor units [2,37].

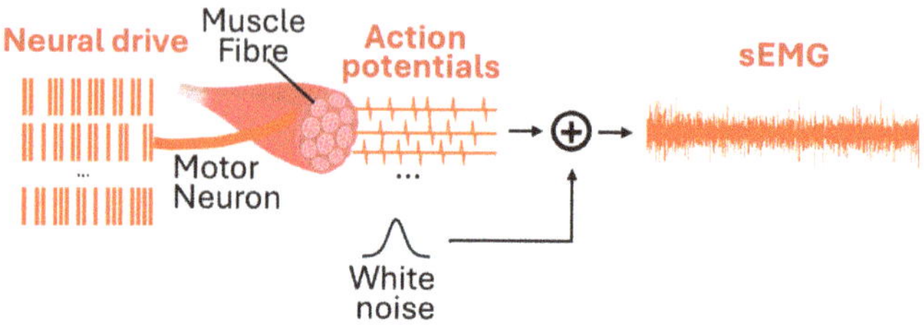

Figure 3. The generation process of an sEMG signal.

The general goal of sEMG-based muscle–machine interfaces is to solve the inverse problem of the forward generation process, specifically to infer the underlying neural drive from the recorded sEMG signal. However, this has been proven to be a challenging and underdetermined problem, particularly when dealing with sparse sEMG signals. To address this, heuristic feature extraction methods are often employed, with sEMG features designed to reflect the physiological mechanisms involved in sEMG signal generation. In general, sEMG features reflect either the signal's energy or its frequency components. Among these, the signal energy and amplitude (low-pass filtered sEMG signals, mean absolute value) are the most commonly used features, as they are associated with both motor unit recruitment and rate coding mechanisms during the sEMG generation process [37]. Frequency-based features, such as the power spectrum, autoregressive coefficients, and the zero-crossing rate, provide more detailed analysis of rate coding [37], the spatial relationship between the electrodes and motor units [35], and muscle fatigue conditions [38]. These frequency-based features have also been found to be more robust in regard to confounding factors, such as changes in the contraction force [6,39] and limb position [7]. Moreover, since each sEMG feature is typically designed to capture a limited aspect of the signal, combining multiple features often leads to improved performance in myoelectric hand gesture recognition compared to using a single feature [22,25].

Building on previous research [7,22,40,41], this study directly utilized eight distinct feature sets, including a new set proposed here, comprising 23 robust sEMG features shown to facilitate sEMG gesture recognition, without connecting them to neuromuscular mechanisms in regard to gesture recognition, which would possibly lead to the capturing of features that are not physiologically valid or relevant. Additionally, seven commonly used and robust feature sets were employed. Each feature set was extracted using a window size of 512 samples (equivalent to 256 ms), with a step size of 50 samples (25 ms).

- **Our proposed extended 23 sEMG feature set (Ext-23):** Mean Frequency (mnf), Cepstrum Coefficient (cc), Power Spectrum Ratio (psr), Marginal of Discrete Wavelet Transform (mdwt), Slope Sign Change (ssc), Auto-Regressive Coefficient (ar), and time-domain power spectral moments (TD-PSR), mean absolute value slope (mavs), Histogram of EMG (hemg), mean absolute value (mav), Zero Crossing (zc), Waveform

Length (wl), Root Mean Square (rms), Integral Absolute Value (iav), Difference Absolute Standard Deviation Value (dasdv), Average Amplitude Change (aac), Log Detector (log), Willison Amplitude (wamp), Myopulse Percentage Rate (myop), V-Order (v), variance (var), Log variance (logvar), and Maximum Fractal Length (mfl).

Other robust feature sets used for benchmarking purposes are as follows:

- **Atzori's feature set:** rms, mdwt, hemg, mav, wl, ssc, and zc;
- **Du's feature set:** iav, var, wamp, wl, ssc, and zc;
- **Hudgins' feature set:** mav, wl, ssc, and zc;
- **Time-domain power spectral moments (TD-PSR):** a set of features that are robust to changes in arm position and contraction force frequency domain features extracted directly from the time domain;
- **Phinyomark's feature set:** mav, wl, wamp, zc, mavs, ar, mnf, and psr;
- **Robust Time-Domain 8 (TD8) [25]:** aac, dasdv, mfl, myop, ssc, wamp, wl, and zc;
- **Robust Time-Domain 8 with Autoregressive Coefficients (TD8-ARs) [25]:** aac, dasdv, mfl, myop, ssc, wamp, wl, zc, and ar.

2.3. Linear Discriminant Analysis and Fisher's Representation

LDA (or Fisher's Discriminant Analysis) is the most commonly used technique for sEMG-based gesture recognition, due to its low computational footprint and its parametric and generative nature. Given a dataset consisting of n samples as column vectors of d dimension $\mathbf{X} = \{\mathbf{x_1}, \ldots, \mathbf{x_n}\} \in \mathrm{R}^{\mathrm{d}\times\mathrm{n}}$, where each sample $\mathbf{x_i}$ corresponds to one of the c classes. Additionally, LDA further assumes that data belonging to class j is of multivariate Gaussian distribution and the covariance of all the classes is equal, i.e., $\mathbf{S_1} = \ldots = \mathbf{S_c} = \mathbf{S}$. Then, the probability that a sample $\mathbf{x_i}$ belongs to class j is determined as [42]:

$$\delta_j(\mathbf{x}) \triangleq \boldsymbol{\mu}_j^\top \mathbf{S}^{-1}\mathbf{x} - \frac{1}{2}\boldsymbol{\mu}_j^\top \mathbf{S}^{-1}\boldsymbol{\mu}_j + \ln(\pi_j) \tag{1}$$

where π_j is the prior probability that a sample belongs to class j. Samples are assigned to the class that has the highest posteriori:

$$y = \underset{j}{\mathrm{argmax}}\,\delta_j(\mathbf{x}) \tag{2}$$

where the classification outlined by (1) and (2) naturally gives rise to a linear decision boundary [42,43]. Additionally, c centroids in the d dimensional input feature space are contained in the subspace of $k \leq c-1$ dimensional when the dataset is zero-centered [42]. Hence, the data can be projected onto this subspace without losing either discriminant information or distribution based on a Gaussian assumption. This subspace is the discriminant subspace. The discriminant subspace span($\mathbf{W}$) where $\mathbf{W} = \{w_1, \ldots, w_k\} \in R^{d\times k}$ can be solved by optimizing the Rayleigh–Ritz quotient:

$$\underset{\mathbf{W}}{\mathrm{argmax}} \frac{\mathrm{tr}\left(\mathbf{W}^\top \mathbf{S_B}\mathbf{W}\right)}{\mathrm{tr}\left(\mathbf{W}^\top \mathbf{S_W}\mathbf{W}\right)} \tag{3}$$

where $\mathrm{tr}(\cdot)$ denotes matrix trace operations, and $\mathbf{S_B}$ and $\mathbf{S_W}$ are the between class and within class covariance matrices, respectively [31]. The optimization objective from (3) is equivalent to:

$$\underset{\mathbf{W}}{\mathrm{argmax}}\,\mathrm{tr}\left(\mathbf{W}^\top \mathbf{S_B}\mathbf{W}\right) \quad \text{s.t.} \quad \mathrm{tr}\left(\mathbf{W}^\top \mathbf{S_W}\mathbf{W}\right) = \mathbf{I} \tag{4}$$

which can be interpreted as finding directions that maximize the between-class variance, while maintaining unitary intra-class variance. Fisher's representation is defined as the projection $\hat{\mathbf{x}} \in R^{k \times n}$ of the sample vector $\mathbf{x}$ onto $\mathbf{W}$, and is expressed as:

$$\hat{\mathbf{x}} = \mathbf{W}^{\top}\mathbf{x} \tag{5}$$

2.4. Hybrid CNN-LDA Framework for End-to-End sEMG-Based Hand Gesture Recognition

Here, we introduce a novel hybrid approach combining CNN and LDA to enhance sEMG-based hand gesture recognition, even under unseen conditions, by approximating Fisher's representation. To this end, we study a simple and straightforward 1D-CNN. The general framework is illustrated in Figure 4, and the detailed configuration of the 1D-CNN model is presented in Table 1. A key feature of the proposed framework is that manual feature extraction occurs only during the training phase. During inference, the hand gestures are predicted directly from the raw sEMG signals. Overall, the model consists of three main components: (1) deep feature extraction, (2) Fisher's approximation, and (3) hand gesture classification (Table 1).

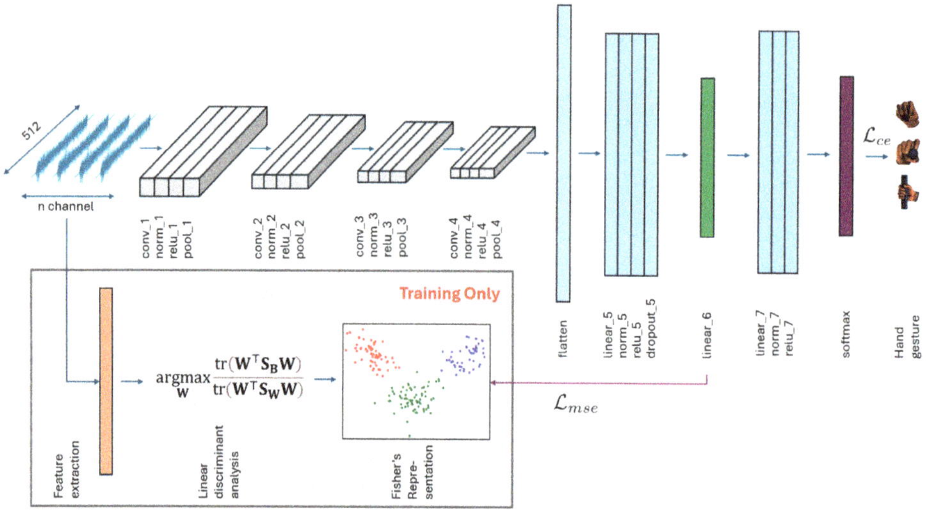

Figure 4. Illustration of the hybrid CNN-LDA framework for end-to-end sEMG-based hand gesture recognition, with manual feature extraction and Fisher's representation used only during the CNN training stage.

To optimize the model parameters, we employed cross-entropy loss, denoted as $\mathcal{L}_{\text{ce}}$, for the discriminative training and mean squared error, $\mathcal{L}_{\text{mse}}$, for the reconstruction loss in approximating Fisher's representation. The cross-entropy loss $\mathcal{L}_{\text{ce}}$ quantifies the dissimilarity between the predicted probability distribution of a sample belonging to class j and the ground truth distribution. $\mathcal{L}_{\text{ce}}$ is given by:

$$\mathcal{L}_{\text{ce}} = -\sum_{i} y_i \log(p_i) \tag{6}$$

where y_i represents the true class label in a one-hot encoded vector, and p_i denotes the predicted probability for class i, as determined by the softmax function. By minimizing the cross-entropy loss, the model is trained to assign higher probabilities to the correct class and lower probabilities to the incorrect classes. To align the latent representation from the CNN with Fisher's representation, we minimize the mean squared error (MSE) $\mathcal{L}_{\text{mse}}$ loss between the output from the linear_6 layer and the features in Fisher's representation. This step forces the CNN to learn a latent representation that closely resembles Fisher's discriminant representation. The MSE loss, $\mathcal{L}_{\text{mse}}$, frequently used in regression tasks, is defined as:

$$\mathcal{L}_{\text{mse}} = \frac{1}{N} \sum_{i=1}^{N} \left(y_i - \hat{y}_i\right)^2 \tag{7}$$

Here, N is the number of samples, y_i is the reference value in Fisher's subspace, and $\hat{y}_i$ is the corresponding latent representation produced by the CNN. The combined loss function of $\mathcal{L}_{\text{ce}}$ and $\mathcal{L}_{\text{mse}}$ is defined as:

$$\mathcal{L} = \alpha \mathcal{L}_{ce} + (1 - \alpha)\mathcal{L}_{\text{mse}} \tag{8}$$

- **Cross-entropy CNN** (CNN-CE, $\alpha = 1$), where the CNN parameters are learned by minimizing the $\mathcal{L}_{\text{ce}}$.
- **Fusion CNN-LDA** (CNN-CEMSE, $\alpha = 0.5$), which simultaneously optimizes both the $\mathcal{L}_{\text{ce}}$ and $\mathcal{L}_{\text{mse}}$ during training.
- **Fisher's approximator** (CNN-MSE, $\alpha = 0$). This model is trained to minimize the $\mathcal{L}_{\text{mse}}$ loss exclusively to obtain a latent representation closely aligned with Fisher's representation. After the model is trained, the weight of the convolution layers up to linear_6 are frozen, and the remaining layers are retrained with cross-entropy loss.

The training and inference of the CNN-CE are both end-to-end processes, using raw sEMG data, while the CNN-CEMSE and CNN-MSE require manual feature extraction during training only. All the 1D-CNN variants were trained using stochastic gradient descent for 60 epochs, with a mini-batch size of 128, a learning rate of 0.01, a weight decay of 0.01, and a dropout rate of 0.2 to further prevent overfitting.

Table 1. Components of 1D convolutional neural network. Fisher's approx. refers to Fisher's approximator layers and clf. refers to classifier layers; k, ch, and strd denote filter kernel size, number of filters, and stride, respectively.

Feature extraction	**conv_1** k = 3, ch = 20	**norm_1**	**relu_1**	**pool_1** k = 3, strd = 3
	conv_2 k = 3, ch = 20	**norm_2**	**relu_2**	**pool_2** k = 3, strd = 3
	conv_3 k = 3, ch = 20	**norm_3**	**relu_3**	**pool_3** k = 3, strd = 3
	conv_4 k = 3, ch = 20	**norm_4**	**relu_4**	**pool_4** k = 3, strd = 3
		flatten		
Fisher's approx.	**linear_5** out = 100	**norm_5**	**relu_5**	**dropout_5** prob = 0.2
		linear_6 out = $n_{gestures}$ 1		
clf.	**linear_7** out = 100	**norm_7**	**relu_7**	**softmax** out = $n_{gestures}$

2.5. Training and Testing Dataset Partitioning

To evaluate the generalization capability of our proposed framework for hand gesture recognition under conditions not encountered during training, we adopted the "train-one-test-all" evaluation scheme. Specifically, the classifiers were trained on hand gestures from a single condition. For testing, the hand gestures from all the available conditions are included. For example, train on P1 test on (P1 to P5) or train on medium force test on (low, medium, high). The training dataset included the first three repetitions from the recorded condition, while the testing dataset comprised all subsequent repetitions of the hand gestures across every recorded condition. This "train-one-test-all" approach helps minimize the user training burden by reducing the amount of data needed.

2.6. Statistical Tests

Where applicable, statistical tests were conducted. Due to the high degree of non-normality in the recognition error results, non-parametric tests were used. Our experiments were designed based on a repeated measures setting, where the result from each individual subject was considered as a single measurement. First, the Friedman test, a non-parametric alternative to the repeated measures ANOVA, was conducted to verify the presence of significant differences between at least two groups. When significant differences were confirmed by the Friedman test, Wilcoxon signed-rank tests with Bonferroni correction were then applied to identify the specific pairs with significant differences. The significance level was set at $\alpha = 0.05$.

3. Results

3.1. Robustness of Fisher's Representation for Hand Gesture Recognition Under Dynamic Conditions Using the TD8-AR Feature Set

Here, we demonstrate the efficacy of Fisher's representation by comparing the recognition error rates of different classifiers in the original feature space and after their transformation into Fisher's discriminant subspace. Seven of the most commonly used classifiers for hand gesture recognition were included in this demonstration, namely LDA, SVM with Linear Kernel, QDA, k-nearest neighbor (k-NN), nearest centroid (CEN), random forest (RF), logistic regression with quadratic kernel (lr quadratic), and multi-layer perceptron (MLP). Furthermore, to demonstrate the impact of the MLP size, we increased the number of hidden layers from one to six, with each layer having 100 perceptrons.

Overall, transforming the data into Fisher's discriminant subspace reduced the recognition error across all the classifiers. In regard to the Limb.Pos. dataset results, the recognition error of the LDA classifier was 24.31% (Figure 5a). For the SVM, the recognition error in the original feature space was 26.46%, which increased to 29.32% when the data was transformed into the LDA subspace. For the QDA, k-NN, and CEN, using the original feature space, the recognition errors all exceeded 30%, with the CEN reaching as high as 38.9%. However, transforming the data into Fisher's discriminant subspace reduced the errors to around 25%. With MLP (Figure 5b), the recognition errors consistently stayed above 30% in the original feature space, ranging from 33.48% for one layer to 31.18% for six layers; however, when transformed into Fisher's subspace, the recognition errors dropped consistently to under 28%.

The results based on the Amp.Force. dataset are shown in Figure 6, where the recognition error for the LDA is 27.3% (Figure 6a). Transforming the data into Fisher's discriminant subspace reduced the recognition errors to approximately 28% for all the classifiers, with the CEN showing a large reduction of 34.09%. For MLP (Figure 6b), in the original feature space, the recognition error increased from 45.13% with one hidden layer to 46.8% with six hidden layers. When transformed into Fisher's discriminant subspace, the recognition error decreased by 17% to approximately 28.41–1.11% higher than that of the LDA.

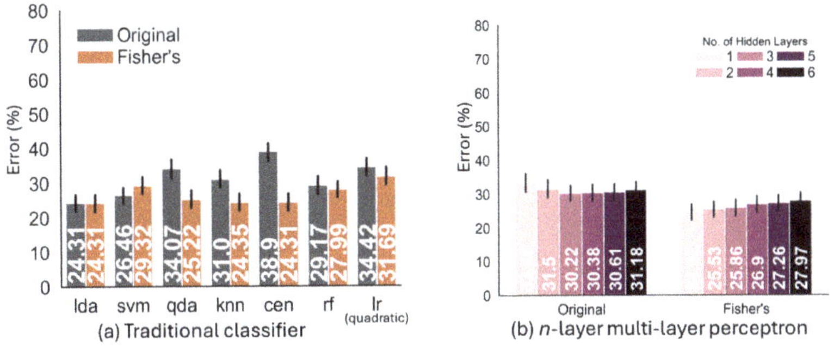

Figure 5. Comparison of recognition error (%) based on the Limb.Pos. dataset using the original TD8-AR feature space and transformed into Fisher's discriminant space for (**a**) seven traditional classifiers and (**b**) n-layers MLP.

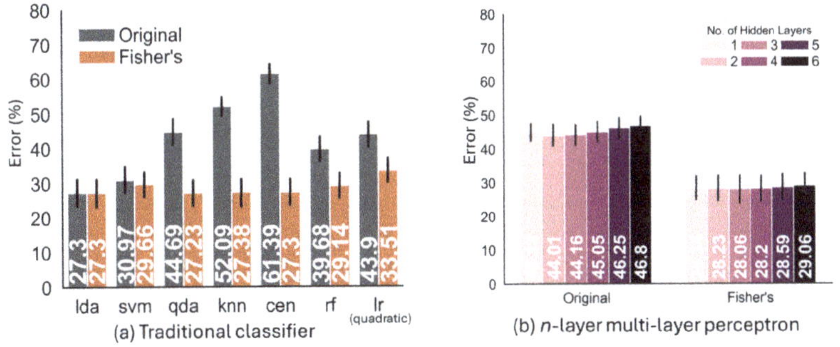

Figure 6. Comparison of recognition error (%) based on the Amp.Force. dataset using the original TD8-AR feature space and transformed into Fisher's discriminant subspace for (**a**) seven traditional classifiers and (**b**) n-layers MLP.

3.2. Recognition Performance of Hybrid Frameworks in Regard to Hand Gesture Recognition Under Dynamic Conditions

3.2.1. Results Based on Limb.Pos. Dataset

Figure 7 presents the recognition errors across eight feature sets based on the Limb.Pos. dataset. The Friedman statistical test identified statistically significant differences between at least one pair of classification methods among all the feature sets ($p < 0.001$). Except for Ext-23, all the feature sets, when trained with the LDA classifier, had significantly lower errors compared to the CNN-CE, which had an error of 34.32% ($p < 0.012$). In regard to LDA, the TD8 feature set recorded the lowest recognition error at 23.81%, outperforming the state-of-the-art TD-PSR [7] set by 0.53%. Meanwhile, the LDA and TD8-AR set raised the recognition error from TD8 by 0.5% to 24.31%. In regard to the hybrid CNN-LDA framework, the CNN-MSE consistently exhibited lower recognition errors and reconstruction losses $\mathcal{L}_{mse}$ than the CNN-CEMSE, with statistically significant differences observed in the recognition errors of the DU, TD-PSR, and TD8 feature sets ($p < 0.041$). When trained with the Ext-23 feature set, the CNN-MSE achieved state-of-the-art performance, with a 22.79% error rate, significantly outperforming the LDA based on the same feature set ($p \approx 0.018$). It is also observed that Fisher's reconstruction loss $\mathcal{L}_{mse}$ was relatively high ($\mathcal{L}_{mse} > 5.0$) based on the Ext-23 feature set for both the CNN-MSE and CNN-CEMSE.

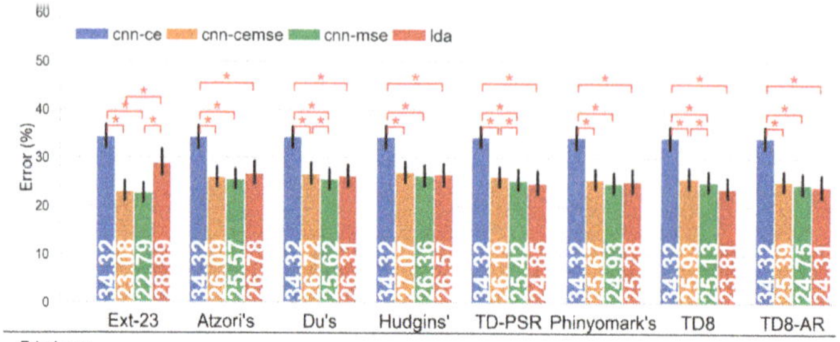

	Ext-23	Atzori's	Du's	Hudgins'	TD-PSR	Phinyomark's	TD8	TD8-AR
Friedman p-value	<0.001*	<0.001*	<0.001*	<0.001*	<0.001*	<0.001*	<0.001*	<0.001*
$\mathcal{L}_{mse}$ CNN-CEMSE	5.41	2.25	1.82	1.6	1.67	2.25	2.2	2.82
$\mathcal{L}_{mse}$ CNN-MSE	5.25	2.11	1.68	1.47	1.53	2.1	2.04	2.64

Figure 7. Comparison of the performance based on Limb.Pos. dataset between 8 different feature sets and 4 classification approaches in terms of recognition error (%), the result of Friedman statistical test with Fisher's reconstruction loss $\mathcal{L}_{\text{mse}}$ by the CNN-CEMSE and CNN-MSE; * indicates statistical significance ($p < 0.05$).

Figure 8 illustrates the recognition errors based on the Ext-23 feature set across 11 subjects, where performance variations by subject were clearly observed. For the CNN-CE, trained end-to-end using the raw sEMG signals, the recognition errors ranged from 25.15% for S9 to as high as 48.27% for S7. Training the LDA model on the Ext-23 feature set did not guarantee enhanced recognition performance over the CNN-CE for all the subjects; notably, the LDA model's error for S10 was 41.5%, 11.5% higher than the CNN-CE. In contrast, the CNN-CEMSE and CNN-MSE significantly reduced the errors across all the subjects compared to the CNN-CE, with the lowest errors recorded for S9 of 13.29% and 13.4%, respectively, for the CNN-CEMSE and CNN-MSE.

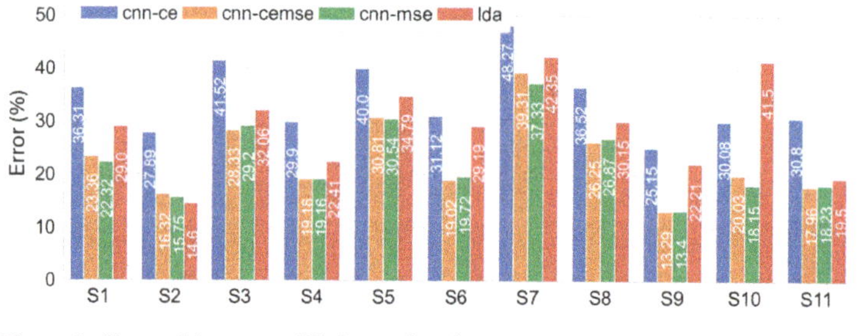

Figure 8. Recognition error (%) for each subject, averaged over all the train–test limb position combinations, using four classification approaches, namely CNN-CE, CNN-CEMSE, CNN-MSE, and LDA, using Ext-23 feature set.

In Figure 9, we can see that the CNN-CEMSE, along with the CNN-MSE and LDA, successfully reduced the recognition error compared to the CNN-CE based on all the train–test combinations, using the Ext-23 feature set. When trained and tested on the same P3 limb position, the CNN-CEMSE achieved the most substantial reduction in the recognition error, decreasing by 6.8% from 8.8% to just 2.0%. When trained and tested on different limb positions, specifically when trained on P3 and tested on P4, the CNN-MSE showed the largest reduction in the recognition errors, decreasing from CNN-CE's 44% to 24.87%. On average, the LDA achieved the lowest error of 2.6% in the same limb position train–test evaluation, marking a 4% improvement over the CNN-CE. While in the case where the tested limb positions differed from the training ones, the CNN-MSE returned the lowest recognition error decrease of 27.71–13.53% compared to the CNN-CE and 7.75% compared to the LDA. Table 2 highlights the recognition performance of our proposed hybrid method compared with other deep end-to-end machine learning approaches for myoelectric hand gesture recognition. By enforcing the linear_6 latent representation to approximate Fisher's representation of the Ext-23 feature set, our proposed CNN-LDA framework based on the CNN-MSE achieved the lowest recognition error across all the evaluation metrics.

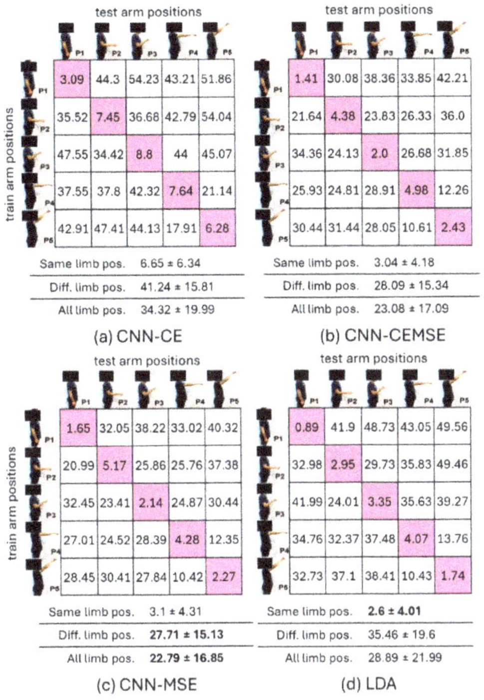

Figure 9. Average inter-limb position recognition error across all 11 subjects with four classification approaches and the Ext-23 feature set: (**a**) CNN-CE, (**b**) CNN-CEMSE, (**c**) CNN-MSE, and (**d**) LDA. Bold values denote the lowest recognition errors.

Table 2. Performance comparison of our proposed hybrid CNN-LDA framework (CNN-MSE) with other deep end-to-end architectures for myoelectric hand gesture recognition based on Limb.Pos. dataset.

Methods	**Same Limb Pos. Error (%)**	**Diff. Limb Pos Error (%)**	**All Limb Pos. Error (%)**
1D-CNN [9] (CNN-CE equivalent)	6.65	41.24	34.32
2D-CNN [9,10]	6.27	38.36	31.94
LSTM-CNN [11]	3.75	34.70	28.51
Multi-stream 1D-CNN [9,12]	3.9	33.32	27.44
Multi-stream 1D-CNN-LSTM [9]	3.82	31.85	26.24
Transformer TC-HGR [13]	17.8	50.89	44.27

Table 9. Performance comparison of our proposed hybrid CNN-LDA framework (CNN-MSE) with other deep end-to-end architectures for myoelectric hand gesture recognition, based on Amp.Force. dataset.

Methods	Same Force Error (%)	Diff. Force Error (%)	All Force Error (%)
1D-CNN [9] (CNN-CE equivalent)	16.98	53.58	41.38
2D-CNN [9,10]	14.11	48.89	37.30
LSTM-CNN [11]	11.42	47.15	35.24
Multi-stream 1D-CNN [9,12]	10.53	47.89	35.44
Multi-stream 1D-CNN-LSTM [9]	11.57	48.75	36.36
Transformer TC-HGR [13]	28.48	59.19	48.95
Transformer Tra-HGR [14]	29.21	54.93	46.36
Transformer Tra-HGR-Fnet [14]	31.49	56.98	48.48
Transformer Tra-HGR-Tnet [14]	51.70	69.35	63.47
Our Hybrid CNN-LDA (CNN-MSE and Ext-23 feature set)	**8.19**	**40.59**	**29.79**

3.3. The Effect of α Hyperparameter Balancing MSE and Cross-Entropy Loss

As shown in Figure 13, we have studied the effect of the hyperparameter α in Equation (8) on the recognition error across two public datasets. It is observed that when $\alpha \leq 0.5$, minimal changes in the recognition performance are seen based on both datasets. However, when the cross-entropy loss starts to become the dominant training loss ($\alpha > 0.5$), an increase in recognition error is observed based on both datasets, highlighting the adverse effects of cross-entropy loss.

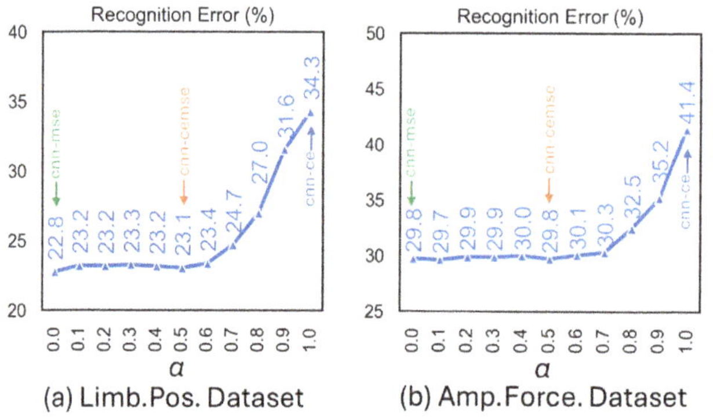

Figure 13. The effect of α in Equation (8) on recognition accuracy of (**a**) Limb.Pos. dataset and (**b**) Amp.Force. dataset, using Ext-23 feature set.

3.4. Evaluation of CNN Training Convergence and Latent Representation

Figures 14 and 15 show comprehensive analysis, comparing three deep CNN training approaches with the conventional LDA, specifically focusing on the Ext-23 feature set. Regarding overall recognition performance, from the 30th epoch onward, the performance of the three CNN models converged, as indicated by minimal reductions in the recognition error (Figures 14a and 15a), based on both datasets. Additionally, the CNN-MSE converged faster than the CNN-CEMSE, based on both datasets, with no signs of overfitting observed at the 60th epoch.

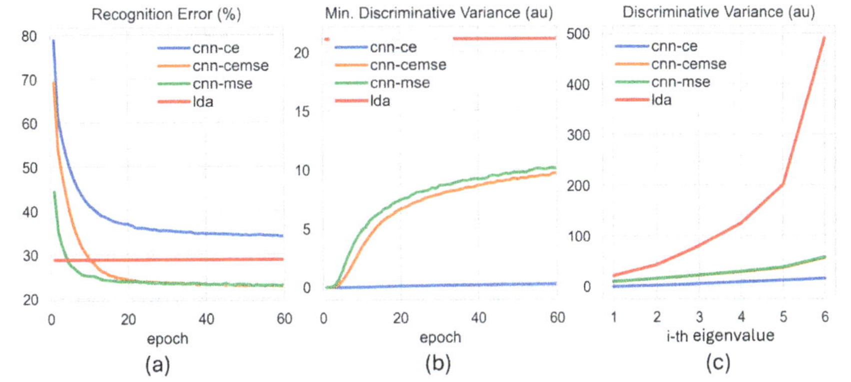

Figure 14. Training convergence in terms of (**a**) recognition error, (**b**) smallest eigenvalue, and (**c**) eigenvalue at 60 epochs for CNN-CE, CNN-CEMSE, CNN-MSE, and LDA, based on the Limb.Pos. dataset and the Ext-23 feature set.

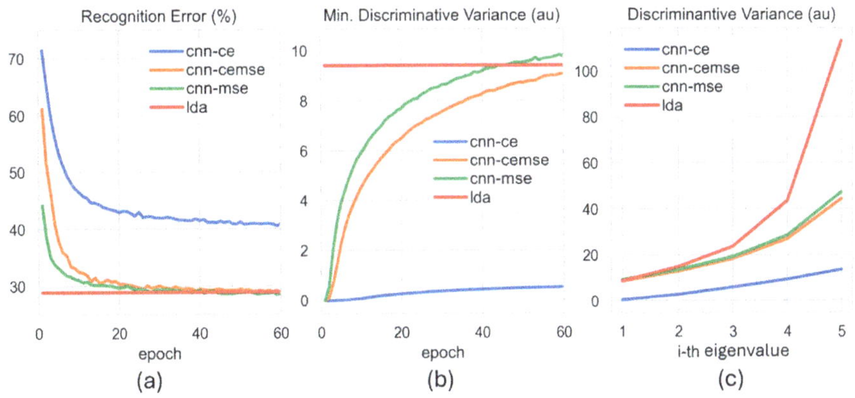

Figure 15. Training convergence in terms of (**a**) recognition error, (**b**) smallest eigenvalue, and (**c**) eigenvalue at 60 epochs for CNN-CE, CNN-CEMSE, CNN-MSE, and LDA, based on the Amp.Force. dataset and the Ext-23 feature set.

Interesting insights were revealed by examining the eigenvalues of the CNN latent representation for the linear_6 layer (Figures 14b,c and 15b,c). The smallest or the first discriminant eigenvalue represents the variance in the most challenging direction for classifying hand gestures. In regard to both datasets, the first eigenvalue of the CNN-CE data exhibited a minimal increase during training (Figures 14b and 15b). However, when using Fisher's reconstruction loss ($\mathcal{L}_{\text{mse}}$), the first eigenvalue of the CNN-MSE and CNN-CEMSE noticeably rises, with the CNN-MSE surpassing the LDA starting from epoch 50th, based on the Amp.Force. dataset (Figure 15b). In regard to the Limb.Pos. dataset, the first eigenvalue of the CNN-MSE and CNN-CEMSE remained smaller than that of the LDA even after 60 epochs. Additionally, the CNN-MSE consistently achieved higher first eigenvalues than the CNN-CEMSE, based on both datasets. With the LDA classifier, significant disparities between the largest and smallest eigenvalues in the embedded space were also observed (Figures 14c and 15c). By approximating Fisher's representation, both the CNN-MSE and CNN-CEMSE mitigated the extreme eigenvalues of the LDA, demonstrating a spectral regularization effect.

To further analyze the spectral regularization effect of our proposed framework, we utilized T-SNE (t-distributed Stochastic Neighbor Embedding, as shown in Figure 16) to illustrate the data embedded in linear_6 and referenced Fisher's representation. T-SNE is a machine learning technique that enables visualization of high dimensional data by reducing the dimensionality of a dataset, while preserving the relative distance between the datapoints. It is evident that there is substantial displacement in the Limb.Pos. dataset (Figure 16a), particularly in regard to the wrist extension and wrist flexion, where the cluster formed by the CNN-MSE and LDA is entirely non-overlapped. In regard to the Amp.Force. dataset (Figure 16b), although not as pronounced as in the Limb.Pos. dataset, there is clear presence of cluster shifts in the spherical grip and thumb flexion data.

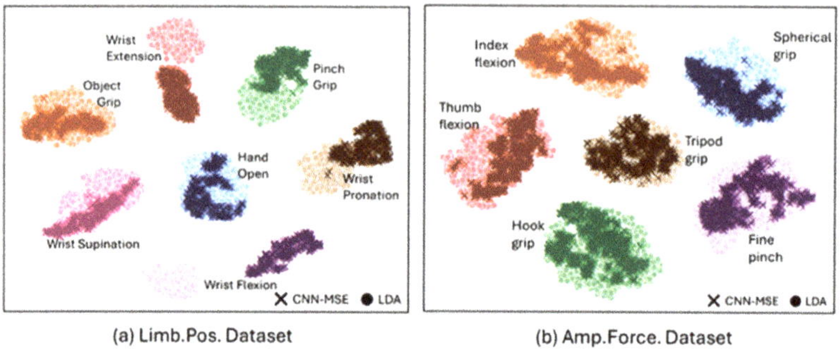

Figure 16. T-SNE visualization of embedded representation of CNN-MSE linear_6 and Fisher's representation on (**a**) S1 trained on P2 limb position based on Limb.Pos. dataset and (**b**) S1 trained on moderate contraction force based on Amp.Force. dataset.

3.5. Comparison of Inference Time

To demonstrate the suitability of our proposed frameworks for the real-time control of prosthetic devices or for other muscle/human–machine interface applications, we evaluated the inference time of our proposed CNN-LDA framework. The inference time was tested on a computer that was equipped with an Intel(R) Core(TM) i7-8750H CPU and an NVIDIA GeForce RTX 2070 GPU. Table 4 presents the inference time for the Amp.Force. dataset. The inference time for the LDA was consistently low, at 0.19 ms per frame, regardless of the input feature set. Feature extraction varied in regard to computation duration, ranging from 0.49 ms per frame using TD-PSR to 16.95 ms per frame using the Ext-23 feature set. By decoupling feature extraction during inference, our CNN-LDA framework offered low real-time processing, at 1.72 ms per frame, for the CNN-CEMSE, CNN-MSE, and CNN-CE.

Table 4. Comparison of inference time between classical LDA with manual feature extraction and the CNN-LDA framework; * CNN includes CNN-CEMSE, CNN-MSE, and CNN-CE.

	Ext-23	Atzori's	Du's	Hudgin's	TD-PSR	Phinyo-mark's	TD8	TD8-AR	CNN *
Feature Dimension	528	272	48	32	48	120	64	120	-
Feat. Extraction (ms/frame)	16.95	5.02	0.83	0.55	0.49	6.80	1.07	2.25	-
Classification (ms/frame)	0.19	0.19	0.19	0.19	0.19	0.19	0.19	0.19	-
Total (ms/frame)	17.14	5.21	1.02	0.74	0.68	6.99	1.26	2.44	1.72

4. Discussion

We have employed the train-one-test-all evaluation scheme to assess the generalization performance of the framework, which is better aligned with real-world conditions. We first highlighted the robustness of the LDA, showing that it consistently outperformed other algorithms in regard to the train-one-test-all evaluation scheme. Notably, the LDA trained with manual feature extraction demonstrated superior performance, not only over traditional machine learning algorithms (Figures 5 and 6), but also over deep 1D convolutional neural networks trained end-to-end with only cross-entropy loss (CNN-CE) (Figures 7 and 10). Furthermore, since the LDA functions as both a classifier and a dimensionality reduction method, transforming the data in regard to Fisher's discriminant subspace significantly reduced the classification error for all the traditional machine learning algorithms.

There are a few possible underlying reasons that may explain this finding. Most machine learning classifiers, except for LDA and QDA, are primarily point based, wherein decision boundaries can be significantly affected by data outliers [44,45]. Algorithms, such as k-NN and SVMs, place high emphasis on hard-to-classify data points [42]. Neural networks trained with cross-entropy have a tendency to heavily penalize incorrect predictions, leading to severe overfitting in regard to outliners [44]. In contrast, the LDA and QDA assume normally distributed data within each class, and their decision boundaries are determined by overall data distributions rather than individual points [43]. Although similar, gesture recognition performance of the LDA and QDA differs significantly, with the QDA showing an over 10% higher error than the LDA (Figures 5a and 6a). While the LDA assumes that all classes have the same variance, leading to a linear decision boundary, the QDA relaxes this homoscedasticity assumption, resulting in a more complex quadratic decision boundary [42]. It has been shown that a simple linear mapping function is effective not only in regard to discrete hand gesture recognition tasks [5], but also in regard to proportional control problems [46,47]. Moreover, gesture consistency varies with the subject's expertise [48,49], and data cluster shifts are expected even under the same conditions [50,51]. Our findings further confirm that the LDA effectively accommodates gestures under new conditions. As a dimensionality reduction method, the LDA's Fisher discriminant subspace is linked to muscle synergy [52], wherein muscle groups coordinate together during movement. We hypothesize that the LDA preserves spatial information related to electrode placement, facilitating an effective muscle/human–machine interface. In related research, [53] proposed a force tolerance model based on muscle synergy reconstruction loss, akin to the LDA's method of assigning hand gestures with the highest probability, as shown in Equation (2).

Based on improved recognition accuracy from transforming sEMG features into Fisher's discriminant subspace, we proposed a novel CNN-LDA framework to approximate Fisher's representation. We tested two variants of our hybrid CNN-LDA framework, the CNN-CEMSE and CNN-MSE, using eight feature sets, across two public datasets. Our results indicate that both variants effectively lowered the recognition error compared to a naive CNN-CE, with improvement ranges from 7% to 11% based on the Limb.Pos. dataset and 4% to 11% based on the Amp.Force. dataset. Notably, based on the Limb.Pos. dataset, we achieved a state-of-the-art performance with the Ext-23 feature set (Figure 7), recording the lowest error of 22.79% with the CNN-MSE, a 2.06% improvement over the TD-PSR [7]. However, based on the Amp.Force. dataset, the CNN-LDA and Ext-23 feature set combination did not achieve state-of-the-art results, with recognition errors 1% higher than the Ext-23 feature set with the LDA, and 2.4% higher than the LDA with Phinyomark's and TD8-AR features (Figure 10). Yet, the result of the CNN-LDA with the Ext-23 feature set remains competitive, showing overall improvements over most of the tested pipelines (Figure 10) and a minimal inference time (Table 4).

Our novel CNN-LDA framework provides many practical features that are suitable for myoelectric-based applications. For every feature set, the relatively high reconstruction error ($\mathcal{L}_{mse} > 0.8$, Figures 7 and 10) induced the spectral regularization effect based on the discriminant eigenvalue structure for linear_6 (Figures 14c and 15c), with a cluster shift in terms of the wrist movements being clearly observable in the t-SNE visualization (Figure 16a). However, since a state-of-the-art performance was achieved based only on the Limb.Pos. dataset using the Ext-23 feature set, further research is needed to understand the relationship between the discriminant eigenvalue structure and generalizability.

The Ext-23 feature set is a concatenation of all the individual features from other effective feature sets, without applying any formal feature selection process. While feature selection can potentially improve recognition performance, even for out-of-distribution hand gestures [25], it is generally a costly and time-consuming process, often requiring manual intervention. Moreover, the resulting feature set is not guaranteed to be generalizable across different datasets. For instance, the TD8 feature set was derived using the Minimum Redundancy Maximum Relevance technique, based on the Limb.Pos. dataset [25]. When trained with the LDA, the TD8 feature set achieved a recognition error of 23.81%, based on the Limb.Pos. dataset (Figure 7). However, based on the Amp.Force. dataset (Figure 10), the same TD8 feature set resulted in the highest recognition error of 37.81%. Moreover, Wei, Dai, Wong, Hu, Kankanhalli, and Geng [41] proposed a multiview deep learning architecture for sEMG-based hand gesture recognition, wherein each input view corresponds to a different sEMG feature set. While the work of Wei, Dai, Wong, Hu, Kankanhalli, and Geng [41] requires explicit computation of each individual feature during inference, our framework does not, resulting in a constant inference time regardless of the feature choice (Table 4). Additionally, by decoupling feature extraction during inference, our CNN-LDA framework enables future integration of robust but computationally intensive features, such as Sample Entropy or Empirical Mode Decomposition [22,54].

Our results also highlighted that cross-entropy loss adversely affected myoelectric hand gesture recognition. As shown in Figures 5 and 6, MLP trained on the original TD8-AR feature space with cross-entropy loss increased the recognition error compared to the LDA, ranging from 6% to 20%. Moreover, the CNN-CEMSE increased the reconstruction loss $\mathcal{L}_{mse}$ across all the features (Figures 7 and 10) and reduced the smallest eigenvalue (Figures 14b and 15b). Moreover, the CNN-CE exhibited only a negligible increase in the smallest eigenvalue as the training converged (Figures 14b,c and 15b,c). This observation aligns with related machine learning findings that cross-entropy favors easily classified classes [44] and is sensitive to noisy datasets [55,56].

In this work, we focused solely on hand gesture recognition using a single modality: the sEMG signal. Multi-modal sensory fusion, i.e., combining sEMG signals with additional sensory inputs, such as pFMG [17,57,58], IMU [30,59], or RGB [18,19], and depth cameras [20], has shown promising results in regard to enhancing sEMG-based hand gesture recognition under dynamic conditions. In general, multi-modal fusion can be approached in two ways. The first concerns sensory complementarity, wherein the sEMG signal is paired with another modality to enhance recognition, as is common with pFMG and IMU [17,59]. The second approach leverages additional modalities to provide contextual information, such as on the arm position [60], usage scenarios [59], grasped object types [18], or wrist orientation [19]. In future work, we aim to explore multi-modal sensing in greater depth to further improve recognition performance under dynamic conditions.

As shown in Figures 7 and 10, recognition performance varies depending on the feature set used. Currently, feature selection is often performed heuristically, typically by combining high-performing features, based on classification accuracy [22] or the ANOVA F-score [25]. However, in our previous study, we observed that criteria, such as the ANOVA F-score, become less reliable under novel conditions [25]. Moreover, there is a lack of detailed analysis on the impact of sEMG signals under dynamic conditions, with only a few notable studies addressing this issue [6,7,38,39]. We believe that a deeper investigation into this impact would be beneficial for developing highly robust and intuitive prosthetic hand control interfaces.

5. Conclusions

We have demonstrated that the LDA and Fisher's discriminant subspace achieved an optimal hand gesture recognition performance under the train-one-test-all evaluation scheme across both the Limb.Pos. and Amp.Force. datasets. Based on this observation, we have proposed a CNN-LDA hybrid framework that approximates Fisher's representation from raw EMG signals. The results from two different public datasets consistently demonstrated that our CNN-LDA hybrid framework outperformed multiple deep learning architectures, trained end-to-end with cross-entropy loss only. When trained with the Ext-23 feature set, our CNN-LDA framework achieved a state-of-the-art recognition error of 22.79%, based on the Limb.Pos. dataset, using the CNN-MSE variant. Additionally, the CNN-LDA framework's imperfect reconstruction of Fisher's representation induced a spectral regularization effect, preventing the occurrence of extreme values of discriminant eigenvalues. By highlighting the robustness of the LDA subspace in regard to sEMG signal covariate shifts and demonstrating that leveraging Fisher's representation can effectively guide CNN training, our framework serves as a foundation for the future development of effective muscle–machine interfaces using deep learning.

Author Contributions: H.L.: Conceptualization, Methodology, Software, Writing—Original Draft, Formal Analysis, Visualization. M.i.h.P. and G.M.S.: Resources, Supervision, Writing—Review and Editing. G.A.: Conceptualization, Resources, Writing—Review and Editing, Supervision, Funding Acquisition. All authors have read and agreed to the published version of the manuscript.

Funding: The research presented in this article was made possible through financial support from the ARC Centre of Excellence for Electromaterials Science (Grant No. CE140100012), the ARC-Discovery Project (DP210102911), and the University of Wollongong.

Institutional Review Board Statement: Ethical approval was not required for this study as it only uses publicly available datasets.

Data Availability Statement: The dataset used in this manuscript is publicly accessible at https://www.rami-khushaba.com/biosignals-repository (accessed on 1 June 2024).

Acknowledgments: During the preparation of this work the author(s) used ChatGPT 4.0 and Quillbot in order to enhance the writing quality. After using this tool/service, the author(s) reviewed and edited the content as needed, and take full responsibility for the content of the published article.

Conflicts of Interest: The authors declare that there are no conflicts of interest.

Abbreviations

The following abbreviations are used in this manuscript:

CNN-CE	Cross-Entropy CNN ($\alpha = 1$)
CNN-CEMSE	Fusion CNN-LDA ($\alpha = 0.5$)
CNN-MSE	Fisher's approximator ($\alpha = 0$)
LDA	Linear Discriminant Analysis
SVMs	Support Vector Machines
QDA	Quadratic Discriminant Analysis

kNN	K-nearest neighbor
CEN	Nearest centroid
LR-quadratic	Logistic Regression with Quadratic Kernel
TD8	Robust Time-Domain 8
TD8-ARs	Robust Time-Domain 8 with Autoregressive Coefficients
TD-PSR	Time-domain power spectral moments

References

1. Cordella, F.; Ciancio, A.L.; Sacchetti, R.; Davalli, A.; Cutti, A.G.; Guglielmelli, E.; Zollo, L. Literature review on needs of upper limb prosthesis users. *Front. Neurosci.* **2016**, *10*, 209. [CrossRef] [PubMed]
2. Yang, D.; Gu, Y.; Thakor, N.V.; Liu, H. Improving the functionality, robustness, and adaptability of myoelectric control for dexterous motion restoration. *Exp. Brain Res.* **2019**, *237*, 291–311. [CrossRef] [PubMed]
3. Kyranou, I.; Vijayakumar, S.; Erden, M.S. Causes of performance degradation in electromyographic pattern recognition in upper limb prostheses. *Front. Neurorobotics* **2018**, *12*, 58. [CrossRef] [PubMed]
4. Hargrove, L.J.; Scheme, E.J.; Englehart, K.B.; Hudgins, B.S. Multiple binary classifications via linear discriminant analysis for improved controllability of a powered prosthesis. *IEEE Trans. Neural Syst. Rehabil. Eng.* **2010**, *18*, 49–57. [CrossRef] [PubMed]
5. Vidovic, M.M.-C.; Hwang, H.-J.; Amsüss, S.; Hahne, J.M.; Farina, D.; Müller, K.-R. Improving the robustness of myoelectric pattern recognition for upper limb prostheses by covariate shift adaptation. *IEEE Trans. Neural Syst. Rehabil. Eng.* **2015**, *24*, 961–970. [CrossRef]
6. Al-Timemy, A.H.; Khushaba, R.N.; Bugmann, G.; Escudero, J. Improving the performance against force variation of EMG controlled multifunctional upper-limb prostheses for transradial amputees. *IEEE Trans. Neural Syst. Rehabil. Eng.* **2015**, *24*, 650–661. [CrossRef]
7. Khushaba, R.N.; Takruri, M.; Miro, J.V.; Kodagoda, S. Towards limb position invariant myoelectric pattern recognition using time-dependent spectral features. *Neural Netw.* **2014**, *55*, 42–58. [CrossRef]
8. Smith, L.H.; Hargrove, L.J.; Lock, B.A.; Kuiken, T.A. Determining the optimal window length for pattern recognition-based myoelectric control: Balancing the competing effects of classification error and controller delay. *IEEE Trans. Neural Syst. Rehabil. Eng.* **2010**, *19*, 186–192. [CrossRef]
9. Le, H.; Spinks, G.M.; in Het Panhuis, M.; Alici, G. Cross-day myoelectric gesture recognition with hybrid multistream CNN-bidirectional LSTM. In Proceedings of the 2025 IEEE International Conference on Mechatronics (ICM'25), Wollongong, Australia, 28 February–2 March 2025.
10. Atzori, M.; Cognolato, M.; Müller, H. Deep learning with convolutional neural networks applied to electromyography data: A resource for the classification of movements for prosthetic hands. *Front. Neurorobotics* **2016**, *10*, 9. [CrossRef]
11. Wu, Y.; Zheng, B.; Zhao, Y. Dynamic gesture recognition based on LSTM-CNN. In Proceedings of the 2018 Chinese Automation Congress (CAC), Xi'an, China, 30 November–2 December 2018; pp. 2446–2450.
12. Wei, W.; Wong, Y.; Du, Y.; Hu, Y.; Kankanhalli, M.; Geng, W. A multi-stream convolutional neural network for sEMG-based gesture recognition in muscle-computer interface. *Pattern Recognit. Lett.* **2019**, *119*, 131–138. [CrossRef]
13. Zabihi, S.; Rahimian, E.; Asif, A.; Mohammadi, A. Light-weight CNN-attention based architecture for hand gesture recognition via electromyography. In Proceedings of the ICASSP 2023-2023 IEEE International Conference on Acoustics, Speech and Signal Processing (ICASSP), Rhodes Island, Greece, 4–10 June 2023; pp. 1–5.
14. Zabihi, S.; Rahimian, E.; Asif, A.; Mohammadi, A. Trahgr: Transformer for hand gesture recognition via electromyography. *IEEE Trans. Neural Syst. Rehabil. Eng.* **2023**, *31*, 4211–4224. [CrossRef] [PubMed]
15. Betthauser, J.L.; Hunt, C.L.; Osborn, L.E.; Masters, M.R.; Levay, G.; Kaliki, R.R.; Thakor, N.V. Limb position tolerant pattern recognition for myoelectric prosthesis control with adaptive sparse representations from extreme learning. *IEEE Trans. Biomed. Eng.* **2017**, *65*, 770–778. [CrossRef] [PubMed]
16. Tchantchane, R.; Zhou, H.; Zhang, S.; Alici, G. A review of hand gesture recognition systems based on noninvasive wearable sensors. *Adv. Intell. Syst.* **2023**, *5*, 2300207. [CrossRef]
17. Zhang, S.; Zhou, H.; Tchantchane, R.; Alici, G. Hand gesture recognition across various limb positions using a multi-modal sensing system based on self-adaptive data-fusion and convolutional neural networks (CNNs). *IEEE Sens. J.* **2024**, *24*, 18633–18645. [CrossRef]
18. Deshmukh, S.; Khatik, V.; Saxena, A. Robust Fusion Model for Handling EMG and Computer Vision Data in Prosthetic Hand Control. *IEEE Sens. Lett.* **2023**, *7*, 6004804. [CrossRef]
19. Cirelli, G.; Tamantini, C.; Cordella, L.P.; Cordella, F. A Semiautonomous Control Strategy Based on Computer Vision for a Hand–Wrist Prosthesis. *Robotics* **2023**, *12*, 152. [CrossRef]

20. Castro, M.N.; Dosen, S. Continuous semi-autonomous prosthesis control using a depth sensor on the hand. *Front. Neurorobotics* **2022**, *16*, 814973. [CrossRef]
21. Khushaba, R.N.; Al-Timemy, A.; Kodagoda, S.; Nazarpour, K. Combined influence of forearm orientation and muscular contraction on EMG pattern recognition. *Expert. Syst. Appl.* **2016**, *61*, 154–161. [CrossRef]
22. Phinyomark, A.; Quaine, F.; Charbonnier, S.; Serviere, C.; Tarpin-Bernard, F.; Laurillau, Y. EMG feature evaluation for improving myoelectric pattern recognition robustness. *Expert. Syst. Appl.* **2013**, *40*, 4832–4840. [CrossRef]
23. Lorrain, T.; Jiang, N.; Farina, D. Influence of the training set on the accuracy of surface EMG classification in dynamic contractions for the control of multifunction prostheses. *J. Neuroeng. Rehabil.* **2011**, *8*, 25. [CrossRef]
24. Franzke, A.W.; Kristoffersen, M.B.; Bongers, R.M.; Murgia, A.; Pobatschnig, B.; Unglaube, F.; van der Sluis, C.K. Users' and therapists' perceptions of myoelectric multi-function upper limb prostheses with conventional and pattern recognition control. *PLoS ONE* **2019**, *14*, e0220899. [CrossRef] [PubMed]
25. Le, H.; Spinks, G.M.; in Het Panhuis, M.; Alici, G. Feature significance and generalizability of myoelectric hand gesture recognition under varying limb positions. In Proceedings of the 2025 IEEE International Conference on Mechatronics (ICM'25), Wollongong, Australia, 28 February–2 March 2025.
26. Akkad, G.; Mansour, A.; Inaty, E. Embedded deep learning accelerators: A survey on recent advances. *IEEE Trans. Artif. Intell.* **2023**, *5*, 1954–1972. [CrossRef]
27. Le, H.; in Het Panhuis, M.; Spinks, G.M.; Alici, G. The effect of dataset size on EMG gesture recognition under diverse limb positions. In Proceedings of the 2024 10th IEEE RAS/EMBS International Conference for Biomedical Robotics and Biomechatronics (BioRob), Heidelberg, Germany, 1–4 September 2024; pp. 303–308.
28. Moslemi, A.; Briskina, A.; Dang, Z.; Li, J. A Survey on Knowledge Distillation: Recent Advancements. *Mach. Learn. Appl.* **2024**, *18*, 100605. [CrossRef]
29. Zeng, J.; Sheng, Y.; Yang, Y.; Zhou, Z.; Liu, H. Cross modality knowledge distillation between A-mode ultrasound and surface electromyography. *IEEE Trans. Instrum. Meas.* **2022**, *71*, 1–9. [CrossRef]
30. Wei, W.; Ren, L.; Zhou, M.; Ma, Z.; Zhao, K.; Xu, X. Improving unimodal sEMG-based pattern recognition through multimodal generative adversarial learning. *IEEE Trans. Instrum. Meas.* **2025**, *74*, 2523520. [CrossRef]
31. Ghojogh, B.; Karray, F.; Crowley, M. Fisher and kernel fisher discriminant analysis: Tutorial. *arXiv* **2019**, arXiv:1906.09436. [CrossRef]
32. Goodfellow, I.; Bengio, Y.; Courville, A. *Deep Learning*; MIT Press: Cambridge, MA, USA, 2016.
33. Drapała, J.; Brzostowski, K.; Szpala, A.; Rutkowska-Kucharska, A. Two stage EMG onset detection method. *Arch. Control Sci.* **2012**, *22*, 427–440. [CrossRef]
34. Jiang, N.; Englehart, K.B.; Parker, P.A. Extracting simultaneous and proportional neural control information for multiple-DOF prostheses from the surface electromyographic signal. *IEEE Trans. Biomed. Eng.* **2008**, *56*, 1070–1080. [CrossRef]
35. Fuglevand, A.J.; Winter, D.A.; Patla, A.E.; Stashuk, D. Detection of motor unit action potentials with surface electrodes: Influence of electrode size and spacing. *Biol. Cybern.* **1992**, *67*, 143–153. [CrossRef]
36. Farina, D.; Merletti, R.; Stegeman, D. Biophysics of the generation of EMG signals. In *Electromyography: Physiology, Engineering, and Noninvasive Applications*; Wiley: Hoboken, NJ, USA, 2004; pp. 81–105. [CrossRef]
37. Fuglevand, A.J.; Winter, D.A.; Patla, A.E. Models of recruitment and rate coding organization in motor-unit pools. *J. Neurophysiol.* **1993**, *70*, 2470–2488. [CrossRef]
38. Kim, H.; Lee, J.; Kim, J. Electromyography-signal-based muscle fatigue assessment for knee rehabilitation monitoring systems. *Biomed. Eng. Lett.* **2018**, *8*, 345–353. [CrossRef] [PubMed]
39. He, J.; Zhang, D.; Sheng, X.; Li, S.; Zhu, X. Invariant surface EMG feature against varying contraction level for myoelectric control based on muscle coordination. *IEEE J. Biomed. Health Inform.* **2014**, *19*, 874–882. [CrossRef] [PubMed]
40. Phinyomark, A.; Phukpattaranont, P.; Limsakul, C. Feature reduction and selection for EMG signal classification. *Expert. Syst. Appl.* **2012**, *39*, 7420–7431. [CrossRef]
41. Wei, W.; Dai, Q.; Wong, Y.; Hu, Y.; Kankanhalli, M.; Geng, W. Surface-electromyography-based gesture recognition by multi-view deep learning. *IEEE Trans. Biomed. Eng.* **2019**, *66*, 2964–2973. [CrossRef]
42. Hastie, T.; Tibshirani, R.; Friedman, J.H. *The Elements of Statistical Learning: Data Mining, Inference, and Prediction*; Springer: Berlin/Heidelberg, Germany, 2009; Volume 2.
43. Ghojogh, B.; Crowley, M. Linear and quadratic discriminant analysis: Tutorial. *arXiv* **2019**, arXiv:1906.02590. [CrossRef]
44. Dorfer, M.; Kelz, R.; Widmer, G. Deep linear discriminant analysis. *arXiv* **2015**, arXiv:1511.04707. [CrossRef]
45. Frénay, B.; Verleysen, M. Classification in the presence of label noise: A survey. *IEEE Trans. Neural Netw. Learn. Syst.* **2013**, *25*, 845–869. [CrossRef]
46. Hahne, J.M.; Biessmann, F.; Jiang, N.; Rehbaum, H.; Farina, D.; Meinecke, F.C.; Müller, K.-R.; Parra, L.C. Linear and nonlinear regression techniques for simultaneous and proportional myoelectric control. *IEEE Trans. Neural Syst. Rehabil. Eng.* **2014**, *22*, 269–279. [CrossRef]

47. Jiang, N.; Vujaklija, I.; Rehbaum, H.; Graimann, B.; Farina, D. Is accurate mapping of EMG signals on kinematics needed for precise online myoelectric control? *IEEE Trans. Neural Syst. Rehabil. Eng.* **2013**, *22*, 549–558. [CrossRef]
48. Bunderson, N.E.; Kuiken, T.A. Quantification of feature space changes with experience during electromyogram pattern recognition control. *IEEE Trans. Neural Syst. Rehabil. Eng.* **2012**, *20*, 239–246. [CrossRef]
49. Stuttaford, S.A.; Dyson, M.; Nazarpour, K.; Dupan, S.S. Reducing motor variability enhances myoelectric control robustness across untrained limb positions. *IEEE Trans. Neural Syst. Rehabil. Eng.* **2023**, *32*, 23–32. [CrossRef] [PubMed]
50. Liu, J.; Zhang, D.; Sheng, X.; Zhu, X. Quantification and solutions of arm movements effect on sEMG pattern recognition. *Biomed. Signal Process. Control* **2014**, *13*, 189–197. [CrossRef]
51. Radmand, A.; Scheme, E.; Englehart, K. A characterization of the effect of limb position on EMG features to guide the development of effective prosthetic control schemes. In Proceedings of the 2014 36th Annual International Conference of the IEEE Engineering in Medicine and Biology Society, Chicago, IL, USA, 26–30 August 2014; pp. 662–667.
52. Vinjamuri, R.; Patel, V.; Powell, M.; Mao, Z.-H.; Crone, N. Candidates for synergies: Linear discriminants versus principal components. *Comput. Intell. Neurosci.* **2014**, *2014*, 373957. [CrossRef] [PubMed]
53. Teng, Z.; Xu, G.; Liang, R.; Li, M.; Zhang, S. Evaluation of synergy-based hand gesture recognition method against force variation for robust myoelectric control. *IEEE Trans. Neural Syst. Rehabil. Eng.* **2021**, *29*, 2345–2354. [CrossRef]
54. Al-Timemy, A.H.; Bugmann, G.; Outram, N.; Escudero, J. Single channel-based myoelectric control of hand movements with Empirical Mode Decomposition. In Proceedings of the 2011 Annual International Conference of the IEEE Engineering in Medicine and Biology Society, Boston, MA, USA, 30 August–3 September 2011; pp. 6059–6062.
55. Zhang, Z.; Sabuncu, M. Generalized cross entropy loss for training deep neural networks with noisy labels. *arXiv* **2018**, arXiv:1805.07836. [CrossRef]
56. Feng, L.; Shu, S.; Lin, Z.; Lv, F.; Li, L.; An, B. Can cross entropy loss be robust to label noise? In Proceedings of the Twenty-Ninth International Conference on International Joint Conferences on Artificial Intelligence, Yokohama, Japan, 7–15 January 2021; pp. 2206–2212.
57. Zhou, H.; Le, H.T.; Zhang, S.; Phung, S.L.; Alici, G. Hand gesture recognition from surface electromyography signals with graph convolutional network and attention mechanisms. *IEEE Sens. J.* **2025**, *25*, 9081–9092. [CrossRef]
58. Oyemakinde, T.T.; Kulwa, F.; Peng, X.; Liu, Y.; Cao, J.; Deng, X.; Wang, M.; Li, G.; Samuel, O.W.; Fang, P. A novel sEMG-FMG combined sensor fusion approach based on an attention-driven CNN for dynamic hand gesture recognition. *IEEE Trans. Instrum. Meas.* **2025**, *747*, 2533413. [CrossRef]
59. Samuel, O.W.; Li, X.; Geng, Y.; Asogbon, M.G.; Fang, P.; Huang, Z.; Li, G. Resolving the adverse impact of mobility on myoelectric pattern recognition in upper-limb multifunctional prostheses. *Comput. Biol. Med.* **2017**, *90*, 76–87. [CrossRef]
60. Scheme, E.; Fougner, A.; Stavdahl, Ø.; Chan, A.D.; Englehart, K. Examining the adverse effects of limb position on pattern recognition based myoelectric control. In Proceedings of the 2010 Annual International Conference of the IEEE Engineering in Medicine and Biology, Buenos Aires, Argentina, 31 August–4 September 2010; pp. 6337–6340.

robotics

MDPI

Article

Neuromorphic Control of Robotic Systems with Numerical Simulations

Abhaya Pal Singh * and Antonio Candea Leite

Department of Mechanical Engineering and Technology Management, Faculty of Science and Technology, Norwegian University of Life Sciences (NMBU), 1430 Ås, Norway; antonio.candea.leite@nmbu.no

* Correspondence: abhaya.aps@gmail.com or abhaya.pal.singh@nmbu.no

Abstract

In this paper, we considered potential benefits of the neuromorphic control technique for solving specific challenges in robotic control. Developing a neuromorphic control system for a robot involves simulating the architecture and dynamics of biological neurons to perform control tasks. This differs from typical control techniques and frequently employs spiking neural networks (SNNs). SNNs are more closely related to our brains than conventional neural networks, as they incorporate temporal dynamics. Biological neurons transmit information using spikes. Neurons do not fire in each cycle, but rather when the membrane potential reaches a predetermined threshold, as in a binary system. When a neuron fires, it transmits a signal to the synapse. The control strategy presented in this paper is based on the Leaky Integrated-and-Fire (LIF) and Generalized Integrate-and-Fire (GIF) neuron models. We designed neuromorphic control systems and utilized three robotic systems as examples. Numerical simulations were used to demonstrate the stability, robustness, and effectiveness of the neuromorphic robot control system design.

Keywords: control; generalized integrate-and-fire; leaky integrated-and-fire; neural networks; robot; spiking neural networks

1. Introduction

Neuromorphic engineering is an emerging field of research as experts combine robotics, artificial intelligence, and brain science to create devices [1] that can function more intelligently and efficiently, particularly in challenging environments. This involves developing circuits that mimic the brain's neural networks. Spiking neural networks (SNNs) inspired by the brain [2] play a crucial role in this process. Unlike traditional computing, SNNs process information through discrete spikes, similar to brain neurons [3], and this makes devices energy efficient, which is crucial for autonomous robots using limited power [4]. Bioinspired synaptic devices have shown promise in artificial intelligence and neuromorphic electronics with reduced energy consumption. Recently in [5], a new synaptic device layout, called the ion-gating vertical transistor (IGVT), has been deployed to perform brain-like perceptions such as artificial vision, touch, taste, and hearing. Real-time perception and decision-making in autonomous driving are being improved by brain-inspired systems [6] that use SNNs. Neuromorphic processors handle data more efficiently [7] than traditional electronics, consuming less power. Neuromorphic control has recently gained attention in robotics due to its suitability for real-time and power-efficient computation. Spiking neural networks (SNNs) can process sensory events and generate motor actions with extremely low latency [8], which has been demonstrated in mobile robots and drones [9], achieving on-chip autonomy. Early neurorobotic systems relied on VLSI-based motion sensorsr [10], and the field has since evolved to incorporate high-resolution dynamic vision sensors (DVS) [11] and neuromorphic processors. Compared to conventional artificial neural networks, SNNs can achieve lower power consumption and reduced communication overhead, making them well suited for embedded robotic applications [12].

There have been many neuromorphic technologies developed in the literature, including electronic, optical, and mixed systems such as the major neuromorphic hardware modalities: digital neuromorphic processors like Intel Loihi [13], IBM TrueNorth [14], SpiNNaker families [15], analog/mixed-signal neuromorphic ASICs [16], and photonic neuromorphic systems like solitonic/photonic networks [17]. In [18], an electrophysiological method-based neromorphic circuit design for copying and pasting is presented, which is a perfect fit to the solid-state memory network where the copied biological neural networks will be 'pasted'. Flexible neuromorphic circuits that mimic natural neural systems are an exciting prospect for next-generation wearable computing, soft robotics, and neuroprosthetics. In [19], the progress of flexible neuromorphic electronics is addressed, from basic foundations, including synaptic features, device structures, and mechanisms of artificial synapses and nerves, to applications for computers, soft robotics, and neuroprosthetics. Neuromorphic models are demonstrating the ability to execute sophisticated machine learning tasks while overcoming structural constraints imposed by software algorithms and electrical designs. The behavior of networks based on solitonic neurons, capable of completing sophisticated tasks such as bit-to-bit information memorization and recognition, is demonstrated in [20,21]. In [22], a compact and energy-efficient LIF neuron circuit-based hardware development is suggested for a high-performance and energy-efficient neuromorphic computing system.

In neuromorphic control, sensory and state information is encoded into spike trains and processed through neuron models to generate control signals. Simple neuron models are preferred in real-time robotics due to hardware and computational constraints [23]. The Leaky Integrate-and-Fire (LIF) and Generalized Integrate-and-Fire (GIF) neuron models offer a balance between biological plausibility, implementation simplicity, and low computational load [24].

The information about the works on the neuromorphic approach in control systems is shown in Table 1 below.

Table 1. The neuromorphic-based control systems.

Neuron Model	Framework	Application
LIF [25]	Loihi neuromorphic chip	Control for robotic arms
General model of spiking neural networks [26]	NeoN (FPGA)	Control for autonomous robotic navigation
LIF [27]	Loihi neuromorphic chip	Obstacle avoidance for autonomous car
LIF [28]	SpiNNaker neuromorphic chip	Learning-based control of humanoid robot
LIF [29]	SpiNNaker neuromorphic chip	Control of four joints BAXTER robot
LIF [30]	Nengo platform [31]	Soft grasping robotic hand
Simple spiking model [32]	Ishii	Learning-based control for surgical task
Izhikevich [33]	NeMo platform [34]	Vision based robotic arm control
aEIF [35]	Working memory (WM) [36]	Flexible cognition in robotics

The objective of this work is to design neuromorphic controllers based on LIF and GIF neuron models and apply them to three robotic platforms of increasing degrees of freedom: (i) a mass–spring–damper system, (ii) a 2-link planar manipulator, and (iii) a six-degree-of-freedom UR3 industrial robot. We extend neuromorphic control to structured robotic manipulators and use Lyapunov stability to analytically integrate it to classical control theory. We derive closed-form Lyapunov-based convergence requirements for LIF/GIF-driven control laws in contrast to most of the SNN-based control literature. We apply the framework to the above-discussed three systems to highlight its scalability. We are motivated by the fact that the neuromorphic controllers are (i) energy-efficient and event-driven: LIF/GIF spiking models compute only when spikes occur, reducing unnecessary processing and energy usage compared to continuous neural models [37]; have a (ii) low-latency response: spiking neurons respond to real-time input through their intrinsic timing dynamics [38], enabling fast reaction to sensory events critical for tasks such as obstacle avoidance and motion control; exhibit (iii) adaptive behavior: encoding information in spike timing and rate, rather than solely in signal amplitude, allows the control system to naturally adapt to environmental changes or disturbances [39] with minimal computation; and have (iv) robustness: the integration and leak properties of LIF/GIF neurons support stable and robust control [40], enabling biological-like compensation for perturbations without significant processing overhead.

In contrast to existing neuromorphic and SNN-based robotic controllers that primarily rely on empirical convergence observations, the controller developed in this work is accompanied by a formal Lyapunov stability analysis. Since the proposed control law generates smooth torque signals through filtered spike trains, the spiking dynamics introduce a bounded approximation error in comparison to traditional continuous control laws. To address this, we demonstrate that the closed-loop dynamics are Input-to-State Stable (ISS) with respect to the approximation residual. This result guarantees that the tracking error remains uniformly bounded even in the presence of modeling uncertainty, external disturbances, and spike-to-torque conversion error. This theoretical guarantee distinguishes the proposed method from prior SNN control formulations that do not provide closed-loop robustness guarantees.

The contributions of this paper are as follows:

- A controller based on LIF and GIF neuron models for the MSD, a 2-link planar robotic manipulator, and the UR3 robotic manipulator,
- Algorithms for numerical simulations of the proposed idea, and
- A Lyapunov-based stability analysis.

The remaining sections of the paper are as follows: Section 2 introduces detailed models of LIF and GIF neurons, followed by the problem formulation in Section 3. Section 4 presents the main results, while Section 5 provides a conclusion.

2. LIF and GIF Neuron Models

The most basic neuron models, such as the LIF and GIF models [41], are nonetheless reasonably realistic despite the complexity of neurons. Let us examine the neuron models and a collection of equations that simulate neuron activity (for more detail, refer to the article by Fourcaud-Trocmé, N. [42]). Before introducing the neuron models, we briefly clarify relevant terminology. Neurons transmit information through action potentials that travel along axons, which are elongated structures responsible for carrying signals to other neurons or muscle cells. Before going in depth, let us understand some terminologies, like axons, which resemble wires and transmit action potentials, which are found in neurons. To determine whether to initiate an action potential, the cell body simply adds up the currents coming from dendrites and synapses. Synapses receive signals from other neurons, and dendrites receive inputs from synapses. As a result, when a neuron receives input from another, it passes through the synapse, dendrites, and cell body before deciding whether to act.

The input current will affect the membrane potential, which is the electrical potential variation between the inside and the outside of the cell. We may now realize the link between current and membrane potential by interpreting the membrane's biophysics as an electrical circuit, as shown in Figure 1.

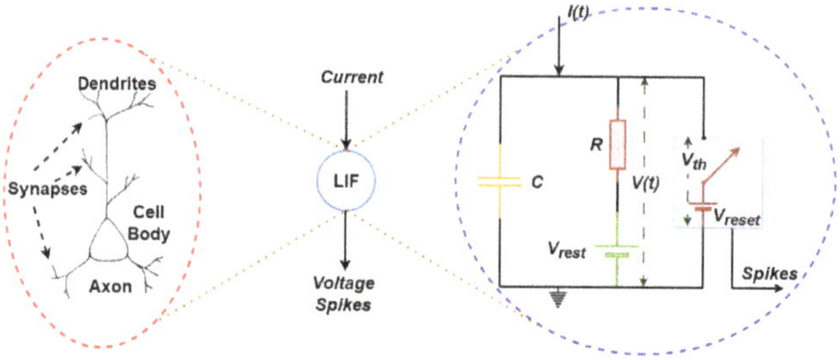

Figure 1. A LIF neuron model and its equivalent electrical circuit.

These physical components are examined using Kirchhoff's law to characterize the current flowing through them. This implies that when current reaches a node, it must pass via one of the node's branches. Therefore, current flowing across the membrane patch either charges the capacitor or passes through the membrane. The leak equilibrium potential is denoted by V_{rest}, the capacitance by C, and the leak resistance by R. When the membrane potential $V(t)$ reaches a specified voltage level, the action potential is triggered. After the action potential is completed, the membrane potential is reset by V_{reset}, and the entire process is restarted.

This is the Leaky Integrate-and-Fire model, and the membrane potential $V(t)$ is described by a first-order differential equation that varies with the input ionic current $I(t)$ over time. There is also a threshold condition: when the membrane potential $V(t)$ crosses that threshold V_{th}, the dynamics stops and restarts after a short time Δ. It is typically the first few milliseconds [43] and creates a fresh action potential. The model equations can be expressed as follows:

$$\tau_m \frac{dV(t)}{dt} = -(V(t) - V_{rest}) + RI(t), \tag{1}$$

where $\tau_m = RC$ is the membrane time constant and if $V(t) \geq V_{th}$, then $V(t + \Delta t) = V_{rest}$.

If the input ionic current increases, the membrane potential will reach the threshold. When this happens, it uses reset and threshold current conditions to stop the dynamics, and the neuron fires. After a Δ time, the dynamics are restarted at their resting potential. If the ionic current remains strong, the membrane potential rises until it reaches the threshold, fires again, and resets, and this is shown in Figure 2. The period between two spikes is known as the inter-spike interval [44], and it mostly influences the cell's firing rate. For a steady current, the inter-spike interval remains constant and only varies when the input ionic current changes.

We now understand the LIF and how the action potential evolves. Consider the LIF extension known as the Generalized Integrated-and-Fire (GIF) model. Let us introduce a current $\omega(t)$, which means that when $\omega(t)$ is positive, $V(t)$ decreases.

$$\tau_m \frac{dV(t)}{dt} = -(V(t) - V_{rest}) + RI(t) - R\omega(t), \tag{2}$$

where $\omega(t)$ is the spike-triggered adaptation current (and decays over time). The spike conditions are when $V(t) \geq V_{th}$, it emits a spike. After the spike $V \leftarrow V_{reset}$, the adaptation current increases by $\omega(t) \leftarrow \omega(t) + \Delta\omega$. This current $\omega(t)$ has the following continuous-time equation [45]:

$$\tau_\omega \frac{d\omega(t)}{dt} = -\omega(t) + \Delta\omega \sum_i \delta(t - t_i), \tag{3}$$

where τ_ω is the time constant of the adaptation. Therefore, the adaptation increases by $\Delta\omega$ each time a spike happens at time t_i.

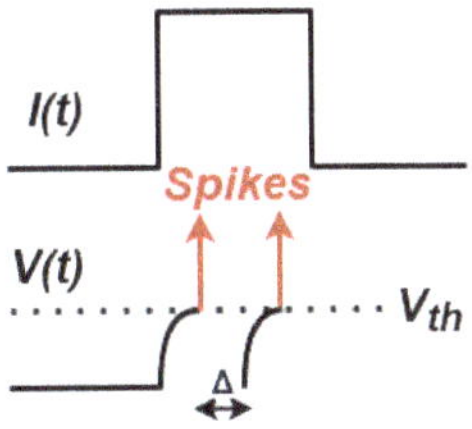

Figure 2. Spikes in LIF: When the input current is strong, the membrane potential gradually rises. Once it reaches the threshold level, the neuron produces a spike. After this spike, the membrane potential is reset for a short period. If the input current remains high, the membrane potential will rise again and produce another spike. This cycle continues as long as the input current is strong enough. When the current decreases and is no longer sufficient to push the membrane potential to the threshold, the spiking stops.

More importantly, the GIF shows spike frequency adaptation. Spike frequency adaptation is the process by which neurons adapt to a certain stimulus [46], implying that the inter-spike interval gradually increases over time when the input remains constant. This can be observed in Figure 3, and it is evident in almost all cells. However, the LIF model is unable to reproduce this phenomenon and consistently maintains the same spike interval for a given input current intensity. As a result, the LIF models roughly represent the complex dynamics of actual neurons, whereas the GIF models attain high accuracy by taking adaptive aspects into account.

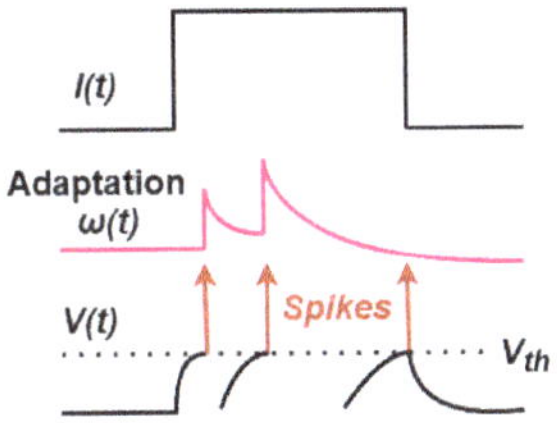

Figure 3. Spikes in GIF: When a neuron's membrane potential exceeds a threshold set in GIF models, spikes are produced. This process is influenced by both an ionic current and a adaptation current. The model outputs a spike when the threshold is achieved, and before integration proceeds, its membrane potential is reset to a lower value. The model computes the membrane potential, which is affected by input currents as well as adaptation current that pulls the potential toward a resting value. A threshold value is continuously compared to this integrated voltage. A spike is fired when the membrane potential reaches beyond this threshold. The membrane potential is immediately reset to a lower value (the reset potential) following the firing of a spike. After that, the integration process resumes using this new value.

3. Problem Formulation

After the neuron models, let us move forward by discussing how to incorporate these neuromorphic techniques into robotic systems. Many applications with fixed-based robotics require multibody dynamics, and the general robotic manipulator with n degrees of freedom can be formulated as [47]:

$$M(q)\ddot{q} + b(q,\dot{q})\dot{q} + g(q) = \tau, \quad (4)$$

where $M(q)$ is the mass matrix, and $(q,\dot{q},\ddot{q})$ are the position, velocity, and acceleration, respectively. $b(q,\dot{q})$ is the Coriolis and centrifugal terms, and $g(q)$ is the gravitational terms and τ is the external generalized forces. The proposed problem definition is as follows:

How can neuromorphic control techniques, that involve spiking neuron control (LIF or GIF), be used to ensure that the robot's joint states $q(t)$ converge to a desired position q_d over time?

The position error of (4) can be found as

$$e(t) = q_d - q(t), \quad (5)$$

and this position error is used as the input for the neuron, and we can convert this error into the input current to the neuron by the expression:

$$I(t) = ke(t), \quad (6)$$

where k is the gain of the input current. This current $I(t)$ will be fed to the neuron(s) to produce a spike (on comparing the threshold voltage V_{th}) representing the input torque (or force) for the robotic system. However, these spikes cannot be used directly on the robotic system and must be translated into a smooth physical control torque (or force) suited for actuating the robotic system. The instantaneous control impulse that a spike generates can be defined as

$$\tau_{unp}(t) = spike(t) \cdot u_{spike}, \quad (7)$$

where τ_{unp} is the unprocessed torque, $spike(t)$ is a binary variable, if $spike(t) = 1$, the neuron fires at time t, and if $spike(t) = 0$, neurons do not fire. u_{spike} is the torque produced per spike, which means that each spike injects a fixed torque u_{spike} into the robotic system. To simulate how actual biological synapses smooth out spikes over time rather than transmitting them instantly, one can employ synaptic filtering [48], also referred to as low-pass filtering in circuit terminology. A first-order differential equation that can be used to illustrate this is as follows:

$$\tau(t) = \tau_{unp}(t) - \tau_s \frac{d\tau(t)}{dt}, \quad (8)$$

where τ_s is the synaptic time constant (in s) and controls the rate at which torque decreases. The $\tau(t)$ represents the filtered control torque to be applied to the robotic system (4) in N-m. The synaptic filter used here is a single-time-constant first-order model; richer synapse models can be incorporated by replacing the filter dynamics with the device model. The ISS proof treats the filter output as a bounded, causal linear operator; thus, if the device's synaptic dynamics remain bounded and causal, the stability argument generalizes. This bridges our controller analysis and synaptic device characterization.

4. Main Results

We will now apply the concept developed in the previous section to three different mechanical systems: mass–spring–damper (MSD) system: canonical second-order system for intuition and closed-form Lyapunov testing; 2-link planar robotic manipulator: demonstrating multivariable control and trajectory tracking; and Industrial UR3 robot arm: industrial

6-DOF manipulator. We chose these mechanical systems to show scalability to real-world robot kinematics and more complex dynamics. All the numerical computations were run in MATLAB 2022a with an Intel Core i7 CPU, 16 GB RAM, and Microsoft Windows 11.

4.1. Mass–Spring–Damper (MSD) System

This section discusses an approach for controlling the mass–spring–damper system that utilizes the Leaky Integrated-and-Fire (LIF) and Generalized Integrated-and-Fire (GIF) spiking neurons to regulate forces, aiming to bring the mass to a target position and maintain it with neuron spikes, thereby emulating neuromorphic control.

The dynamics of the MSD can be written as

$$m\ddot{x}(t) + b\dot{x}(t) + kx(t) = u(t), \tag{9}$$

where m is the mass, b is the damping coefficient, k is the spring constant, and $u(t)$ is the neuron-driven control force. Consider that this MSD system exerts an input force that stabilizes the entire system at a desired position x^t. Then, the equation of motion of the system can be written as

$$m\ddot{x}(t) + b\dot{x}(t) + k(x(t) - x^t) = u(t), \tag{10}$$

Let us assume the system is critically damped, with $b = 2\sqrt{km}$, where the solution reaches the target without overshoot in the shortest possible time.

Neuromorphic Controller Design for MSD System

Designing via LIF neuron model: We revisit the concept we introduced in Section 2: evaluating the position error and feeding it as a current to the LIF neuron to generate spikes. Then, from (5), we can write

$$e(t) = x^t - x(t), \tag{11}$$

and from (6)

$$I(t) = k \cdot e(t). \tag{12}$$

The current (12) will be used to generate the LIF spikes after passing (1) and the conditions. These spikes are translated to an unprocessed force using the expression represented in (7). This unprocessed force is then passed through the Equation (8) to generate the force that stabilizes the MSD system. The pseudo-code presented in Algorithm 1 ensures that the MSD system stabilizes and executes as expected using the LIF neuron model.

Designing via GIF neuron model: The same steps are required to follow as in LIF i.e., calculating (11) and (12). After getting (12), it is passed to the GIF dynamics (2) and the conditions to generate a spike. In the case of GIF, after a spike, the adaptation current changes as per (3). These spikes are translated to an unprocessed force using the expression defined as (7). Equation (8) uses the unprocessed force to generate the force needed to stabilize the MSD system. Algorithm 2 provides pseudo-code to stabilize the MSD system exactly as expected using the GIF neuron model.

Algorithm 1 Numerical simulation algorithm employing the LIF model to control the MSD system

Initial conditions: Membrane potential $V = 0$, System states $x = \dot{x} = 0$
Model Parameters: $\tau_m, R, k, V_{th}, V_{rest}, V_{reset}, u_{spike}, \tau_s$
for i = 1 to T **do**
  Compute the tracking error $e(t)$ using (11)
  Calculate the ionic input current $I(t)$ from $e(t)$ using (12)
  Update the LIF membrane dynamics using Equation (1)
  Set $V(t) = V(t) + \Delta V$
  if $V(t) \geq V_{th}$ **then**
    Generate Spike: $spike(t) = 1$
    $V \leftarrow V_{reset}$
  else
    No Spike: $spike(t) = 0$
  end if
  Compute the synaptic response time constant τ_{unp} using (7)
  Use τ_{unp} in (8) Pass this τ_{unp} and compute the control force
  Apply this control force to the MSD dynamics
end for

Algorithm 2 Numerical simulation algorithm employing the GIF model to control the MSD system

Initial states: Membrane potential $V = 0$, System states $x = \dot{x} = \omega = 0$
Model Parameters: $\tau_m, R, k, V_{th}, V_{rest}, V_{reset}, u_{spike}, \tau_s, \tau_\omega, \Delta\omega$
for i = 1 to T **do**
  Compute the tracking error $e(t)$ using (11)
  Calculate the ionic input current $I(t)$ from $e(t)$ using (12)
  Update the GIF membrane dynamics using Equation (2)
  Set $V(t) = V(t) + \Delta V$
  Set $spike = 0$
  if $V(t) \geq V_{th}$ **then**
    Generate Spike: $spike(t) = 1$
    $V \leftarrow V_{reset}$
    $\omega(t) = \omega(t) + \Delta\omega$
  else
    No Spike: $spike(t) = 0$
  end if
  Compute the synaptic response time constant τ_{unp} using (7)
  Use τ_{unp} in (8) Pass this τ_{unp} and compute the control force
  Apply this control force to the MSD dynamics
end for

Numerical simulations obtained via the Algorithms 1 and 2 are compared in Figure 4.

The numerical simulation and Figure 4 show that the neuromorphic control system designed for the MSD system, utilizing the LIF and GIF neuron models, efficiently tracks the target. The GIF performs better than the LIF in terms of the quick settling of the MSD system because of the adaptation current, and can also be seen in the following video: https://youtu.be/SbPHr_Y2VdI.

Stability and robustness analysis of the designed neuromorphic control: To introduce the uncertainty and disturbance in the model, let us say that the model of the MSD system takes the form

$$m(t)\ddot{x}(t) + b\dot{x}(t) + kx(t) = u(t) + \zeta(t), \tag{13}$$

where $m(t)$ is a time-varying uncertain mass, $\zeta(t)$ is the bounded disturbance, and all other terms are defined the same as in (9). We define the tracking error as (11) and feed this

$e(t)$ to the dynamics of the LIF or GIF neuron models through (12). The LIF spikes will be produced using this current $I(t)$, following (1) and the criteria. The expression (7) is used to transform these spikes to an unprocessed force. This unprocessed force of (8) is then used to create the force that stabilizes the MSD system of (13). The numerical simulation for LIF and GIF was provided by adapted Algorithms 1 and 2 which are shown in Figure 5.

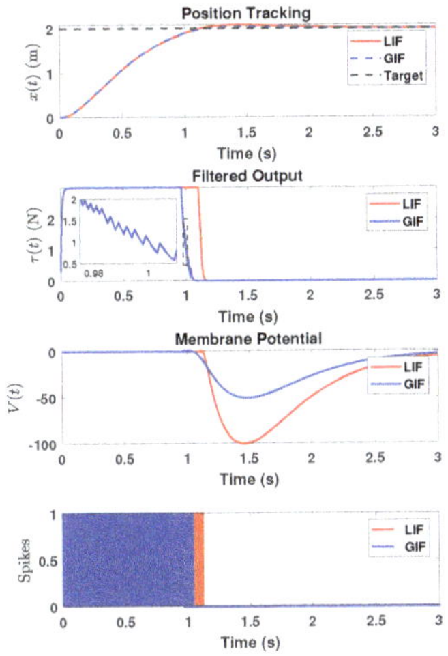

Figure 4. LIF and GIF neuromorphic control comparison for the MSD system. Panel 1 (**top**) illustrates the LIF and GIF technique for position tracking; Panel 2 illustrates the time-varying filtered output using the LIF and GIF models; Panel 3 illustrates the membrane potential change; and Panel 4 illustrates the spike generation utilizing the LIF and GIF neurons.

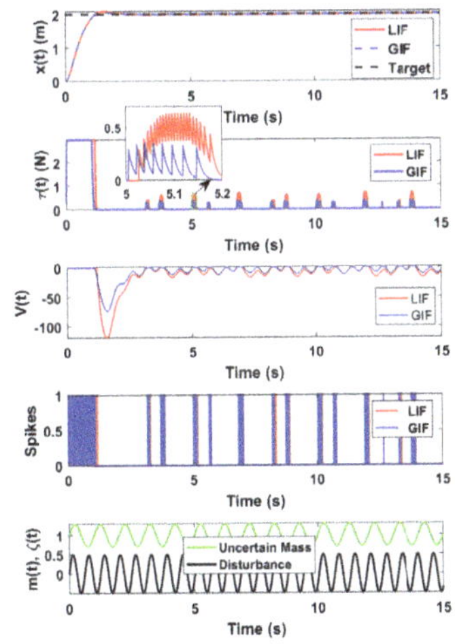

Figure 5. LIF and GIF neuromorphic robust control comparison for the MSD system. Panel 1 (**top**) shows the robust position tracking using the LIF and GIF technique; Panel 2 displays the time-varying filtered output using the LIF and GIF models, and the green color part is enlarged; Panel 3 shows the change in membrane potential; Panel 4 shows the spike generation using the LIF and GIF neurons; and Panel 5 shows the uncertainties and disturbances.

Figure 5 shows that the LIF or GIF control for the MSD system can handle changes in system parameters and uncertainties while tracking the desired trajectory. Let us prove the robust stability of the system by Lyapunov-based analysis. The neuromorphic controller generates its torque command through the weighted and filtered accumulation of discrete spike events. This mechanism inherently approximates the ideal continuous control law. Therefore, the resulting closed-loop dynamics include an additional bounded disturbance term corresponding to the spike approximation error and synaptic filtering residual. To ensure that this approximation does not degrade stability, we analyze the system using a Lyapunov function. By showing that the derivative of the Lyapunov function is negative outside a small neighborhood determined by the approximation bound, we establish input-to-state stability (ISS). Consequently, the tracking error remains bounded for all time, even in the presence of modeling uncertainty and external disturbances. Lyapunov techniques provide a rigorous method for demonstrating boundedness and convergence for nonlinear, time-varying systems with bounded disturbances [49]; they enable us to treat spike-filter approximation errors as bounded perturbations and establish ISS properties. Define a sliding surface that makes the system error go to zero in time by

$$s(t) = \dot{e}(t) - \lambda e(t). \tag{14}$$

Let us choose a Lyapunov candidate function as

$$V(t) = \frac{1}{2}s^2(t), \tag{15}$$

then

$$\dot{V}(t) = s(t)\dot{s}(t). \tag{16}$$

Evaluating $\dot{s}$, we receive

$$\begin{aligned} \dot{s}(t) &= \ddot{e}(t) + \lambda \dot{e}(t) \\ &= \frac{1}{m(t)}(b\dot{x}(t) + kx(t) - u(t) - \zeta(t)) - \lambda \dot{x}(t). \end{aligned} \tag{17}$$

Multiplying (17) by $s(t)$, we receive

$$\begin{aligned} \dot{V}(t) = s(t)\dot{s}(t) &= \frac{s(t)}{m(t)}(b\dot{x}(t) + kx(t) - u(t) - \zeta(t)) - s(t)\lambda\dot{x}(t), \\ &= \frac{s(t)}{m(t)}(-b\dot{e}(t) + k(x^t - e(t)) - u(t) - \zeta(t)) - s(t)\lambda\dot{e}(t), \end{aligned} \tag{18}$$

Assuming that the spikes output $u(t) \approx -k_a e(t) - b_a \dot{e}(t)$ (k_a is the proportional gain from the spikes and b_a is derivative gain that arises from the rate-of-rise of the membrane potential [50]) as the filtered output of LIF or GIF neurons behaves like a PD controller over time (a simulation to show this approximation is present in Appendix A), we have

$$u(t) \approx -k_a e(t) - b_a \dot{e}(t). \tag{19}$$

Using (19) in (18), we have

$$\dot{V}(t) = (\frac{-(b + b_a)s(t)}{m(t)} + \lambda)\dot{e}(t) + \frac{-(k + k_a)s(t)}{m(t)}e(t) - \frac{\zeta(t)s(t)}{m(t)}. \tag{20}$$

Now using (14), we have

$$\dot{V}(t) = (\frac{-(b + b_a)s(t)}{m(t)} + \lambda)(s(t) - \lambda e(t)) + \frac{-(k + k_a)s(t)}{m(t)}e(t) - \frac{\zeta(t)s(t)}{m(t)}. \tag{21}$$

With further mathematical manipulation and simplification, we have

$$\dot{V}(t) \approx \frac{1}{m(t)}(-\alpha s^2(t) + s(t)\zeta(t)), \tag{22}$$

where $\alpha = k_a + k - \lambda(b_a + b - m(t)\lambda)$. Taking the disturbance term $s(t)\zeta(t)$ from (22) and from the Young's inequality [51], we have

$$s(t)\zeta(t) \leq \frac{\epsilon}{s}s^2(t) + \frac{1}{2\epsilon}\zeta^2(t), \tag{23}$$

and we have

$$\dot{V}(t) \leq \frac{1}{m(t)}(-(\alpha - \frac{\epsilon}{2})s^2(t) + \frac{\zeta^2(t)}{2\epsilon}), \tag{24}$$

where ϵ is a small quantity so as to make $\alpha - \frac{\epsilon}{2} > 0$. The quadratic term contributes to the system's dissipative and stable behavior, providing input-to-state stability (ISS) with a bounded disturbance. We can write (24) as

$$\dot{V}(t) \leq -\beta(t)V(t) + \delta(t), \tag{25}$$

where $\beta(t) = \frac{2(\alpha - \epsilon/2)}{m(t)}$ and $\delta(t) = \frac{\zeta^2(t)}{2\epsilon m(t)}$. Using (25) and a bounded and strictly positive $0 < m_{min} < m(t) < m_{max} < \infty$, we are able to conclude that (i) if there is no disturbance, i.e., $\zeta(t) = 0$, then $\delta(t) = 0$, showing that the system decays exponentially and is asymptotically stable; and (ii) if $\delta(t) > 0$, $V(t)$ decreases but is offset by the term $\delta(t)$, it results in bounded behavior. The state (in this case, tracking error) stays bounded in response to bounded input disturbances, and even in cases when mass remains uncertain, the error $e(t)$ converges to a neighborhood of zero.

Adaptive Control Design for MSD System

Let us consider designing adaptive control, such as that proposed by Slotine and Li in [49], for the MSD system to compare the results of this MSD control system with the LIF type of neuromorphic control strategy for the MSD system.

The plant model will take the form (9). Let the output $x(t)$ of the plant track a reference model $x_{rm}(t)$ while estimating the unknown mass m adaptively, and let us assume that the system follows a second-order behavior explained by the following expression.

$$\ddot{x}_{rm}(t) + \lambda_1\dot{x}_{rm}(t) + \lambda_2 x_{rm}(t) = \lambda_2 r(t), \tag{26}$$

where x_{rm} is the desired position, $r(t)$ is the reference input, and λ_1, λ_2 are design constants that affect the speed and the damping of the system response. Equation (26) is chosen as a critically damped second-order reference for design comparison to the plant (MSD is inherently second-order). In adaptive control, it is standard to choose the reference model with the same relative degree as the plant to ensure achievable tracking dynamics. Let us also define the tracking errors as follows:

$$\tilde{x}(t) = x(t) - x_{rm}(t),\ \dot{\tilde{x}}(t) = \dot{x}(t) - \dot{x}_{rm}(t), \tag{27}$$

and we want this error to become zero following a critically damped second-order system dynamics shown by the equation below:

$$\ddot{\tilde{x}}(t) + 2\lambda\dot{\tilde{x}}(t) + \lambda^2\tilde{x}(t) = 0. \tag{28}$$

Taking the derivation of the velocity error of (27) and using (28), we can evaluate

$$\ddot{x}(t) = \ddot{x}_{rm}(t) - 2\lambda\dot{\tilde{x}}(t) - \lambda^2\tilde{x}(t), \tag{29}$$

This expression (29) is the real acceleration that the system should follow to track the reference smoothly.

The control law can be defined by

$$u(t) = \hat{m}v + b\dot{x}(t) + kx(t), \tag{30}$$

where $\hat{m}$ is the current guess (estimation) for the mass. Let us define the sliding surface that will guarantee that the tracking error decays exponentially to zero in time, with the expression:

$$s = \dot{\tilde{x}}(t) + \lambda\tilde{x}(t), \tag{31}$$

where λ is the convergence rate, and the mass adaptation law should follow the Lyapunov energy-based stability theory given by

$$\dot{\hat{m}} = -\gamma s v, \tag{32}$$

where γ is the adaptation rate, and the sign ensures the stability of the tracking error. The proof of (32) can be found in Appendix B.

The LIF/GIF controller converges with less control effort than adaptive control (see Figure 6), particularly in cases where the mass parameters are unknown. Furthermore, GIF neurons have smoother control transients due to adaptation current $\omega(t)$, which reduces overshoot. It can be concluded that while the LIF and GIF controllers achieve the same goal with comparable tracking performance but with noticeably less control effort, the adaptive controller generates a significantly larger initial torque magnitude and sustained control magnitude.

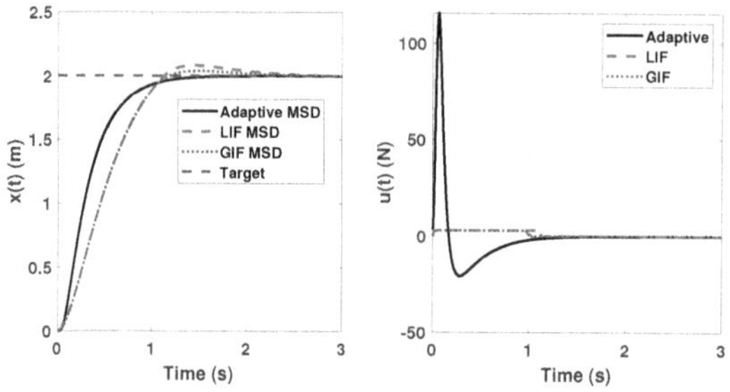

Figure 6. Comparison of adaptive, LIF, and GIF controllers for the mass–spring–damper (MSD) system. (**Left**) tracking response $x(t)$: all three controllers show comparable transient characteristics and settling times, closely following the reference (dashed black). (**Right**) control input $u(t)$: compared to neuromorphic controllers, the adaptive controller (solid black) generates a significantly larger initial torque peak and higher net control effort. While attaining similar tracking, LIF (red) and GIF (blue dotted) result in lower peak torque and time-integrated control (area under $u(t)$).

4.2. A 2-Link Planar Robotic Manipulator

The dynamics of a 2-link planar robotic manipulator that is shown in Figure 7 can be found as

$$M(q)\ddot{q} + B\dot{q} = \tau, \tag{33}$$

where these terms represent the same meaning as in (4). The aim here is to design a control law that makes the robot arm reach a set point (target). In this section, an approach for controlling the 2-link planar robotic manipulator is presented that utilizes the LIF and GIF spiking neurons to regulate torques, aiming to bring the arm to a target position and maintain it with neuron spikes, thereby emulating neuromorphic control.

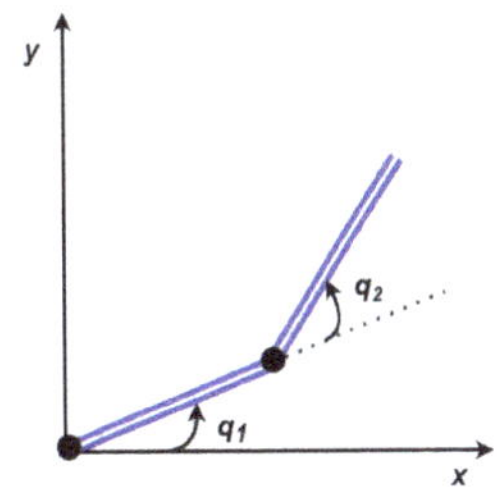

Figure 7. A 2-link planar robotic manipulator.

Neuromorphic Controller Design for 2-Link Planar Robotic Manipulator System

Designing via LIF neuron model: We will follow the same steps as in Section 4.1, evaluating the joint angle error and feeding it as a current to the LIF neuron to generate spikes. We can write

$$e_i(t) = q_i^t - q_i(t), \tag{34}$$

and

$$I_i(t) = k \cdot e_i(t), \tag{35}$$

where $i \in 1, 2$, the joint numbers for the considered system. The current (35) will be used to generate the LIF spikes after passing (1) and the conditions. These spikes are translated to an unprocessed torque using the expression represented in (7). This unprocessed torque is then passed through Equation (8) to generate the filtered torque that makes the 2-link robotic manipulator reach the targeted position. Following the pseudo-code presented by Algorithm 1 and adapting to the 2-link planar robotic manipulator dynamics ensures that this system follows the target and executes as expected using the LIF.

Designing using GIF Neuron Model: Follow the same steps as for the LIF. After obtaining (35), it is directed to the GIF dynamics (2) and the requirements for generating a spike. After a spike, the adaptation current changes according to (3). These spikes are translated to an unprocessed torque using the expression specified as (7). Equation (8) utilizes the unprocessed torque to generate the torque required to move the 2-link robotic manipulator to the target position. Modifying the Algorithm 2 according to the 2-link planar manipulator dynamics ensures this system reaches the targeted position as intended using the GIF model.

Figure 8 compares numerical simulations produced by the modified Algorithms 1 and 2 to represent the 2-link arm. The neuromorphic control for this system, which uses the LIF and GIF neuron models, effectively tracks the target, as demonstrated by the numerical simulation. Since the adaptation current allows the system to settle faster, the GIF performs better than the LIF.

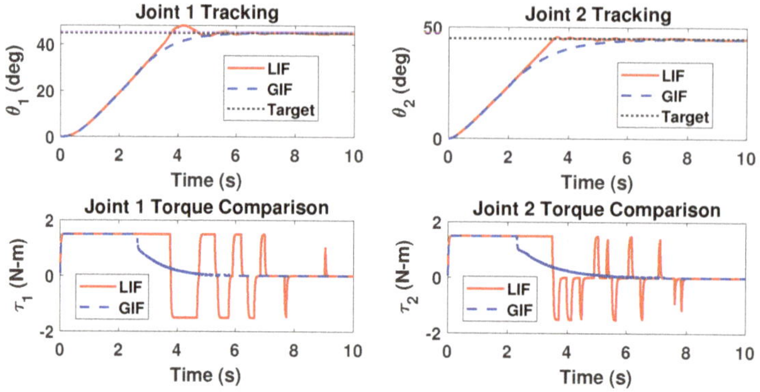

Figure 8. Comparison of LIF and GIF controllers for the 2-link robotic system. Tracking response $\theta_1(t)$ and $\theta_2(t)$ (**top**): the settling time of the LIF and GIF control is almost the same and following the reference trajectory (dashed black). Control input $\tau_1(t)$ and $\tau_2(t)$ (**bottom**): compared to GIF control, the LIF control has higher net control effort.

The trajectory tracking from the LIF and GIF neurons in reaching the target position is depicted in Figure 9 of the 2-link arm.

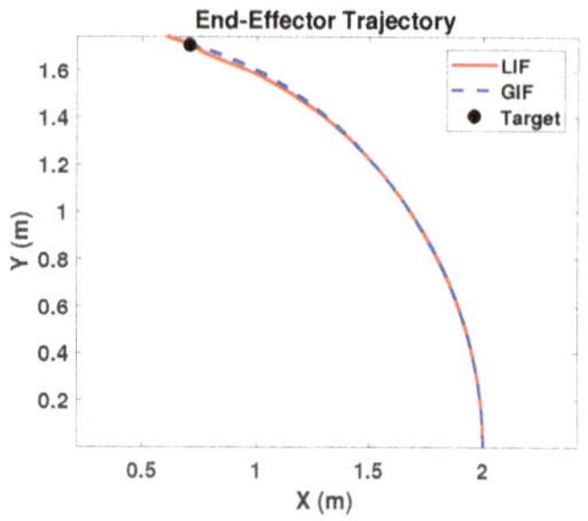

Figure 9. End effector trajectory tracking using LIF and GIF neromorphic models.

A video showing the trajectory movement of the 2-ink planar robotic manipulator from the initial position to the target is shown at the link: https://youtu.be/82K47K3WILw. The proposed neuromorphic control methodology is scalable to robotic manipulators with multiple degrees of freedom (DOF). Appendix A describes how the proposed neuromorphic controller architecture scales linearly in degrees of freedom (DOF). Appendix A also describes how the proposed neuromorphic controller architecture scales linearly in degrees of freedom (DOF).

Let us also compare the results from the adaptive control of the 2-link robotic system with the LIF/GIF control by providing the simulation results as follows.

The LIF/GIF controller converges with less control effort than adaptive control (see Figure 10). It can be concluded that while the LIF and GIF controllers achieve the same goal with comparable tracking performance but with noticeably less control effort, the adaptive controller generates a significantly larger initial torque magnitude and sustained control magnitude.

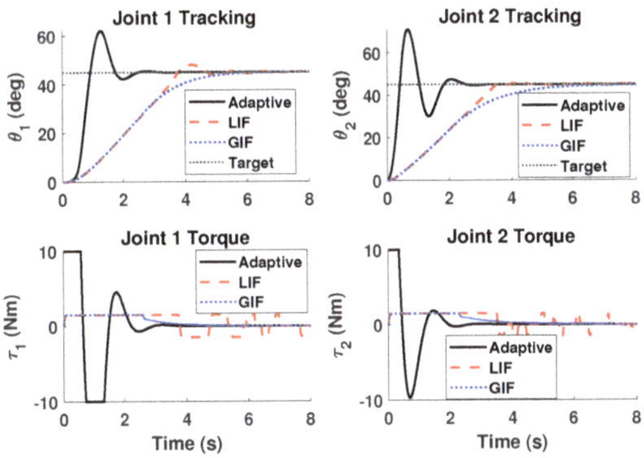

Figure 10. Comparison of adaptive, LIF, and GIF controllers for the 2-link robotic system. Tracking response $\theta_1(t)$ and $\theta_2(t)$ (**top**): the settling time of the adaptive control is better than the LIF and GIF control and following the reference trajectory (dashed black). Control input $\tau_1(t)$ and $\tau_2(t)$ (**bottom**): compared to neuromorphic controllers, the adaptive controller (solid black) generates a significantly larger initial torque peak and higher net control effort. While attaining tracking of the reference trajectory, LIF (red) and GIF (blue dotted) result in lower peak torque.

4.3. An Industrial UR3 Robot Arm

Let us design the neuromorphic control that sets the joint angles of a UR3 robot arm to the target joint angles. We will be using the same analysis that we have for the MSD and the 2-link planar manipulator. The six-joint angle error will be fed as the current to the LIF and GIF neurons. Depending on the current $I_i(t)$ where $i \in 1, 2, \ldots, 6$, the number of joints, the spikes will be generated corresponding to LIF and GIF neuron models. Then, depending on these spikes, a controlled input is derived that controls the movement of these joints to the target position. Figure 11 compares numerical simulations produced by the modified Algorithms 1 and 2 to represent the UR3 robotic arm. The neuromorphic control for this system, which uses the LIF and GIF neuron models, effectively tracks the target, as demonstrated by the numerical simulation.

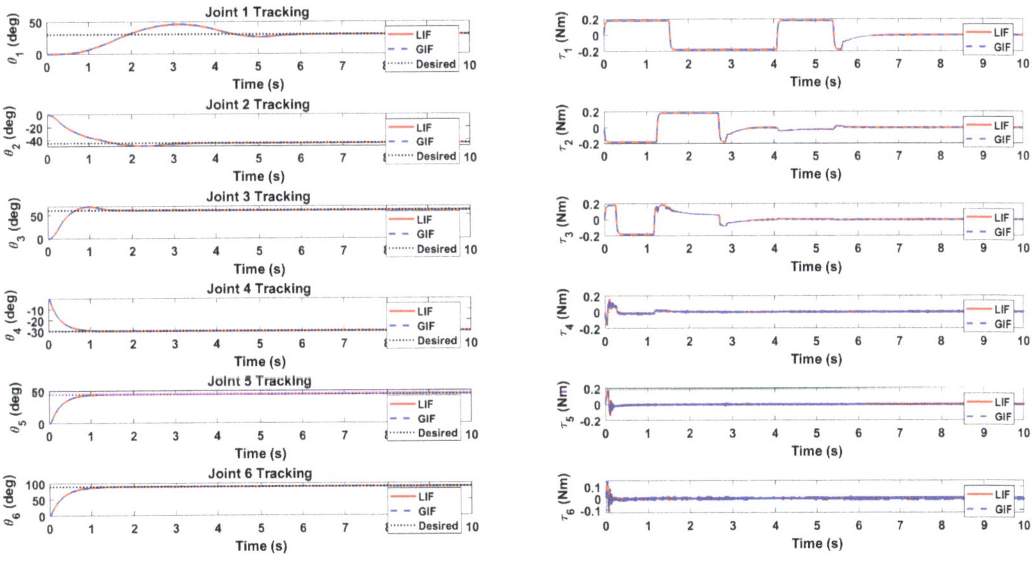

Figure 11. LIF and GIF neuromorphic control comparison for the UR3 robot arm.

5. Conclusions

The use of neuromorphic control based on spiking neural networks for controlling various robotic systems is demonstrated in this paper. The LIF and GIF neuron model was utilized to mimic neuromorphic control and develop a control law for the three systems: a UR3 robotic arm, a 2-link planar robotic manipulator, and a mass–spring–damper system. The efficiency of the neuromorphic control is demonstrated in the paper through the stability and robustness analyses using the Lyapunov-based theory. Additionally, two algorithms are provided to carry out the numerical simulations to verify the developed approach. To compare the outcomes of the neuromorphic control methods, an adaptive control is also presented. According to the results, the adaptive control method is less effective than the LIF and GIF in terms of control effort.

Spiking neural networks (SNNs) have the potential to improve autonomy and adaptability in dynamic situations, making them important in robotics, especially for increasing degrees of freedom and industrial applications. In the future, we aim to develop a fully adaptive SNN controller on neuromorphic hardware by interfacing it to a physical robot arm and optimizing it further to increase performance metrics in real-world scenarios with reduced latency.

Author Contributions: Conceptualization, A.P.S.; methodology, A.P.S.; software, A.P.S.; validation, A.P.S.; formal analysis, A.P.S.; investigation, A.P.S.; resources, A.P.S.; writing—original draft preparation, A.P.S.; writing—review and editing, A.C.L.; supervision, A.C.L.; project administration, A.C.L. All authors have read and agreed to the published version of the manuscript.

Funding: This work is supported by NMBU and the Research Council of Norway through the project SFI Digital Food Quality (DigiFoods), project number 309259.

Data Availability Statement: No new data were created or analyzed in this study. Data sharing is not applicable to this article.

Acknowledgments: During the preparation of this manuscript, the authors used Quillbot (free online version) to improve syntax, and paraphrasing in certain sections of the paper to provide a clear overview. The authors have reviewed and edited the output and take full responsibility for the content of this publication.

Conflicts of Interest: The authors declare no conflicts of interest.

Abbreviations

The following abbreviations are used in this manuscript:

LIF	Leaky Integrate-and-Fire
GIF	Generalized Integrate-and-Fire
MSD	Mass Spring Damper
SNN	Spiking Neural Networks
ANN	Artificial Neural Networks
UR3	Universal Robot (Model 3)

Appendix A

Each neuron spike generates a short force pulse in both LIF and GIF-based control systems, and the control force $\tau(t)$ is the filtered sum of these pulses, and is given by (8). The LIF neuron receives an input current of $I(t)$ and its membrane potential evolves as (1). The bigger the error $e(t)$, the faster the membrane potential $V(t)$ approaches the threshold, resulting in more frequent spikes. So, (i) larger $e(t)$ results in a higher spike rate and more force; (ii) a small $e(t)$ results in a low spike rate, which requires less force. Hence, the spike rate is proportional to $e(t)$.

If the error $\dot{e}(t) > 0$ grows, the input current $I(t)$ increases over time. This accelerates the increase in membrane potential, resulting in shorter inter-spike intervals. Therefore, when $\dot{e}(t) > 0$, spiking is faster; and when $\dot{e}(t) < 0$, spiking is slower. This generates differential feedback, in which the change in spike frequency provides information about $\dot{e}(t)$. This behavior is comparable to derivative control and becomes more obvious after synaptic filtering, which smoothens the spike pulses into a signal that resembles a PD controller output. Hence, we can approximate the spiking-based control as (19).

After some starting time, the neurons' output will nearly match the PD output, so the filtered spike-based control behaves similarly to a PD. The simulation shown in Figure A1 demonstrates exactly what we have described in this Appendix.

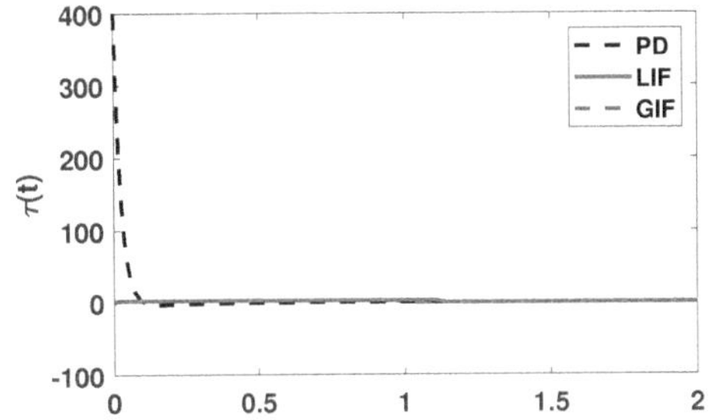

Figure A1. Behavior of LIF and GIF neurons compared to a PD control.

For an n-DOF manipulator governed by

$$M(q)\ddot{q} + C(q,\dot{q})\dot{q} + G(q) = \tau, \tag{A1}$$

the spiking control law is applied per joint as a distributed population of spiking neurons:

$$\tau_i = \tau_{s,i}(t), \tag{A2}$$

where $\tau_{s,i}(t)$ is the spike-induced torque command generated by a LIF or GIF neuron population corresponding to the joint i. Since each joint population operates independently, the number of neurons and synapses grows linearly with DOF. The cross-coupling terms (A1) are treated as bounded uncertainties and thus enter the Lyapunov derivative through the disturbance term $d(t)$.

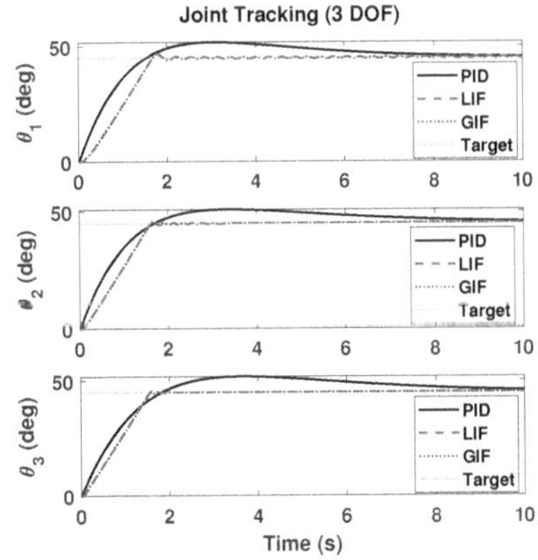

Figure A2. Scaling of DOF of the robot and performance comparison with PID.

Additional simulations for a three-DOF planar robot shown in Figure A2 confirm that the neuromorphic controller maintains stable tracking when the DOF is scaled with the settling time mentioned in Table A1 below shows that the LIF/GIF-based control gives good settling time compared to the PID control (a comparison with ANN is also shown in Appendix C).

Table A1. Performance comparison of the LIF, GIF, and PID control.

Controller	Settling Time (θ_1 s)	Settling Time (θ_2 s)	Settling Time (θ_3 s)	Computational Time (s)
PID	6.2	6.3	6.4	0.03
LIF	1.64	1.5	1.2	0.04
GIF	1.6	1.5	1.2	0.04

These values were obtained on MATLAB simulation and indicate that the LIF/GIF controllers run comfortably below 50 ms per joint.

Appendix B

Define the Lyapunov function as follows to ensure that the system is stable and $\tilde{x} \to 0$

$$V = \frac{1}{2}s^2 + \frac{1}{2\gamma}\tilde{m}^2, \tag{A3}$$

where $\tilde{m} = \hat{m} - m$ is the mass estimator, $\gamma > 0$, and s is defied by (31).

Taking the first derivative of (A3),

$$\dot{V} = s\dot{s} + \frac{1}{\gamma}\tilde{m}\dot{\tilde{m}} \implies s\dot{s} + \frac{1}{\gamma}\tilde{m}\dot{\hat{m}}. \tag{A4}$$

Now, let us evaluate $\dot{s}$ from (31),

$$\dot{s} = \ddot{x} - \ddot{x}_{rm} + \lambda(\dot{x} - \dot{x}_{rm}) \tag{A5}$$

Using (9), (29), (30), and (A5), we receive

$$\dot{s} = \frac{\tilde{m}}{m}v. \tag{A6}$$

So, from (A4) and (A6), we have

$$\dot{V} = s\frac{\tilde{m}}{m}v + \frac{1}{\gamma}\tilde{m}\dot{\hat{m}}. \tag{A7}$$

For stability and convergence, it is obvious to choose the mass adaptation law equal to

$$\dot{\hat{m}} = -\gamma s v, \tag{A8}$$

and hence $\dot{V} \leq 0$ as long as $\hat{m} \to m$ and the system is stable.

Appendix C

This appendix gives a comparison between the presented approach and an ANN-based controller. The results are illustrated using two figures (Figures A3 and A4), followed by a summary comparison table.

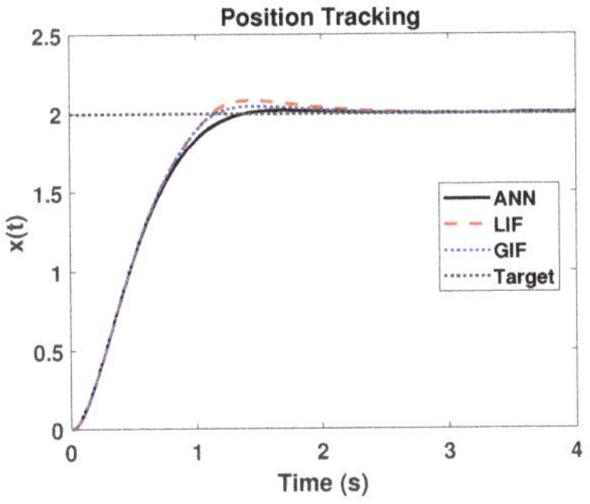

Figure A3. LIF/GIF MSD performance comparison with ANN.

The performance of ANN vs LIF/GIF of Figures A3 and A4 is summarized in the following Table A2.

Table A2. Performance comparison of the LIF, GIF, and ANN control.

Controller	MSD System		2-Link System		
	Settling Time $x(t)$ (s)	Computation Time (s)	Settling Time $\theta_1(t)$ (s)	Settling Time $\theta_2(t)$ (s)	Computation Time (s)
ANN	1.3	0.013	4.2	2.5	0.12
LIF	1.1	0.010	4.2	3.3	0.04
GIF	1.1	0.010	5.5	5.5	0.06

From the table above, it can be observed that the LIF/GIF model requires less computational time compared to the ANN to receive similar to better responses.

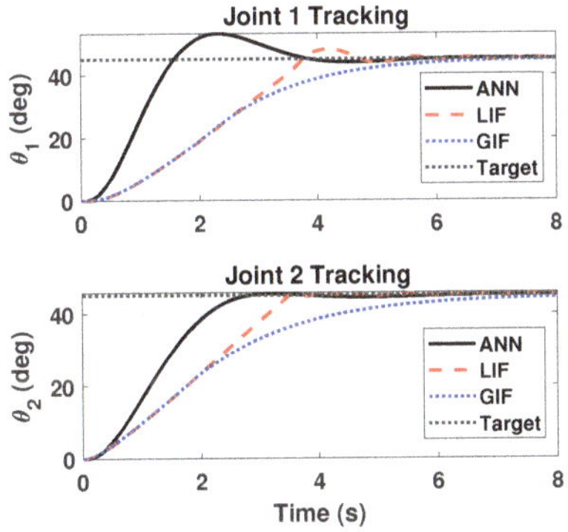

Figure A4. LIF/GIF 2-link performance comparison with ANN.

References

1. Kudithipudi, D.; Schuman, C.; Vineyard, C.M.; Pandit, T.; Merkel, C.; Kubendran, R.; Aimone, J.B.; Orchard, G.; Mayr, C.; Benosman, R. Neuromorphic computing at scale. *Nature* **2025**, *637*, 801–812. [CrossRef]
2. Muir, D.R.; Sheik, S. The road to commercial success for neuromorphic technologies. *Nat. Commun.* **2025**, *16*, 3586. [CrossRef]
3. Zheng, H.; Zheng, Z.; Hu, R.; Xiao, B.; Wu, Y.; Yu, F.; Liu, X.; Li, G.; Deng, L. Temporal dendritic heterogeneity incorporated with spiking neural networks for learning multi-timescale dynamics. *Nat. Commun.* **2024**, *15*, 277. [CrossRef] [PubMed]
4. Liu, J.; Lu, H.; Luo, Y.; Yang, S. Spiking neural network-based multi-task autonomous learning for mobile robots. *Eng. Appl. Artif. Intell.* **2021**, *104*, 104362. [CrossRef]
5. Merces, L.; Ferro, L.M.M.; Nawaz, A.; Sonar, P. Advanced Neuromorphic Applications Enabled by Synaptic Ion-Gating Vertical Transistors. *Adv. Sci.* **2024**, *11*, 2305611. [CrossRef] [PubMed]

6. Bartolozzi, C.; Glover, A.; Donati, E. Neuromorphic sensing, perception, and control for robotics. In *Handbook of Neuroengineering*; Springer Nature: Singapore, 2023; pp. 1635–1665.
7. Jiang, J.; Kong, D.; Hu, C.; Fang, Z. Fully asynchronous neuromorphic perception for mobile robot dodging with loihi chips. *IEEE Trans. Autom. Sci. Eng.* **2025**, *22*, 12802–12815. [CrossRef]
8. Paredes-Vallés, F.; Hagenaars, J.J.; Dupeyroux, J.; Stroobants, S.; Xu, Y.; de Croon, G.C. Fully neuromorphic vision and control for autonomous drone flight. *Sci. Robot.* **2024**, *9*, eadi0591. [CrossRef]
9. Vitale, A.; Renner, A.; Nauer, C.; Scaramuzza, D.; Sandamirskaya, Y. Event-driven vision and control for UAVs on a neuromorphic chip. In Proceedings of the 2021 IEEE International Conference on Robotics and Automation (ICRA), Xi'an, China, 30 May–5 June 2021; IEEE: Piscataway, NJ, USA, 2021; pp. 103–109.
10. Indiveri, G. Neuromorphic analog VLSI sensor for visual tracking: Circuits and application examples. *IEEE Trans. Circuits Syst. II Analog. Digit. Signal Process.* **2002**, *46*, 1337–1347. [CrossRef]
11. López-Osorio, P.; Domínguez-Morales, J.P.; Perez-Peña, F. A Neuromorphic Vision and Feedback Sensor Fusion Based on Spiking Neural Networks for Real-Time Robot Adaption. *Adv. Intell. Syst.* **2024**, *6*, 2300646. [CrossRef]
12. Yang, Y.; Bartolozzi, C.; Zhang, H.H.; Nawrocki, R.A. Neuromorphic electronics for robotic perception, navigation, and control: A survey. *Eng. Appl. Artif. Intell.* **2023**, *126*, 106838. [CrossRef]
13. Lin, C.K.; Wild, A.; Chinya, G.N.; Cao, Y.; Davies, M.; Lavery, D.M.; Wang, H. Programming spiking neural networks on Intel's Loihi. *Computer* **2018**, *51*, 52–61. [CrossRef]
14. Hsu, J. IBM's new brain [News]. *IEEE Spectr.* **2014**, *51*, 17–19. [CrossRef]
15. Furber, S.B.; Lester, D.R.; Plana, L.A.; Garside, J.D.; Painkras, E.; Temple, S.; Brown, A.D. Overview of the SpiNNaker system architecture. *IEEE Trans. Comput.* **2012**, *62*, 2454–2467. [CrossRef]
16. Murmann, B. Mixed-signal computing for deep neural network inference. *IEEE Trans. Very Large Scale Integr. (VLSI) Syst.* **2020**, *29*, 3–13. [CrossRef]
17. Zhang, J.; Dai, S.; Zhao, Y.; Zhang, J.; Huang, J. Recent progress in photonic synapses for neuromorphic systems. *Adv. Intell. Syst.* **2020**, *2*, 1900136. [CrossRef]
18. Ham, D.; Park, H.; Hwang, S.; Kim, K. Neuromorphic electronics based on copying and pasting the brain. *Nat. Electron.* **2021**, *4*, 635–644. [CrossRef]
19. Park, H.L.; Lee, Y.; Kim, N.; Seo, D.G.; Go, G.T.; Lee, T.W. Flexible neuromorphic electronics for computing, soft robotics, and neuroprosthetics. *Adv. Mater.* **2020**, *32*, 1903558. [CrossRef]
20. Bile, A.; Tari, H.; Fazio, E. Episodic memory and information recognition using solitonic neural networks based on photorefractive plasticity. *Appl. Sci.* **2022**, *12*, 5585. [CrossRef]
21. Bile, A. *Solitonic Neural Networks*; Springer Nature: Cham, Switzerland, 2024.
22. Jooq, M.K.Q.; Azghadi, M.R.; Behbahani, F.; Al-Shidaifat, A.; Song, H. High-performance and energy-efficient leaky integrate-and-fire neuron and spike timing-dependent plasticity circuits in 7nm FinFET technology. *IEEE Access* **2023**, *11*, 133451–133459. [CrossRef]
23. Aitsam, M.; Davies, S.; Di Nuovo, A. Neuromorphic computing for interactive robotics: A systematic review. *IEEE Access* **2022**, *10*, 122261–122279. [CrossRef]
24. Harkin, E.F.; Béïque, J.C.; Naud, R. A user's guide to generalized integrate-and-fire models. In *Computational Modelling of the Brain: Modelling Approaches to Cells, Circuits and Networks*; Springer International Publishing: Cham, Switzerland, 2021; pp. 69–86.
25. Polykretis, I.; Supic, L.; Danielescu, A. Bioinspired smooth neuromorphic control for robotic arms. *Neuromorphic Comput. Eng.* **2023**, *3*, 014013. [CrossRef]
26. Mitchell, J.P.; Bruer, G.; Dean, M.E.; Plank, J.S.; Rose, G.S.; Schuman, C.D. NeoN: Neuromorphic control for autonomous robotic navigation. In Proceedings of the 2017 IEEE International Symposium on Robotics and Intelligent Sensors (IRIS), Ottawa, ON, Canada, 5–7 October 2017; IEEE: Piscataway, NJ, USA, 2017; pp. 136–142.
27. Viale, A.; Marchisio, A.; Martina, M.; Masera, G.; Shafique, M. Carsnn: An efficient spiking neural network for event-based autonomous cars on the loihi neuromorphic research processor. In Proceedings of the 2021 International Joint Conference on Neural Networks (IJCNN), Shenzhen, China, 18–22 July 2021; IEEE: Piscataway, NJ, USA, 2021; pp. 1–10.
28. Rast, A.D.; Adams, S.V.; Davidson, S.; Davies, S.; Hopkins, M.; Rowley, A.; Stokes, A.B.; Wennekers, T.; Furber, S.; Cangelosi, A. Behavioral learning in a cognitive neuromorphic robot: An integrative approach. *IEEE Trans. Neural Netw. Learn. Syst.* **2018**, *29*, 6132–6144. [CrossRef]
29. de Azambuja, R.; Klein, F.B.; Stoelen, M.F.; Adams, S.V.; Cangelosi, A. Graceful degradation under noise on brain inspired robot controllers. In Proceedings of the International Conference on Neural Information Processing, Okinawa, Japan, 20–24 November 2025; Springer International Publishing: Cham, Switzerland, 2016; pp. 195–204
30. Tieck, J.C.V.; Secker, K.; Kaiser, J.; Roennau, A.; Dillmann, R. Soft-grasping with an anthropomorphic robotic hand using spiking neurons.*IEEE Robot. Autom. Lett.* **2020**, *6*, 2894–2901. [CrossRef]

31. Bekolay, T.; Bergstra, J.; Hunsberger, E.; DeWolf, T.; Stewart, T.C.; Rasmussen, D.; Choo, X.; Voelker, A.R.; Eliasmith, C. Nengo: A Python tool for building large-scale functional brain models. *Front. Neuroinform.* **2014**, *7*, 48. [CrossRef] [PubMed]
32. Zhou, T.; Wachs, J.P. Early turn-taking prediction with spiking neural networks for human robot collaboration. In Proceedings of the 2018 IEEE International Conference on Robotics and Automation (ICRA), Brisbane, Australia, 21–25 May 2018; IEEE: Piscataway, NJ, USA, 2018; pp. 3250–3256.
33. Zahra, O.; Navarro-Alarcon, D.; Tolu, S. A neurorobotic embodiment for exploring the dynamical interactions of a spiking cerebellar model and a robot arm during vision-based manipulation tasks. *Int. J. Neural Syst.* **2022**, *32*, 2150028. [CrossRef] [PubMed]
34. Fidjeland, A.K.; Roesch, E.B.; Shanahan, M.P.; Luk, W. NeMo: A platform for neural modelling of spiking neurons using GPUs. In Proceedings of the 2009 20th IEEE International Conference on Application-Specific Systems, Architectures and Processors, Boston, MA, USA, 7–9 July 2009; IEEE: Piscataway, NJ, USA, 2009; pp. 137–144.
35. Berberian, N.; Ross, M.; Chartier, S. Embodied working memory during ongoing input streams. *PLoS ONE* **2021**, *16*, e0244822. [CrossRef]
36. Takeda, K.; Funahashi, S. Prefrontal task-related activity representing visual cue location or saccade direction in spatial working memory tasks. *J. Neurophysiol.* **2002**, *87*, 567–588. [CrossRef]
37. Gao, P.; Adnan, M. Overview of emerging electronics technologies for artificial intelligence: A review. *Mater. Today Electron.* **2025**, *11*, 100136. [CrossRef]
38. Bartolozzi, C.; Indiveri, G.; Donati, E. Embodied neuromorphic intelligence. *Nat. Commun.* **2022**, *13*, 1024. [CrossRef]
39. Marrero, D.; Kern, J.; Urrea, C. A novel robotic controller using neural engineering framework-based spiking neural networks. *Sensors* **2024**, *24*, 491. [CrossRef]
40. Javanshir, A.; Nguyen, T.T.; Mahmud, M.P.; Kouzani, A.Z. Advancements in algorithms and neuromorphic hardware for spiking neural networks. *Neural Comput.* **2022**, *34*, 1289–1328. [CrossRef]
41. Teeter, C.; Iyer, R.; Menon, V.; Gouwens, N.; Feng, D.; Berg, J.; Szafer, A.; Cain, N.; Zeng, H.; Hawrylycz, M. Generalized leaky integrate-and-fire models classify multiple neuron types. *Nat. Commun.* **2018**, *9*, 709. [CrossRef]
42. Fourcaud-Trocmé, N. Integrate and fire models, deterministic. In *Encyclopedia of Computational Neuroscience*; Springer: New York, NY, USA, 2015; pp. 1441–1448.
43. Pozzorini, C.; Mensi, S.; Hagens, O.; Naud, R.; Koch, C.; Gerstner, W. Automated high-throughput characterization of single neurons by means of simplified spiking models. *PLoS Comput. Biol.* **2015**, *11*, e1004275. [CrossRef] [PubMed]
44. Moreno-Bote, R.; Parga, N. Response of integrate-and-fire neurons to noisy inputs filtered by synapses with arbitrary timescales: Firing rate and correlations. *Neural Comput.* **2010**, *22*, 1528–1572. [CrossRef] [PubMed]
45. Geminiani, A.; Casellato, C.; D'Angelo, E.; Pedrocchi, A. Complex electroresponsive dynamics in olivocerebellar neurons represented with extended-generalized leaky integrate and fire models. *Front. Comput. Neurosci.* **2019**, *13*, 35. [PubMed]
46. Liu, Y.H.; Wang, X.J. Spike-frequency adaptation of a generalized leaky integrate-and-fire model neuron. *J. Comput. Neurosci.* **2001**, *10*, 25–45. [CrossRef]
47. Schilling, R.J. *Fundamentals of Robotics: Analysis and Control*; Simon & Schuster Trade: New York, NY, USA, 1996
48. Moreno, R.; Parga, N. Response of a LIF neuron to inputs filtered with arbitrary time scale. *Neurocomputing* **2004**, *58*, 197–202. [CrossRef]
49. Slotine, J.J.E.; Li, W. *Applied Nonlinear Control*; Prentice Hall: Englewood Cliffs, NJ, USA, 1991; Volume 199, p. 705.
50. Stagsted, R.; Vitale, A.; Binz, J.; Bonde Larsen, L.; Sandamirskaya, Y. Towards neuromorphic control: A spiking neural network based PID controller for UAV. In Proceedings of the Robotics: Science and Systems 2020, Virtually, 12–16 July 2020.
51. Li, Y.; Xu, N.; Niu, B.; Chang, Y.; Zhao, J.; Zhao, X. Small-gain technique-based adaptive fuzzy command filtered control for uncertain nonlinear systems with unmodeled dynamics and disturbances. *Int. J. Adapt. Control Signal Process.* **2021**, *35*, 1664–1684. [CrossRef]

robotics

MDPI

Article

A Synergistic Rehabilitation Approach for Post-Stroke Patients with a Hand Exoskeleton: A Feasibility Study with Healthy Subjects

Cristian Camardella [1,*], Tommaso Bagneschi [1], Federica Serra [1], Claudio Loconsole [2,1] and Antonio Frisoli [1]

[1] Institute of Mechanical Intelligence, Scuola Superiore Sant'Anna, 56127 Pisa, Italy; t.bagneschi@santannapisa.it (T.B.); f.serra@santannapisa.it (F.S.); claudio.loconsole@unimercatorum.it (C.L.); a.frisoli@santannapisa.it (A.F.)

[2] Department of Engineering and Science, Universitas Mercatorum, 00186 Rome, Italy

* Correspondence: c.camardella@santannapisa.it

Abstract

Hand exoskeletons are increasingly used to support post-stroke reach-to-grasp, yet most intention-detection strategies trigger assistance from local hand events without considering the synergy between proximal arm transport and distal hand shaping. We evaluated whether proximal arm kinematics, alone or fused with EMG, can predict flexor and extensor digitorum activity for synergy-aligned hand assistance. We trained nine models per participant: linear regression (LINEAR), feedforward neural network (NONLINEAR), and LSTM, each under EMG-only, kinematics-only (KIN), and EMG+KIN inputs. Performance was assessed by RMSE on test trials and by a synergy-retention analysis, comparing synergy weights from original EMG versus a hybrid EMG in which extensor and flexor digitorum measure signals were replaced by model predictions. Results have shown that kinematic information can predict muscle activity even with a simple linear model (average RMSE around 30% of signal amplitude peak during go-to-grasp contractions), and synergy analysis indicated high cosine similarity between original and hybrid synergy weights (on average 0.87 for the LINEAR model). Furthermore, the LINEAR model with kinematics input has been tested in a real-time go-to-grasp motion, developing a high-level control strategy for a hand exoskeleton, to better simulate post-stroke rehabilitation scenarios. These results suggest the intrinsic synergistic motion of go-to-grasp actions, offering a practical path, in hand rehabilitation contexts, for timing hand assistance in synergy with arm transport and with minimal setup burden.

Keywords: robotics; exoskeleton; muscle; synergy; rehabilitation; stroke; hand; pattern; regression; machine learning

1. Introduction

Impairments of hand function are among the most disabling consequences of stroke and critically limit independence in activities of daily living (ADLs) [1,2]. Over the past two decades, robotic technologies for upper-limb rehabilitation have proliferated in both research and clinical environments with the aim of delivering highly repetitive, task-oriented, and measurable therapy [3–5]. Large meta-analyses and reviews indicate that electromechanical and robot-assisted training can improve arm function and strength and, in some cases, ADLs, although clinical effect sizes and the translation to meaningful functional gains remain debated and appear sensitive to device design and dosing parameters [6–9].

A key lesson emerging from rehabilitation robotics and human–robot interaction is that assistance must be intuitive and patient-cooperative to sustain engagement and improve usability [5,10]. In wearable orthoses, the bottleneck is often the intention detection strategy (IDS), the algorithmic interface that maps user signals to device actions, which strongly affects robustness, timing, workload, and acceptance in daily use [10]. IDSs used in practice span surface electromyography (sEMG), kinematic sensing, manual triggers, and brain–computer interfaces (BCIs), each with distinct trade-offs in setup burden, reliability, and responsiveness [10–13].

Hand-specific robotic devices include end-effector systems and wearable exoskeletons/gloves designed for therapy and, increasingly, for assistance [3,12,14,15]. These devices can be either rigid or soft, depending on the clinical case and the rehabilitation scenario. Soft hand exoskeletons are very-well adaptable and versatile but they may struggle in achieving high forces, especially on hands with a high spasticity, and they usually feature more complex systems for closed-loop control [16,17]. Rigid exoskeletons may be less adaptable but they can convey high forces and they are, in most of the cases, more bulky but with a more precise and simple control schemes [18]. Control strategies for these devices can be grouped as follows. (i) EMG-driven control: widely used to trigger hand opening/clos ing via onset thresholds or pattern-recognition models; however, EMG onset detection is non-trivial in noisy, post-stroke signals, and performance can degrade with fatigue and spasticity [19–21]. (ii) Kinematics-driven control: local finger/wrist angles or inertial measurements are used to infer grasp states; in bilateral modes, sensors on the unaffected hand command the paretic-hand exoskeleton (master–slave mirroring) [22]. (iii) BCI-driven control: motor-imagery BCIs coupled to hand robots have shown promising clinical signals in controlled trials and systematic reviews, yet deployment remains constrained by robustness and setup-time issues [10,23]. (iv) Mirrored/bimanual strategies: robot-mediated mirror therapy and bilateral training replicate the movement of the unaffected hand on the affected side; these approaches can modulate cortical activation but, by design, do not infer intention from the paretic limb [22,24,25].

Neuroscience and motor-control studies emphasize that reach-to-grasp is a coordinated behavior in which proximal arm transport and distal hand shaping are tightly coupled via task-dependent synergies [1]. Post-stroke, interjoint coordination and the timing of grasp relative to arm transport are often disrupted [1,2]. These insights motivate control policies that fuse proximal and distal information to assist the hand in synergy with the arm. While there are demonstrations of integrated reach-to-grasp assistance combining a multi-joint arm exoskeleton with neuromuscular stimulation of the hand [26], recent reviews of hand exoskeletons and wearable soft devices primarily catalogue EMG-, kinematics-, BCI-, and mirrored-control schemes, with little emphasis on controllers that explicitly exploit shoulder–elbow kinematics to synchronize hand opening/closing with the phases of reaching [10–13]. In many clinical and research systems, hand assistance is still triggered by discrete events (e.g., EMG onset, decoded MI, button press, or mirrored command) that are largely independent of concurrent arm motion.

Natural prehension is a coordinated behaviour in which proximal arm transport and distal hand shaping are temporally coupled; for example, hand closure typically begins during the deceleration phase of the transport [27,28]. After stroke, this coupling is disrupted, with altered timing and longer deceleration phases during reach-to-grasp [2,29]. These observations motivate assistance strategies that respect arm–hand synergies rather than treating the hand in isolation.

https://doi.org/10.3390/robotics15010021

A second, complementary pillar is the role of temporal contingency in driving neuroplasticity. Paired associative stimulation (PAS) shows that precisely timed pairing of afferent input with cortical stimulation induces Hebbian, timing-dependent changes in corticospinal excitability in humans [30–32]. Related work demonstrates rapid, training-induced reorganization of motor representations with short bouts of practice [33]. Together, these studies support the principle that the closer the temporal coupling between intention, movement, and afferent feedback, the stronger the plasticity response.

Clinical neurorehabilitation technologies that make feedback contingent on intention align with these principles. In chronic stroke, brain–computer interface (BCI) control coupled to functional electrical stimulation (FES) produced significantly greater and lasting upper-limb recovery than sham FES, with concomitant neuroplastic signatures [34]. By contrast, a multicentre randomized trial comparing cyclic NMES, EMG-triggered NMES, and sensory stimulation for the paretic hand found no superiority of EMG-triggered over cyclic stimulation; notably, participants in the EMG-triggered arm were instructed to relax during stimulation, effectively unpairing intention and afferent consequences [35]. These findings underscore that mere event triggering is insufficient unless intention and feedback are closely time-locked.

Beyond local hand feedback, somatosensory inputs and movements from adjacent limb segments can modulate hand motor pathways, providing a rationale for synergy-level contingency. Heteronymous reflex pathways link muscles across the upper limb [36,37], and cutaneous/proprioceptive inputs alter hand corticospinal excitability [38–40]. Forearm/hand posture and ongoing movement further shape cortical drive to intrinsic and extrinsic hand muscles [41,42]. In parallel, bilateral/bimanual paradigms that exploit interlimb coupling show beneficial effects on post-stroke motor outcomes [43]. Collectively, these data indicate that pairing hand assistance with phase-specific signals from the moving arm (and, where appropriate, from the contralateral limb) is biologically plausible and clinically relevant.

Building on these principles, we frame and evaluate intention-prediction strategies that use EMG, proximal arm kinematics, or their fusion to trigger hand exoskeleton open/close in synergy with ongoing arm transport during functional reach-to-grasp. This design places the controller within a contingency-informed framework, time-locking assistance to volitional state and to intersegmental context, which prior experimental and clinical evidence identifies as favourable for inducing and consolidating motor plasticity [30,33,34].

The state of the art thus reveals a relative lack of intention-decoding approaches that leverage proximal arm kinematics, alone or fused with EMG, to coordinate hand assistance with ongoing arm transport during goal-directed tasks. Addressing this gap is consistent with patient-cooperative control principles and could improve timing and naturalness of assistance during functional reach-to-grasp [5,10].

The objective of this study is to develop and evaluate an intention–prediction strategy for a hand exoskeleton that can support post-stroke opening and closing in synergy with arm motion during goal-directed actions (e.g., grasping a bottle). Specifically, we compare multiple machine-learning (ML) techniques trained to predict hand open/close from three input conditions: (1) sEMG alone, (2) kinematics from a sensorized 3-DoF arm carrying the exoskeleton at the end of the kinematic chain, and (3) a multimodal fusion of EMG and arm kinematics. Our research questions are does fusing arm-kinematic context with EMG improve the accuracy and timing of open/close predictions, compared to single-modality baselines, for controlling a hand exoskeleton during functional tasks? Are such predictions suitable to feed a hand exoskeleton control in an actual rehabilitation setting? Can such a control retain the original arm/hand patterns during grasping?

 https://doi.org/10.3390/robotics15010021

The contributions of this work are (i) a comparative evaluation of several ML intention-decoding pipelines across EMG-only, arm-kinematics–only, and multimodal inputs for dynamic and synergistic hand exoskeleton control; (ii) an experimentally validated online control strategy that uses the best predictor (in terms of trade-off between performance, simplicity of setup, and complexity of the model) to drive timely, task-consistent assistance of hand opening/closing while the arm moves.

2. Materials and Methods

2.1. Participants

Eight adult participants took part in the study (N = 8; height 182.0 ± 7.2 cm; arm length 54.8 ± 4.6 cm; forearm length 27.8 ± 3.3 cm; hand length 19.7 ± 1.1 cm; hand width 8.3 ± 0.7 cm; age 31.6 ± 2.6 years). Participants have been selected to cover a broad range of hand and arm sizes, rather than on a broader age range, which are the variables that are most related to the wearability of the hand exoskeleton. Hand length, for instance, goes from a minimum of 17.4 cm to a maximum of 20.5 cm. Arm length and forearm length as well go respectively from a minimum of 45.0 cm and 20.0 cm, to a maximum of 60.0 cm and 30.1 cm. All subjects reported to be right-handed.

2.2. System Description

Rehabilitation Platform with the Hand Exoskeleton

The system used in this study is a wheeled rehabilitation platform that has been designed to accommodate different exoskeletons on the end-effector. A passive, sensorized 3-DoF arm served as the end-effector support, constrained to move on the horizontal plane (see Figure 1). The dominant-arm forearm was secured to the end-effector via a rigid forearm support. On the end-effector of the sensorized arm, the HandExos hand exoskeleton is mounted: it features four under-actuated finger modules (with a parallel kinematics that constrain their motion on the horizontal plane) with an independent thumb module, five linear electromagnetic actuators (Actuonix Miniature Linear Motor P16-50, Victoria, BC, Canada), a control unit, and it is mainly composed by 3D printed mechanical parts. Control electronics was embedded in the structure of the device at the hand dorsum, including amplification and digital conversion of the force sensors signals, signal processing and control on a microcontroller unit (Teensy 4.1 carrier board with ARM Cortex-M7, Sherwood, OR, USA), native Ethernet connection with the system platform, and drivers of the actuators with H-Bridge ICs (Texas Instruments DRV8833, Dallas, TX, USA). The user can wear the hand exoskeleton inserting, for each of their fingers excluding the thumb, their proximal and middle phalanxes in two C-shaped components that can be removable, thanks to its sliding insertion in the aforementioned finger kinematic structure, and also with different sizes. These mechanical user–machine interfaces grant the orthogonal transmission of forces from the human to the hand exoskeleton and vice versa.

2.3. Hand Exoskeleton Low-Level Control Architecture

The low-level loop is a proportional position controller: the error $e = P_{\text{ref}} - P_{\text{curr}}$ is amplified by a gain K_p to form a drive command V_{ref} (see Figure 2). A static nonlinearity models actuator dead-zone and saturation, and the command is applied to an H-bridge PWM stage that powers a linear actuator. The actuator–mechanism is represented as two cascaded integrators. Position feedback P_{curr} is measured by a linear potentiometer mounted on the actuator, scaled by a gain k and low-pass filtered to suppress sensor and PWM ripple before being subtracted from P_{ref}. The chosen filtering and control loop adds a non-relevant delay to the actuation system, being quantified overall to be 30–50 ms. Let $P_{\text{ref}}(t)$ be the position setpoint and $P(t)$ the measured position. The feedback is low-pass

 https://doi.org/10.3390/robotics15010021

filtered and scaled (filter $F(s)$ with impulse response $f(t)$, scalar k). The drive-to-position dynamics of the H-bridge–actuator–mechanism are denoted $G(s)$ (e.g., two integrators with gain). Linearizing the static nonlinearity after the proportional stage, the closed-loop transfer is

$$\frac{P(s)}{P_{\mathrm{ref}}(s)} = \frac{K_p\, G(s)}{1 + K_p\, G(s)\, k\, F(s)}\,.$$

The actual command sent to the drive includes the dead-zone/saturation map $\phi(\cdot)$ and reads

$$V_{\mathrm{ref}}(t) = \phi\Big(K_p\big[P_{\mathrm{ref}}(t) - k\,(fP)(t)\big]\Big)\,,$$

where K_p is the proportional gain, fP denotes convolution, and $V_{\mathrm{ref}}(t)$ is applied to the PWM H-bridge. This cascaded structure provides closed-loop position tracking with bounded velocity and current via the drive saturation.

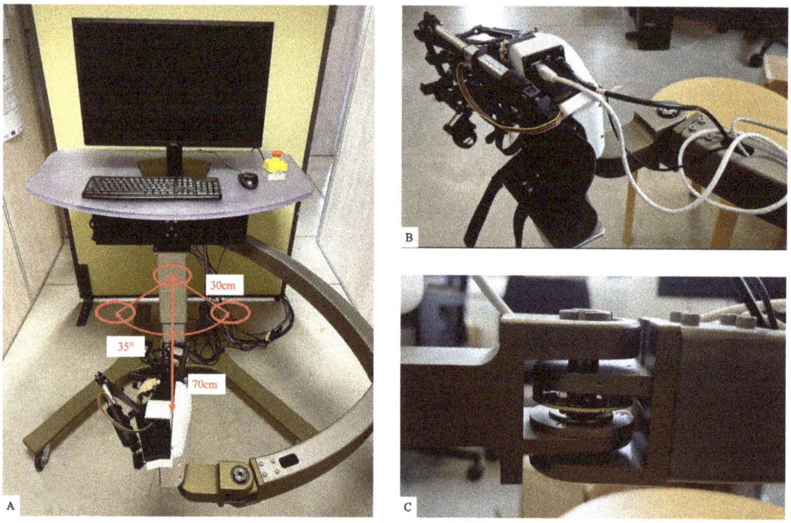

Figure 1. Rehabilitation platform: (**A**) platform and real-world position of the bottles to grasp; the hand exoskeleton has been disabled and configured with a fully-opened kinematics to avoid interactions during the hands-free experiment while keeping the subject's forearm fixed in position thanks to the forearm support attached to it, (**B**) detail of HandExos and forearm support, (**C**) detail of encoder.

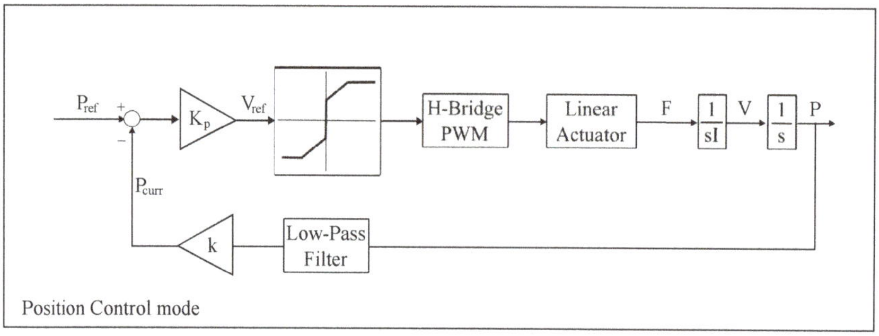

Figure 2. Low-level control scheme of the hand exoskeleton, implementing position control of each independent finger, and replicated for each under-actuated finger. The system that outputs the position of the linear actuator through the two integrators is internal to the actuator itself.

https://doi.org/10.3390/robotics15010021

Setup Sensors

Three bottle locations were defined on the workspace: one central position, one at $-35°$ (right of center), and one at $+35°$ (left of center), all at the same radial distance from the subject. Surface EMG (sEMG) was acquired at 2222 Hz using a Delsys wireless system equipped with Quattro and Avanti sensors (Delsys Inc., Boston, MA, USA) and Ag/Cl electrodes. Twelve muscles were monitored: anterior (AD), middle (MD), and posterior deltoids (PD); pectoralis major (PM); infraspinatus (INF); teres major (TM); biceps brachii (short head, BS); triceps brachii (long head, TL); brachioradialis (BR); extensor digitorum (ED); flexor digitorum (FD); and abductor pollicis brevis (APB). A representation of the electrodes placement is shown in Figure 3. Joint angles and the end-effector position of the 3-DoF passive arm were sampled at 100 Hz using RLS Orbis absolute encoders mounted at each joint.

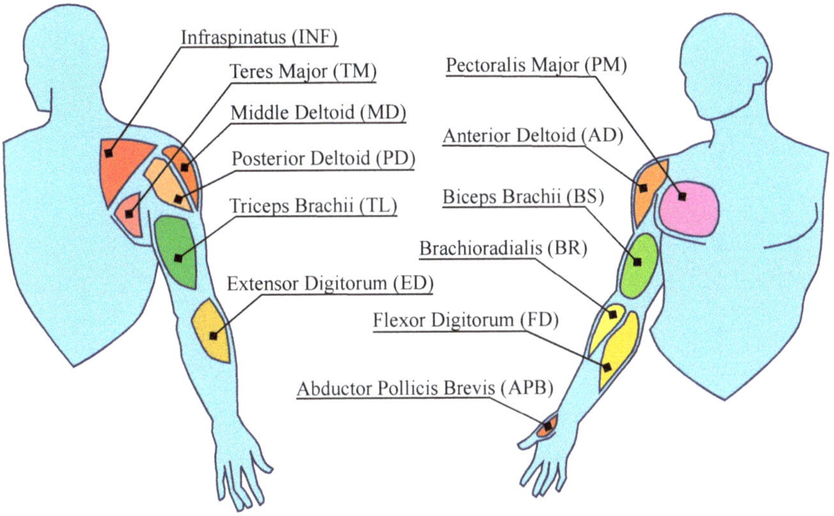

Figure 3. Targeted muscles to measure EMG activity during go-to-grasp back and forth actions. Back (**left**) and Front (**right**).

2.4. Offline Experimental Protocol

Participants were seated on a chair positioned in front of the HandExo rehabilitation platform. After electrode placement, each participant performed maximum voluntary contraction (MVC) trials used for subsequent normalization of EMG amplitudes: these trials include flexion/extension of the shoulder, internal/external rotation of the shoulder, flexion/extension of the elbow, and open/close of fingers. Participants then donned the wrist splint and were guided to a standardized initial posture: the wrist center located 70 cm from the central bottle, with the elbow configured so that the central bottle could be reached at full elbow extension (see Figure 1). For each of the three bottle locations (center, $-35°$, $+35°$), participants completed 7 reach-to-grasp-and-return trials, starting from the initial position, reaching to grasp the bottle, and returning to the initial position. In total, each participant performed $3 \times 7 = 21$ trials.

2.5. Data Acquisition and Synchronization

EMG and kinematic data streams were synchronized and temporally aligned offline to a common time base. All data processing and modeling were conducted in MATLAB R2023b (MathWorks, Natick, MA, USA). Raw EMG signals underwent the following steps: (i) normalization to each muscle's MVC, (ii) full-wave rectification, (iii) band-pass

https://doi.org/10.3390/robotics15010021

filtering in the 3–250 Hz range, and (iv) envelope extraction via low-pass filtering at 1 Hz. Unless otherwise specified in subsequent sections, all muscles followed the same preprocessing pipeline. Joint angles from each of the three revolute joints and the end-effector Cartesian position of the passive arm were sampled at 100 Hz from the RLS Orbis absolute encoders. No additional filtering was applied beyond that required for synchronization and model input formatting.

2.6. Prediction Target and Modeling Overview

The modeling objective was to predict the (preprocessed, MVC-normalized) amplitudes of ED and FD during reach-to-grasp movements. To emulate assistive use, predictions are intended to drive a hand exoskeleton during reach-to-grasp tasks within a serious-game environment that mirrors the physical setup (virtual bottle positions in the game replicate the three recorded physical locations i.e., center, -35°, $+35^\circ$). We trained three algorithmic families:

1. Linear regression (LR),
2. Nonlinear regression using a feedforward neural network (NN),
3. Long short-term memory network (LSTM).

Each algorithm was trained under three input conditions:

1. EMG-only,
2. Kinematics-only,
3. EMG+Kinematics.

This yielded a total of $3 \times 3 = 9$ models per participant. The EMG input set consisted of the electromyographic signals from all channels except the target ED and FD channels, resulting in 10 EMG features. The Kinematics input set included 10 kinematic channels describing the movement trajectories: end-effector position and velocity (4 channels) and joint angles and velocity (6 channels, having 3 DoF on the passive arm). The combined EMG+Kinematics input set was formed by concatenating the 10 EMG features (excluding channels 6 and 7) with the 10 kinematic features, yielding a total of 20 input features. In all cases, the models were trained to predict the EMG activity of channels 6 and 7. Model hyperparameters and feature construction are detailed in the next subsection. For each participant and each bottle location, the 7 trials were split into 3 for training, 2 for validation, and 2 for testing. Splits were performed at the trial level to prevent temporal leakage between sets. Unless otherwise noted, models were trained and evaluated in a within-subject manner using these subject-specific splits.

2.7. Architectures and Settings

In this work, three classes of models were compared for the estimation task: linear regression, nonlinear regression, and recurrent neural networks of the Long Short-Term Memory (LSTM) type. These models have been chosen to preliminary investigate the feasibility of the aforementioned rehabilitation approach, selecting the most common ones in literature, in the EMG signals estimation tasks, with increasing complexity. Thus, the comparison of the algorithms is either not intended to be extensive or to aim at finding the best model for the proposed task, but rather to give to the reader an objective evaluation of the performance of the synergistic go-to-grasp rehabilitation approach, on which specific future optimization can be run.

Three regression models were trained to estimate electromyographic activity in channels 6 and 7 from different sets of input features. The first model was a linear regression with ridge regularization, implemented as two independent least-squares regressors (one for each channel). The second model was a non-linear regression approach based on gradient boosting of regression trees (LSBoost), which aggregates the predictions of multiple

https://doi.org/10.3390/robotics15010021

shallow regression trees to capture non-linear input–output relationships. The third model was a recurrent neural network using a long short-term memory (LSTM) architecture to model the temporal dynamics of the signals. The LSTM network consisted of a sequence input layer with dimensionality equal to the number of features, a first LSTM hidden layer with 100 units, a dropout layer with 20% probability, a second LSTM hidden layer with 50 units, a fully connected layer with two output units corresponding to the target channels, and a regression layer with a mean squared error loss function. The network was trained with the Adam optimizer for a maximum of 100 epochs using a mini-batch size of 8, a learning rate of 10^{-3}, and gradient thresholding set to 1. Validation data were used to monitor performance and prevent overfitting. These specific settings have been set to build a moderate-capacity, regularized sequence model appropriate for smooth EMG envelopes: two LSTM layers provide enough capacity to model temporal dependencies without moving into an over-parameterized regime; dropout equals to 0.2 is a standard regularizer for small datasets, while mini-batch size increases the number of weight updates per epoch when training data are limited. Finally the gradient thresholding set to 1 is included specifically to prevent rare exploding-gradient events in recurrent optimization, which is a common setting in the state of the art.

2.8. *Performance Metrics*

Given the time-continuous nature of the target signals, models accuracy was quantified using the root mean squared error (RMSE) between the predicted and measured EMG envelopes of FD and ED. For a given muscle m and trial with N time samples, let $y_m(t)$ denote the measured (MVC-normalized, enveloped) EMG and $\hat{y}_m(t)$ the model estimate. The RMSE is

$$\mathrm{RMSE}_m = \sqrt{\frac{1}{N}\sum_{t=1}^{N}\left(\hat{y}_m(t) - y_m(t)\right)^2}. \quad (1)$$

We report $\mathrm{RMSE}_{\mathrm{FD}}$ (flexor digitorum) and $\mathrm{RMSE}_{\mathrm{ED}}$ (extensor digitorum) separately; summary values within a condition are obtained by averaging across trials (and, where indicated, across the two target muscles).

2.9. *Statistical Analysis*

To assess differences in estimation accuracy, we compared the root mean squared error (RMSE) across factors Model (Linear, Nonlinear, LSTM) and Input type (EMG, Kinematics, EMG+Kinematics). Because of the limited sample size and potential violations of normality, we employed a non-parametric two-way analysis based on the Scheirer–Ray–Hare test, a rank-based extension of the Kruskal–Wallis test suitable for factorial designs. RMSE values were first converted to ranks, and the sums of ranks were partitioned into main effects for Model, Input type, and their interaction. For each term we computed the corresponding H statistic, degrees of freedom, and p-value using the chi-square approximation. To quantify effect sizes in a way robust to ties, we reported rank-based eta squared (η^2_H) and epsilon squared (ϵ^2). These measures are defined as the proportion of variance in ranks attributable to each factor, with ϵ^2 providing a less biased estimate. Interaction effects were carefully checked: in cases where cross-cell rank dispersion was essentially zero (for example, nearly identical medians across cells), the H statistic approached zero and effect sizes were reported as zero rather than undefined.

2.10. *Muscle Synergy Analysis and Rationale*

Because the controller is intended to operate in synergy with arm transport during reach-to-grasp, we verified that replacing the two missing channels (ED, FD) with model predictions does not alter the subject's original low-dimensional muscle coordination.

 https://doi.org/10.3390/robotics15010021

To this end, we compared muscle synergies extracted from the original EMG against those from a hybrid EMG in which channels 6–7 were replaced by the model estimates. Preserving synergy structure supports the physiological plausibility of the predictions and their suitability for synergy-informed assistance. For each participant, we concatenated the EMG envelopes from the test set only (all test trials and repetitions) into a nonnegative matrix $X \in \mathbb{R}_{\geq 0}^{M \times T}$ with $M = 12$ channels and T time samples at 2222 Hz. Two versions were formed: (i) X_{real}: original EMG (all real channels), and (ii) X_{hyb}: the same matrix where channels 6 and 7 (ED and FD) were replaced by the corresponding model predictions (per model and input condition). All signals were those used for evaluation (MVC-normalized, rectified, 3–200 Hz band-pass, and 4 Hz envelope). Muscle synergies were computed by non-negative matrix factorization (NMF), seeking

$$X \approx WH, \qquad W \in \mathbb{R}_{\geq 0}^{M \times r}, \quad H \in \mathbb{R}_{\geq 0}^{r \times T}, \tag{2}$$

where r is the number of synergies, W contains time-invariant synergy weights, and H their time courses. For each $r \in \{1, \ldots, 8\}$ we ran NMF with 20 random initializations (MATLAB R2023b, `nnmf`, multiplicative updates, max 500 iterations) and retained the factorization with the smallest reconstruction error. We computed the global variance accounted for (VAF) as

$$\text{VAF}(r) = 1 - \frac{\|X - \widehat{X}_r\|_F^2}{\|X\|_F^2}, \qquad \widehat{X}_r = W_r H_r, \tag{3}$$

and selected the dimensionality by the 90% rule,

$$r^\star = \min\{ r : \text{VAF}(r) \geq 0.90 \}.$$

Dimensionality was determined separately for X_{real} and X_{hyb}. To assess preservation, we (i) compared the VAF curves $\text{VAF}_{\text{real}}(r)$ vs. $\text{VAF}_{\text{hyb}}(r)$ and (ii) verified whether $r^\star_{\text{hyb}} = r^\star_{\text{real}}$. Because NMF solutions are column-permuted, we matched synergies between W_{real} and W_{hyb} using a permutation that maximized overall column-wise similarity. For similarity we used cosine similarity:

$$s(W_i, \widehat{w}_j) = \frac{w_i^\top \widehat{w}_j}{\|w_i\|_2 \, \|\widehat{w}_j\|_2}, \qquad w_i, \widehat{w}_j \in \mathbb{R}_{\geq 0}^{M}. \tag{4}$$

The optimal one-to-one pairing was found by maximizing the cumulative cosine similarity. We report per-subject mean cosine similarity $\bar{s}$ across the $r^\star$ matched pairs, and aggregate $\bar{s}$ across subjects, models, and input conditions.

2.11. Online Test of the Hand Exoskeleton: High-Level Control Strategy

The control strategy can be designed trying to mimic fingers extensor and flexor antagonists muscles behaviour. Considering a typical position control (a control output between 0 and 1, where 0 stands for fully-closed hand exoskeleton kinematics, and 1 stands for fully-open hand exoskeleton kinematics) the control strategy can be designed as follows: when both are at rest, the fingers closing amount is at mid-way (i.e., 0.5), when flexors are active close the hand $(0.5 - k_f u(1))$ and when extensors are active open the hand $(0.5 + k_e u(2))$. Finally the reference position for the control law can be written as follows:

$$P_{ref} = 0.5 + k_e e_{est} - k_f f_{est} \tag{5}$$

where e_{est} and f_{est} are low-bounded to zero and k_e and k_f are tuned considering the maximum amplitude of ED and FD in healthy subjects, so that $k_e e_{est} <= 0.5$ and $k_f f_{est} <= 0.5$. The k_e and k_f coefficients are subject-specific and depend on the normalized values of EMG

 https://doi.org/10.3390/robotics15010021

signals of ED and FD. They can be re-tuned for lower residual activations for post-stroke patients. Basically, the control strategy can be imagined to be in such a way that each finger is pulled by two antagonist springs, one pulling towards the full opening (i.e., the extensor) and one pulling towards the full closing (i.e., the flexor). To summarize, the model predicts the extensor and flexor muscle activity, which are e_{est} and f_{est} respectively, and it feeds the computation of the reference position for each of the linear actuator of the hand exoskeleton, i.e., P_{ref}, that is eventually used in the control scheme.

Online Experimental Protocol

After implementing the control law on the hand exoskeleton (see Section 2.11), 3 out of 8 subjects repeated the go-to-grasp experiments while wearing the exoskeleton: in this test, the subject was instructed to simply get close to the bottle and passively follow the assistance of the hand exoskeleton during pre-shaping and closing actions. In an actual setup with post-stroke patients, EMG placement timing cannot be ignored, thus, in testing the online control not only performance but also usability has been considered. For this reason, to simplify the setup, to make implementation simpler and given the extracted performance of the offline tests (see Figure 4), only the LINEAR model with kinematics inputs was used. Right after the end of the offline experiment and consequent training of the model on the subject's data, coefficients and bias of the linear model were used in the online tests. Before testing the online control, an estimation of the prediction delay, in the case of the LINEAR model with KIN inputs, has been performed, in order to ensure that the actuation can be delivered on time to the user while approaching the object to grasp. The delay has computed first detecting the index where a 10% variation of the initial value of the channel occurs both on the measured signal and the prediction and then calculating their difference, dividing it by the sampling frequency.

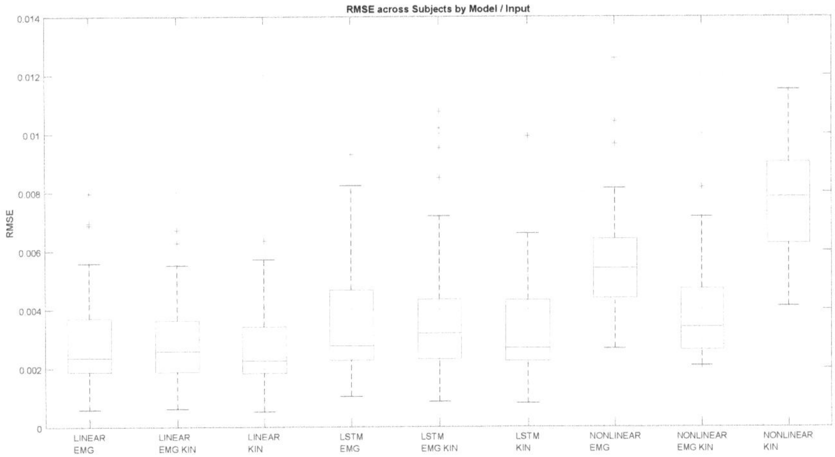

Figure 4. RMSE distributions (computed on the normalized signal) across all subjects for all models and input types. Each boxplot is a performance distribution built on the RMSE on the test set, having the red line as the median, the blue box as the 1st and 2nd quartiles, and whiskers as the 3rd and 4th quartiles. Red crosses show outliers.

3. Results

3.1. Offline Prediction Accuracy Across Models and Inputs

Across eight participants and 168 trial-level observations, descriptive RMSE for the combined target (ED+FD) showed that LINEAR and NONLINEAR models produced low errors for all inputs, while LSTM errors were larger and more input-sensitive (see Figure 4).

https://doi.org/10.3390/robotics15010021

Channel-wise patterns (reported for completeness) were approximately consistent with the combined metric and they have been reported in Tables 1 and 2.

Table 1. RMSE (extensor digitorum, ch. 6) across subjects: mean ± SD.

Model	EMG	EMG_KIN	KIN
LINEAR	0.0035 ± 0.0023	0.0032 ± 0.0017	0.0032 ± 0.0017
LSTM	0.0063 ± 0.0025	0.0090 ± 0.0020	0.0042 ± 0.0018
NONLINEAR	0.0043 ± 0.0027	0.0040 ± 0.0018	0.0044 ± 0.0023

Table 2. RMSE (flexor digitorum, ch. 7) across subjects: mean ± SD.

Model	EMG	EMG_KIN	KIN
LINEAR	0.0017 ± 0.0013	0.0017 ± 0.0013	0.0019 ± 0.0017
LSTM	0.0057 ± 0.0017	0.0103 ± 0.0080	0.0033 ± 0.0009
NONLINEAR	0.0020 ± 0.0016	0.0020 ± 0.0016	0.0026 ± 0.0024

A Scheirer–Ray–Hare (rank two-way) test on combined RMSE (factors: Model, Input) yielded a highly significant main effect of Model ($H = 123.76$, $df = 2$, $p < 1 \times 10^{-20}$, $\eta^2_H = 0.287$, $\epsilon^2 = 0.283$), a significant main effect of Input ($H = 7.39$, $df = 2$, $p = 0.0249$, $\eta^2_H = 0.017$, $\epsilon^2 = 0.012$), and a significant Model × Input interaction ($H = 30.96$, $df = 4$, $p = 3.12 \times 10^{-6}$, $\eta^2_H = 0.072$, $\epsilon^2 = 0.063$). The interaction reflects the disproportionate degradation of LSTM with EMG-rich inputs (EMG, EMG_KIN) relative to KIN, whereas LINEAR and NONLINEAR varied little across inputs (see Figure 5).

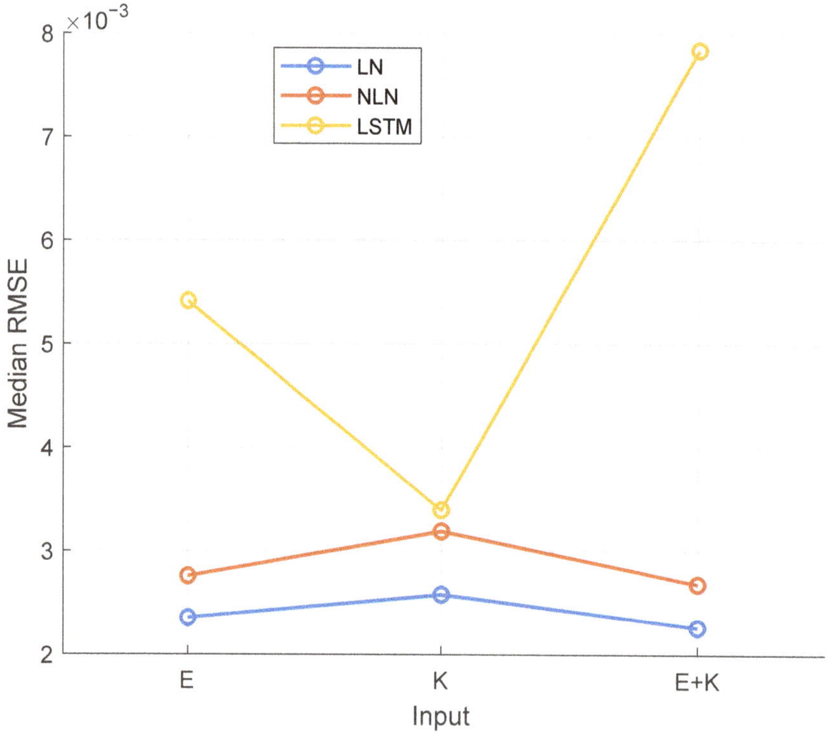

Figure 5. Model × Input interaction on combined RMSE (mean ± SEM).

https://doi.org/10.3390/robotics15010021

3.2. Synergy Retention with Predicted Channels

Using NMF on test-set EMG and replacing channels 6–7 with model predictions to form a hybrid EMG, we compared synergy weight matrices W via cosine similarity. Across {model, input} cells (Figure 6), median similarities clustered high for LINEAR and NONLINEAR (typically 0.85–0.89) with low-to-moderate dispersion. LSTM showed input sensitivity: KIN yielded the highest similarities (mean 0.873 ± 0.023, median 0.868), while EMG_KIN was lowest (mean 0.825 ± 0.020, median 0.845), with wider interquartile ranges. Aggregated over inputs, mean similarities were LINEAR 0.874 ± 0.010, NONLINEAR 0.876 ± 0.012, LSTM 0.846 ± 0.013. Aggregated over models, KIN achieved the highest mean similarity 0.869 ± 0.0117, versus EMG 0.864 ± 0.0132 and EMG_KIN 0.863 ± 0.0108.

Mean VAF curves for original vs. hybrid EMG largely overlapped across the synergy range (Figure 7); the 90% VAF criterion was reached at $r \approx 6$ on average (overall $r = 6.06 \pm 0.75$, median 6). At the selected dimensionality r, the average VAF difference $\Delta\text{VAF} = \text{VAF}_{\text{hyb}} - \text{VAF}_{\text{true}}$ was small overall (0.00456 ± 0.0159), with model/input breakdowns indicating minor, condition-dependent shifts: LINEAR showed higher VAF in the hybrid (EMG $+0.0267 \pm 0.0116$, KIN $+0.0177 \pm 0.00746$, EMG_KIN $+0.0169 \pm 0.00926$); NONLINEAR yielded small negative deltas (KIN -0.00703 ± 0.00508, EMG -0.00819 ± 0.00347, EMG_KIN -0.00545 ± 0.00556); LSTM deltas were near zero to mildly negative for KIN/EMG_KIN (KIN -0.00589 ± 0.0150, EMG_KIN -0.000312 ± 0.0146) and mildly positive for EMG ($+0.00673 \pm 0.0151$). Taken together, the synergy dimensionality was preserved (no systematic shift in r), and synergy composition was largely retained, with the highest retention observed for KIN inputs and for LINEAR/NONLINEAR models.

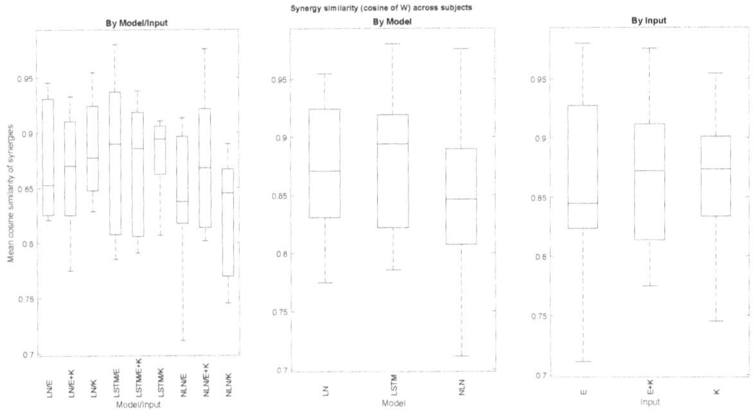

Figure 6. Across-subject cosine similarity between synergy weights (W) from original vs. hybrid EMG, by model/input.

3.3. Preliminary Real-Time Control of the Hand Exoskeleton

Before evaluating the online control performance, an estimation of the actuation delay has been computed, without including any lag deriving from the electromechanical system itself, but only considering the prediction delay. On the LINEAR model with KIN inputs, the delay has been calculated to be 279 ± 397 ms with a median value of the distribution that includes all trials and all subjects equal to 147 ms. Furthermore, for reproducibility purposes, the values used for k_e and k_f are here reported, as mean and std values on the tested population: k_e was set to 0.0022 ± 0.0027 and k_f was set to 0.0049 ± 0.0072. Preliminary results on the real-time hand exoskeleton synergistic go-to-grasp control can be found in Figure 8. Differently from what expected, only on a single case out of 6 (2 channels and 3 trials) the amplitude of EMG signals were lower in the online test (i.e., wearing the

 https://doi.org/10.3390/robotics15010021

hand exoskeleton) compared to the offline test. Across the three bottle-placement trials, the offline condition showed extensor digitorum RMS values between 0.0036 and 0.0055 with standard deviations between 0.0015 and 0.0043, and flexor digitorum RMS values between 0.0035 and 0.0061 with standard deviations between 0.0026 and 0.0046. In the online condition, the extensor digitorum RMS values ranged from 0.0035 to 0.0079 with standard deviations from 0.00086 to 0.0045, while the flexor digitorum RMS values ranged from 0.0093 to 0.0274 with standard deviations from 0.0073 to 0.0221.

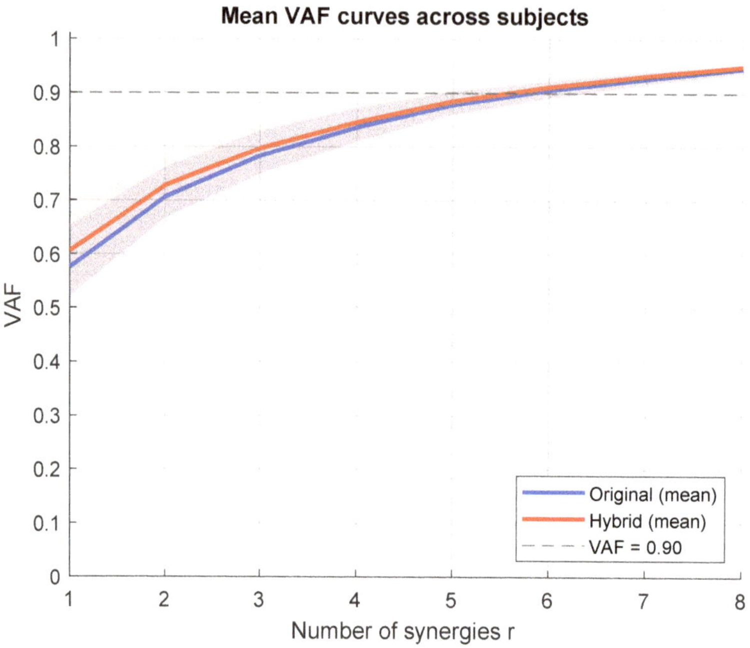

Figure 7. Mean VAF curves (the shaded band represents the variability across subjects) for original and hybrid EMG; dashed line marks 90% VAF.

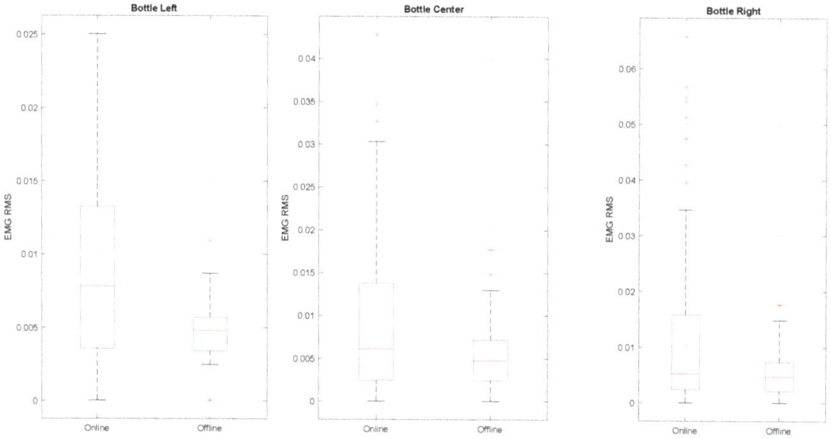

Figure 8. Comparison of EMG RMS between online and offline tests in the three experimental trials. Distributions come from three subjects and seven repetitions per trial. The red line is the median, the blue box represents the 1st and 2nd quartiles, and whiskers represents the 3rd and 4th quartiles. Red crosses show outliers.

 https://doi.org/10.3390/robotics15010021

These numerical differences indicate higher RMS amplitudes in the online condition for both muscles, with the most pronounced increase observed in the flexor digitorum channel. Concerning muscle synergies, a comparison has ben performed between the synergies extracted during the offline task (without the exo) and the online task (with the exo), on the three subjects (see Figure 9). For the bottle–left trial, the offline (NoExo) centroids showed: C1 dominated by DELT P (weight $\approx$ 0.9), C2 by DELT M ($\approx$0.8–0.9), C3 by DELT A ($\approx$0.85–0.9), C4 with larger loading on TRI LAT and BIC SH (both $\approx$0.55–0.7, with INFRASP $\approx$ 0.6), and C5 by BRACH ($\approx$0.9). Online (Exo) retained the deltoid-dominated clusters (C1 DELT P $\approx$ 0.9, C2 DELT M $\approx$ 0.9, C3 DELT A $\approx$ 0.7) but showed a redistribution in the remaining modules: C4 emphasized TERES MAJ/BIC SH ($\approx$0.7–0.9), whereas C5 became pectoral-dominant (PECT M $\approx$ 0.9). For the bottle–center trial, offline synergies were organized as C1 DELT P ($\approx$0.9), C2 DELT M ($\approx$0.9), C3 TRI LAT ($\approx$0.9–0.95), C4 DELT A ($\approx$0.9), and C5 BRACH ($\approx$0.7–0.8); online preserved the deltoid structure (C1/C2/C3 with DELT P/DELT M/DELT A at $\approx$0.7–0.9) and increased the contribution of scapular/rotator muscles, with C4–C5 highlighting TERES MAJ/INFRASP (both approaching $\approx$ 0.9). For the bottle–right trial, offline clusters again emphasized DELT P (C1 and C5, both $\approx$0.9–0.95), DELT M (C2 $\approx$ 0.6–0.7), TRI LAT (C3 $\approx$ 0.95), and DELT A (C4 $\approx$ 0.9); online retained the deltoid pattern (C1/C2/C3/C4) and exhibited stronger pectoral/teres-major loadings in C5/C4 (PECT M and TERES MAJ each $\approx$0.9). Overall, across targets the deltoid-dominated modules were retained from offline to online, while the remaining clusters showed moderate reweighting toward shoulder–scapular muscles (pectoral, teres major, infraspinatus) under the hand exoskeleton assistance.

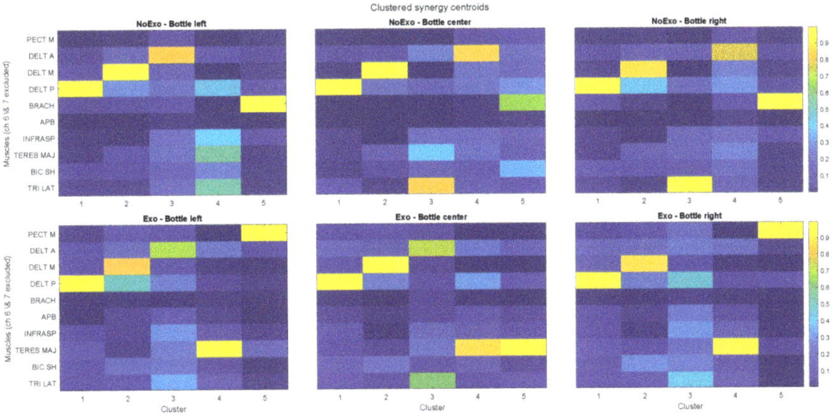

Figure 9. Clustered muscle-synergy centroids for offline (NoExo, **top row**) and online (Exo, **bottom row**) conditions across the three trials (**left**, **center**, **right**). For each condition $\times$ trial, EMG from three subjects was factorized by NMF (channels 6 and 7 removed, corresponding to extensor and flexor digitorum), the resulting synergy vectors were pooled and clustered with *k*-means (cosine), and the $K = 5$ cluster centroids are shown as heatmaps. Color encodes the muscle weight (0–1). The layout allows direct comparison of synergy composition between NoExo and Exo for each target location.

4. Discussions

4.1. Models and Flexor/Extensor Activity Prediction

We compared three intention-prediction families (LINEAR, NONLINEAR, LSTM) trained on three input configurations (EMG, KIN, EMG_KIN) to estimate the EMG envelopes of ED and FD for synergy-aligned control of a hand exoskeleton during reach-to-grasp. The rationale was twofold: first, to align assistance with the natural coordination between arm transport and hand shaping described in motor-control studies of prehension

 https://doi.org/10.3390/robotics15010021

and in post-stroke kinematic evidence of disrupted coupling [2,27–29]; second, to exploit temporal contingency between intention, movement, and sensory consequences, a known driver of plasticity in humans and a feature of assistive paradigms that show stronger gains when feedback is intention-locked [30–35].

Two consistent trends emerged. First, model choice strongly influenced performance: LINEAR and NONLINEAR produced similarly low errors across inputs, whereas LSTM errors were larger and markedly input-dependent (rank two-way on combined RMSE: Model, $H = 123.76$, $df = 2$, $p < 10^{-20}$; Model × Input, $H = 30.96$, $df = 4$, $p = 3.12 \times 10^{-6}$). Second, input type also mattered: across models, KIN yielded the lowest average RMSE, and adding EMG (EMG or EMG_KIN) did not systematically improve accuracy (Input, $H = 7.39$, $df = 2$, $p = 0.0249$). The interaction reflects the disproportionate degradation of LSTM with EMG-rich inputs relative to KIN, whereas LINEAR and NONLINEAR varied little across inputs (see Figure 5). These findings are compatible with intention–detection literature for wearables: EMG-driven control can be responsive but is sensitive to electrode placement, skin impedance, fatigue, and calibration drift, with non-trivial setup burden and dedicated hardware [10,19,21]; kinematic signals from encoders, IMUs, or camera tracking are faster to set up and typically more stable over repeated practice [11–13,22]. In this light, the best predictor for clinical deployment may balance accuracy with setup time, cost, and reliability. Our results suggest that a simple linear or shallow nonlinear model on arm kinematics can achieve low errors suitable for driving open/close assistance, consistent with reports with previous works that lightweight regressors, not specifically using kinematic inputs, suffice when features are informative and stable [44,45]. Deep or recurrent architectures are prominent in EMG decoding when large training sets and high-density arrays are available [21], but performance can degrade with limited data and non-stationarity, helping to explain the LSTM pattern observed here. A plausible reason the LSTM underperformed in our setting is the mismatch between model capacity and the effective amount of training data available per condition, combined with optimization difficulties induced by long, high-resolution sequences. Although recurrent networks can, in principle, exploit temporal context, in our protocol each participant contributes only a limited number of independent trials per target to learn the mapping, while the LSTM architecture (two recurrent layers with a relatively large number of units) has enough flexibility to fit trial-specific idiosyncrasies rather than stable task-invariant structure. In small-data regimes like this, the variance of the estimator becomes dominant: the LSTM can inadvertently learn noise and non-stationarities (e.g., envelope fluctuations or trial-to-trial changes) that do not generalize to test trials, whereas simpler linear models are implicitly regularized and therefore remain more robust. In addition, the LSTM is trained on time series derived from signals acquired at very different native sampling rates (high-rate EMG then smoothed into an envelope versus lower-rate kinematics), which can yield long effective sequences once synchronized. Long sequences make recurrent optimization more sensitive to vanishing/exploding gradients; consequently, stabilizing choices such as gradient thresholding/clipping and dropout, while necessary, can bias learning toward overly smooth dynamics and reduce the ability to capture sharper transitions in muscle envelopes. In such a scenario, the LSTM may converge to conservative, smoothed predictions that appear qualitatively reasonable but incur higher pointwise error, particularly when the relationship between inputs and outputs is largely instantaneous (or adequately captured by shallow nonlinearities), limiting the advantage of a memory-based model. In any case, the goal of this study was not to perform an optimization of hyperparameters of the LSTM, but rather investigate and compare plausible different models, and to test the one with a good trade-off between complexity of models, setup simplicity, and predicting performance.

https://doi.org/10.3390/robotics15010021

Existing control strategies for hand exoskeletons include EMG triggers or pattern recognition, kinematic thresholds, mirrored or bilateral strategies, and BCI-driven intents [11–13,15,22,25]. Most of the hand exoskeletons, both rigid and soft, found in literature employ an EMG-driven control, relying on residual muscle activity at a distal level, making the actuation of the robotic device not possible in case of severe impairments or high spasticity. Of course the availability of hand muscles activity grant higher motion prediction accuracy and suitable actuation delays, but it requires bulky, uncomfortable, and time-consuming EMG setups. BCI–robot or BCI–FES paradigms produce clinically meaningful gains versus control conditions in randomized trials and meta-analyses [23,34]; mirror or bilateral schemes modulate cortical activation and can be implemented with simple sensors [24]. Across the forearm/hand digitorum literature, EMG estimation has been tackled with markedly different inputs and modeling assumptions: for isometric gripping, Mogk and Keir derived regression equations that predict normalized forearm activation levels (including extensor digitorum communis) primarily from grip force and wrist/forearm posture, reporting RMSEmodel approximately 8.9–11% MVE (with EDC around 11% MVE) and variance explained that was higher for flexors (>70%) than extensors (up to 60%), without any explicit treatment of prediction delay, synergy constraints, or reliable prediction error metric in non-maximal voluntary contraction [46]. Furthermore, the usage of either grip force or wrist posture is not a feasible rehabilitation approach for a patient with a severe lesion on the distal segment. In contrast, synergy-based approaches treat EMG structure itself as low-dimensional: Ajiboye and Weir used NMF-derived muscle synergies learned from a subset of static ASL hand postures and showed that as few as 11 postures could define an 8-dimensional synergy framework achieving $>=$90% prediction (variance explained) of EMG patterns across 33 held postures, explicitly preserving synergy structure [47]. Extending synergies to dynamic/non-isometric hand function, Cole and Ajiboye extracted time-invariant synergies from static and dynamic datasets and evaluated reconstruction by variance accounted for (VAF), finding that three functional synergies achieved $66.0 \pm 4.9\%$ VAF (vs $42.5 \pm 4.4\%$ chance), again inherently synergy-preserving [48]. None of these works performed an actual real-time control and latency estimation of the actuation. Furthermore, the real-time usage of muscle synergies assume that EMG setup are included in the protocol which is not practical in daily clinical scenarios. Musculoskeletal inverse-dynamics studies instead estimate model-based muscle activity/activation proxies from measured kinematics: Melzner/Engelhardt et al. drove a detailed hand model with task kinematics from seven dynamic hand movements and evaluated agreement to EMG via timing-based metrics—computing on-/off-set time differences (mean 0.58 s) and weighted kappa—thereby providing an explicit timing discrepancy measure that functions as a practical "delay" indicator between simulated and measured activity [49]. Nevertheless, this approach assume that hand motion is preserved, since motion capture data is used in the inverse-dynamics based model, which makes it unsuitable for post-stroke rehabilitation scenarios. Standard pipelines typically trigger hand assistance from local hand or wrist events or mirrored commands without explicitly synchronizing open/close with ongoing shoulder–elbow transport. The present strategy contributes by leveraging proximal kinematics to time hand assistance within a reach-to-grasp phase structure, a design aligned with the neurophysiology of prehension and contingency principles [2,27–30], and related to hybrid arm–hand systems that assist transport and grasp together [26]. The proposed model achieved 30% RMSE on average compared to the typical contraction level during pre-shaping extension and prehension (corresponding to less than 1% of the MVC). To the best of authors' knowledge, there are no studies in literature that performs EMG estimation of flexor and extensor digitorum during dynamic tasks.

https://doi.org/10.3390/robotics15010021

4.2. Muscle Synergies Retention Analysis on the Offline Test

We examined whether replacing the two target channels with model estimates preserves each subject's low-dimensional coordination. Cosine similarity between synergy weights (W) from original versus hybrid EMG remained high: for LINEAR and NONLINEAR, median values across inputs typically fell in the 0.83–0.91 range. LSTM was more input-sensitive, with KIN yielding the highest similarity (median ≈ 0.91) and EMG_KIN among the lowest (medians ≈ 0.83–0.85), accompanied by wider dispersion. Thus, even when pointwise estimation errors differ, the predicted channels tend to integrate coherently with the subject's synergy structure, particularly when only kinematics are used as inputs. This coherence accords with reports that upper-limb activations during reach-to-grasp can be captured by a few task-related synergies coupling proximal and distal groups [26,27].

VAF curves for original and hybrid EMG overlapped and crossed the 90% threshold at approximately six synergies on average, with negligible differences in VAF at the selected dimensionality. The low-dimensional control space therefore was neither inflated nor collapsed by channel replacement, an important property for synergy-informed assistance and for interpretable monitoring of recovery. Together with known intersegmental interactions (heteronymous reflex links and posture-dependent changes of corticospinal excitability) [36–42], these findings support the feasibility of hybrid synergies in which hand channels are inferred from proximal context without corrupting global coordination. In practice, this enables two complementary selection criteria for an online controller: choose the model with the lowest RMSE, or, when preserving natural coordination is prioritized (for training transfer or decoding robustness), choose the model and input that best retain synergy structure even if pointwise error is slightly higher. In our data, KIN-based inputs offered an attractive trade-off on both fronts.

For a synergy-aligned hand exoskeleton designed for frequent outpatient use, a pragmatic recipe follows from these results. First, prioritize proximal kinematics (encoders or IMUs, or camera-based tracking) for minimal setup burden and stable signals [11–13,22], adding EMG only when a clear incremental benefit is demonstrable for a given user and task [10,19–21]. Second, begin with linear or shallow nonlinear regression and escalate complexity only if data volume and stability justify it. Third, gate open/close by transport phase estimates (for example, onset of deceleration) to respect prehension timing [27,28] and to maximize intention–feedback contingency, a factor linked to stronger plastic changes [33–38]. Finally, monitor not only task scores and RMSE but also synergy changes (for example, cosine similarity of W, VAF and the selected number of synergies) as a proxy of physiological plausibility during training.

4.3. Real-Time Hand Exoskeleton Go-to-Grasp Control

The kinematics-driven linear model ran stably in real time across all targets (left/center/right), and the clustered synergy maps indicate that assistance did not disrupt the proximal coordination underpinning reach-to-grasp. Using the elbow of the k-means sum-of-distances curve, the slope flattened at about five clusters, adopted as the common dimensionality for comparison. With that choice, offline (NoExo) and online (Exo) centroids showed closely corresponding patterns across trials, deltoid groupings and pectoralis–biceps–triceps couplings remained salient, and brachioradialis and scapular rotators loaded similarly in homologous clusters, despite exclusion of the two hand-muscle channels (see Figure 9). This qualitative preservation tracks well with prior reports that upper-limb robotic assistance tends to exert limited effects on synergy structure in healthy subjects and during aided reaching, with most spatial weights conserved and only modest adjustments in specific muscles or amplitudes [50–52] . Similar "module preservation with modulation" has also been observed in lower-limb robot-aided locomotion, supporting the

 https://doi.org/10.3390/robotics15010021

broader view that exoskeletons often leave the fundamental modular organization intact while altering timing or gain [53].

In contrast, the RMS boxplots for flexor and extensor digitorum during the same online sessions showed higher medians and markedly wider dispersion than offline for all targets, with several large outliers. A likely contributor is timing misalignment between the healthy user's internally learned reach-to-grasp synergy, a well-consolidated cortico-spinal pattern, and the position-controlled exoskeleton. If a mismatch happens between what the subject would do and what the exoskeleton actually does, the subject basically opens or closes the hand against the exoskeleton (equivalent to an isometric contraction); this causes an increase of the EMG activity of the aforementioned muscles: even small early/late triggers can make the user generate forces that are not perfectly aligned with the imposed motion, promoting co-contraction and elevated EMG. Consistent with this interpretation, the estimated controller features a prediction delay for the LINEAR+KIN model, computed prior to online testing (see Section 2.11). Delays of this magnitude can span a meaningful fraction of the transport–hand-shaping sequence, particularly near closure onset, increasing the risk of user–robot opposition and explaining the broader RMS dispersion. Mitigations follow directly: reduce algorithmic latency (shorter windows, lighter filtering, pipelined processing), incorporate explicit movement-phase estimation to anticipate open/close timing, and add online adaptation of assistance gain and compliance (e.g., impedance control) to absorb small timing errors. A brief per-subject calibration of timing and gain before training could further temper peaks while preserving the synergy coherence observed in the heatmaps. Nevertheless, it represents a limited criticality, since it is not likely to happen with a post-stroke patient with a low residual muscle activity, as it would be used as a fully-passive exercise.

In rehabilitation scenarios, the proposed kinematics-only intention predictor is attractive because it avoids EMG setup (skin prep, electrode placement, recalibration) and remains usable when distal EMG is weak or unreliable, common in patients with severe finger paresis or spasticity. For users who contribute little voluntary hand drive and largely allow the exoskeleton to transport the arm, opposition forces against a position-controlled device are expected to be lower, which should mitigate the timing-mismatch effects we observed in healthy subjects (elevated, more variable finger-muscle RMS). In other words, a more passive distal strategy can reduce user–robot "tug-of-war," while proximal kinematics still provide a stable, high-SNR cue for synchronizing hand opening/closing with transport. Clinically, this could translate into simpler sessions (faster donning, fewer sensors), easier deployment in outpatient and home settings (IMUs/encoders or camera tracking suffice), and broader eligibility, including patients with minimal hand activation who cannot tolerate EMG-driven triggers. At the same time, maintaining engagement remains essential: progressive assistance, impedance/compliance tuning, and brief per-patient timing calibration can help personalize the controller so that it supports movement without overriding it, preserving the arm–hand coordination we saw in the synergy maps while limiting unintended co-contraction.

4.4. *Applicability of the Proposed Method in Post-Stroke Rehabilitation Contexts*

One interesting discussion point regards the applicability of the proposed methodology on the target population, i.e post-stroke patients. There are many examples in the literature showing that muscle synergies, which reflect co-contraction patterns on coordinated movements, are more likely to be disrupted after stroke [45,54,55]. This element may prevent the proposed methodology to be applied, since models cannot be trained after the stroke onset. If the coordinated pattern is disrupted on post-stroke patients but it existed prior stroke it means that it is reasonable, from a rehabilitation point of view,

 https://doi.org/10.3390/robotics15010021

trying to restore it to give back to patients the previous coordinated movement. In this case one strategy could be to involve the healthy limb: in an actual rehabilitation setup, this coordinated pattern can be extracted from the healthy hand and arm and used to train a model and finally to actuate the hand exoskeleton worn on the affected hand. The approach of using the healthy limb to rehabilitate the impaired one is a well-established practice in neuro-rehabilitation, for example in mirroring setups. This approach assumes that the impaired side, which can be dominant or non-dominant, shares common patterns with the healthy one: Flindall and Gonzalez in a 2013 study [56] have shown no significant differences in kinematic measurements, such as peak velocity, movement time, and deceleration phase time, between left and right hand during pick-and-place tasks; in another study by Grosskopf et al. [57] comparable kinematic features resulted from dominant and non-dominant arms during prehension tasks. The maximum hand aperture during pre-shaping seems to be the only relevant difference, that is a tunable parameter on the presented hand exoskeleton device. These results suggest that the proposed approach could be applicable to the target patient population, although it is an hypothesis that needs to be validated in a pilot study. Nevertheless, results shown in this work mainly represent an advancement on the hand rehabilitation technology, without any clinically relevant outcome.

4.5. Limitations

This study has a couple of limitations. First, the sample size is small (N = 8), which limits generalizability; nevertheless, the between-subject standard deviations of the performance metrics were modest, suggesting relatively low variation across subjects in this dataset. Secondly, although the presented methodology was designed to be used in rehabilitation setups with post-stroke patients, the current study is a feasibility study with healthy subjects only, to be intended as a pre-clinical evaluation of the synergistic control strategy on a hand exoskeleton. Finally, the presented methodology is not suitable in those cases in which the hand opening and closing is decoupled from the arm transport action, for example in static hand operations or object manipulations. Robotic rehabilitation setups with hand exoskeletons can, thus, combine different control strategies to target goal-directed reach-to-grasp actions and manipulation ones separately in different sessions.

5. Conclusions

This study compared linear, shallow nonlinear, and recurrent predictors trained on EMG, arm kinematics, and their fusion to estimate flexor and extensor digitorum activity for synergy-aligned hand exoskeleton control during reach-to-grasp. The main findings are (i) model choice strongly affected accuracy, with linear and shallow nonlinear models yielding the lowest RMSE and LSTM showing larger, input-sensitive errors; (ii) kinematics alone provided the most favorable accuracy–setup trade-off, with the lowest average RMSE and no additional sensor burden; and (iii) in the offline analysis, substituting the two target channels with model predictions largely preserved each subject's muscle-synergy composition and dimensionality, supporting the physiological plausibility of the inferred signals.

Beyond the offline benchmark, we demonstrated real-time feasibility: a kinematics-driven LINEAR model controlled the hand exoskeleton during go-to-grasp with three subjects and three target locations. Control was stable across trials, but the distal EMG (flexor/extensor digitorum) showed higher and more variable RMS online than offline, consistent with occasional timing mismatches between the user's reach-to-grasp pattern and the position-controlled device. These observations motivate delay-aware scheduling of open/close events, brief per-subject timing calibration, and adaptive compliance/assistance gains to absorb small phase errors while maintaining coordination with arm transport.

https://doi.org/10.3390/robotics15010021

From an implementation standpoint, these results continue to favor kinematics-based sensing with simple regressors as a practical baseline for intention detection when the goal is to synchronize hand opening and closing with arm transport phases. For rehabilitation scenarios, the approach is appealing in patients with limited hand mobility, where distal drive is weak and interaction forces with a position-controlled device are expected to be smaller; in such cases, the model's reliance on proximal kinematics can still coordinate assistance while reducing interference from involuntary or fatigued finger activity.

Future steps include expanding closed-loop tests to larger healthy cohorts, then piloting on post-stroke patients, testing robustness across sessions and users, benchmarking against established controllers (e.g., EMG-threshold or mirrored control), and adding neural endpoints to probe whether synergy-aligned timing enhances training-related plasticity.

Author Contributions: Conceptualization, C.C. and T.B.; methodology, C.C.; software, C.C.; validation, C.C. and T.B.; formal analysis, C.C.; investigation, C.C.; resources, C.C., T.B. and F.S.; data curation, C.C., T.B. and F.S.; writing—original draft preparation, C.C. and T.B.; writing—review and editing, C.C., T.B. and C.L.; visualization, C.C.; supervision, A.F.; project administration, C.L. and A.F.; funding acquisition, C.L. and A.F. All authors have read and agreed to the published version of the manuscript.

Funding: This project has been funded under the National Recovery and Resilience Plan (NRRP), Mission 4 Component 2 Investment 1.1—Call for tender No. 104 published on 2 February 2022, by the Italian Ministry of University and Research (MUR), funded by the European Union–NextGenerationEU—Project Title "AVATAR: Enhanced AI-enabled Avatar Robot for Remote Telepresence"—CUP J53D23000860006, D53D23001490008—Grant Assignment Decree No. 960 adopted on 30 June 2023 by the Italian MUR.

Institutional Review Board Statement: The study was conducted in accordance with the Declaration of Helsinki, and approved by the Scuola Superiore Sant'Anna Review Board (protocol aoproval number 15/2021). Participants were briefed on the procedures and provided their written informed consent before the experiments.

Informed Consent Statement: Informed consent was obtained from all subjects involved in the study.

Data Availability Statement: The original data presented in the study are openly available in FigShare at 10.6084/m9.figshare.30051970.

Acknowledgments: The authors would like to thank all participants for the time given to take part in this study. During the preparation of this manuscript/study, the author(s) used ChatGPT 5 for the purposes of summarizing and rephrasing. The authors have reviewed and edited the output and take full responsibility for the content of this publication.

Conflicts of Interest: The authors declare no conflicts of interest.

References

1. Collins, K.C.; Kennedy, N.C.; Clark, R.A.; Pua, Y.H. Kinematic components of reach-to-target movement after stroke: A systematic review and meta analysis. *Front. Neurol.* **2018**, *9*, 472. [CrossRef]
2. Choi, H.; Park, D.; Rha, D.W.; Nam, H.S.; Jo, Y.J.; Kim, D.Y. Kinematic analysis of movement patterns during a reach-and-grasp task in stroke patients. *Front. Neurol.* **2023**, *14*, 1225425. [CrossRef]
3. Maciejasz, P.; Eschweiler, J.; Gerlach-Hahn, K.; Jansen-Troy, A.; Leonhardt, S. A survey on robotic devices for upper limb rehabilitation. *J. Neuroeng. Rehabil.* **2014**, *11*, 3. [CrossRef]
4. Chien, W.t.; Chong, Y.y.; Tse, M.k.; Chien, C.w.; Cheng, H.y. Robot-assisted therapy for upper-limb rehabilitation in subacute stroke patients: A systematic review and meta-analysis. *Brain Behav.* **2020**, *10*, e01742. [CrossRef] [PubMed]

https://doi.org/10.3390/robotics15010021

5. Dalla Gasperina, S.; Roveda, L.; Pedrocchi, A.; Braghin, F.; Gandolla, M. Review on Patient Cooperative Control Strategies for Upper-Limb Rehabilitation Exoskeletons. *Front. Robot. AI* **2021**, *8*, 745018. [CrossRef] [PubMed]
6. Mehrholz, J.; Pohl, M.; Platz, T.; Kugler, J.; Elsner, B. Electromechanical and robot-assisted arm training for improving activities of daily living, arm function, and arm muscle strength after stroke. *Cochrane Database Syst. Rev.* **2018**, *9*, CD006876. [CrossRef]
7. Rodgers, H.; Bosomworth, H.; Krebs, H.I.; van Wijck, F.; Howel, D.; Wilson, N.; Aird, L.; Alvarado, N.; Andole, S.; Cohen, D.L.; et al. Robot assisted training for the upper limb after stroke (RATULS): A multicentre randomised controlled trial. *Lancet* **2019**, *394*, 51–62. [CrossRef] [PubMed]
8. Banyai, A.D.; Brișan, C. Robotics in physical rehabilitation: Systematic Review. *Healthcare* **2024**, *12*, 1720. [CrossRef]
9. Park, J.M.; Kim, J.U.; Hong, S.C.; Cho, Y.H.; Hong, B.T.; Kim, K.T.; Park, J.H.; Kim, J.S. Effects of Robot-Assisted Therapy for Upper Limb Rehabilitation After Stroke: An Umbrella Review of Systematic Reviews. *Stroke* 2025, *Advance online publication*. [CrossRef]
10. Gantenbein, J.; Dittli, J.; Meyer, J.T.; Gassert, R.; Lambercy, O. Intention detection strategies for robotic upper-limb orthoses: A scoping review considering usability, daily life application, and user evaluation. *Front. Neurorobotics* **2022**, *16*, 815693. [CrossRef]
11. Bardi, E.; Bruschetta, M.; Fontanelli, A.; Foresti, M.; Meli, E.; Ridolfi, A.; Allotta, B. Upper limb soft robotic wearable devices: A systematic review. *J. Neuroeng. Rehabil.* **2022**, *19*, 121. [CrossRef]
12. Kabir, R.; Sunny, M.; Ahmed, H.; Rahman, M. Hand Rehabilitation Devices: A Comprehensive Systematic Review. *Micromachines* **2022**, *13*, 1033. [CrossRef]
13. du Plessis, T.; Djouani, K.; Oosthuizen, C. A Review of Active Hand Exoskeletons for Rehabilitation and Assistance. *Robotics* **2021**, *10*, 40. [CrossRef]
14. Schabowsky, C.N.; Godfrey, S.B.; Holley, R.J.; Lum, P.S. Development and pilot testing of HEXORR: Hand EXOskeleton Rehabilitation Robot. *J. Neuroeng. Rehabil.* **2010**, *7*, 36. [CrossRef]
15. Ko, M.J.; Chuang, Y.C.; Chen, H.Y.; Tzeng, Y.L.; Lin, Y.C. The Application of Soft Robotic Gloves in Stroke Patients: A Systematic Review and Meta-Analysis of Randomized Controlled Trials. *Brain Sci.* **2023**, *13*, 900. [CrossRef]
16. Shi, X.Q.; Heung, H.L.; Tang, Z.Q.; Li, Z.; Tong, K.Y. Effects of a soft robotic hand for hand rehabilitation in chronic stroke survivors. *J. Stroke Cerebrovasc. Dis.* **2021**, *30*, 105812. [CrossRef]
17. Lu, Y.; Li, H.; Lai, J.; Wang, J.; Yu, Y.; Lu, T.; Wei, X.; Wang, H.; Song, A. Adjustable Rigid-Soft Wearable Hand Robot With Magnetorheological Cable-Driven Mechanism for Grasping Assistance. *IEEE Trans. Neural Syst. Rehabil. Eng.* **2025**, *33*, 3053–3064. [CrossRef]
18. Sarac, M.; Solazzi, M.; Frisoli, A. Design requirements of generic hand exoskeletons and survey of hand exoskeletons for rehabilitation, assistive, or haptic use. *IEEE Trans. Haptics* **2019**, *12*, 400–413. [CrossRef] [PubMed]
19. Carvalho, C.R.; Fernández, J.M.; del Ama, A.J.; Barroso, F.O.; Moreno, J.C. Review of electromyography onset detection methods for real-time control of robotic exoskeletons. *J. Neuroeng. Rehabil.* **2023**, *20*, 141. [CrossRef]
20. Cho, G.; Yang, W.; Lee, D.; You, D.; Lee, H.; Kim, S.; Lee, S.; Nam, W. Characterization of signal features for real-time sEMG onset detection. *Biomed. Signal Process. Control* **2023**, *84*, 104774. [CrossRef]
21. Meyers, E.C.; Gabrieli, D.; Tacca, N.; Wengerd, L.; Darrow, M.; Schlink, B.R.; Baumgart, I.; Friedenberg, D.A. Decoding hand and wrist movement intention from chronic stroke survivors with hemiparesis using a user-friendly, wearable EMG-based neural interface. *J. Neuroeng. Rehabil.* **2024**, *21*, 7. [CrossRef] [PubMed]
22. Chen, Y.; Yang, Z.; Wen, Y. A soft exoskeleton glove for hand bilateral training via surface EMG. *Sensors* **2021**, *21*, 578. [CrossRef]
23. Cervera, M.A.; Soekadar, S.R.; Ushiba, J.; Millán, J.d.R.; Liu, M.; Birbaumer, N.; Garipelli, G. Brain-computer interfaces for post-stroke motor rehabilitation: A meta-analysis. *Ann. Clin. Transl. Neurol.* **2018**, *5*, 651–663. [CrossRef] [PubMed]
24. Kim, D.H.; Lee, K.D.; Bulea, T.C.; Park, H.S. Increasing motor cortex activation during grasping via novel robotic mirror hand therapy: A pilot fNIRS study. *J. Neuroeng. Rehabil.* **2022**, *19*, 8. [CrossRef]
25. Kueper, N.; Kim, S.K.; Kirchner, E.A. Avoidance of specific calibration sessions in motor intention recognition for exoskeleton-supported rehabilitation through transfer learning on EEG data. *Sci. Rep.* **2024**, *14*, 16690. [CrossRef]
26. Grimm, F.; Naros, G.; Gharabaghi, A. Closed-Loop Neuroprosthesis for Reach-to-Grasp Assistance: Combining Adaptive Multi-Channel Neuromuscular Stimulation With a Multi-Joint Arm Exoskeleton. *Front. Neurosci.* **2016**, *10*, 284. [CrossRef]
27. Jeannerod, M. The timing of natural prehension movements. *J. Mot. Behav.* **1984**, *16*, 235–254. [CrossRef] [PubMed]
28. van de Kamp, C.; Zaal, F.T.J.M. Prehension is really reaching and grasping. *Exp. Brain Res.* **2007**, *182*, 27–34. [CrossRef]
29. Thrane, G.; Sunnerhagen, K.S.; Murphy, M.A. Upper limb kinematics during the first year after stroke: The stroke arm longitudinal study at the University of Gothenburg (SALGOT). *J. Neuroeng. Rehabil.* **2020**, *17*, 76. [CrossRef]
30. Stefan, K.; Kunesch, E.; Cohen, L.G.; Benecke, R.; Classen, J. Induction of plasticity in the human motor cortex by paired associative stimulation. *Brain* **2000**, *123*, 572–584. [CrossRef]
31. Wolters, A.; Schmidt, A.; Schramm, A.; Zeller, D.; Naumann, M.; Kunesch, E.; Benecke, R.; Reiners, K.; Classen, J. Timing-dependent plasticity in human primary somatosensory cortex. *J. Physiol.* **2005**, *565*, 1039–1052. [CrossRef] [PubMed]

 https://doi.org/10.3390/robotics15010021

32. Arai, N.; Müller-Dahlhaus, F.; Murakami, T.; Bliem, B.; Lu, M.K.; Ugawa, Y.; Ziemann, U. State-dependent and timing-dependent bidirectional associative plasticity in the human SMA-M1 network. *J. Neurosci.* **2011**, *31*, 15376–15383. [CrossRef]
33. Classen, J.; Liepert, J.; Wise, S.P.; Hallett, M.; Cohen, L.G. Rapid plasticity of human cortical movement representation induced by practice. *J. Neurophysiol.* **1998**, *79*, 1117–1123. [CrossRef] [PubMed]
34. Biasiucci, A.; Leeb, R.; Iturrate, I.; Perdikis, S.; Al-Khodairy, A.; Corbet, T.; Schnider, A.; Schmidlin, E.; Zhang, H.; Bassolino, M.; et al. Brain-actuated functional electrical stimulation elicits lasting arm motor recovery after stroke. *Nat. Commun.* **2018**, *9*, 2421. [CrossRef] [PubMed]
35. Wilson, R.D.; Page, S.J.; Delahanty, M.; Knutson, J.S.; Gunzler, D.D.; Sheffler, L.R.; Chae, J. Upper-Limb Recovery After Stroke: A Randomized Controlled Trial Comparing EMG-Triggered, Cyclic, and Sensory Electrical Stimulation. *Neurorehabilit. Neural Repair* **2016**, *30*, 978–987. [CrossRef] [PubMed]
36. Manning, C.D.; Bawa, P. Heteronymous reflex connections in human upper limb muscles in response to stretch of forearm muscles. *J. Neurophysiol.* **2011**, *106*, 1489–1499. [CrossRef]
37. Lewis, G.N.; McNair, P.J. Heteronymous Ia-afferent connections in the upper limb following stroke. *Muscle Nerve* **2010**, *41*, 71–77. [CrossRef]
38. Käelin-Lang, A.; Cohen, L.G.; Wassermann, E.M.; Brasil-Neto, J.P.; Hallett, M.; Cohen, D. Modulation of human corticomotor excitability by somatosensory input. *J. Physiol.* **2002**, *540*, 623–633. [CrossRef]
39. Vargas, C.D.; Olivier, E.; Craighero, L.; Fadiga, L.; Duhamel, J.R.; Sirigu, A. The influence of hand posture on corticospinal excitability during motor imagery: A transcranial magnetic stimulation study. *Cereb. Cortex* **2004**, *14*, 1200–1206. [CrossRef]
40. Rogić Vidaković, M.; Kostović, A.; Jerković, A.; Šoda, J.; Russo, M.; Stella, M.; Knežić, A.; Vujović, I.; Mihalj, M.; Baban, J.; et al. Using Cutaneous Receptor Vibration to Uncover the Effect of Transcranial Magnetic Stimulation on Motor Cortical Excitability. *Med. Sci. Monit.* **2020**, *26*, e923166. [CrossRef]
41. Perez, M.A.; Rothwell, J.C. Distinct influence of hand posture on cortical activity during human grasping. *J. Neurosci.* **2015**, *35*, 4882–4889. [CrossRef]
42. Garcia, M.A.C.; de Carvalho, T.S.; Matsuda, R.H.; Baffa, O.; Imbiriba, L.A.; Souza, V.H. Forearm posture affects the corticospinal excitability of intrinsic and extrinsic hand muscles in dominant and nondominant sides. *J. Appl. Biomech.* **2024**, *40*, 316–322. [CrossRef] [PubMed]
43. Stewart, K.C.; Cauraugh, J.H.; Summers, J.J. Bilateral movement training and stroke rehabilitation: A systematic review and meta-analysis. *J. Neurol. Sci.* **2006**, *244*, 89–95. [CrossRef]
44. Camardella, C.; Junata, M.; Tse, K.C.; Frisoli, A.; Tong, R.K.Y. How many muscles? Optimal muscles set search for optimizing myocontrol performance. *Front. Comput. Neurosci.* **2021**, *15*, 668579. [CrossRef]
45. Camardella, C.; Tse, K.C.; Frisoli, A.; Tong, R.K.Y. Investigating muscle synergies changes after rehabilitation robotics training on stroke survivors: A pilot study. In Proceedings of the 2020 42nd Annual International Conference of the IEEE Engineering in Medicine & Biology Society (EMBC), Montreal, QC, Canada, 20–24 July 2020; IEEE: New York, NY, USA, 2020; pp. 3731–3734.
46. Mogk, J.P.; Keir, P.J. Prediction of forearm muscle activity during gripping. *Ergonomics* **2006**, *49*, 1121–1130. [CrossRef]
47. Ajiboye, A.B.; Weir, R. Muscle synergies as a predictive framework for the EMG patterns of new hand postures. *J. Neural Eng.* **2009**, *6*, 036004. [CrossRef] [PubMed]
48. Cole, N.M.; Ajiboye, A.B. Muscle synergies for predicting non-isometric complex hand function for commanding FES neuroprosthetic hand systems. *J. Neural Eng.* **2019**, *16*, 056018. [CrossRef] [PubMed]
49. Melzner, M.; Engelhardt, L.; Simon, U.; Dendorfer, S. Electromyography-Based validation of a musculoskeletal hand model. *J. Biomech. Eng.* **2022**, *144*, 021005. [CrossRef]
50. Pirondini, E.; Coscia, M.; Marcheschi, S.; Roas, G.; Salsedo, F.; Frisoli, A.; Bergamasco, M.; Micera, S. Evaluation of the effects of the Arm Light Exoskeleton on movement execution and muscle activities: A pilot study on healthy subjects. *J. Neuroeng. Rehabil.* **2016**, *13*, 9. [CrossRef]
51. Cancrini, A.; Baitelli, P.; Lavit Nicora, M.; Malosio, M.; Pedrocchi, A.; Scano, A. The effects of robotic assistance on upper limb spatial muscle synergies in healthy people during planar upper-limb training. *PLoS ONE* **2022**, *17*, e0272813. [CrossRef]
52. Scano, A.; Chiavenna, A.; Malosio, M.; Molinari Tosatti, L.; Molteni, F. Robotic assistance for upper limbs may induce slight changes in motor modules compared with free movements in stroke survivors: A cluster-based muscle synergy analysis. *Front. Hum. Neurosci.* **2018**, *12*, 290. [CrossRef]
53. Gizzi, L.; Nielsen, J.F.; Felici, F.; Moreno, J.C.; Pons, J.L.; Farina, D. Motor modules in robot-aided walking. *J. Neuroeng. Rehabil.* **2012**, *9*, 76. [CrossRef] [PubMed]
54. Roh, J.; Rymer, W.Z.; Perreault, E.J.; Yoo, S.B.; Beer, R.F. Alterations in upper limb muscle synergy structure in chronic stroke survivors. *J. Neurophysiol.* **2013**, *109*, 768–781. [CrossRef] [PubMed]
55. Dipietro, L.; Krebs, H.I.; Fasoli, S.E.; Volpe, B.T.; Stein, J.; Bever, C.; Hogan, N. Changing motor synergies in chronic stroke. *J. Neurophysiol.* **2007**, *98*, 757–768. [CrossRef] [PubMed]

 https://doi.org/10.3390/robotics15010021

56. Flindall, J.W.; Gonzalez, C.L. On the evolution of handedness: Evidence for feeding biases. *PLoS ONE* **2013**, *8*, e78967. [CrossRef]
57. Grosskopf, A.; Kuhtz-Buschbeck, J.P. Grasping with the left and right hand: A kinematic study. *Exp. Brain Res.* **2006**, *168*, 230–240. [CrossRef]

 https://doi.org/10.3390/robotics15010021

MDPI AG
Grosspeteranlage 5
4052 Basel
Switzerland
Tel.: +41 61 683 77 34

Robotics Editorial Office
E-mail: robotics@mdpi.com
www.mdpi.com/journal/robotics

www.ingramcontent.com/pod-product-compliance
Lightning Source LLC
LaVergne TN
LVHW070456061126
851858LV00011B/246
* 9 7 8 3 7 2 5 8 8 2 2 7 4 *